THE ABRIDGED DIARIES OF

Charlotte Perkins Gilman

Midnight ——— Morning—

The clocks ring 12.

With no pride, with little hope, with uncertain occasional happiness, with no glad energy and living power; with no faith or nearly none, but still, thank God! with firm belief in what is right and wrong; I begin the new year.

Let me recognize fully that I do not look forward to happiness; that I have no decided hope of success.

So long must I live.

One does not die young who so desires it.

Perhaps it was not meant for me to work as I intended. Perhaps I am not to be of use to others.

I am weak.

I anticipate a future of failure and suffering. Children sickly and unhappy; Husband miserable because of my distress; and I ——————! of

I think sometimes that it may be the other way; bright and happy; but this comes oftenest; holds longest. But this life is marked for me, I will not withdraw; and let me at least learn to be uncomplaining and unselfish. Let me do my work and not fling my pain on others.

THE ABRIDGED DIARIES OF

Charlotte Perkins Gilman

Edited by Denise D. Knight

University Press of Virginia / Charlottesville and London

THE UNIVERSITY PRESS OF VIRGINIA
Copyright © 1998 by the Rector and Visitors
   of the University of Virginia
All rights reserved
Printed in the United States of America

First published 1998

⊗ The paper used in this publication meets the minimum
requirements of the American National Standard for Information
Sciences—Permanence of Paper for Printed Library Materials,
ANSI Z39.48–1984.

Library of Congress Cataloging-in-Publication Data
Gilman, Charlotte Perkins, 1860–1935.
   The abridged diaries of Charlotte Perkins Gilman / edited by
Denise D. Knight.
      p.   cm.
   Abridged ed. of: The diaries of Charlotte Perkins Gilman, 1994.
   Includes bibliographical references and index.
   ISBN 0-8139-1796-4 (paper : alk. paper)
      1. Gilman, Charlotte Perkins, 1860–1935—Diaries.   2. Women
authors, American—19th century—Diaries.   3. Women authors,
American—20th century—Diaries.   4. Feminists—United States—
Diaries.   I. Knight, Denise D., 1954–   .   II. Gilman, Charlotte
Perkins, 1860–1935.   Diaries of Charlotte Perkins Gilman.
III. Title.
PS 1744.G57Z463   1998
818'.403—dc21
[B]
                                                         97-43274
                                                            CIP

Frontispieces: Diary entry of December 31, 1883–January 1, 1884, and
photograph of Charlotte Perkins Stetson, age thirty-three. (Courtesy
of the Schlesinger Library, Radcliffe College)

CONTENTS

ACKNOWLEDGMENTS

THE STAFF AT THE Arthur and Elizabeth Schlesinger Library on the History of Women in America, and particularly Eva S. Moseley, Curator of Manuscripts, deserves my sincere thanks for facilitating my research on the original two-volume edition of the Gilman diaries, from which this project was drawn.

I am also deeply grateful to Boyd Zenner and Nancy C. Essig at the University Press of Virginia for their support of this project.

As always, I am indebted to my husband, Michael K. Barylski, for sharing my interest in Gilman's life and literature.

INTRODUCTION

O N DECEMBER 25, 1875, Charlotte Anna Perkins's older brother, Thomas, gave to her a small leather-bound Excelsior diary as a Christmas present. Inside, he inscribed:

> Within this book, if *every day*
> You entry make of some import,
> On Christmas next, to you I say
> I'll give one dollar. *Naught if naught.*

> Each entry must *upon the day*
> *'Tis entered, entered be.*
> If this rule's broke and is not kept,
> Thou shalt get naught from me.

Fifteen-year-old Charlotte enthusiastically accepted her brother's offer with "sincere thanks," and the next week she began a practice—the making of daily entries of "some import"—that would continue over much of the next twenty-eight years.

Charlotte Perkins Gilman's biography has been well documented in numerous writings.[1] Even a brief overview of her life reveals a remarkable woman who overcame incredible obstacles to become one of the most celebrated leaders of the turn-of-the-century women's movement. Born on July 3, 1860, in Hartford, Connecticut, Charlotte Anna Perkins was the great-niece of author and abolitionist advocate Harriet Beecher Stowe. Her childhood was characterized by loneliness, isolation, and poverty, particularly after her father, a gifted but temperamental librarian and fiction writer, abandoned the family when Charlotte was nine. Contributing to her emotional insecurity was her mother's tendency to withhold affection, which left Charlotte exceedingly wary of personal relationships. Moreover, the Perkinses' precarious economic condition forced the family to move nineteen times in just eighteen years.[2] The constant uprooting left Charlotte Perkins with only four years of formal schooling, "among seven different schools," which ended when she was fifteen (*Living*, p. 18). Her father's love of books, however, propelled her own intellectual curiosity, and Charlotte became largely self-educated as a result. She frequented the public library and joined the Society for the Encouragement of Studies at Home, where she avidly read about ancient history and civilizations. She also solicited advice from her estranged father about which books might best prepare her to serve society.

The trials of Charlotte Perkins's childhood helped, in fact, to prepare her for the life that lay ahead: they fostered an incredibly strong individual spirit, a unwavering desire for independence, and an enduring devotion to hard work. By the time she was twenty-one, Charlotte had decided the direction that her life would take: she would contribute something meaningful to humanity. In her autobiography, *The Living of Charlotte Perkins Gilman*, most of which was written at the age of sixty-five, she remembered it this way: "From sixteen I had not wavered from that desire to help humanity which underlay all my studies. Here was the world, visibly unhappy and as visibly unnecessarily so; surely it called for the best efforts of all who could in the least understand what was the matter, and had any rational improvements to propose" (p. 70).

Healthy, productive, and secure in a loving relationship with her longtime friend Martha Luther, Charlotte was set to conquer the world. In a letter to Martha, she affirmed her desire to forgo the traditional roles of wife and mother in favor of cultivating her intellect. In her mind the two were mutually exclusive. "I am really glad not to marry," she wrote. "*I have decided.* I'm *not* domestic and I don't want to be. Neither am I a genius in any special sense, but a *strong-minded* woman I will be."[3] Martha satisfied Charlotte's craving for intimacy and affection, and Charlotte believed that her relationship with Martha would even "make up to me for husband and children and all that I shall miss."[4] With Martha in her life, Charlotte seemed genuinely content. Her autobiography offers a summary of the relationship that she and Martha shared: "With Martha I knew perfect happiness. We used to say to each other that we should never have to reproach ourselves with not realizing this joy while we had it; we did, thoroughly. We were not only extremely fond of each other, but we had fun together, deliciously. . . . Four years of satisfying happiness with Martha, then she married and moved away" (*Living*, p. 80). Charlotte was devastated by Martha's decision to marry. "It was the keenest, the hardest, the most lasting pain I had yet known," she wrote (p. 80).

Then in January 1882, as Charlotte was still coming to terms with her loss of Martha, she was introduced to Charles Walter Stetson, a handsome young Rhode Island artist who promptly proposed marriage. Charlotte quickly declined, convinced that marriage would destroy her plans to contribute to the improvement of society. While holding the conviction that women should be able to combine marriage, motherhood, and career, the preservation of "self" became a key concern. In a letter to Stetson, Charlotte wrote, "My Individual Self, the Soul I hope you will meet when we are dead, is a thinking creature, and I hate to lose its cleareyed strength for even a moment."[5] Again and again, in letters to Stetson, Charlotte expressed the fear that marriage would bring an end to her independence. "My life is one of private aspiration and development, and of public service which only awaits to be asked. . . . I will give and give and give you *of* myself, but never give myself to you or any man," she wrote (*Endure*, pp. 29–30). Walter Stetson persisted for nearly two years, however, and finally, after he had suffered a "keen personal disappointment,"[6] Charlotte agreed to marry him, despite serious reservations. The marriage, predictably, was a failure.

The chronic depression that would plague Charlotte for most of her adult life had its origins in her engagement and subsequent marriage to Walter Stetson. While numerous entries both in her diaries and in Stetson's reveal a marriage characterized by discord from the outset, Charlotte rather dubiously remarked in her autobiography, "We were really very happy together." And then, a qualifier: "There was nothing to prevent it but that increasing depression of mine" (*Living*, p. 87). The depression persisted, and within several weeks after the wedding, Charlotte discovered that she was pregnant.

"A lover more tender, a husband more devoted, woman could not ask," she wrote of Walter Stetson. Still, "a sort of gray fog drifted across my mind, a cloud that grew and darkened" (*Living*, pp. 87–88). Ironically, more than two years before their marriage, Charlotte had informed Walter of her priorities and had clearly articulated the conflict she was confronting: "As much as I love you I love *WORK* better, & I cannot make the two compatible. . . . It is no use, dear, no use. I am meant to be useful & strong, to help many and do my share in the world's work, but not to be loved" (*Endure*, p. 63). Despite Walter's best efforts to make Charlotte feel loved, her depression only deepened. If Charlotte had found marriage and work incompatible, impending motherhood, which would require the forfeiture of any remnants of freedom, promised to be a recipe for disaster.

Katharine Beecher Stetson was born on March 23, 1885, just ten and a half months after Charlotte and Walter were married. The depression that Charlotte experienced continued to escalate following Katharine's birth, and over the next several months, Charlotte became dangerously despondent. A friend, fearing that Charlotte was going insane, funded her stay at a Philadelphia sanitarium where she underwent the "rest cure," a new and experimental treatment for nervous prostration. During her six-week stay, the twenty-six-year-old Charlotte was fed, bathed, read to, massaged; in short, all responsibility (and hence, all power and control) was taken away. At the end of her stay, she was pronounced well, sent home, and told by her physician, Dr.

S. Weir Mitchell, to: "Live as domestic a life as possible. Have your child with you all the time. . . . Lie down an hour after each meal. Have but two hours' intellectual life a day. And never touch pen, brush or pencil as long as you live" (*Living*, p. 96).

Charlotte Stetson returned home and attempted to follow the doctor's prescription; within weeks, she was on the verge of a nervous breakdown. Biographers have documented how the tremendous subjugation of her own desires—to work and to help humanity—in favor of fulfilling the socially prescribed roles of wife and mother resulted in her brush with total insanity. Fortunately, Charlotte was able to pull herself together, seek a separation from her husband, and move to California, where she began to thrive. For the first time, she would be free to answer her calling.

Although she had begun, tentatively, to develop her skills as a writer by producing a handful of poems and articles during the early years of her marriage, her career flourished after she arrived in California. In 1890 alone, the first year of her "freedom," Charlotte Stetson produced thirty-three articles and over twenty poems. She became interested in the Nationalist movement and began her work as a public speaker, lecturing to women's clubs and becoming active in the Pacific Coast Women's Press Association. For several months she edited the *Impress*, a small family weekly. Her continuing struggle with poverty and the demands placed upon her by her burgeoning but ill-paying career made it increasingly difficult for her to provide adequately for Katharine. In 1894, the year her divorce became final, Charlotte arranged to send her daughter to live with her ex-husband and his new wife (Charlotte's lifelong friend, Grace Channing). After her daughter's departure Charlotte Stetson spent much of the remainder of the 1890s on the lecture circuit, speaking on socialist issues and on women's rights throughout the United States and in England.

In 1898 Charlotte produced her groundbreaking work, *Women and Economics*, which brought her international acclaim. In 1900 she married her first cousin, George Houghton Gilman, and the marriage lasted for thirty-four happy years, until Houghton's sudden death from a massive cerebral hemorrhage. During the early years of their marriage, Katharine lived with Charlotte and Houghton much of the time and alternately with her father and stepmother, Grace.

Throughout the first part of the twentieth century, Charlotte Gilman's incredible prolificacy continued (see the introduction to chapter 6 for more discussion of Charlotte's activities after 1900). She produced numerous books of sociological import, several novels, hundreds of short stories and poems, and her autobiography. Nearly all of her writing touched on human rights in one way or another. For seven years, from 1909 to 1916, she single-handedly wrote, edited, and published the *Forerunner*, a progressive monthly magazine of some 21,000 words per issue. In 1922 Charlotte and Houghton Gilman moved to Norwich Town, Connecticut, where she continued to write and to lecture occasionally. In 1932 Charlotte Gilman learned that she had inoperable breast cancer, and in 1935 she ended her life, citing among other reasons her diminished "power of service" to contribute meaningfully to society (*Living*, p. 333).[7]

The diaries that Charlotte Perkins Gilman kept throughout much of her life are not characterized by any kind of conscious literary style. She was not in the least concerned with producing a set of documents that could be lauded for their sophisticated eloquence or artistic effect. Rather, the diaries provide an often unpolished record of daily events. "My purpose in diary-keeping, since girlhood, was not at all to make revelations of feeling, though[t], or of incidents not readable by other people," she wrote in *The Living of Charlotte Perkins Gilman* (p. 244). The purpose, instead, was to document the "small detail[s]" of a life (p. 244), and indeed, the diaries offer a revealing look at the day-to-day activities of a woman who struggled against overwhelming odds to attain a respect and popularity as an author and lecturer. At times confessional, at times startling, at times mundane, Charlotte's "old friend" or "beloved journal" offers a rare opportunity for the reader simultaneously to study nineteenth-century domestic life in general and to witness the consequences of one woman's rebellious rejection of the exclusionary limitations imposed by the "cult of domesticity" in particular. The domestic scenes around which many of the entries are centered would likely be deemed too marginal for inclusion in a man's diary; for the nineteenth-century female diarist, however, records of such activities were considered noteworthy and invariably safe to write down. But Charlotte supplements her record of domestic life in nineteenth-century America with a variety of unrestrained protests and spirited assertions. She damns those who oppose women's rights, castigates her young husband for attempting to "mould" her, sympathizes with another "victim" whose husband used his "'marital rights' at her vital expense," reviles the drudgeries of housework, and derisively condemns feminine vanities on the pages of her diaries. From an early age it was apparent that Charlotte Perkins Gilman would not conform to societal expectations of appropriate roles and vocations.

On the whole Charlotte Gilman's diaries serve as a barometer of her state of mind: when she was feeling well, the entries are bright, animated, and often humorous; when she was experiencing her low "grey" periods, the entries are stark, eclipsed, sometimes cryptic. Charlotte's emotions, as presented on the pages of her diaries, are often understated. As she noted in *The Living of Charlotte Perkins Gilman*, the decision to withhold some of the most personal details of her interior world was a conscious one. In reviewing the diaries at the age of sixty-five, for example, during the process of writing her autobiography, Gilman was "amused by [the diary's] paucity of material which might be eagerly looked for by—well, a newspaper-minded person" (p. 244). Although she was enormously affected by various events in her life—the deaths of loved ones, her decisions to marry, her long separations from Katharine— the diary entries depicting these turning points are frequently, and intentionally, guarded: they often consist of rather flat and factual reports that obscure the pain, the fear, the ambivalence that Charlotte actually experienced. There is, in fact, often a striking dichotomy between the living Charlotte and the voice that emerges on the pages of her journal.

The reality of Charlotte's life was that it was often complicated by intense emotional entanglements. The public persona that she cultivated from an early age, however, was strong, rational, and very much in control. Her exclusion from the diaries of the details of her intensely personal experiences, particularly after 1887, was deliberate: it was designed to protect the vulnerable part of herself that was at odds with the carefully constructed public image. Ever mindful of the imposing curiosity of the "newspaper-minded person," she preferred, instead, to capture on the journal pages "the living" in which she was engaged. Nevertheless, page after page of the diaries tells us much about the reality of her existence: the poverty, the hardships, the anxiety, the insecurity, the despair, the hysteria, the anger. But in addition to the many trials, we also witness the triumphs and strengths: the intellectual growth, the fiesty spirit, the fierce determination, the drive to effect social change, the kindness, and the compassion.

Interestingly, Charlotte documented the majority of her most intimate thoughts not on the pages of her diaries—the traditional forum for confessional writing—but on odd scraps of paper that she kept in a folder marked "Thoughts & Figgerings" and in personal correspondence and in poetry. Many of those writings have been collected in the appendixes in this edition, and they provide an extraordinary glimpse into the private Charlotte—often enormously insecure, often suffering from emotional paralysis, often self-reflective to a fault—a markedly different woman from the self-confident public persona. The striking dichotomy between the two selves—the public figure and the private woman—emerges on the pages of the appendixes. It is here that we see much of the sensuality, the passion, the desperate efforts to reclaim her health that contributed to the shaping of Charlotte's life.

The Abridged Diaries of Charlotte Perkins Gilman document the highs and lows in the life of a brave and intelligent woman. The selections included in this edition chronicle the experiences that marked turning points through nearly twenty years of Charlotte's life: her on-again, off-again romantic interest in the charming Brown University undergraduate Sam Simmons, (and occasionally in his brother, Jim); her intense love of Martha Luther and the subsequent pain of losing her; her ominous premonition that her marriage to Charles Walter Stetson would prove a disaster; her unbridled contempt for Stetson as she left for Philadelphia to undergo Dr. Mitchell's rest cure. They also depict her mother's losing battle with cancer, her own struggle with chronic and often debilitating depression, her love for Adeline ("Delle") Knapp, her reacquaintance with her first cousin and future husband, Houghton Gilman, and, of course, the realization of her dream: to "find out what ailed society" and to improve it (*Living*, p. 182).

The early entries included in this edition are somewhat different in content and mood from the later entries, those written after her nervous breakdown. (No diaries exist for the two-and-a-half-year period immediately preceding, during, and following the breakdown in 1887.) The Charlotte of the early diaries tends to be somewhat more introspective, more methodical, and more playful, although certainly some of these characteristics are, at least in part, a function of age.

The sparse little diary for 1890, the first postbreakdown record and the least developed of all of the diaries, is a remarkable document; its understated entries paradoxically capture a rather dramatic transformation in Charlotte as she finally started to take control of her life. As the year progresses, the brief entries gradually reflect more confidence, more stamina, and certainly more output in her literary endeavors. Charlotte commented in *The Living of Charlotte Perkins Gilman* on that "scrappy little . . . diary" (measuring only 2⅛ by 5⅜ inches) that she "tried to keep that first year [in California]" and particularly on the large gaps that exist. "The blanks were the drowned time, not even sense [enough] to make . . . scanty notes," she wrote (pp. 114–15). The entries for the remainder of the 1890s, in contrast, show a woman still plagued by episodes of depression but generally calmer, more in control, more decisive, and far more independent. Together, the diaries document a life where periods of incredible productivity were juxtaposed with months of intellectual paralysis.

When Charlotte Stetson was preparing to travel to Philadelphia for treatment at Dr. Mitchell's sanitarium, she expressed regret that she would have to leave her diary behind: "I have kept a journal since I was fifteen, the only blanks being in these last years of sickness and pain. I have done it because it was useful. Now I am to go away for my health, and shall not try to take any responsibilites [*sic*] with me, even this old friend."[8]

Eventually, after she had achieved fame, Charlotte Perkins Gilman abandoned the practice of keeping diaries. "These diaries are a nuisance," she complained in the autobiography. She continued: "Page after page of those dismal 'downs' with the cheerfully welcomed 'ups.' Record of writing, record of lecturing, record of seeing people, record of housework. After 1903 I gave up the fat three by six kind, with two days to a page, and took to thinner ones, with seven days on a page . . . with the right hand page for cash account. These are big enough to set down engagements, train time, and such necessities" (p. 294). It is almost as if after having documented the climb, Charlotte Gilman no longer needed her "old friend." Besides, she had a new friend in the person of her second husband, George Houghton Gilman, and he acted as her advocate, her companion, her confidant until his death in 1934.

But the diaries served a useful purpose. They fulfilled Charlotte Gilman's need—indeed her "responsibility" if we are to heed her word choice as she headed to Philadelphia—to document even the most trivial events as evidence of her "living." The living in which Charlotte Perkins Gilman engaged, and on which she based the title of her autobiography, is not exclusive to the work that she contributed to society; the living that she experienced was as much a result of her day-to-day activities as it was standing on a platform before a large crowd. The diaries are, above all, a validation of her life; they offer tangible evidence that it did, indeed, have value and meaning.

Charlotte Perkins seemed to sense, in fact, that she would someday be famous. In an extraordinary letter to her brother Thomas at the age of twenty-two (see Appendix B), she predicted the mark she would make on the world: "I have ideas and theories which time will develope. . . . Bye and bye when I know much more and hold such place in society as I will hold, perhaps I might write you letters that would be of some use. But now I am only acquiring knowledge, . . . and my 'ideas and theories' change and change as the years go by." She relied heavily on her diaries in documenting those changes as she wrote her autobiography some forty-two years later.

My objective in publishing *The Abridged Diaries of Charlotte Perkins Gilman* is to compile a streamlined edition featuring selections that best illustrate both Gilman's struggles and her triumphs and to make it available to the widest possible audience: scholars, researchers, students, and general readers. Moreover, I hope the abridged edition will continue to facilitate research, to broaden our knowledge of Charlotte Gilman's life, to open the growing field of personal writings to further inquiry and investigation.[9]

NOTES

1. See, in particular, Mary A. Hill's biography, *Charlotte Perkins Gilman: The Making of a Radical Feminist, 1860–1896* (Philadelphia, 1980); Ann J. Lane's *To Herland and Be-*

yond: The Life and Work of Charlotte Perkins Gilman (New York, 1990); and Gary Scharn-horst's *Charlotte Perkins Gilman* (Boston, 1985).

2. Charlotte Perkins Gilman, *The Living of Charlotte Perkins Gilman* (1935; rpt. Madison, Wis., 1990), p. 8.

3. To Martha Luther, July 29, 1881, Rhode Island Historical Association.

4. To Martha Luther, July 24, 1881, Rhode Island Historical Association.

5. To Charles Walter Stetson, Jan. 29, 1882, quoted in Mary A. Hill, ed., *Endure: The Diaries of Charles Walter Stetson* (Philadelphia, 1985), p. 36. Stetson routinely recopied Charlotte's letters verbatim into his private journals to be "doubly sure" of their preservation.

6. See chap. 7 for further discussion of Charlotte's decision to marry Walter Stetson.

7. On the evening of Aug. 17, 1935, Charlotte Perkins Gilman ended her life by inhaling chloroform, preferring it, she said, to dying of cancer (*Living*, p. 334). Gilman's death mask, which was made by Charlotte's daughter, Katharine Stetson Chamberlin, is part of the Charlotte Perkins Gilman collection at the Schlesinger Library. Although the cancer had caused her face to become emaciated, Gilman wore a determined and contented expression at the time of her death.

8. Diary entry, April 18, 1887.

9. Readers wishing the full unabridged diaries should consult the two-volume edition, *The Diaries of Charlotte Perkins Gilman* (Charlottesville, Va., 1994). That edition begins on Jan. 1, 1876, and continues virtually uninterrupted (except for occasional omissions or infrequent breaks, most notably after the birth of Charlotte's daughter, Katharine Beecher Stetson) until April 19, 1887, the day before twenty-six-year-old Charlotte Stetson left for Dr. Mitchell's sanitarium to undergo the rest cure for nervous prostration. After a break of more than two and a half years, the unabridged diaries resume on Jan. 1, 1890, and continue, with more frequent and more substantial breaks, until May 3, 1903, at which point they abruptly end. Thereafter, beginning in 1904, Charlotte Gilman preferred to keep engagement books rather than diaries.

A NOTE ON THE TEXT

T HE PURPOSE OF this edition is to make available to scholars, researchers, and students a streamlined version of the personal diaries and journals of Charlotte Perkins Gilman, with representative selections from the various periods of her life.

Included in this edition are selections written between January 1, 1879, and March 12, 1935. (There are no extant diaries for 1888, 1889, and 1895.) The selections illustrate Gilman's development from a restless, high-spirited, and rather opinionated young woman to a mature, internationally known author and lecturer whose words and wisdom touched thousands of lives as she attempted to effect social change. Omitted material within a day's entry is indicated with ellipses, and long breaks during which Gilman neglected to make diary entries are identified with a bracketed note in the text.

Because the role of an editor is to be less interpretive than objective, I have attempted, in the chapter introductions, to retain a fair degree of neutrality while still providing as background an appropriate amount of historical and biographical contextualization. Readers wishing to have a fuller psychological profile of Charlotte Gilman should consult full-length biographies.

Texts for this edition were excerpted from my two-volume edition, *The Diaries of Charlotte Perkins Gilman* (Charlottesville, Va., 1994), which were originally drawn from microfiche copy; the transcribed version of the two-volume set was then verified against the original diaries housed at the Schlesinger Library. In only one instance was it impossible to verify the transcribed copy against the original text: the journal for 1880–81 has been missing from the Gilman collection for several years, according to the Curator of Manuscripts at the Schlesinger Library, Eva S. Moseley. Whether the diary was stolen or misfiled is unknown; efforts to locate it, however, have been unsuccessful. The 1880–81 journal transcription was, therefore, edited against the microfiche copy.

The editorial method I used was a conservative one: my purpose has been to reproduce Gilman's original text insofar as typographical conventions allow. Gilman's spelling, capitalization, often erratic (and sometimes missing) punctuation, underlinings, indentations, and abbreviations have been preserved. In cases where parts of words are missing because of damaged or mutilated text in the extant diaries, I have attempted to reconstruct the passage based on the partial word. Where there is any question, however, as to the content

of the text, I have indicated the missing text with *"msm"* (manuscript mutilated) in brackets. In cases where text is indecipherable, I have included a
bracketed *illegible*. On rare occasions I have inserted missing punctuation
within brackets to enhance readability. I have also occasionally inserted words
within brackets for clarification of a particular passage. Any conjectural readings are indicated by a bracketed question mark. Only where something in
the original may appear to be a printer's error have I included a bracketed *sic*.
Gilman was a particularly poor speller; even the names of friends and/or
acquaintances were frequently misspelled; Charlotte occasionally would use
variant spellings of a name within a single entry. Particularly noteworthy
is Gilman's frequent misspelling of her daughter Katharine's name (as "Katherine") in the months following her birth.

Charlotte not only had difficulty in spelling names; she occasionally had
difficulty remembering people. "I haven't the faintest memory . . . of most of
the names in the diary, but the record shows the kind of calls I had, from all
kinds of people. . . . I do not, can not, hold in mind a fraction of the innumerable people I have met" (*Living*, pp. 134, 261). Her circle of friends and
acquaintances was indeed wide; I have identified and annotated those people
with whom Charlotte shared a close relationship, those with whom she spent
a substantial amount of time, and those who were well known enough to
be included in *Webster's Biographical Dictionary*. A few people, however, remain unidentified, primarily those to whom there is infrequent or only brief
mention.

In addition to having a wide circle of friends, Charlotte was an avid reader,
and on the pages of her diaries she alludes to literally hundreds of works that
she read. I have annotated works according to specific criteria. Annotation has
not been provided for: (*a*) works that are widely recognized (e.g., Whitman's
Leaves of Grass); (*b*) historical works and biographies where the title conveys
a strong sense of the content (e.g., *A History of Egypt*); (*c*) works for which
Charlotte has included title *and* author (e.g., Olive Schreiner's "Heaven");
(*d*) works (primarily short fiction, poems, and essays) appearing in popular
press magazines for which no index is available. Otherwise, I have identified
as many of the less-well-known works as possible. At times, however, it was
impossible to locate obscure or incomplete titles.

As a rule, I have not provided annotation for Charlotte Gilman's own works,
except where publication information is particularly noteworthy. Readers
wishing complete publication histories of Gilman's works are referred to Gary
Scharnhorst's virtually complete listing, *Charlotte Perkins Gilman: A Bibliography* (Metuchen, N.J., 1985). The bibliography also lists information on published reports of Gilman's lectures.

Charlotte used numerous abbreviations in the diaries; I have expanded, with brackets, the first use of an abbreviation, left the abbreviation intact thereafter, and provided at the end of this section a list of those she most commonly used. Numbers occasionally included at the beginning of an entry record the time that she arose that particular day. Dates have not been standardized; they have been reproduced as they appear in the original diary. Where Charlotte included drawings and illustrations that were impossible to reproduce in the text, a note has been provided to that effect in a separate section entitled Textual Notes. Any of Gilman's own editorial emendations which were awkward to include in the text (particularly words that were written and subsequently crossed out) have also been documented in the Textual Notes. An asterisk in the text of the diary signals that there is a textual note. These notes have been arranged chronologically by year and date.

In addition to the Textual Notes, a full set of Explanatory Notes is included in a separate section. Except where they can be located in a standard dictionary, allusions to places, people, events, words, or objects that might be unfamiliar to the contemporary reader or that might benefit from clarification have been elucidated to make the text more accessible.

Also included in this edition are two appendixes. Contained in these appendixes are a variety of writings by Charlotte (and some by Walter Stetson), many of which are being published for the first time. They elucidate Gilman's life; in many cases, they enlarge upon what is only hinted at on the pages of the diaries. The enormous passion between Charlotte and Walter Stetson, for example, which is rather tempered in the diaries, is plainly apparent in the private writings appended to this edition. Appendix A contains selections from "Thoughts & Figgerings," a collection of miscellaneous perceptions or objectives that Gilman occasionally jotted onto little scraps of papers and eventually compiled into a folder. Appendix B contains verses, letters, and miscellaneous writings that either are tucked into the diaries or are alluded to in the text but located elsewhere (either in volumes 21 or 22 of the Gilman Papers or in an unprocessed addendum to the collection).

The abridged diaries are arranged chronologically; the only substantive alteration I have made is to divide the text into six chapters (which tend to mark significant events, milestones, or other transitions in Charlotte Gilman's life) and to include titles and contextualizing commentary for each chapter.

COMMON ABBREVIATIONS IN THE DIARIES

Ath.:	Athenaeum
Aunt C.:	Aunt Caroline
Dr. C.:	Dr. Channing
gym. *or* gymn.:	gymnasium
H. *or* Ho.:	Houghton
h'k'f *or* h.d.k.f.; *or* han'ch'fs:	handkerchief(s)
Lit.:	Literature
M.:	Martha [Luther]
Mr. L.:	Mr. Lane
N. E. Mag.:	*New England Magazine*
Pub. Lib.:	Public Library
S.F.:	San Francisco
Scrib.:	*Scribner's* magazine
sen.:	senior
S.& M.:	Small & Maynard
S.P.C.:	Socialist Purity Club
S.P.S.:	Socialist Purity Society
S. S.:	Sunday School
T.:	Thomas [Perkins]
W.:	Walter
W.J.:	*Woman's Journal*
Xtian:	Christian

THE ABRIDGED DIARIES OF

Charlotte Perkins Gilman

ONE

"As lonely a heart as ever cried"

January 1, 1879–January 10, 1882

WHEN CHARLOTTE PERKINS received her first diary from her brother Thomas at the age of fifteen, her entries were characteristic of what one might expect from any typical teenaged girl: accounts of her love life, of her childish feuds with her brother, of her power struggles with her mother, Mary, and occasionally, of her ambivalent feelings toward her estranged father, Frederick Perkins. But it was the object of her infatuation, a young actor in a local theater company, William S. Daboll, who received much of the attention on the pages of Charlotte's diary for 1876, even though the two never met: "I saw him! I saw him! My own, dear, darling, lovely, handsome, tall, graceful, splendid, glorious, excruciating, gorgeous, Willie Daboll! Bless him! Bless him! Bless him! & he saw me! Hurrah!"* Charlotte also experienced the thrill of anticipation: "Willie has been in Worcester . . . & is coming here! In 'As You Like It'! And *I'm* going!!! Just think of it! It's too lovely to happen! To sit & see him for a whole evening! I can't believe it possible!" And over the next several days, a series of sightings: "Oh I wish I could get acquainted with him!" "Oh be joyful! I saw my darling 4 times. And he saw me! And I blushed! What should I do if I was introduced?" "[S]aw my darling . . . I love him more & more every day. I hope he will always be happy." Day after day the pages of Charlotte's first diary chronicle the hope, the ecstasy, and, inevitably, the profound disappointment of young love.

"Oh Dear! is it never going to be anything more?" "W. S. D. has been seen walking with a lady on Westminster St. several times. Alas! poor Charlotte! T'is false! Prove it!" And then, toward the end of the year: "I went down St. & saw him! He visibly sneered! I am devoured with grief."

---

*Unless otherwise noted, all quotations in the chapter introductions are taken from entries within that chapter. Excerpts from letters are taken from unpublished correspondence in the collection of Gilman Papers at the Schlesinger Library, Radcliffe College.

While the year 1877 brought an end to her heartache over the unrequited love of Willie Daboll, the diary entries remained strikingly similar, although somewhat less melodramatic, as Charlotte approached her eighteenth year in Providence, Rhode Island. Cousin Arthur Hale, who was attending Harvard University, became Charlotte's primary romantic interest, and the two exchanged frequent letters. During a visit to Boston in early 1877, the two cousins enjoyed some cozy time together: "A[rthur]. & I go to see the 'Scarlet Letter.' Had a nice time. Then lunched on gingerbread in the seclusion of the red parlor. The friendly A. evidently likes his little cousin." But Charlotte's interest in Arthur wasn't very serious, and there were plenty of other callers who were vying for her attention during 1877 and 1878. Still, Charlotte grew impatient whenever Arthur failed to keep in touch. In June, for example, she remarked in her diary, "Guess Arthur is 'sick or in prison.' What can ail him?" The next day, her loneliness was apparent. "I wish I had a 'feller,'" she wrote. Finally, two days later, she received a card from Arthur. "The dear boy sends me his photo. He *is* homely. But so nice!" By the end of 1878, she had lost her interest in him altogether. "I like him less and less unfortunately," she wrote on December 28. "He grows homlier and homlier. . . . I wouldn't mind that if he would only dress well, and was not so conceited."

While matters of the heart were prominent among Charlotte's confessions in her juvenile diaries, so too was her tendency to exaggerate the most mundane and trivial of events, particularly those which threatened her self-image as she stood stranded on the shaky threshold between adolescence and womanhood. A few days before her seventeenth birthday, for example, Charlotte was chagrined by a comment made by a friend's father. "Mr. Carpenter mortally offends me by thinking I was about 15! And I *seventeen* next Tuesday!" And later that summer, "Twilight conversation with mother on all sorts of potent grave and reverend subjects. Verily I am grown exceeding old." And the next year: "Mother & I go to see Mary Anderson in Romeo & Juliet. Very fine indeed, but alas. At eighteen I am already losing my delight for the theatre. It is a pity."

But in addition to anxieties about age and identity, also embedded in the pages of Charlotte's teen diaries are subtle allusions to the work ethic which was already beginning to form and which would influence so dramatically her future years. "Have taken a fancy to work hard and be very smart," she wrote in March 1877. And in August she chided herself for wasting precious time: "What a wasted day! I have accomplished nothing. Neither learned anything, or grown any. Home and work is best." In October, after a particularly hard wash day, the seventeen-year-old Charlotte altered Benjamin Franklin's familiar maxim to fit her own burgeoning feminism: "Go to bed at 7!! Early to bed, and early to rise, makes women healthy contented and wise," she wrote cheerfully. While much of Charlotte's work during her adolescence was of the domestic kind—sewing, washing dishes, cleaning house, and the like—she also tried her hand briefly at employment outside of the home. In December 1877, for example, she worked as a cashier for a few days, and in late 1878 she was employed for two weeks by a Mr. Tingley, of a marble works company, to help in the design of marble monuments.

In September 1878 a friend of her parents began encouraging Charlotte to attend the Rhode Island School of Design, which was to open in Providence that fall. Her father was unusually supportive: "Go to the School of Design by all means, and learn all you can. You could not do a better thing," he wrote to Charlotte. She promptly enrolled as a member of the day class for 1878–79. A few weeks after classes commenced, Charlotte herself began teaching art to others. At the age of eighteen, Charlotte Anna Perkins was already educating people: offering encouragement and teaching them how. It was a pattern which would last a lifetime.

At the beginning of 1879, Charlotte abandoned her commercial diary in favor of a journal, which would allow her unrestricted space for making entries. The year 1879 also marked the beginning of a subtle shift away from the juvenile nature of the diaries, as Charlotte began to grow—intellectually, socially, artistically. Still, we see both sides of the girl/woman. On the one hand, Charlotte was earnestly practicing a course of self-improvement, not unlike Benjamin Franklin's plan for moral perfection: she was trying to make herself less egotistical, attempting to outgrow laziness, and, most importantly, exercising control over her own life. On the other hand, she could still be incredibly childlike, writing some of her diary entries entirely in verse (see, for example, the entry dated January 9, 1879) or naively dismissing the gravity of the diptheria which she and Thomas both contracted early in the year. Still, 1879 was, in many ways, a turning point for Charlotte. It marked the beginning of her lifelong friendships with Martha Luther and Grace Channing, and late in the year a visit to her aunt Katie Gilman reacquainted Charlotte with her twelve-year-old cousin, Houghton, whom she would marry some twenty-one years later.

Charlotte's friendships continued to blossom in 1880 when Martha Luther introduced her to the brothers Jim and Sam Simmons, with whom she would share a long, if turbulent, friendship. But on-again, off-again relationships aside, Charlotte had more serious matters with which to contend, particularly the poverty against which she and her mother, Mary, were constantly struggling. Brother Thomas had moved to Nevada in the fall of 1879 to work as a surveyor (*Living*, p. 92), and father Frederick Perkins, who was living in Boston, rarely offered financial support to his estranged family. Charlotte attempted to contribute whatever monies she could to the household budget, but there were some rather lean times. After an entry noting the receipt of seventy cents, for example,

Charlotte added simply, "It goeth to squench our hunger." Fortunately, in late 1880 Charlotte learned that an aunt had bequeathed $66 to her and Thomas. Though it was a small sum, it would carry the family through the current financial shortfall.

By the age of twenty, Charlotte Perkins was a popular young woman with a keen sense of humor and a restless spirit. She and her mother, Mary, were often at odds, and Mary's provincialism would frequently leave Charlotte irritable or sullen. Sometimes, however, her moodiness was fueled by the reality of the Perkinses' poverty: her inability to afford new shoes, for example, caused extreme physical discomfort, and in the cold, snowy month of January, she went barefoot in the house after her old, shabby shoes finally wore out. Even when she and Mary appeared to be getting ahead financially, their "prosperity" was invariably short-lived.

To help her mother pay the bills, Charlotte devised various strategies for earning an income. In addition to running a small day school with her mother, Charlotte found that her classes at the Rhode Island School of Design were paying off. Orders for her dainty, hand-painted stationery were a steady, though insubstantial, source of income; moreover, in collaboration with her cousin Robert Brown, Charlotte was successful in designing advertising cards for Soapine, a household cleaning product made by the Kendall Manufacturing Company of Providence. While the business was not particularly lucrative, it enabled Charlotte to contribute, at least nominally, to the family earnings. Private art lessons given by Charlotte also yielded some much-needed cash. At the same time that she was teaching others, however, Charlotte continued her own education by enrolling in classes, attending lectures, and spending countless hours at the public library and the local athenaeum reading and studying on her own.

During this period, Charlotte's friendship with Martha Luther blossomed, and the two of them were often joined in their activities by Sam and Jim Simmons. The Simmons brothers were frequent guests at the Perkins house where they enjoyed whist parties and lively conversations. But although Charlotte's circle of friends was constantly enlarging, she still suffered from episodes of loneliness. On Christmas night of 1880, Charlotte had a particularly hard time dealing with the holiday letdown, which seemed to amplify her sense of isolation. In a verse included in her December 25 entry, Charlotte's self-pity is apparent.

In reality, Charlotte's life was not as bleak as she suggested that Christmas evening. While Martha and the Simmons brothers were welcome companions, Charlotte also enjoyed the company of some of Rhode Island's most prominent families. Among them were the Dimans, headed by Brown University history professor J. Lewis Diman, who died on February 3, 1881, after a short illness. Less than three months later, his daughter, May Diman, whom Charlotte described as the "most utterly charming" member of her circle of friends (*Living*,

p. 49), was killed after she was thrown from a horse. Her death occurred as the Perkinses were settling into a new, more spacious house, which understandably tempered Charlotte's enthusiasm for the "wholly advantageous" change that the move was intended to signal. Although Charlotte tried to "preserve the appearance of composure" at May Diman's funeral, the death of her friend left her sad and shaken.

Shortly after May's death, the friendship between Charlotte and Martha Luther deepened. On the morning of Saturday, May 14, the two went shopping together in downtown Providence and purchased "a pair of lovely little bracelets" that they each vowed to wear as a "badge . . . of union"—a symbolic acknowledgment of their mutual trust and affection. The rest of the day they spent in "tranquil bliss," after Martha "surreptitiously" stole up to Charlotte's room where they passed a quiet afternoon. "With Martha I knew perfect happiness," Charlotte reflected years later in *The Living of Charlotte Perkins Gilman* (p. 78).

The "perfect happiness" that she shared with Martha compensated, in part, for the lack of affection shown Charlotte by her mother, whose own disappointments in "early love" caused her to withhold "all expression of affection as far as possible" (*Living*, p. 10). "Looking back on my uncuddled childhood it seems to me a sad mistake of my heroic mother to withhold from me the petting I so craved. . . . Denied that natural expression, my first memory of loving any one . . . and immeasurably the dearest, was Martha. We were closely together, increasingly happy together, for four of those long years of girlhood. She was nearer and dearer than any one up to that time," Charlotte wrote (p. 78).

Indeed, because love had been elusive all of her life, Charlotte's emotional investment in her relationship with Martha was enormous. Extant correspondence reveals the extent of her trust in, and dependence upon, Martha. To Martha, Charlotte could reveal vulnerabilities that to the rest of the world she would keep concealed. "Fancy me strong and unassailable to all the world beside, and the coming down and truckling to you like a half-fed amiable kitten," she wrote to Martha on July 3, Charlotte's twenty-first birthday. The letter underscores the striking dichotomy between Charlotte's public and private personas and reveals a pattern which would characterize many of her adult relationships.

In addition to writing long letters to Martha, who was away for much of the summer, Charlotte assumed the bulk of the domestic responsibilities in the Perkins household, since her mother, Mary, was frequently debilitated by chronic headaches. But Charlotte also found time to cultivate her own interests, reading Emerson and Tennyson, studying Latin, painting cards for compensation, and learning to play the piano "to the dire distress of [her] friends." She also made substantial progress in convincing Dr. John P. Brooks that Providence needed a "Ladies Gymnasium." Thanks to her skills of persuasion and her tireless campaign to recruit potential members, the gymnasium project was soon under way.

Through all of her various experiences that summer, Charlotte's friendship with Martha remained her strongest tie. Still, she had no shortage of male companionship during the summer of 1881. Among her callers was Sidney Putnam, who would introduce Charlotte to Charles Walter Stetson in early 1882.

In general, Charlotte's spirits during the summer of 1881 were high; she felt strong, cheerful, and optimistic. "My circle widens," she noted in the middle of August. "Life may be happier than I thought." Just two days later, on August 15, Charlotte wrote Martha a letter reaffirming her love for her—and apparently looking for reassurance that Martha felt the same way. "I think it highly probable (ahem) that you love me however I squirm, love the steady care around which I so variously revolve, love me and will love me—why in the name of heaven have we so confounded love with passion that it sounds to our century-tutored ears either wicked or absurd to name it between women? It is no longer friendship between us, it is love," she wrote. But Charlotte's dream of continuing to share mutual love and "perfect happiness" was shattered when Martha returned to Providence late that summer with the news that she had become enamoured of one Charles A. Lane of Hingham, Massachusetts. By the first of November, Martha was engaged to be married.

Charlotte was devastated, confiding to Sam Simmons that the loss of Martha was analogous to the amputation of a limb (see her letter dated November 14, 1881, in Appendix B). To her diary she confessed "lov[ing] the damsel," and several entries reflect the depth of her despair as a result of Martha's betrayal: "O my little girl! My little girl," she cried. The loneliness and pain as she "struggle[d] with [her] grief" was enormous. Charlotte tried to fight back, verbally "spar[ring] with the enemy," Charles Lane, but with little success. "Pleasant," she wrote bitterly, "to ring at the door where you've always been greeted with gladness; to be met by the smile that you value all others above—to see that smile flicker and vanish and change into sadness because she was met by *your* presence instead of her love."

As a way of coping with her grief, Charlotte immersed herself in work, establishing a lifelong pattern that would repeat whenever she was faced with loss or pain. She kept busy finalizing plans for the Providence Ladies Gymnasium and joining the Union of Christian Work where she spent her Saturday evenings. She also began confiding more in Jim and Sam Simmons and attempted to work through her sadness in letters and poems. Still, she would sometimes break down after seeing Martha home; at other times, she would reduce Martha to tears by making her feel guilty. In a poignant poem (see Appendix B for complete text) that Charlotte wrote to Martha on the subject of their permanently altered friendship, she particularly mourns the loss of their former intimacy:

> Think dearest, while you yet can feel the touch
> Of hands that once could soothe your deepest pain;

Think of those days when we could hardly dare
Be seen abroad together lest our eyes
Should speak too loud. * * There is no danger now . . .

By Christmas Day, 1881, Charlotte seemed to feel somewhat better: "I am very tired, but not much hurt by the work & pain of the past two months, & begin to see light again." Charlotte ended the year lamenting the loss "of a perfect friendship," but she also celebrated the growth that had resulted from the pain. "I am stronger, wiser and better than last year, and am fairly 'satisfied,' as to the years work," she wrote. "I have learned much of self-control & consideration of others. . . . My memory begins to show the training it has had, I can get what I want when I want it, pretty generally. Most of all I have learned what pain is. Have learned the need of human sympathy by the unfilled want of it, and have gained the power to *give* it, which is worth while."

As to the new year, Charlotte looked forward, however uncertainly, to a fresh start. Less than two weeks later, she was introduced to Charles Walter Stetson, a man who would change her life forever.

Jan. 1st. 1879.

Having kept a diary for three years, and not liking a set space, I herewith begin on a journal.[1]

It feels good.

Gentle reader, wouldst know me? Verily, here I am. 18 years old. 5 feet, 6½ in. high. Weigh some 120 lbs. or thereabouts. Looks, not bad. At times handsome. At others decidedly homely. Health, Perfect. Strength amazing. Character——. Ah! Gradually outgrowing laziness. Possessing great power over my self. *Not* sentimental. Rather sober and bleak as a general thing. At present I am not in love with anybody; I don't think I ever shall be.

I arose late this morning and was somewhat lazy. Am committing Macaulay[']s Horatius to memory. Skate all the afternoon with T. Fourth trial. (1st this year). Really progress. Thomas goes in the evening to a church-social-New-Years-party affair, but on account of an unpleasant eminence of a ruddy hue on my fair brow, and the unsuitableness of my one dress, and the necessity for early rising tomorrow, and lack of inclination to go, I stay at home. Fix things for school tomorrow, and christen my new inkstand and beloved Journal. . . .

Jan. 3rd.

Windy and *very* cold. But with fresh air to feed the fire I carry a furnace inside which keeps me warm. Make a great step in drawing. i.e. learn to grasp the spirit of the thing and draw that. Really improved on my copy. . . .

Jan. 4th. 1879.

. . . I have decided that I *will* get married. Whereas before, I thought it more likely that I should not. Purpose: Happy man and Noble Family. "Our Sistah! Oh! has spoken!"

Jan. 9th.

All through the muggy morning we were snug and warm within, but the snow was drop, drop, dropping on the muffled roof of tin. And now through the long evening we still are snug within, but the rain is drip, drip, dripping on the sounding roof of tin. . . . I endeavor to poetize, with but indifferent success.

Tues. Jan. 14th. 1879.

. . . Am overtaken, greeted, and affably conversed with by Mrs. Putnam. Subject "Sydney." [2] Messieur Thompson denotes his arrival by an ambiguous card, and follows it by his noble prescence. . . . He is fair to average.

Jan. Wed. 15. 1879.

. . . (Private.) Mentally canvass young Thompson. Ans. Won't do.

Jan. Saturday. 25th. 1879.

. . . Morning at Essay Club. Very pleasant. Quite distinguish myself in discussion. Saunter home in balmy sunshine, eating snowball. . . .

{Jan. 27th}

Behold a day is lost! in this wise. On Monday eve, at half past six, I departed with lord Keach to our unfortunate sleighing party. It rained. We rode in a moving wagon on runners. . . . Great fun in the sleigh. They put the lantern out! Oh-o-o! Stop at Ryder's house North Attleboro. Supper. then dance till one or after. I didn't dance but was besought thereto. . . . Rode home in pitch darkness, and damp warmness. "Lie still Miss Perkins"!!!! Potter home in the wet at 4.30 A.M.

Wednesday. Jan. 29. 1879.

. . . Thomas owns to sore throat.

Thursday. Jan. 30. 1879.

Annie Aborn calls at school and expresses great grief that I did not go last night. It is pleasant to be missed, but I do not regret it. . . . Ride home in the car, laden with claret & oranges for Thomas. He is worse. We bring down the little bed into the dining room, and make it as cosy and comfortable as possible. Dr. B[arrows]. arrives in hack at about 7.45. Pronounces it a case of diptheria. "And gave him bitter medicine." Poor little boy.

Saturday. Feb. 1. 1879.

Am awakened at 6.30. by T. who bangs incessantly and will not be appeased. If I leave the room he plaintively cries "Hi!" til I reappear, and when I am out will not be consoled. . . .

Sunday. Feb. 2nd.

Patient better. Toil and moil. John Willie appears at door and inquires for patient. Aunt Caroline³ appears at door and enquires for patient. Robert Brown call[s] and invites me to go to church with him. Refuse on account of patients and contagion. Spit of snow. Cold.

Tuesday. Feb. 4th.

. . . Doctor says T. is all right now. Begin to write valentine. Mother went out for the first time since T. was sick. Having after much toil arrived at a state where pain and pleasure are nearly immaterial to me I now resolve to practice Duty for a while. Without the slightest doubt that as I progress it will grow easier and pleasanter till I shall never be tempted to forsake it. Of course some slips are to be expected, but I long ago learned not to be discouraged by them. A steady struggle if never wilfully relaxed, is invincible in such matters. . . .

Friday 7th.

. . . As I put on a damp nightie last night, and then sat round in nothing else, I have a not sore, but lame throat today. My worthy family very scared, consign me to a knarly grave. But I work all the afternoon, take camphor on sugar, dress up in fine array, wear wool wadding round my neck, eat ice, sip beef tea, and promise to be all well tomorrow. Thomas goes out after oranges in the evening. . . . If it were not for mother I had just a [*sic*] lief "go out" as not. As a tired child drops asleep, I could lay down my arms, and stop the endless battle, in this world, without any feeling but calm content. but I won't, for her sake; and—I blush to own it, because I should be pointed out as an example of foolhardy recklessness.

Sat. 8.

Alack and welladay! I have succumbed! Doctor here this A.M. Got it bad. . . .

Monday 10.

O-ho! Almost gone. feel quite well. . . . Mrs. Smith . . . wants me to come and visit her as soon as I am well. (As if I was sick! Why I havn't had a pain enough to call one, *no sore throat!*; not sick in bed!!! Call that *Diptheria?*)

Wed. Feb. 12.

The worthy and venerable doctor did not arrive as usual. Natheless I subsist in peace without out [*sic*] him. and sip up all my toothsome draughts with infinite relish. . . . Am unnecessarily lazy.

Feb. Thursday. 13. 1879.

Last visit of ye ancient physician. . . .

Friday. Feb. 14. 1878. {sic}

No Valentines! No regrets. . . . Mother is scared and blue. Her throat *is* sore. I believe I have no heart.

Feb. Sat. 15. 1879.

Mother has got it now. . . . Doctor here. Aunt C[aroline]. calls, all in a bluster, wants us to have a nurse. Not so. . . . Work some for a convalesent.

Sunday. 16.

Thomas sat up all night. I slumbered ingloriously. But then I needed it as I am not strong yet, and have all the work to do. . . . By dint of obstinate sitting up, and no persuasion, I am gratified to see TAP [Thomas A. Perkins] take a nap. From 8 to 12. Then I wake him.

Mon. 17.

. . . Mother is very cross and fretty. As for me, I weep.* Pretty business. She sends me to bed at 8.

Wednesday. 19th.

. . . My time is principally occupied about now, in playing Go-Bang and Parcheesi with mother. Egotism should be excused in a journal. . . . I am by no means satisfied with my present condition. *Not circumstances.*

Thursday. Feb. 20.

Perform in their appointed order the various menial offices belonging to my present condition. . . .

Saturday. 22.

Hurrah! Go to the Essay Club! Read my Valentine. Make the acquaintance of my double, Miss. Blake, and Miss. Carrie Hazard (E-r-mense!)[4] She assaulteth me and demandeth my residence with purpose to call. Aha! I shall diligently encourage the Hazards one and all. For why? They are agreeable. They are smart. i.e. intelligent. They are (two of them) noble youths. They have a country residence in Peacedale. They have (here we come to it) *Saddle Horses*!!!

Monday. 24. 1879

Return to school and greet them with "My gallant crew; good mor-o-r-ning"! Am received with great joy, or the semblance thereof. . . . As for cash account, it would be objectless just now. I possess precisely 8 cents. . . .

Wednesday. 26. 1879.

Sweep all around. Change our bed back again into our own room, and replace Thomases in the dining room. He is sick again. Dr. Barrows says it is a rheumatic affection of the lungs. Exposure before he was entirely strong; the cause. He can hardly move or breathe for the pain. Mother has gone to take a nap, and I am "watching" in state. He asks for nothing but water. . . .

Thursday. 27. 1879.

Thomas is worse this morning. A torturing cough sets in. A little easier at night. Dr. Barrows A.M. Son P.M. Write to father about it. . . .

{March} 2nd.

. . . I write father telling Thomas was worse, and asking him to come and see him.

March. Monday. 3rd. 1879.

. . . Postman with letter from father saying he will come if it is necessary! . . .

Thursday. 6.

. . . I wish I had some one to fight with. Possessed of reason. How blind people are! Here I never had anything to complain of in mother with the exception of—modes of speech; and it seems to be all that she has against me, yet one would think I was the worst of criminals to here my accusations at times. And Thomas too! One would think he had enough to answer for without molesting me. I must really abolish all desire for comfort or any sort of happiness if I expect to have any peace. Things look black tonight. A person who has a good creed and does not follow it is a weak fool. . . .

Saturday. 8. 1879.

. . . I read "House and Brain"[5] to mother. We were both permeated with cold chills. I like it. The mere contact with such clear strong ideas, the even mythical possibilities of the human will, have roused me from my enervating course of novel reading during these sick times. I long for science again. That is a weak girlish expression, "but it will serve." Spring on the south, wild wicked wintry wind on north side of anything.

Wed. March. 26.

[*Charlotte was in Boston visiting friends and relatives, including her father. She arrived there on March 24.*]
Read Daisy Miller. . . . Go to tea at Aunt Es. Arthur appears, and escorts me to see Fechter[6] in The Howard Atheneaum. "Monte Cristo."

Sat. 29th.

No bells were rung, so we rose late, and I presided over a second breakfast, with W.[7] at the foot. Engage the lordly youth in a game of beanbags. Touching Farewells and he departs for Cambridge. . . . Am blue, and weepse. Rather enjoy it. . . . Persuade papa to put me on the train. He does so, but does not contribute the ticket. Mildly attempt to flirt with gorgeous neighbor in cars, but perceiving his station from "Yes, Miss," congeal. . . . Bring home a heavy cold.

Friday 4th. April. 1879.

. . . Go over in high feather to teach the evening scholars. With the fair Miss. Angel as co-assistant. Grand success as teacheress. We escort each other to our respective cars. Thus have I disdained the festivities at the chapel, and entered on a life of toil.———

Mon. 7th.

Privy conference with Mr. Barry. Confidential. Proposition—Teach evening school next winter, (6 hours a week for 8 months), return; $75.00, Certificate of vast value, and the years tuition in Day School free! We consider it. . . . Write to father.

Mon. April 14. 1879

. . . Robert Brown calls. . . . Makes an extravagant offer to pay my board next winter if there is no other way for me to accept Mr. Barry's proposal. I think I see myself! People do not give something for nothing. Generosity without reason, is as bad as anything else in like case. . . .

Tues. 15.

Accept Mr. Barry's offer, recklessly. . . .

Sat. May 3rd. 1879.

. . . Stop in with Carrie Hazard and Ada Blake at the college Library. Wash dishes, dress, and go per invitation of morning to dine at the Hazards. Stop for Ada. The friendly Arthur was the attraction. It appears that that beloved seraph had brought a copy of Monte Christo, and come to the Boston depo to give it me and bid me good bye when I left Boston!! I wish he had been in time. I should have had a pleasanter journey. I am escorted to dinner by the noble Fred Hazard in great state. . . . The friendly Arthur desires to walk home with me, but F. Hazard supervenes. Come home, denude, re-dress, and make bread. . . .

Thurs. 15.

Ride to school in open car model. Mary Channing brings me two letters, one from her father, the other from Aunt Isabella Hooker. She wants us to go there, take their house, boarding them for rent, and enough others [*sic*] boarders to keep them all. Small chance of a fortune, but a comfortable home. It would be very nice in some ways. A large handsome, house and grounds, less of the unpleasant if more actual work. All our friends & people,—a change of air, scene, &c,—. On the other hand, here goes my school of Design arrangements, and all the friends and acquaintances I have just begun to form.

Farewell to my well-loved Miss Salisbury, to the serene Hazards, Ada Blake, and the other Clubbists. To all our pleasing cousins, and —to—"Kellup"![8] But as more there than sufficient counteraction, behold the gentle Gillett. Aha! Aha! . . .

Fri. {May} 16.

Rain. Vegetation joyous in consequence. Mother & I ride down together to see ye circus. There isn't any. Meet her after school. dine at Café. Get gloves for me & other things. Purchase tea rosebud to paint. But Martha Luther[9] arrives and I don't. She stays to tea. . . .

Thur. {May} 22.

. . . See Martha Luther. . . . Martha Luther and her mother call. Robert Brown came over at about 3 to take me to ride. "O no, I had to sew carpets." No, my friend, the length & breadth & the height of it are equal, and you won't do. . . .[10]

Thurs. 29.

. . . Call at Channings to enquire for Grace.[11] Better. See Mary. She exhibits picters to praising parents. May Diman has had an accident.[12] Horse fell on her. Not expected to live. Last day of school. . . . Grand farewell. . . .

Tues. June 3rd.

. . . I am blessed with a cold sore of such amazing size & hideous aspect as to strike terror to all beholders.
Oh it is grievous.*

Thurs. 19. 1879.

Sew with startling rapidity all the morning, crawl into the last dress almost before it is done, and speed me away to Boston. Meet Caleb on my way down. Tell him of my coming glories. Arrive all right. Am met by papa who who {sic} will give me no definite hopes of another year of support; merely saying that he don't know what his affairs will be next fall. He bestows on me by request, a pair of white kids as a birthday gift; and see me into a Cambridge car. Received with much joy. . . .

Fri. June. 20. 1879.

. . . Whom do I see but the saintly Almy. I straightway address him with "Neighbor, neighbor, how art thee?" to which the bright youth answers instantly "Very well as you may see." . . .

Thurs. June. 26. 1879.

Pleasant morning call from Edward. He gives me his photograph; choice of 6. I calmly inform him that I like him better that {sic} A[rthur]. And he blandly replies that I "had better restrain my ardor," as in a year or two he will be just like him!

Fri. 27 June. '79.

. . . Arthur arrived; not having received my letter at all. We play one game of whist much to A's disgust, and then I converse pleasingly with him till 10.30. I tell him about my lovers and lovees, planting him as the second of the latter. Which confidence he reciprocates by telling me of his four, of whom I was the second also. And all before Miss C! It was truly absurd. but I gained my point; we understand each other now, and rest on a calm super-flitatious [*sic*] ground. Much comfort will ensue. Possibly reinstatement. He seemed to enjoy it immensely. . . .

Mon. 30. 1879.

. . . Arrange letters & sich. P.M. read some of A[rthur]'s, & do 'em up in blackedged paper, singing mournful ditties about the perfidy of mankind. He sent me his picture this A.M. acknowledged by next mail.

Tues. July 1st. 1879.

. . . Am immersed in gloom — natural consequence of my late festivities

Thurs. July 3. 1879.

My 19th birthday. No gifts but those beforehand. Celebrate by having teeth filled. Rather enjoy it. Stop at Browns. Stop at M. Luthers. Card from her. Thomas goes off on three days cruise. Mother & I play bezique by moonlight! (*Pain* is a sure cure for——)

Wed. July 16. 1879.

Letter from Marthar Luther. Answer it. Am blue. Very blue. Lively thunder storm.

Thurs. July 17.

. . . Letter from father & Nellie. Father chose the "stylish" photo. and says in effect that I had better learn to dance if I want to certainly, but he don't like it. Nellie says "when can we come?" Oh-ho! And Almy is to be there! Hi-yi! We go Sat. Mother & I call on May Diman. I am invited to tea tomorrow. . . . Oh I am filled with friskiness[.]

Sun. July 20.

[*Charlotte was visiting Matunuck, Rhode Island, on the beach.*]
. . . We go out, a lot of us one day, Nellie and Miss L. paint, the boys swim, and I trot off and go to sleep under a tree quite romantically. Am prosaically discovered by Edward who awakes me up with a "Hullo! here she is." I refer it to the toadstool we ate to see if it was or not. . . . Edward surrounds me so

I don't care for the interloper. Nice boy, E. I like him in a grandmotherly sort of way.

Sun. {Aug.} 24.

Sleep till 11.30. Lizzie Brown over. Stays to tea. Robert subsequently. Go to walk with him. Pitch dark Grove. Attempts a mild embrace. *First time* from *any* man! Quench his advances with much coolness. Becomes respectful, even awestruck. Hot.

Monday Sept. 1.

. . . Hattie & I *Sleep on the roof*! Make up a sumptuous couch of comforters & things on the slant. *Very comfortable*. So nice to wake up and see the moon and the sky. And flitting mosquitoes between me and the moon.

Tues. 16. 1879.

. . . Begin to systematize the ideas on athletics I have held for years with the assistance of Blakies "How to get Strong."

Present measurements:

Chest.	31 in.	Upper arm.	10–11.
Waist.	27 in.	Fore arm.	9–10
Thigh.	14–19.	Calves.	13.
Weight.	——		

Thurs. Oct. 30. 1879.

Walk down with May. Stop at dentists, and walk up with Martha. I love the pussy. Horrid windy.

Mon. Nov. 3. 1879.

Hurry & scurry to get Thomas off. Mother & he down st. buying at a great rate. Trunk, valise, soap, candles, watches, etc. He goeth about & calleth on relations. I drop in on Martha P.M. Snow this morning, 1 in. deep! little more at 10 P.M. I don flannel & rue it, but endure. Cold.

Sat. Nov. 8.

Letter from Aunt Kate Gilman.[13] Bessie *died* last Thursday morning! Of an affection of the heart. The dear little girl got my last letter, when to weak to read, and held it in her hand or kept it by her all day! I am so glad she did not have to fret for the absence of it. . . .

Sat. Nov. 15. 1879.

Stop for Martha and go down street. Telegraph yes to Aunt K[ate Gilman].

Mon. Nov. 17. 1879.

On New York boat. 10.40 P.M. Rise betimes. hie down to depot and start for Norwich. No one at station so travel by the aid of friendly stranger to Aunt

Ks. She immediately arrays me in complete suit of Bessie's clothes.* To my amazement and surprise she hales me away to N. Y. Houghton & Francis very nice. Aunt K. delightful.

Tues. Dec. 2nd. 1879.

. . . Aunt Katie Gilman is dead!

Thurs. Dec. 4th. 1879.

Letter from Houghton. . . .

Christmas. 1879.

A Glorious & entire success! The best Xmas I remember. Retired at 12.5 this morning & rose at 5.30. Sweep and toil. . . . Entertainment opened at 7 P.M. all lovely. My costume charming. More presents all round than anyone expected. . . . All lovely. All pulled their crackers & wore their hats. All happy. Robert in an hour or so. O I am so tired!

[1880]

Cambridge. 11. odd P.M. Thurs. Jan 1st. 1880!

. . . Come home at 11 or near it, regretting not having said goodbye to Greeley, and, can I believe my *senses*, find that identical youth artlessly happening by as we get out of the back!!! Am going to a museum with him tomorrow!————I never was so courted and entertained and amused & done for in all my little life. It seems as if the memory of today would last me in solid comfort through all the ills that flesh is heir to. I thought nothing was needed to my happiness when I rode home, and then to find Lewis Greeley actually loitering about to see *Me!* I cannot understand it. Not that I mean him in especial, but the attention.————The—the—why to think of its being *me!*

Boston. Jan 2nd. 1880.

Mr. Greeley, whom I have really begun to wish was a blonde, arrived at 9.30 or thereabouts, and he & I traverse the zoological & archealogical museums. Very enjoyable. He rode in with me, as I did not return for more farewells, and sought to prevail on me to go to the opera with him Mon. Then capitulated to Sat. I left it uncertain and dashed his hopes by a note this P.M. Letter from Mother which induces me to arrange for return on Sat. 4. P.M. train. As I shall be accompanied by May Diman it will be pleasant. . . .

I wonder,————, if,————,————,. Time will show. O, I had a call from Nellie. . . . Dear Nellie. I think I've had enough. Work will seem pleasant. And swainlessness? Guess I can stand it.

Tired, body and soul.

Providence.
Sat. Jan 3rd. 1880.

Note from the gentle Greeley, regretting failure of opera scheme. Very respectful gentlemanly note. "Miss Perkins." "Yours ever." . . . Find a gorgeous New Years card from "Henry Alford Short." Jacket, N.Y. Card, & his card. All in a box. Beuteous. And I never saw him but once! Truly, my cup runneth over. . . .

Friday January 23. 1880.

Refrained like a fool, from going to school,
As mamma with a headache appeared,
But was grieved to remain, for she suffered no pain
the moment the weather had cleared.
6 cents I did spend, on three pinks to the end
of enhancing L. G.'s valentine,
and the rest of the day, spent in painting the spray,
with effect most uncommonly fine.
Went round to see Ray, at two P.M. today,
to get means for our next months survival;
Had a letter from T. full of pleasure and glee,
announcing his boxes arrival.
Left the dishes to Belle, who delighteth full well
on some pretext to come in & stay,
And by Bolan the gifted our ashes were sifted
and the cellar cleaned up for small pay.

Saturday. January 24. 1880.

. . . Anna & Annie Westcott in. Martha too. Wants us to come down this evening. . . . Whist. One Simmons appears. James Simmons, friend of Marthas. . . . Smart youth.

Mon. Feb. 9th. 1880

. . . Sit peacably down to sew, when who should call but Jim Simmons, Samuel Simmons son! I feel quite set up, for we never asked him to call, except with Martha. Not that he amounts to much, but he's a caller!*

Sat. Feb. 14.th. 1880

Arise and diddle about in full expectation of Valentines. Get 4 . . . . 2 Pretty cards from the girls, A funny letter from George Bissell. . . . And a mysterious epistle in ardent verse from some unknown individual. Hazards suspected.

Call at Martha's. She is better, going to matineé this P.M., and was quite pleased with my valentine. Is innocent of the mysterious one. . . . Meet mother at car, and get home just in time to receive a most interesting telegram. From the pleasing Almy, who sends a three verse Valentine in answer to mine. And so bright! And so witty! And so delightfully immediate! And so complimentary to come by telegraph! I am more pleased than if I had had 40. . . . 9 P.M. A ring at the bell. I descend. I open the door. No one there. I see a letter on the step. I claw at it. No effect. I claw at it again. I surmise. I examine my lily fingers. Chalk! Not a circumstance! O I am so pleased! . . .

Wed. Feb. 18th. 1880

. . . Call on Martha. Jim Simmons, Samuel Simmons' Son called in my absence, and invited me to go to a concert tonight! He's getting as frequent as the bat.

Sunday. March. 14th. 1880.

. . . Go to hear father lecture at Beethoven Hall. On Voltaire. Very good[.] [S]aw and conversed with him. Found Martha there and sat by her. . . .

Tuesday. March. 23rd. 1880.

My respected papa returns the rent bills mother sent him. . . .

Wednesday. March. 31st. 1880.

. . . Aunt C. in. Mutually read "Jolly" [14] all day, and make gawks of ourselves over the last of it. Weep and snivel consumedly. I break down, and mother reads and sobs while I stand by the stove drying my handkerchief. I don't see why it is any worse to cry over a book than to laugh over it. And bogus emotion is better than real, for it leaves no sting.

Wednesday. April 14th. 1880.

Arise betimes. Spry. 2nd invitation to Junior X. *"James D. Simmons."* Oh yis! Oh yis! . . .

Wednesday. May 12. 1880.

Am considerably under the weather. . . . Letter from father. Says "D.G." will appear in the N. E. J[ourna]'l of Ed'tn.[15] Very good. . . .

Saturday the 22nd of May. 1880.

. . . New England Journal of Education from father, with my first appearance in print therein. "To D xxx. G xxx."

Monday. June 28th. 1880.

Am quite "feak & weeble," and so much indisposed that my kind host send for the Doctor. A stately and agreeable man. He leave meddi; and says to go to bed, but I don't. . . .

Saturday. July 3rd. 1880.

My twentieth birthday. Kisses a plenty. Eke a V [dollar bill]. Three for mother & two for me. . . .

Tues. August. 17th. 1880.

. . . Who should call but the gentle Jim! Quite "feak and weeble." Were glad to see him.

Mon. Aug. 23rd. 1880

. . . Mr. S. Simmons calls. I learn of him many things. secridly.

Friday. August 27th. 1880.

> . . . I chanced upon the guileless Sam,
> and home with me he walked,
> He was as quiet as a clam,
> although I talked and talked.
> Invited him to Sunday's tea,
> he actually refused!
> But we'll have Jim, for really we
> not often are so used.

Wednesday. Sept. 22nd. 1880.

. . . Go to Martha's. Get much satisfaction. Discovering from her that the infant Samuel has made her a mother confessor in part, I abandon my scruples and "tell her all." It appears that Sam really considers himself insulted and forbidden the house. Insulted! And here I have refrained from telling my most intimate friend on account of his feelings forsooth! And the stealthy Jim has known the whole business all the while! I wash my hands of 'em. Just let me catch him alone—perhaps I may induce him to reconsider. . . .

Thursday. Sept. 23rd. 1880.

Joy to the brave! (And the bold faced.) All is well. . . . Do several errands, and guilelessly happening into that blessed Post Office meet the recreant Sam. Bow. Give chase. Easily overtake. Excuse myself, and request a few moments conversation. He gladsomely leaveth his office an hour too early, and walketh home with me. I give him a large piece of my mind. He is finally convinced; as who could help being? The thing is entirely cleared up, and I feel very comfortable in my mind. Ma chére mama however is mortally enraged, and loads me with opprobrium. I answer not a word, and she is comparatively benign by bedtime. . . .*

Friday Sept. 24th. 1880

. . . Martha over in the morning. Dear little chick. Grub and scrub, dress up and go to Ada's. Learn of handmaid that she is over here via George. Scurry home. Mother had met and kept her. She brought me 7 pair of four button *Gloves*. All shades dressed and undressed. I walk home with her and she furthermore bestows upon me a pair of black silk stockings & a silver headed comb; balls on top. Lovely. I admire, extol and gratitudinize in fine style. Stop

at door and have a word with Martha. Come home ready to drop, and raven-
ously hungry. Nice hot dinner all a cooking. Very tired.

Wednesday. Oct 6th. 1880.

Martha's birthday. I give her a horse chestnut, a pear, an apple, a needlecase, a
fetich in many wrappers, the pocket atlas which Sam gave her yesterday and
left here last night, and the M. letter which unfortunately didn't come. I spent
the day with her from 1 to 6. . . .

Friday Oct. 15th. 1880

Bright sunrise but cloudy morning, to my infinite disgust. . . . I don my
flannel and call for Martha. Jim cometh for us and we seek the Bridge. Sam
joins us there, only to inform us that he wasn't going! He certainly invited
me, and Martha thought he was going as much as I. I was wroth at first, but
the first glimpse of blue water was enough, and I haven't enjoyed a day more
this summer. Such flames of maple and sumach; such emptiness of blue above,
and placidity of blue below; such warm glowing sunlight; the tumbling rapids, and cool shadows————— O it was the perfection of autumn glory in sight
sound and *feel*. And we thoroughly enjoyed it. Reached Soccanosset at about
3.10. and then down through all the loveliness with the great round white
moon and Jupiter looking at us. A feast indeed. Home by 9.30. . . .

Thurs. Oct. 28th. 1880

. . . Robert comes, and we produce between us some designs for advertising
cards. Soap business.[16]

Tuesday. Nov. 23rd. 1880.

. . . Mother wants to go and see the Rawsons, but I hang fire, and Lo! A call
from Sam. I open on him in full force with a "triangular row." Rake over the
whole business from beginning to end, and settle up with mutual satisfaction.
He departs in friendly mood, and all is serene. Selah!

Thurs. Dec. 23rd. 1880

. . . Had a letter from George Bissell today. It appears that there was some
bank stock of Aunt Nancy's left around somewhere, which has just come to
light, and Thomas & I have some $66.00 coming. Good enough. Therefore
will I spend Carrie's five for Christmas & sich, and be gay.——

Christmas Day.
Saturday December 25th. 1880.

Late and Lazy. Martha over A.M. She bringeth me a white fan, & two ties.
I love her. The postman brings me many cards[;] one from Jim. Where's
Sammy? We go around to Mary's at 1. Grand tree there for Alice *And* the
family. All seemed happy but regret that Anna could not be there. I had a

gorgeous fan from Ada, a very handsome book from Robert, and lots of splendor that I hadn't expected, A stamp box from Grandpapa Carpenter. My little
bottle paid. Ten dollar check from Carrie Hazard. Droves of cards. See Xmas
book. Mother goes up to Anna's to stay over Sunday, ye nurse going home for
Xmas. I come home and find a card from Sam. Prettiest of all. Quiet evening
making up accounts & enumerating presents. I have dispensed some 80 gifts
to some 25 people, 40 to mother. I have had about 40 myself, cards inclusive.
I am dreadfully tired.
Not quite such a success as last Xmas, but very jolly.

9 P.M.

Christmas night, and all alone!
All alone in the quiet room
With the lamplit space and the shadowy gloom
In the distant corners. Overhead
Aunt Caroline has gone to bed
Tired out with the week before.
Mother has gone to Anna's to stay
Over Sunday. Thomas away
in Nevada. Never a friend
Christmas night with me to spend.
It makes me cry. I've worked away
Getting ready for Christmas Day
Got up mornings and sat up nights
Lots of work and losts of fun
Getting presents for every one;
Had no end of presents myself——
And now at nine o'clock at night
To be all alone — it isn't right.
There's a dreary whirling wind outside
Over the common bare and wide;
And a snowy ground and a cloudy sky
And nothing but a clock that ticks
Till each vibration stabs & pricks.
A clock that ticks and a lamp that burns
With blinks & flickers and starts by turns.
And a little girl with her feet in a chair,
And tearstained cheeks and tumbled hair
And tired eyes like the soul inside
And as lonely a heart as ever cried.

Thurs. Dec. 30th. 1880.

Snow very deep, and cold as Labrador. 6, 4, zero, as the day advances. Heavy snow, deep every where, & drifted besides. Our gas which was so deliciously unsatisfactory last night, won't go at all tonight. But we rejoice in a lamp. . . .

[1881]

Saturday
January 1st. 1881.

Go down St. stopping at Martha's, Ada's, and the Hazards. . . . I think I must have that bête noir[1] of my childhood, chillblains! My feet swell after walking, and are hot and achy. Can't get my shoes on hardly. Poor little me! . . . We begin our year with a quiet solitary evening. Not bad for a change. I shall be very very glad to go to Boston and see some more people. Verily my soul weareth of the swains incumbent. I am tired. I am sleepy. I am *not* energetic. I do not progress. Not a bit. Oh dear————.
The happiest time of day is————bedtime.

Wednesday. Jan. 5th. 1881.

Up very betimes and swear over the kitchen fire for an hour or so. Never, never, never again will I attempt to cook a new fire out of an old one. Fresh snow four of [*sic*] five inches deep over the already drifted landscape. I go out and shovel, assisted by the genial though elderly "Pa Willey." Martha over on business. (To illustrate a parodiacal joke for her Aunt Sarah.) Sweep bedroom and kitch[en]. Apply snow to my miserable little toes, which were totally insensible to the cold thereof, and settle the question after the swelling went down. Corns, *not* chillblains. One on the outside and two between each little toe! . . .

Thurs. 6th.

Up early. Mother scalds her right wrist with boiling fat. A bad burn. Flour and hammemelis, as we had no plaster. Seems to get well. Snow again last night, very heavy. Thaws and mists all day. Go over to school. .75 [cents]. Get some cornplaster. . . . Call at Martha's for a minute. Home and fix up for Martha's Whist Party this evening. Mother wouldn't let me go without her, and wouldn't go herself on account of the nasty weather and walking. I have a good cry, and don't get over it yet awhile. Aunt Caroline an interested auditor.

Saturday. Jan. 8th. 1880. {sic}

Rather late. Get breakfast & sprinkle clo[thes]. Do up all the work by ten. Trip on the board outdoors and saturate myself with hot water &—more water. And not a drop of hot water in the house! Take a shampoo under the faucet and go out to freeze my head. Lecture Club. Bishop Clarke holds forth on motion in etymology. Trot down st, and get salmon & orange & an account book. . . . Stop at Martha's. She is not well. Stay to dinner. . . .

Monday. Jan. 10th. 1881.

Clean up draw[er] and table in kitchen. Iron a little. Sew a little. Read to mother out of Harper's "Mrs. Flint's married experience." A most edifying tale. Do up dinner dishes barefoot, as I have done before, for I can not stand up in any of my old shoes even. Ablute. Chrochet. Write to T. O we did want to play whist tonight.

Friday. Jan. 14th. 188. {sic}

. . . Crochet and [read] "The Confessions of a Frivolous Girl."[17] Jim calls. Argue as of old. *He* held my yarn.

Sunday. January 16th. 1881.

. . . [W]e all go over to Grace Church. Hot and sleepy, stick a friendly pin into myself as an exhilarator.[18] Ride back and stay to dinner. A little loving talk with Ada, and she and her happy swain, whom I begin to like, walk home with me.[19] They come in and stop a bit. . . . Our water has frozen again, although we turned it off yesterday. I do a little mending while Aunt C. finishes "The Confessions." I can't say I enjoyed the book much—yes, I think I did though; it seems singularly truthful and exact. Put me quite in a moralizing mood. Write to T. . . .

Monday. January 17th. 1881.

Up and going at 5. Sweep parlor, dining room and kitchen. All else as usual. Water still frigid, & it is growing colder tonight too. . . . Ablute, pretense of crocheting, casino with Aunt C. and so to bed with a thankful heart. We havn't been so rich in a long time. Thomas has given Mother all his $62.00 even as I did, but instead of bills this will do some good. Then I have plenty of cards ahead, a large order from Ada, a dollar from Martha's Aunt Sarah, and what is the most surprising a dollar & a half clear after the market man was paid! Oh it does feel good.

Friday. January. 21st. 1881.

7! Mes enfants only bring me a dollar. A wild northeast snowstorm sets in, and I carry Jessie Budlong all the way home, from the corner of Waterman st. *With* a big umbrella. . . . All serene "thereaway." Clarence thinks I'll never marry. Peut-être-pas.[20] Says they're afraid of me. I hate a fool! Snow turns to rain, and we have a nasty night. I worked some on the cards, but I can't seem to get hold of them at all this time. A pleasant evening with "A Fair Barbarian."[21] In Scribner's.

Sunday, Jan. 30th. 1881.

7.30!! Do the ironing. Light snow. Darn things. Aunt C. after her daily trip Annawards reads "Sevenoaks"[22] quite persistently. Nice book. Robert over. Cards. Aunt C. goes to bed. I inform R. on his departure that I am "getting to like him ever so much." Wonder if he misunderstands?

Tuesday. February 1st. 1881.

6.20. Long busy day of drawing. Get a lot of sketches done. Go to sleep bolt upright in my chair three times. Sleepy work. Chrochet and read for an hour or so when Jim and Sam arrive and we play whist. Sam and Aunt C. 4 to our three. He had several ingenious excuses for bringing his friend here t'other night. Said "he was a respectable bachelor, and as I was getting along——"! Said he dropped in on him, wanted to play whist, and as he hadn't anywhere else to bring him he brought him here! Very pretty, very pretty! Aunt C. delighted in him, and scorneth the Right Honorable James D.

Thurs. Feb. 3rd. 1881.

. . . Prof. J. Louis Diman died this afternoon.[23] Malignant ensephelus.

Friday. February 4th. 1881.

6.30 —7. *Slept warm.* With my feet under 14 thicknesses of blanket. Warmer weather too. Paint marguerites with good success. Do a bit on cards. Aunt C. got along with a dinner out (being down st.) and I got along without a dinner. Manufacture an unsatisfactory rice pudding. . . .

February 6th. 1881.

. . . Martha over. A very pleasant time with her. We meet in lots of places. She has made me a lovely and most convenient little pincushion (by request.) . . . Aunt C. begins "The Guardian Angel"[24] while I piously crochet. Robert comes. Cards. I am tired.

Mon. Feb. 7th. 1881.

7! Bah! A lazy wasted miserable mispent day. Shall I never outgrow the fascination of a book! Here I started that "Angel" to myself, then let Aunt C. read it aloud because I knew she liked to, then go and read it all through today, wasting precious hours of work and now listen with hypocritical interest while that deluded lady goes all over it again. Paint less than one card. . . .

Tuesday, February 8th. 1881.

Up at 5. Work on Archery cards with some application, and finish 'em. . . . R. isn't satisfied of course, so I needs lug my poor little cards back again. Then meet Martha, see her off in the train to Auburn, get some brown paper, and "My Wayward Partner,"[25] and splash home. I haven't worn rubbers this winter, nor won't.

Wed. Feb. 9th. 1881.

7. O it is hotter than blazes! I draw all day more or less, design for curtains etc. Martha over for an hour or so. Aunt C. goes around to Mary's after dinner, I go after her, and we are overtaken by the Simmonses as we return. They stay uncomfortably until ten, and then go gladly away. . . . Those chaps are bad enough single, but dreadful together.

Sunday. Feb. 13th. 1881.

7. Biscuit and mackerel as usual. Clean up a bit. . . . Martha arrives. She goes off with my wayward partner (mysterious phrase!) Send valentine to Ada, & a bit of a card to May. Beans and rice pudding. Robert. Cards. "Great heavens! Is it any harm to hug your cousin?"* Oui mon ami, il est. Quelquefois.²⁶

Tuesday. Feb. 15th. 1881.

. . . Jim appears. Invites me to go to see the Pirates of Penzance, Boston Ideal Company, next Saturday. Will I? Of course I will. Whist two games apiece, and Aunt C. and Robert whitewash us once. No progress on cards tonight.

Thurs. February 17th. 1881.

6. Get the work all done by 9. . . . Walk down st. with M. . . . Shop. . . . Get likewise a pair of boots; similar to my present dilapidated pair. (Not similar in delapidation.) Feel very nice with my new purchases. . . . Home, paint, draw, rest, work on bonnet, & receive Robert as aforetime in the kitchen. Aunt C. retires. R. Brown offers to grow cousinly & affectionate in loneliness & proximity. "And I? And I? What shall I do? for all is vain. No book will rule, no frown deny, no words restrain. Nor any reason reach his mind to make him take his arm from me; or could they I should be inclined to let them be." I feel very dirty and ashamed of myself. He only had his arm on the back of my chair (& me); and he's a cousin, but natheless it wasn't right in me to let him, and I won't any more!

Saturday. February 19th. 1881.

. . . Jim arrives in due time & we promenade over to see "The Pirates of Penzance." Boston Ideal Opera Company. Prov. Opera house. I christen my new coat and bonnet. Look well and feel well. Barker (Ben) sat right behind us. I was glad. Walk both ways. Jim carrys everything and is irreproachable. Nice boy, Jim. I haven't been to the theatre since a year ago New Year's night. Enjoyed it immensely.

Thursday. February. 24th. 1881.

6 to 6.20. Do up housework, array myself in purple and fine linen, & depart. Stop at exhibit at Mary's. Call for Martha & take a Brook St. car. Am ushered by Horace Burney. A very gorgeous affair. 8 bridesmaids & 8 ushers. Maids in

creamy white bunting stuff, little straw hats, & flowers in pairs, wild roses, tulips, lilacs, & buttercups. Ushers in dark blue neckties. Ada in enough veil and orange flowers for ten, looked like a houri of course. Several miles of train. The Professor[27] gave her away. Trot back with M. petrifying Sam on the way, leave her to proceed homeward, & attend the reception. *Very* select. A gorgeous refection. See all the folk I please, & have plenty of time to kiss Ada & scowl at Another. Don't fancy any of the ushers. Hobnobbed with fair Coatses, was reasonably attended on, & chatted with the astute Marian for a season. Ada put on a meek travelling dress, and departed at about II amidst a shower of rice & an old shoe. I have a box of wedding cake. Leave among the last, & stop at M.'s on way home. Tired mother at Marys. Clarence was down this morning to get my already exhausted aunt, as mother's right arm has given out, strain or some such. I find her at Mary's. Come home & get good dinner, wash dishes, dress, sew a bit, and expect Sam. Didn't come. Drat him! . . .

Tuesday. March 1st 1881.

'"Late! late! So late!"' half past seven or eight! Being in a season of moroseness & depression I laboriously grovel through the work and then help mother make an old dyed black silk for me. Pretty pretty. . . .

Friday. March. 4th. 1881.

Arise morosely in our 6th consecutive day of all-pervading gloom. Wash the accumulated dishes of four meals. Mrs. Springer comes down after Aunt C.'s rent, and after some powow we all enthuse over taking her house root & branch. I especially am highly elate at the prospect.

Friday, March. 11th. 1881.

. . . Martha over. . . . Verily I love the damsel. . . .

Sunday. March. 13th. 1881.

My laziness abashes my consience stricken soul, for save a pan of ashes & a single hod of coal, I've been an idle loafer through the livelong day, and on the bed & sofa have whiled the hours away. . . .

Monday. March. 14th. 1881.

. . . Go down to Martha's, Atheneum, down st. & home in my new boots. Ow! Robert over. Cards. He and mother start out on a pie speculation, 15 cts. apiece.[28]

Monday. 28th. March. 1881.

. . . Call from May, who imbibes a soft custard & some tarts with much joy, and accompanies me as far as Prospect St. . . . Carry my orange to Martha, who bites it with great glee. Dear little chick. I can't stand my feet much longer, went about a quarter of an inch into the epidermis without touching meat. . . .

Friday. April 1st. 1881.

. . . I go down to Martha's at about 3. Read her some "Phantasmagoria." [29] Solemn consultation apropos of cousinly caresses, wherein the chicken helps me to decide rightly. Glad to make her of some use. . . .

Saturday. April. 16. 1881.

Clear, bright, and beautiful at last. Do a lot of work. Mr. Bolan comes, and he and I lift the parlor stove with a fire in it. Carpets all up. Mother & Aunt C. go up to the house, and I take *everything* out of the front entry, and take up that and the stair carpet. . . .

Friday. April 22nd. 1881.

4.30. The dirtiest and hardest day's work yet, & the most done All my duds and Thomas' duds, and all the bureau drawers. I work from before sunrise till 8 with about an hour & a half out for meals. *14 hours*! Am tired and concious of a back. Glad I've got one to be concious of. . . .

Tuesday. April 26. 1881.

5. Mother gads about with carpet men, & Mrs. Nolan & I clean & pack at home. Much done. Mrs. Thomas calls at the door. Helen comes in state, and brings some *wall paper*. (Widder Brown much impressed, stares after her over the gate.) I go up and gloat in the new house. (Sent Helen up there, great, awestruck.) Guess she found we had wallpaper enough. It is lovely up there. Spend half hour 8–8.30 glaring out of Thomas' window. Fruitless. no sneaks.

Wednesday, April. 27th. 1881.

. . . Last night in the little home where we have lived so contentedly for five changing years! Longer than I ever lived anywhere in my life. I am more glad than sorry for a thousand reasons. The step is wholly advantageous and the new house charming in every respect. So goodbye to ungraded "Coonville," and ho! for fresh fields and pastures new! [30]

Thurs. April. 28th. 1881.

Wake at 4. Work swift and immeasurable. Mother goes up with the stove men, and I domineer over Mrs. Nolan and Katie to my hearts content. Then she comes back, the moving wagons arrive, and I go up, and, assisted by Aunt Caroline, and backed up by Mrs. Springer, see to the disposal of all our household truck. Never did we have so much furniture before, that hole below was vastly smaller than this, and not too crowded; but this spacious edifice fairly efferveces with upholstery and stuff. Oh but it's lovely! And oh but it's fine!

Old Mr. Carpenter stopped here with Anna, and wandered about the house with evident delight. Mrs. Springer hirples up and down stairs, and revels in our comfort and splendor. Miss Murphy comes with my new dress, and is also impressed. Mary drops in later, and is as pleased as all of 'em are.

Oh! the dear beautiful little house! How did we ever live so long and contentedly in the "hole below"?

But I'm tired, tired, tired, and shall sleep the sleep of the righteous tonight. Nor I won't get up till morning!

Friday. April. 29th. 1881.

7.20. Get things much arranged, dishes in particular. Such a lot of 'em. . . . [I]n the evening about 8 o'clock, Mrs. Henry Carpenter was in to tell me that May Diman was thrown from her horse at about 7 P.M. and *killed*! I don't believe it yet for they said the same thing before, when she was thrown. But O, her mother!

Saturday, April 30th. 1881.

True. All true. Ben Barker was with her and got off scott free! Poor Man! Mrs. Diman herself said that he is the most to be pitied.

x x x x

. . . The dreadful accident is on every one's tongue, the city rings with it. Oh dear.

Mary & Alice in. Jim and Sam come over as requested and open all the book boxes. Put up most of 'em. 12 o'clock!

Sunday, May 1st. 1881.

. . . Am very tired. I can't write down much about May now, statements conflict too much.

Monday. May 2nd. 1881.

. . . Charlotte Hedge comes. I go with her to May's funeral. The dear girl looked as lovely as ever she did, in white silk and white roses. Great white casket and pedestals, (not trestles). For all it was so private the house was full to overflowing, and all were friends. The clergyman stood on the stair landing. Beautiful services, and a house full of tears. Poor Will Bogert sat right opposite me, and I think he must have loved her, for he covered his face with his hat all through the services, and shook with suppressed sobs. Fred Hazard came and sat by him, and laid a strong hand on his, for which I was grateful. As for me I found I couldn't stand the music, and took refuge in the "Sorrows of Amelia" and the "rivers and lakes of Mane." Which treatment enabled me to preserve the appearance of composure. Why should I sit and drivel to no purpose?

Dear May! I could have kissed her but for folk.[31] Edward Hale was down, and went home on the 2 o'clock train with Miss Charlotte. I walked down with her, and saw the post all strewn with sand to hide the blood stains, and the great hole in the fence where Barker's horse went through. People looking over. . . . Walk swiftly home again. Nap. Dinner. Mr. Stillwell called. No whist.——

Tuesday. May. 10th. 1881.

Up early, and engage in upholstery & miscellaneous chores. Get the chambers partially arranged. Letter from C. Hedge. Go down st. via Martha's, & accompanied by her. Sherbet. Lends me "The Story of Avis." . . .[32]

Saturday May 14th. 1881. *

Whisk through my work and go to Martha's. Go down st. and shop with 'em. Martha & I get a pair of lovely little red bracelets with gold acorns dependent theron, to be worn by us as a badge, ornament, bond of union, etc. 20 cts. And I superintend her shopping to great pecuniary advantage. Home to dinner. Martha comes surreptitious over P.M., I let her in unseen, she prowls up to my room, and we spend the afternoon in tranquil bliss. I trim her hat, and she hems my pillocase. She returns as invisibly as she came, at which I am exalted. . . .

Sunday. May 15th. 1881.

. . . Robert here. I get awfully cross over cards. I do *hate* waste, in work or anything else. And I get cross over mother's having invited Robert to go on the Pawtuxet! Robert Brown of all persons in the world to go with Helen Hazard, and now! *Yah*!

Monday. May. 16th. 1881.

Up betimes and very industrious before breakfast. . . . We get a letter from Thomas. He has been sick, had a mountain fever, and wants to borrow two hundred dollars. I write to G. Bissell and trot down St. to post it. Met Jim. Trot back and write to T. . . .

Wednesday. May 18th. 1881.

Get up in time to get the breakfast table, at least. Letter from G. Bissell. He won't let me have it, the pig![33] Says he has so many drains on his pocket book that he must stop somewhere! Good place to stop! Mother & Aunt C. go out and I snooze on the rug for two hours or more. Manage to draw a little. Martha over. Brings me a lovely little pink toilet cushion. Mrs. Springer comes down to keep company with Aunt C. while mother and I trudge down to the Carpenter's and see about that money. Mr. C. agrees to let us have it and is extremely kind. Also he walks home with us, and comes in awhile.

Tuesday. May. 24th. 1881.

Up at 5.30. Cloudy and threatening, fog & northeast wind, but clears, and we all set out in high style. Sam meets us at the bridge, and we get to Pawtuxet at 11. Row up to the spring and lunch in comfort and luxury, straggle off in the woods with Sam, and enjoy ourselves generally. Go higher up, drift down, Get hoards of flowers, and home in the 6 o'clock car. Mary Brown & family in the car. Sam comes home with us, *Takes tea*! and plays a rubber of whist. Very pleasant day.

Monday. May. 30th. 1881.

. . . Mother & Aunt C. go to the woman suffrage convention, and I go and invite Miss Manchester to spend the evening with me. Then I go to Martha's, meet her, & drag her over. . . .

Saturday June 11th. 1881.

. . . Mother still dolorous and ailing, we *must* get her off somewhere for a rest. Long letter from Thomas. Martha over & Mother & Aunt C. out. Paint and "fiddle." I can play on the painner!!! I can play the "Campbells are Coming"; and some of The White Cockade. Onehandedly. To the dire distress of my friends. . . .

Sunday. June 12th 1881.

Sat up in a comforter and watched the total eclipse of a bright full moon. Dozed and woke alternately and saw it all. Worth seeing, too. . . .

Thurs. June 16th. 1881.

Really fair weather but still cool. Up bright & early and finally finish those whales. Get 'em down to Edwards by 9. . . . Ride home. Miss Briggs in car. She kindly lends me another h'k'f when I desecrate mine, my gloves, dress, car step, and the surrounding county. Home very wilted, and snooze continuously.

Saturday July 2nd 1881.

Up at 4. Make cake and otherwise labor. We learn by John Arnold of Garfield's assassination.[34] He is not dead yet, I believe. Mother & Aunt C. gad incessantly, Mrs. Springer flitters in and out, and I go over to Martha's, (calling on Mabel Hill, out;) and stay to tea. Last day of minority.

Sunday July 3rd. 1881.

Up at 4. My 21st birthday. I am the richer by two white skirts from Aunt C. Some candy & strawberries from Frau Springer, a dress, two tin cups, five jars, a metalic hair brush, two speckled neck ruffles, twenty one cents, and a great bunch of hothouse flowers from Mother, and a lovely basket full of flowers from—Richie! Make sponge cake and labor generally. Hot.

July 4th. Monday. 1881.

Up before *light*. Compose innumerable sandwiches & pack spongecake, pound-cake, & lemons etc. . . . We assemble on the bridge, Mother, Lizzie Brown, Annie Townsend, Sophie Aborn, Miss Manchester, Martha & I, Henry, Foster, Theo, Mr. Seagraves, Harry Manchester, Richie, & by great good luck Knight Richmond who was in the Pawtuxet car. I enjoyed him more than any of 'em. Delicious lunch, and very jolly time, save two showers, one tremendous, with the biggest hail stones I ever saw.* Martha, Knight, and I crouch under our umbrellas out on the meadow through the worst of it. . . .

Tuesday. July 5th. 1881.

. . . Mrs. Springer gave me a pretty cameo ring which I wear on my engage-ment finger & mystify all therewith.

Wednesday July 6th. 1881.

. . . Martha over. I go down st., meet her at the boat, & we sail down to Rocky Point and back. Delicious. . . . Go home with M. of course. . . . Mr. Stillwell comes, feasts upon cake and spends the evening. The elders retiring on ac-count of coolness, we sit on the moonlit steps and talk of love & marriage. He's quite nice & sensible when you get at him.

Friday. July 15th. 1881.

. . . Sam calls. I wouldn't give 2 cents for him one way or the other.

Saturday Aug. 13th. 1881

. . . Go to Squantum with Mary Carpenter. . . . The most enjoyable day I've had for a long time. My circle widens. Martha, Cassie, Retta, Mary—life may be happier than I thought. Letter from Martha on return.

Saturday Sept. 10th. 1881.

. . . Introduce "le chat" into my study, and snooze together. The tiredest day I've had for a long time.

*Thurs. Sept. 14th. {sic} * 1881.*

. . . See Dr. Brooks about a Ladies Gymnasium and find him very much inter-ested.[35] Shows me large room. I try the lift & reach 300 lbs. . . .

*Saturday. Sept. 24th. 1881.**

6 or so. M[artha]. spent the night. Retired at ten. Asleep ere 12. I plainly state my grounds, and we consent to divide if needs must. She went home before breakfast. . . .

Sunday. Sept. 25th. 1881.

6 just. Bake & have all done by 9. Sunday School. Church. Mr. Lane of Hingham is interesting Martha now.[36] . . .

Monday. Sept. 26th. 1881.

President Garfield's funeral services. More black than there was for Lincoln. . . . Martha & Mr. Lane stop for me and we infest the Manchester's. Mr. L[ane]. sings—well. Jolly time. . . .

Tuesday. Sept. 27th. 1881.

6. School in earnest. Very good. Grace is every way ahead. Mother returns. Cut out & baste my work dress waist. Martha over. O very well Mr. Lane!, very well. Walk home with her. Arithmetic Latin etc.

Wed. Sept. 28th. 1881.

. . . Edward over. I *hate* to spend an evening in enforced torpor. No exercise of any sort and yet no rest. No conversation worth the name, no ideas; and yet not even room for reverie. I'll have a house of my own yet, and choose my own society. Latin. *Hot.*

Saturday. Oct. 1st. 1881.

. . . Stop to see Dr. Brooks. All things in turn for the "Providence Ladies Gymnasium." Hurrah. . . .

Sunday Oct. 2nd. 1881.

. . . Go to Martha's. She wont go to church, and I stay. Jim calls there. We discuss great things, and on the way home he touched my very soul. "There's something greater than Right & Justice." "Oh? And what's that?" "Love." . . .

Thurs. Oct. 6th. 1881.

. . . Meet Martha down st. Ride home & tea with her. Bible Class. I enjoy playing escort. *Lovely* night. Call from Grace Channing & her cousin.

Sunday. Oct. 9th. 1881.

. . . Martha's young man at church. Jim walks home with me. Keep him an hour in deep discussion. . . .

Monday. Oct. 10th. 1881.

. . . Martha called. I was out. Jim comes over and helps me on my arithmetic. I am not tired, but those brains of mine are. Query. Weariness settled in the weakest place?

Saturday. Oct. 29th. 1881.

. . . Go to M[artha]'s. . . . Stay to a fine tea. Am closeted with Mrs. L[uther]. & change my views a bit. Tell M. to go ahead. Kiss her.[37]

Sunday. Oct. 30th. 1881.

. . . Mr. Woodbury preaches a sermon of which I heard little, being principally occupied in not crying. Walk home with M. . . . Speak to M. a moment wishing her joy of her All Hallow'een. . . . O my little girl! My little girl.

Tues. Nov. 1st. 1881.

. . . Martha over. She hath a ring. I have a pain. Give her my blessing. Write to Sam and tell him all about it. Post the same. . . .

Sat. Nov. 5th. 1881.

. . . Stop at the Hazard's and at Martha's. Saw Mr. Lane and congratulated him. Pleasant, to ring at the door where you've always been greeted with gladness; to be met by the smile that you value all others above—to see that smile flicker and vanish and change into sadness because she was met by *your* presence instead of her love!

Sun. Nov. 13th. 1881.

. . . Sam comes over and takes me for a short walk. Fall in with M[artha]. & Mr. L[ane]. . . . Spar with the enemy.

Tues. Nov. 15th. 1881.

. . . Darn a bit & study a *wee* bit. Spend an hour in the chilly twilight up at my window, and have my crucial struggle with my grief. Victory. Too utterly worn out to do anything in the evening but write down my "state o' mind." Bed at 9.

Monday. Dec. 12th. 1881.

. . . Stop at Martha's to supper. O my little girl!

Tues. Dec. 20th. 1881.

. . . Mrs. Luther calls. Martha calls. Read her my poem.[38] She weeps & wants it. Paint jolly little black & grey panels. Mr. Stillwell calls. Whist. . . .

Fri. Dec. 23rd. 1881.

. . . We receive a miraculous & unaccountable Xmas present. ½ bll. of flour, no end of sugar, heaps of coffee, piles of apples, a box of crackers, a box of raisins, six boxes of sardines, & 3 great jars of the best olives! Can't imagine the donor. . . .

Christmas Day.

. . . Very fine & jolly. Everybody surprised & delighted. I gave but little, & received in all:

1 Card & h'k'f from C. Hedge.
2 Martha's Photo.
3 2 N.gowns from Aunt C.
4 Red headed needles from Mother.
5 Pocket book from Anna.
6 Card from Helen.
7 $10.00 from Mrs. Blake.
8 Gold pencil from M.
9 H'k'f's in box from Aunt C.
10 Silver pin from Mag.
11 Silver umbrella from Anna.
12 Carved leaf pencil holder from Jim.
13 Grand card from Sam.
14 2 chemiloons from Mother.
15 Necktie from Ray.
16 Necktie from Lizzie.

Cake & coffee. Dead tired. Come home early & fix up the presents & room. Send note apropos of "orgie" to "Mr. James Samuel D. R. Simmons Jr." Shortly Sam arrives God bless him! and spends the evening. Whist. We beat 'em 8 games & they the 9th. So thoughtful and kind of him to come over. I owe all my good time this Christmas to him. Well, it's over. I have paid all the bills & have ten dollars odd in hand. I am very tired, but not much hurt by the work & pain of the past two months, & begin to see light again.

Friday. Dec. 30th. 1881.

7.50. Sew on Gym. suit. Carry lent books over to Martha's. Out. Leave 'em with inscription.

> "Some books & things for you dear, once kindly lent to me;
> I have had pleasure from them all, & now with thanks for great & small
> I bring them back to thee.
> I'm rather glad you're out dear, I write without a sigh,
> And miss the taste of bitter tears, the hopeless glimpse of dear lost years
> I'd have if you were by"   C. A. P.

. . . My heart aches and I am tired. What then? I can live and work.

Sat. Dec. 31st. 1881.

It is after midnight, but I write natheless. . . .

A year of steady work. A quiet year, and a hard one. A year of surprising growth. A year internally dedicated to "discoveries and improvements. A year in which I knew the sweetness of a perfect friendship, and have lost it forever. A year of marked advance in many ways, and with nothing conspicuous to regret. I am stronger, wiser and better than last year, and am fairly "satisfied," as to the years work.

I have learned much of self-control & consideration of others. Often think before I speak, and can keep still on occasions. My memory begins to show the training it has had, I can get what I want when I want it, pretty generally.

Most of all I have learned what pain is. Have learned the need of human sympathy by the unfilled want of it, and have gained the power to *give* it, which is worth while.

This year I attained my majority—may I never loose [*sic*] it!

[1882]

[*The following "resolution" immediately precedes the first diary entry for 1882.*]
I have on my mind this year three cares. (So far.)

1. Others first.
2. *Correct* & *necessary* speech only.
3. Don't waste a minute!

If I can form the groundwork of these habits in a year, it will be well. Furthermore, I wish to form a habit of *writing* as much as I can.

Monday. January 2nd. 1882.

Up at 6:15. Deep snow and drifted. Cold. Shovel and broom before light. . . . *Glorious* night. Cold, clear, full moon, universal snow. Enjoy it. Start to eat supper, but Martha & Mr. Lane arrive, and he sings to us. Funny & nice. Good day, with a few mistakes.

Tuesday. Jan. 10th. 1882.

. . . Martha over. Mr. Putnam appears and invites me to go to Mr. Stetson's studio with him, and eke to an art thing tomorrow night.[39] Accept the latter. . . .

TWO

"In Duty, Bound"

January 11, 1882–April 30, 1884

ON JANUARY 11, 1882, CHARLOTTE accompanied her friend Sidney Putnam
to an evening lecture given by a handsome young Providence artist,
Charles Walter Stetson. Still reeling from the loss of Martha, Charlotte was in a
state of emotional vulnerability. Her reactions to meeting Stetson, however, were
decidedly noncommittal. "I like him and his pictures," she wrote simply. And a
couple of days later, "It's a new thing to me to be admired."

Stetson's feelings for Charlotte, in contrast, quickly turned serious: just two
and a half weeks after they met, he proposed marriage. Charlotte promptly declined. A few days later she composed "An Anchor to Windward," a narrative
documenting her "Reasons for living single" (see Appendix B). Foremost among
the reasons she cited was her desire for independence. "I am fonder of freedom
than anything else. . . . I like to be *able* and *free* to help any and every one, as I
never could be if my time and thoughts were taken up by that extended self—a
family. If I were bound to a few[,] I should grow so fond of them, and so busied
with them that I should have no room for the thousand and one helpful works
which the world needs."

It is also likely, however, that Charlotte feared being hurt yet again. Her father had abandoned the family, her mother had withheld the love that she had
craved, and Martha had committed her love to someone else. Denying herself a
serious relationship was one way to avoid more pain. Throwing herself into work
would be less risky, on an emotional level, and more rewarding, she felt, on a
professional level.

Although she held the conviction that women should be able to combine
marriage, motherhood, and career, Charlotte also recognized the personal cost
should she decide to marry. "I felt strongly that for me [marriage] was not right,
that the nature of the life before me forbade it, that I ought to forego the more

intimate personal happiness for complete devotion to my work," she wrote in her autobiography (*Living*, p. 83). Undeterred by Charlotte's refusal of marriage, however, Walter Stetson remained a persistent suitor.

During the spring of 1882, Charlotte continued to assert her independence, by working out at the gym, by reading Mill's *The Subjection of Women*, and by wistfully longing for a "home of [her] own." At the same time, however, and despite her best efforts to the contrary, she and Walter grew increasingly close. They exchanged letters, went for long, leisurely walks together, and wrote each other tender and passionate poems (see Appendix B). "There was the pleasure of association with a noble soul, with one who read and studied and cared for real things, of sharing high thought and purpose, of sympathy in many common deprivations and endurances," she wrote. "There was the natural force of sex-attraction between two lonely young people" (*Living*, p. 83).

Despite the mutual attraction Charlotte struggled with ambivalence when she recalled her earlier resolve to live single and to devote her life to public service. The extent of her emotional dilemma becomes pronounced when we read the love poems that Charlotte and Walter exchanged (see Appendix B). The passion the two shared is apparent; the problem was that it was incompatible with Charlotte's view of how she wanted her life to evolve. She constantly struggled between the pull of the two forces. Whenever the fear of commitment became too intense, Charlotte would enumerate for Walter the reasons that they should part company. She was invariably relieved, however, whenever a proposed separation failed to materialize.

Charlotte's ambivalence toward her relationship with Walter stemmed from a number of concerns. The pain of Martha's rejection, coupled with her mother's tendency to withhold maternal affection, left Charlotte understandably wary of emotional involvements. Also, her resistance toward the traditional roles of wife and mother was rooted in her genuine desire to serve humanity, a philosophy that was taking shape long before she was introduced to Walter Stetson. But that did not make her dilemma any easier. The depth of Charlotte's conflict is apparent in the letters written to Walter during the early weeks of their acquaintance: "You give me rich new happiness which bids fair to make up for the dear love, which I have lost," she wrote in late January (*Endure*, p. 37).

Clearly, one advantage that a relationship with Walter offered was that it helped to fill the void that had been left by Martha's departure. At the same time, however, Charlotte was terrified by the prospect of surrendering her "self" for love. "O my dear! my dear! the more I love you, and the more I grow accustomed to the heaven of your love, the less I wish for anything further. . . . You *must* believe that I love you. . . . But much as I love you I love *WORK* better, & I cannot make the two compatible," she lamented in late March (*Endure*, pp. 62–63). Within a day or two, however, she was wavering again, and by the middle of April, Charlotte believed that she had grown "to understand . . . the full benefit of love" (p. 66).

On the whole, the spring months during which Charlotte and Walter Stetson spent time together were generally pleasant, and Charlotte reported passing several *"very* happy" evenings in his company. But the ambivalence remained. The magic of new-found love notwithstanding, she still looked forward with much anticipation to her summer vacation in Ogunquit, Maine, when they would finally be apart.

Charlotte left Providence for Maine on July 1, 1882. There she enjoyed long, lazy days — loafing, sketching, watching the sun set, and corresponding with Martha, Walter, and various friends. A few days after her return to Providence on July 24, Charlotte spent a "pleasant evening" with Walter, and despite her increasingly frequent expressions of ambivalence, she was overjoyed to see him. On August 14, she left again, this time for twelve days at Martha's Vineyard.

Her happiest moments of the trip seemed to occur in the six days during which Martha Luther joined her at the Vineyard. Indeed, she seemed elated to have Martha to herself: "Meet Martha on the wharf at 12.45 or so. . . . Long pleasant ride, so glad to see her. Dinner, lots, & then we make tracks for & on the beach. I swim & disport myself as usual — catch a fish! She seems to like it. 'A bite' on return & bed. Bless her!"

When the vacation finally ended, Charlotte enjoyed another "pleasant ride" back to the wharf, with Martha seated securely upon her lap. By the time she returned to Providence on August 26, the summer was nearly over, and she and Walter had spent more time apart than together.

Over the next several weeks, however, she and Walter were together often. Walter began painting Charlotte's portrait, but he was unhappy with the result (see "The Painting of *The Portrait*" in Appendix B). Walter was frustrated by his failure to capture Charlotte's beauty adequately; nevertheless, he and Charlotte clearly enjoyed their time together in his studio. And although time must have been at a premium as her wedding day approached, Martha accompanied Charlotte to nearly every studio sitting.

In an attempt, perhaps, to deflect the pain she felt over being spurned by Martha in favor of Charles A. Lane, Charlotte used the quiet moments in the studio to boast about her own future plans of a life with Walter. According to Walter, "She talked . . . to Miss Martha about *our* lives, about *we* had before us," he reported in his diary (*Endure*, p. 98). "She said it all in a way which showed how decided she was that it all would be," he continued. By focusing on her own future, which was, in reality, still very much in limbo, Charlotte was better able to cope with the imminent loss of Martha. In truth, Charlotte was still vacillating on whether she could — or even wanted to — conform to the traditional roles of wife and mother. Bantering about it with Martha, however, helped to diminish her pain. Indeed, at the same time that she braced herself for Martha's wedding, Charlotte valiantly tried to be supportive, escorting Martha to the dressmaker's shop and often dropping in at her home to share a cup of tea or a few stolen moments before Martha would finally, and irrevocably, belong to another.

On October 5, 1882, Martha Luther married Charles Lane. Despite her insistence that she enjoyed the wedding, Charlotte's discomfort with the traditional wedding day rituals was apparent. She helped Martha with last-minute preparations, stood next to her during the "grand and solemn" ceremony, held her bouquet, and then kissed Martha as "Mr. Lane" stood by. When she and another wedding guest, Mabel Bridges, simultaneously caught Martha's bouquet, Charlotte relinquished it without hesitation, since Mabel, she reported, "cared more [for the bouquet] than I." Since Charlotte's brother, Thomas (who was living out west), had also gotten married the previous evening, Charlotte was undoubtedly anxious to reaffirm her independence. Work, and not marriage, despite her occasional disclaimers to the contrary, remained her first priority.

Within a month, however, Charlotte had once again changed her mind. She loved Walter, but she was terrified of commitment. She wanted to be free, yet she enjoyed their time together. She desperately wanted to work, but she feared that within the confines of marriage, Walter would not allow it.

On December 31, 1882, Charlotte reflected on the year just passed: "My last act in the old year was to kneel at my bedside in shame & repentance, with hot tears and self-abasement." Charlotte clearly felt that she had failed by wavering in her resolve to contribute meaningfully to the "world's work," as she had vowed to do in "An Anchor to Windward," written early in the year. She therefore renewed her resolve to work. Yet by early February a wedding seemed inevitable as Mary Perkins suggested that Charlotte and Walter board in the downstairs tenement of her house. Money, however, was a valid concern. Walter's income from the sale of artwork was negligible and sporadic, and Charlotte earned little from her various self-employments. Predictably, there was an escalation in tensions and tears. Charlotte needed to affirm her independence, and Walter resisted it every step of the way. The simmering conflict finally erupted. Just three days after Charlotte had refused to accept a friend's gift of Whitman's *Leaves of Grass* because she had promised Walter that she would not read it (he felt that Whitman's sexual allusions were vile), the two parted company for a period that lasted five weeks.

Charlotte's sadness during this separation was intensified by the death of one of her young day school pupils, Isabel Jackson. Charlotte's emotional pain was exacerbated by the lingering emptiness left by Martha's departure and her sadness over her estrangement from Walter. "The least line of kindred thought in poetry brings all the ache and tears," she confided to her diary, "but by myself I wont think about it." By the end of April, although she was managing to pass some pleasant evenings, she still felt devastated by the loss of Walter. The feeling was mutual, and on May 14, 1883, the two reconciled.

The next day, May 15, Charlotte was approached by the mother of Isabel Jackson, the young student who had died just weeks before. Mrs. Jackson proposed that Charlotte serve as governess to Isabel's young brother, Eddie. When the plans were finalized in late May for Charlotte to commence work in July, she could hardly contain her excitement. The position seemed to offer precisely the kind of independence that she had been seeking. Charlotte ran "gaily home" to trumpet the news, but her mother and Aunt Caroline received it "with disapprobation." Undeterred by their disapproval, however, Charlotte maintained her high spirits all through the following week. "Felt particularly happy in the still warm moonrise. Awake early, still thankful and glad." And just a few days earlier, she had agreed—very suddenly—to marry Walter. The May 20 allusion to her decision is brief and matter-of-fact, betraying the ambivalence that Charlotte was undoubtedly working hard to suppress: "Walter. I have promised to marry him. (Robert called.) Happy." Whatever romantic notions she may have entertained about her impending employment and her subsequent marriage, they carried her happily through the next several weeks.

In her autobiography Charlotte remains vague about her sudden decision to marry Walter Stetson: "At one time when he had met a keen personal disappointment, I agreed to marry him. After that, in spite of reactions and misgivings, I kept my word, but the period of courtship was by no means a happy one," she wrote (p. 83). Walter, however, was more candid about the "keen personal disappointment" that he had suffered. He confides to his journal his decision to solicit from a friend, American art editor and author Charles de Kay, an opinion about the quality of the sonnets that he frequently wrote during spare moments (*Endure*, pp. 187–90). Walter apparently fancied himself a serious poet, and he was devastated by de Kay's assessment that his verse was mediocre at best, that it should be considered a source of "amusement of vacant hours, not a serious matter for publication" (p. 187). A passionate man, Walter poured onto the pages of his journal his humiliation over his fatuous belief that the sonnets had aesthetic merit. His depression, undoubtedly exacerbated by mounting debts as he struggled to survive on an emerging artist's salary, lasted for days. He wrote an impassioned plea to Charlotte, imploring her to burn the sonnets that he had previously sent. So tortured was Walter by his friend's criticism, and so shaken was his confidence, that he began to doubt the value of all of his artistic endeavours, even burning his old journal, consisting of "939 pages of foolscap" (p. 189). When Walter went to visit Charlotte later that evening, she was so affected by his emotional state that she vowed to marry him. (A couple of days later, she pleaded with Walter that he not force her to burn his sonnets, and he agreed; several of those that survive appear in Appendix B).

A few days later, before leaving Providence for a week's visit to Martha Lane and other friends in Massachusetts, Charlotte and Grace Channing, with whom she was spending more and more time since Martha's departure, paid a visit to Walter at his studio. "Dress and go for Grace Channing, and we call on Walter. She was much pleased with him and his work. Which pleased me much, as I value her, & any favorable criticism is an agreeable change." Years later, Grace would become the new Mrs. Stetson after Walter's divorce from Charlotte.

On June 30 Charlotte left Providence again, this time for a two-week visit to Ogunquit, Maine. She passed her time reading, sketching, napping on the rocks, and spending a good deal of time with her friend Conway Brown, who would die from a self-inflicted gunshot wound less than six months later. Charlotte's diary reported that during a walk on July 9, young Conway had allowed her to "try his revolver," and she was pleased to have hit "4 shots out of 10." She also spent time with Conway counseling him and comforting him as he confided to her his suicidal impulses. (Charlotte's grief upon learning of his death is reflected in her diary entry of January 1, 1884. Later than summer, Charlotte learned that Sidney Putnam, who had introduced her to Walter, had drowned. Walter speculated that Putnam's death may have been a suicide; see *Endure*, pp. 221–22.)

After returning to Providence, Charlotte began work as Eddie Jackson's governess on July 16. She proudly remarked on her new arrangement in her diary. "Become a hireling as I phrase it for the admiration of my friends, at 5.35 [P.M.]," she wrote contentedly. She and Eddie seemed to hit it off immediately, and they spent hours playing billiards, baseball, and battledore. Charlotte also taught him sewing, reading, math, and drawing, and she was obviously pleased with the relationship that she and Eddie shared. But by early August, during which time she accompanied the Jackson family to Moosehead Lake, Maine, her patience with Eddie was wearing thin. "His mother *says* he must go to bed at 8, but lets him play come-as-you-come & sit up & sit up till almost nine!" Two days later she commented disparagingly, "Can't say I love these folk." By August 29 the honeymoon was clearly over, and by September 9 Charlotte wanted out of the arrangement. "Eddie rather ruder than usual to me. Can I stand it all winter? 'M-m-m!" As it turned out, however, Mrs. Jackson announced a few days later that she planned to enroll Eddie in school that winter, which meant that Charlotte would be out of a job. Charlotte was overjoyed; the ten weeks with Eddie, "a despicable boy," had seemed like an eternity. As she drolly remarked in her autobiography over forty years later, she "learned more about the servant question in that time than most of us ever find out" (p. 69).

On October 2 Charlotte returned to Providence. "Leave bundles [in the depot] & go straight to Walter. A happy morning," she wrote. But almost inevitably, the happiness only postponed the pain. Just days after Charlotte's return from Moosehead Lake, Walter revealed to her his growing anxiety over his lack of financial preparedness for marriage. He even briefly contemplated giving up his art for an occupation that would be more dependable and lucrative. Within a day or two, however, he had a change of heart, and he and Charlotte continued to plan their wedding.

Walter's precarious financial situation, however, continued to fuel his anxiety. When Charlotte visited his studio in late October and proposed that they marry before the year's end, Walter's frustration at the bleak reality of his economic condition was obvious. "It seemed almost wicked in me not to join in her enthusiasm, but I could not," he confided to his diary (*Endure*, p. 241). For her part, Charlotte coped with her growing unrest by immersing herself in a variety of activities: she worked out at the gymnasium, continued to teach painting, frequented the library, and learned French. But while her days were full, Charlotte continued to be haunted by her own reservations about the drawbacks of marriage. On November 9 her misgivings were projected through her artistic expression, when she painted a "lugubrious picture of 'The Woman Against The Wall,'" which Walter described as "a literal transcript of her mind" (p. 244). In an attempt to confront some of her misgivings, Charlotte confided her fears to such friends as Retta Clarke and Jim and Sam Simmons, whom she found only marginally helpful. With Sam Simmons, for instance, she talked late into the night about women's rights, but to her utter disappointment she found him unsympathetic and narrow-minded.

As a form of catharsis, perhaps, for her growing uncertainty about the impending marriage, Charlotte composed a poem during this time, which significantly marked her first adult publication. "In Duty, Bound" was a lamentation on the loss of individualism in marriage (see Appendix B). The poem depicts the "wasting power," the death of "high ideals," and the broken spirit that Charlotte felt one must endure in marriage. If her painting of 'The Woman Against The Wall' was a literal transcript of Charlotte's mind, "In Duty, Bound" was even more so. The metaphors of bondage and isolation are powerful; images of pain and despair are etched into every line.

When Charlotte learned that the *Woman's Journal* had accepted the poem for publication, she commented simply, "No pay, but it's a beginning." And it did mark the start of an incredibly prolific writing career that would span much of the next fifty-two years. But the poem also marked the beginning of the most difficult period of Charlotte's life, as her ill-fated marriage to Walter Stetson drew near.

After having "been miserable in divers ways for weeks," Charlotte left on December 26 for a visit to Martha and Charles Lane and their four-and-a-half-month-old son in Hingham, Massachusetts. Although she enjoyed seeing Martha again, the old pain of abandonment mercilessly resurfaced when the two young parents left Charlotte "sitting up in [a] lonely state" so that they could retire, alone, for the evening.

On December 29, 1883, Charlotte returned to Providence. As the year drew to a close, Charlotte reflected on the year just passed. Her entry of December 31 is both prophetic and chilling.

The old, familiar feelings of loneliness and isolation resurfaced in full force. With her wedding just a few months away, Charlotte documented her increasingly frequent manic-depressive episodes, the "waves of misery" that were interspersed with brief and, to Charlotte's mind, inexplicable periods of happiness. In the final hours of that cold New Year's Eve, she perceived just how susceptible her relationship with Walter made her to the depression that was beginning to govern her life. "Let me not forget to be grateful for what I have" she wrote. "Some strength, some purpose, some design, . . . And some Love. Which I can neither feel nor believe in when the darkness comes," she wrote.

Chief among Charlotte's concerns that night was the growing fear—despite his reassurances to the contrary—that in marrying Walter she would be sacrificing her life's work, "to be of use to others." So profound was her pain as the new year approached that she was visited by a bold and defiant death wish, tempered only by her reluctance to hurt those who loved her. "I would more gladly die than ever yet; saving for the bitter agony I should leave in the heart of him who loves me. And mother's pain," she wrote.

New Year's Day, 1884, however, brought the tragic news of the suicide of Conway Brown, a friend with whom Charlotte had spent considerable time during her previous summer's stay in Ogunquit, Maine. Charlotte understood Brown's suicide; she could sympathize with his "mental misery." His death, in fact, only reinforced Charlotte's conviction that life could only have meaning when one has "enough real work" through which "to preserve one's self-respect."

Yet, despite her understanding of Conway Brown's suicide, the death of so many of Charlotte's friends in the three years before her wedding to Walter Stetson had to have contributed to her growing unrest. The theme of loss—both actual and symbolic—was consistently reinforced. Since early 1881 Charlotte had attended the funerals of numerous people who had somehow shaped her life: Professor Lewis Diman, May Diman, Sidney Putnam, Isabel Jackson, Conway Brown. During that same period she had also accompanied her mother to numerous other funerals: a neighbor's young infant had died, as had a close family friend, Mr. Manchester, as well as two of Mary's friends, Mrs. Stimpson and Walter Smith. Their deaths forced Charlotte to reassess her own life. Her conclusions were grim. "One does not die young who so desires it," she wrote somberly.

Soon after Conway Brown's funeral, Charlotte tried to alleviate her despondency by immersing herself in her daily activities: painting, teaching, and exercising at the gym. At the same time she continued to write for publication. In early January her poem about a "fallen" woman, "One Girl of Many," was accepted for publication in *Alpha*. But even the triumph of publication was eclipsed by the shadow of ever-increasing doubts. Charlotte began to consciously suppress her misgivings: "Bed after 12, trying to forget personal misery in thought for others," she wrote just four months before her wedding. And on March 9: "Am lachrymose. Heaven send that my forebodings of future pain for both be untrue."

Still, however portentous her doubts, Charlotte seemed to enjoy decorating the rooms in which she and Walter would live. As the wedding day approached, they abandoned their plans to live with Mary Perkins in favor of renting a suite of rooms on the second floor of a house owned by a Dr. Wilcox: "Betake myself to the house, where I remain from 9 till 12, while gas men, stove men, other men and a boy bring divers things to our domicile. Walter arrives and remains with me. I sweep up the parlor. The stove is magnificent and color of paint and paper highly satisfactory. We exult in the prospect before us."

On May 2, 1884, Charlotte and Walter Stetson would enter their newly decorated quarters as husband and wife.

Wed. Jan. 11th. 1882.

6.40 Snow on my face on waking. Shovel paths. Only Florrie. She stays to dinner. Lu over. Wash "heap" dishes. Go to store & Mabel Hills with Lu. Dress up, and go to a lecture on etching by Charles Walter Stetson, with "Sidney." *Rather* a waste of time. He brought me a piece of sugar cane. . . .

Thurs. Jan. 12th. 1882.[1]

. . . Meet Mr. Put[nam]. at Riders and go to Mr. Stetson's studio. I like him and his pictures. Ath. Forgot the etching Mr. S. gave me, & went back after it. He was out. . . .

Sat. Jan. 14th. 1882.

. . . Call at Mr. Stetson's for my proof. Sidney there. Miss Arnold comes in. All go, & I have a twilight tête-a-tête with Charles Walt. Like him. It's a new thing to me to be admired. . . .

Sat. Jan. 21st. 1882.

. . . Letter from Mr. Stetson with invitation to a concert next Wed. (Shall go.) . . .

*Sun. Jan. 22nd. 1882.**

. . . Mr. Stetson calls. We are left alone, and have a nice talk. I introduce myself as fully as possible, and he does the same. We shake hands on it, and are in a fair way to be good friends. . . .

Mon. Jan 23rd. 1881. {sic}

. . . Find a letter from my new friend. It's worth while to wait for some things. . . .

Wed. Jan. 25th. 1882.

7.10. Warmer. Lazy day. Wash all the dishes. Loaf a bit. Dress up and go to concert at the Art Club with Herodotus.[2] Snows. The youth advances. Home by ten. Sam here. I value him.

Sun. Jan. 29th. 1882.

7.15. Stay at home & get diner. Mother a bit better. Charles Walt. appears. Mary in. Go to church alone. Jim sees me home.
I have this day been asked the one question in a womans life, and have refused.[3]

Friday February 3rd. 1882.

6.45. . . . Go to the Morse's & so to the Reading Club at Miss Waterman's. Am "Mrs. Rogers" in "Esmeralda." Quite a gathering of big bugs. Am introduced to divers. . . . Cover myself with glory by my performance. Am inordinately complimented by all hands. . . .

Sat. Feb. 4th. 1882.

. . . See Carrie Hazard [at library], & she drives me over to Martha's. Stay there to dinner, & have a nice talk with M. Home in a rapidly increasing snow storm. Sup, "hilt my kirtle above my knee," and go to the Boy's Room regardless of family obloquy. Splendid storm. . . .
Martha says that if she dies I must bring up her children. Somewhat of a compliment.

Sunday. February 5th. 1882.

7.5. A tremendous snowstorm! I dig through drifts waist deep. No cars at all, but a snowplough with *14* horses and another thing with 8 at 2.15. 30 men or so with 'em. *Tremendous* snowstorm. Charles Walt arrived about 4. Stays to tea, and seems to enjoy himself.

Mon. Feb. 13th. 1882.

6.45. Go to have tooth filled, and don't have it; as I had not time enough. Utilize the half hour in reading, at the dentist's, a 30-page-letter from Mr. Stetson. Autobiographical, and interesting. . . .

Sun. Feb. 19th. 1882.

. . . Jim [here] . . . and at 4.30 or so Mr. Stetson arrives. Very unhappy to find me engaged, and won't stay to tea. Gives me his photo. Fine. Martha & Mr. L. arrive at 5.40 about. . . . Gay tea party. . . . Jim was the life and soul of the party, and helped mother a lot. . . . Tired. Why can't they all be friends like the Simmonses?

Fri. Feb. 24th. 1882.

. . . Pub. Lib. & get "The Subjection of Women." J. S. Mill.[4]

Tues. Feb. 28th. 1882.

6.25. Letter from Herodotus. Went calmly through all the lessons till recess before reading. . . . Hour at the Gymn. . . . . Hour at the Ath. Solid study too. Home gaily ater [*sic*] 12 hours work. Herodotus here. He had invitation to the Hazards "tea" Thurs. & want to inquire concerning the same. Bit of talk, but he has to go. Read an atom, sup, *Sam* called, so that I could not write! Whist till 10.20. Then he stayed till 11. Helped me in my arithemetic though. Tired, which I was *not* a bit when on my way home after 12 hours work.

Wed. March. 8th. 1882.

. . . Home via Martha's. Mr. Stetson here. Mother invites him to come & stay with me as she & Aunt C. go out. He does so, bringing Rossetti's poems (P.M. call). Sam calls, but goes ere long. Queer sort of evening—unsatisfactory.

Tues. March. 14th. 1882.

. . . Letter from Herodotus. . . . Home, sup, write note to He. to thank him for good store of fine stationery he sent me today. Sidney does not appear, but Herodotus does, just for a moment, to ask me if he might bring his friend MacDougal[5] to see me on Friday. *Course!* Read an hour or so.

Friday March. 17th. 1882.

. . . Mr. Stetson & Mr. MacDougal call. Like the latter amazingly. Gay sort of time.

Sat. March. 18th. 1882.

6. Start out at 8.40, stopping for Miss Hill. Get half an hours exercise, and then, in stepping on a chair, to mount the piano, to set the clock, at Miss Hill's request, I clumsily fall, and give myself a violent bruise and profusely bleeding cut just in the "middle." Sit 'round a while, with cold wet towels in abundance; get advice from Dr. Brooks, and ride home serenely, in a horse car. Am blest with an entire holiday till Thurs.! Houp la! . . .

Sun. March. 19th. 1882.

Rise at 12.30 or so. Bathe & dress up. Sit around serenely. Lu calls. Martha & Mr. Lane call. . . . He. gives me Rossetti & certain moneys in an envelope to "keep for him." Is much concerned.

Tuesday. March. 21st. 1882.

7.30. Write to He. Paint a *little*. Dr. Tyney calls. Examination highly favorable, two dollars. Says she would have sewed it if she had seen it Sat. Diet embargo removed. . . . Herodotus stops in for a few moments. I give him a letter recommending departure. He goes. Jim calls. He. returns, has a few moments talk with me, and things slide on once more. But it was a long hour between 7.30 & 8.30, when I thought he had gone, and gone to stay. I could have stood it though for I thought it right—if *he* did.

Sunday. March. 26th. 1882.

11.40! Last day of delicious idleness. Write to C. A. Hedge. Dine. Wash dishes. Herodotus arrives. Real nice time. In honor of his 24th birthday yestreen. . . . Mr. Stetson & I compare colds. His ahead.

Tuesday. March. 28th. 1882.

. . . Mr. McDougal & Herodotus. A horribly incongruous evening. Whist & Biblical criticism in the same small room. Mr. M. plays. Mr. Stetson is sick— faint, & goes out to lie down. He might not have come over. Threatened pneumonia. O when shall I have a home of my own! 12.20

Monday. May 1st. 1882.

Because t'is Spring I needs must sing
My joy I cannot smother,
The grass is green, the sky is blue,
And I am I and you are you
And we have found each other!
Then what care we for Fate's decree
It *must* be one or t'other,
And if we live or if we die
Still you are you and I am I
And still we have each other! . . .

Thurs. May. 4th. 1882.

5.30! Letter from He. Stop at his Studio to leave him mine. . . . Gym. Ride to the Ath. with Helen Gammell. Read. Joined there by Walter, & we take an extended walk and then spend the evening at Martha's. Very pleasant, *very*. Home ere ten. Sup.

Sun. May. 21st. 1882.

. . . Our first summer day. Martha & Mr. Lane call. Herodotus arrives. We walk about ten miles, & get a lot of flowers. . . .

Mon. May. 22nd. 1882.

4. Paint violets and bell wort. School. Letter from Carrie Hazard with check for $10.00 for my summer vacation. I seem likely to have one. . . .

Fri. May. 26th. 1882—

. . . Sam talks to me as I wish he had six or eight weeks ago. He is a friend worth having.

Sat. May. 27th. 1882 —

. . . Had a letter from Thomas! Dear boy! He is going to be married. Write him, & send best wishes & violets to the dame. . . .

Sun. June 25th. 1882.

6.50. *Hot.* Loaf all day. Good Shampoo. Read & doze P.M. Mr. Stetson comes back from Phil. & spends the evening. . . . *Hot! Hot! Hot!*

Mon. June 26th. 1882.

. . . He. appears, nice time till lo! Edward, & then Jim, who wouldn't come up the steps at all, but stayed down below and argued on instinct vs. reason. He. gets a little mad at sophism & pigheadedness. I'm too used to it to mind. He attempts a little explanation with mother but in vain. Needs some practice to get along with her — or a Simmons.

Thurs. June 29th. 1882.

. . . [C]all on Mrs. Diman. Get a lot of roses. Home, sup, and dress up in tissue skirt, bunting overthing, lace, pearls, silver stars, bracelets & rose. A party for one. Charles Walt. appears, & enjoys it. He says goodbye at 10.45. I love him.

Saturday July 1st.

5.5 Pack. . . . Hack at 8.45 & off. . . . Reached Wells late & tired, no one to meet us. Engaged a sort of Black Maria & rode 9 miles or so up and to Augunquit. Big bare boarding house, close to the rocks and surf. Hot supper, eat little, snooze and talk & recite & tell stories till trunks come at 10. *Bed.*

Monday. July 3rd. 1882.

4.30, but retire again. 6.45. Go fishing after breakfast. Catch two. Write to He. Dine on lamb killed today! Sleep two hours on the rocks P.M. & sketch in pencil a very little. Go sit on rocks with all of 'em till nearly 9. . . . Come in when it rains, & have a little music in the keroseney parlor. See a dull moon rise. bed at 10 or so. Have left my flannel sack outsomewhere. Coldsores. 22 years old! Good!

Tues. July 4th. 1882.

7. No signs of celebration save a few subdued firecrackers. Paint my first out door sketch. Pretty good. Icecream for dinner, & both fish & chicken! . . . Write to Mrs. Smith, & this:

> I sit at my ease & gaze on the seas
> Three things before me lie;
> The rock where I sit, the sea under it,
> And the overarching sky.
> The rocks iron brow is the life I have now;
> Too hard for peaceful rest;

Too warm in the sun, too cold when there's none
Uncomfortable at best.
The wide ocean comes next; now quiet, now vext;
It wants me, to hold & to keep;
It looks pleasant & warm—but there might come a storm—
And the ocean is pathless & deep.
And above hangs the dome of our dear future home
To be ours if we work through the day:
But these rocks hide the sun, the azure is gone—
Even Heaven looks misty & grey.

Came back under the cliff, supper, & evening on the rocks, enlivened with firecrackers. (Found flannel sack.)

Mon. July 24th. 1882.

Awake at 3.30, in at 4, got hat etc., crawled down over roof & pillar, & took a walk with Kate. Saw the sun rise & got a lot of gorgeous flowers. Roses & daisies for Miss G. Back to house, fix flowers, bathe, & pack. Last visit to rocks with Kate. Breakfast. Off at 8 or so, amidst general bewailment. Hot ride to station, & hot ride to Boston, diversified by amusing children. Transfer trunk for 25 cts, and ride over to Prov. station in horse car. . . .

Thurs. July 27th. 1882.

. . . Sam and I sat & talked till 11.20. I'm very fond of Sam. He's a good friend for any girl.

Sat. July 29th. 1882.

. . . Bathe and dress. Mr. Stetson returns. Glad to see him. Pleasant evening on steps.

Wed. Aug. 2nd. 1882.

6.30. Letter from He. . . . As I finish He's letter, he arrives, and a nice time we have of it. He tears up his—the bad thing! unwarrantedly. We look over "Talks on Art," & I read him "The Well Bred Girl."

Thurs. Aug. 3rd. 1882.

. . . Go to Martha's & have a very pleasant talk. Much of Dr. Keller of Boston. I am glad such women live.

Sunday Aug. 13th. 1882—

6.45 or so. Get clothes & things all ready. . . . Robert over to tea. Gives mother $2.00 for the vineyard,[6] good of him. C. W. later, we go out to post letter, & take quite a walk. A pleasant evening, I'm really getting fond of him. He gives me a stylograf.

Mon. Aug. 14th. 1882.

4.30. Pack & fix. . . . 8 o'clock train, reach New Bedford at 10 or so, & get to the Vineyard by a little after 12. . . . I spend afternoon in the hammock & arranging things. . . . Write to Martha.

Tues. Aug. 15th. 1882.

6 or so. Slept in the cupola on a canvas cot. Like it *amazingly*. Always wanted to sleep in a cupola. Am pursued by the children who adore me straitway. All go to the beach, & I have a fine swim with May. Go up in the tower & view the country round. . . . Go to the hotel & watch them dance, go & have a cream, stop and hear music at one of the cottages. Home by 10, & gladly retire.

Wed. Aug. 16th. 1882.

6. . . . Letter from Love.[7] Can come tomorrow. . . .

Thurs. Aug. 17th. 1882.

5. Go to beach & have a nice bath, diving off raft, etc. Out by 6. Home with suit, breakfast, snooze in hammock, amuse Bess, pack, bit of cake for lunch, & am off with Jophanus at 1.30 or so. Pleasant ride of about 8 miles. Arrive, get acquainted with Love, & start for the beach. Supper at 5.30 to 6, & go & watch sunset from the shores of oyster pond. Like the place—much.

Sun. Aug. 20th. 1882.

6. Read in orchard all day. An elderly caller there, who asked questions. Finished "Bella," & read a book on beauty, some Mosses from an Old Manse, a little of Sesame & Lilies, & some old Littells.[8] Card from Martha.

Mon. Aug. 21st. 1882.

. . . Meet Martha on the wharf at 12.45 or so & walk back with her & Miss H. Jophanus waiting for us, she writes a postal, and we set off. Long pleasant ride, so glad to see her. Dinner, lots, & then we make tracks for & on the beach. I swim & disport myself as usual—catch a fish! She seems to like it. "A bite" on return & bed. Bless her!

Sat. Aug. 26th. 1882.

3.50. Finish packing. Pay bill—$8.00. Breakfast. Off to the Bluffs with M. on my lap. Pleasant ride. . . .

Mon. Aug. 28th. 1882.

6. Sew. Get splendid letter from Thomas. Sit down and answer it—32 pages. . . . Home here & find Sidney (I had stopped & saw his mother in her yard, & met him at the gate.) A pleasant call, I talking in great style. He seems pleased.

Fri. September 1st. 1882.

. . . Stop for Martha & give 1st sitting at Walter's studio. Very pleasant time indeed. . . .

Thurs. Sept. 7th. 1882.

. . . Stop for Martha, out, meet her at Rider's, & then to studio. Have to wait half an hour for Charles. Stay till 12.15. Discuss Malagawatch project.[9] Dine with M. . . .

Fri. Sept. 22nd. 1882.

6. Write to Thomas. Little opening with mother to the effect that things I thought mine were not. Surrender claim to the large mirror, mother's portrait, gold bracelets, locket, & divers other things. A very mean business. . . .

Sat. Sept. 23rd. 1882.[10]

O God! My God! I thank thee For a day well spent!
I thank thee for the happiness Which thou has sent!
I thank thee & I pray thee To help me so to live
As to deserve the blessing Thou didst give

Wed. Oct. 4th. 1882

2.30! Down stairs & out doors to look for comet. Not risen. Nap on lounge & wake at 4.30 or so. Up then, and a beauty. Wake the other folks to see it. General admiration. Bed afterward and don't rise till near seven. . . . Thomas married tonight.[11]

Thurs. Oct. 5th. 1882.

6.30. Dressmake. . . . Dress in white bunting and get to Martha's by 12. Put on her flowers for her, and otherwise assist, Mrs. Sullivan doing the "maid" to perfection. I stand by her during the ceremony, hold her bouquet and kiss her next to Mr. Lane. Mr. Slicer was perfect;—very grand and solemn. Introduced to Mr. & Mrs. Lincoln of Hingham. A satisfactory refection, furnished by Ardoene. Really enjoyed myself. Help Martha change her dress, hand around the rice, carry home wedding cake, preserve one of her rosebuds, catch her bouquet, (as also did Mabel Bridges, and I let her have it, I had the bud & she cared more than I,) and throw the slipper (one of my own old ones, small & pretty) so that it lights airily on top of the carriage, and stays there till they all disappear in the distance. Go home with Lu, (run for a car for Mabel Bridges,) & dressmake till dark. Read & write.

Wed. Oct. 11th. 1882.

. . . Letters from Charles, & Martha. The little girl is happy. . . .

Tues. Oct. 17th. 1882.

. . . Whisk down st. stopping at Ada's with ulster. Meet Miss Gladding in coach & go to Studio. Lo! Mother is there! An unpleasant call, with the poor picture severely criticized.[12] Then Miss G. takes me up to Annie's. . . . Home just in time to find Kate Bucklin. She makes a long call and engages the palette. Talk with mother. She thinks we'd better marry & come here to board. (I don't). Write to Walter and post it. . . .

Fri. Nov. 3rd. 1882.

. . . Kate [Bucklin] comes. Brings me a grand edition of Robert Browning— uncut! I am *pleased*. She stays to tea, mother & Aunt go to Marys, & we have a pleasant everning. I have to stop altogether in reading "A Blot on the 'Scutcheon,"[13] for crying! Home with Kate.

Sat. Nov. 4th. 1882.

. . . Go to Miss Gladdings till 6.15 or so. An old Dr. Fuller there. I had a bite of *guava*—didn't think much of it. Miss G. is disappointed in me because I want to marry as I do! I feel a little blue—very.

Sun. Nov. 19th. 1882.

. . . Walter comes at 6.30. Glad, *glad* to see him. Sam stops & takes hepatica & others. Robert calls but is relegated to back room with the ladies. Long happy evening with Walter who stays till 11.

Mon. Nov. 20th. 1882.

. . . Walter joins me on Main st. & walks home with me. Mother asks him to stay to tea & go down with me. He does. Reads me a letter of Mrs. Cressons. I love him. . . .

Wed. Nov. 29th. 1882.

7–10. Fly around, & nearly miss my 8.30 train. Walter joins me and we ride to Boston in a dismal N. E. snowstorm. He sends off my bag & leaves me at Mrs. Smith's. A nice time with her, & lunch; then he comes for me in a Herdic, & we look at pictures in Wms. & Everetts for an hour or so. Then Martha stops for me, we bid adieu to C. W. & take a car to the vicinity of her mothers. Pleasant call there, & then take two cars to Aunt Emilie's. Houghton & Francis[14] there. Quiet evening, games with the boys, Edward arrives late. Bed between 9 & 10.

Thurs. Nov. 30th. 1882.

7.10. Church A.M. & a good sermon, very. Home & "dressup." I was a military gentleman, so was Houghton; Edward Queen Elizabeth, Bertie a fair damsel, Phil & Robbie Orientals, Aunt Susie a Zuni Indian. Uncle E. a judge, & Aunt

E, a fine lady. Splendid dinner. Then sit around till six, & then some other people come, Rogers, & Bissells, &c. & we masqueraders a act ballads & things. Virginia Reel & all kinds of fun. A Morton Mitchell & Alice M. arrive later. I've outgrown this kind of fun.

Sun. Dec. 10th. 1882.

. . . Walter at near 8! Desire him to read over his last letter to me. Then I discuss it with him with good effect. Happy half hour thereafter.

Wed. Dec. 20th. 1882.

. . . For a wonder Walter comes, & we have a pleasant evening together. I show him picters and he likes 'em. Give him the panel I made for a Xmas gift. Likes it much. . . .

Christmas Day.
Mon. Dec. 25th. 1882

5 A.M. Up, and busy doing up bundles, Retire at 1. Rise at 7.35. Have a surprise at breakfast; a silk umbrella, head of lavonarola & "Romola"[15] from Kate Bucklin, & two nightdresses from mother & some pretty cards. Harry Manchester stops & leaves me a ridiculous paintbox & some verses & a real pretty card. I breakfast under my umbrella, a gorgeous black silk one with a stick handle. Paint on Sam's card. Go to Mary's at 1.45. Annie Westcott there and the Carpenters. A very jolly time, my poetry proving very acceptable. Mother gave me Don Quixote, Robinson Crusoe, AEsops Fables, Alice through the Looking Glass, & The Princess & Curdie! Anna & Clarence an Emerson Calendar & Birthday Book, Mary a tidy, Ray a pretty wodden Box, Robert Brown little extension gold pen, Aunt C. splendid travelling bag & little fan in a stick. Card from Harold Childs. Came home, met Robert, Jim called & brought me a lovely little corner bracket, Japanese. Pack. Very pleasant Xmas. Walter comes & we take a walk in the dim moonlight. Goes at 10.

Fri. Dec. 29th. 1882.

Mr. Lane has the pleasure of calling me to breakfast, and enjoys it. Martha not very well, so I wait on her and really make myself useful. Read her "A Blot on the 'Scutcheon" till we are both sobbing, and she won't hear any more. She sleeps nearly all the afternoon till I prevail on her to take a little walk. . . .

Sunday Dec. 31st. 1882.

. . . My last act in the old year was to kneel at my bedside in shame & repentance, with hot tears and self-abasement. From which I rose resolved to pray no more for a season but to work again.

And so to sleep at eleven or so.

[1883!]

Tues. Jan. 2nd. 1883.

. . . A little Jackson girl called to see about painting lessons in the morning, and I go down and see her mother about. Am to have her twice a week. . . . Supper. Dress myself in fine array, & go to see "Iolanthe" with Walter. Enjoy it. Like it. Like to go with him. Home serenely, and he stops and has some supper as he had no time for one before. . . .

Sun. Feb. 11th. 1883.

6.40. More snow. . . . Clean some paths. . . . Wait a bit, & then Walter. Mother proposes a grand new arrangement to which we joyfully accede. We take the house & things, downstairs tenement that is, & live here for the present while she goes out west.

Mon. Feb. 12th. 1883.

. . . Call on Carrie Hazard who goes to Aiken S. C. on Wed. She gives me $5.00 to *buy things for Walter.* I love her much. She is a noble & beautiful woman. Home, wrote a little to Walter. . . .

Wed. Feb. 21st. 1883.

. . . Letter from Walter. He and his parents call in state, & they stay while he & I go & see the Hayden exhibition of etchings. Stop at the studio in the glorious moonlight. Then home & he stays till 10.30.

Tues. March. 6th. 1883—

. . . Card from Martha and letter from Walter announcing the fact that he is not to have the sale he expected. Doll & Richards advise having the pictures worked off privately instead. Walter is sad enough. Write long letter to comfort him. . . .

Sun. March. 18th. 1883.

. . . Practice Easter songs in the church. Walk around the square with some of the boys, giving perapatetic instruction. A Mr. Haywood drones in Mr. Slicers place. . . . Jim to dinner, & stays till 6.30! . . . Do nothing but wash the dishes & talk with Jim, partly on business. Dress, not down to let Walter in. Find him with an anagram. Spend an hour in that divertisement & then talk till 10.45 in the parlor. Tears.[16] Bed by 11.30.

Fri. March. 23rd. 1883—

. . . Go to hear Julia Ward Howe on Maternity. Not new, but good.[17] . . .

Thurs. April. 5th. 1883—

. . . Go to Gym. Run mile. . . . [G]o to Grace Channing's. Mr. O'Connor had left for me a beautiful new copy of "Leaves of Grass." Walt. Whitman is an intimate friend of his. I am obliged to decline, as I had promised Walter I would not read it. . . .

Sun. April 8th. 1883.

5.30. Mend petticoat & write most of a sermon for the boys. Was off in good season, had on spring suit & waterproof, felt unusually clean and nice in every way, and met a female who confidently remarked, "I presume you're a livin'-out girl, aren't you?" Such is human vanity. Home alone. . . . Bit of a nap, . . . read Rossetti. Dress. Walter. We have the back room & wood fire. He is not coming any more.[18] Went at 11.15.
(Simply to anticipate the parting & save pain.)
Dear Love! Shall I come back?

Tues. April. 10th. 1883.

. . . Alone all P.M. & paint on Soapine card. Wash dinner dishes. Sew. (My pain & sorrow is all behind & underneath as yet. The least line of kindred thought in poetry brings all the ache and tears, but by myself I wont* think about it.) Sam calls, and then Ben Wells. Whist. Wearisome.
Sun. April 15th. 1883.
. . . [W]rite 4 sheets to Walter. Read a little Rossetti. Cry a good deal. Bed before 11.

Tues. April. 17th. 1883.

5.30. This day died at 3.20 A.M. Isabel Jackson. Her mother sends me a note at breakfast time, enclosing a gold pen I left there, and a cuff-pin I let Bella wear one day. Answer in time for the postman. Florrie. Write a little poem to Mrs. Jackson.[19] Dine lightly alone. . . . Beg a few snowdrops which I take to Mrs. Jackson with my verses. The little brother comes to the door. O I am grieved to lose her!

Wed. April. 18th. 1883.

. . . Evening watching Belinda,[20] who became a happy mother at 10.30. Again at 11 or so, and again, I don't know when, as I went to bed and to sleep with the furry family snugly ensconced at the foot of the bed. Read a little.

Thurs. April 26th 1883.

. . . Find that Walter has been here, expecting to find me out, and left note, & sonnets. Answer. Not in bed before 11.35 or so.

Sat. April. 28th. 1883.

. . . Mother tries to talk to me about Mr. Stetson, & blames him somewhat. I refuse to give any information.

Fri. May. 11th. 1883.

5:20–30. Make fire, etc. Murder a kitten with chloroform & bury it in the back yard.[21] . . .

Mon. May. 14th. 1883.

. . . Go to see Mrs. Jackson about lessons to Eddie. Poor little woman! Home. Sup. Mix bread. Walter calls! O I was *glad* to see him! Jim comes with an order. I excuse myself and stay with Walter. Goes at 10.30. . . .

Tues. May 15th. 1883.

. . . Write note to Walter. Am unhappy. . . . Lesson 1st to Eddie Jackson. Prospect of being his governess. . . . [B]ed by 10.40. The first night I have cried because I couldn't help it. That is couldn't help *wanting* to.

Thurs. May. 17th. 1883.

. . . Walter comes, bless his heart! Happy evening. Goes at 10.30 – 45.

Sat. May. 19th. 1883.

. . . Copy article on gym. Take it to Journal office. Mr. Danielson, (edtr.) not in. (Give it to Dr. Brooks & he don't want to offer it. Send it to Carrie Hazard to put in if she will.) Gym. & work well. . . .

Sun. May. 20th. 1883.

. . . Retta calls for a few minutes, but can't see her to speak to. Sup. Dress. Walter. I have promised to marry him. (Robert called.) Happy.

Wed. May 23rd. 1883

. . . My article on Prov. Ladies Gym. comes out in the Journal. Note from Carrie Hazard saying she had sent it. . . . Walter comes, bless him; happy evening. . . . Mrs. Jackson called & wants me to come and see them about the governess plan.

Thurs. May. 24th. 1883.

. . . Go and see the Jacksons. Am engaged as governess for Eddie to begin in July. Run gaily home to tell. Sam here. News received with disapprobation by mother and Aunt. . . .

Sat. May 26th. 1883.

5. Bed last night at a little after 11. Felt particularly happy in the still warm moonrise. Awake early, still thankful and glad. Wash dishes and go to the first Annual exhibition of Prov. Ladies Gymnasium. . . .

Monday. June 4th. 1883 —

4.30. Pack. Do usual housework all but dishes. Off before 8. . . . Take 8.30 train & doze all the way. Arrange toilet in station (Boston) and eat chocolates & banana, & read. Walk up to Dr. Keller's. Wait over an hour contentedly. Good talk with her, personally & professionally. She drives me down to get my bag, then to notify Mr. Smith, & then out to her beautiful home in Jamaica Plain. A delicious lunch, and then I am operated upon by Dr. Betts, who "depilates" me & otherwise attends to my complexion. Then drive about with Dr. Keller, dear woman, and join Mr. Smith in the train at 4.55. Come to West Dedham, drive through lovely scenery to Mrs. Lockes, and after tea and a letter to Walter & card to mother and talk with Mrs. Smith go quietly to bed. Still warm and sweet, with the soft June air blowing through my room, and the low country sounds outside.

Wed. June 6th. 1883.

6. Pack bag. Breakfast. . . . Then we drive to the station & I start for Boston. . . . Arriving in Boston I make a leisurely toilet and a leisurely dinner at the station, then visit the Art Museum & sketch Venus; then by divers cars to Rebeccas. She is out, not expecting me until tea time, but I am well received and given icewater and Pilgrims Progress. Go to her room and dress, she comes, and we have pleasant talk. Supper. Upstairs to open windows & we have more talk. George comes up, and Helen, and I repeat poetry and we talk. Very pleasant evening. Sleep with Retta, going to sleep while she was waiting for sage remarks. A woman I love & trust. Strength Purity & Courage.

Thurs. June 7th. 1883.

7.30. More talk with Retta. Pack bag. Off by ten. Ride to Kneeland st. & start for Old Colony station, but am ensnared by the Boston and Albany and leave my things there, also getting my ticket for Hingham—as I thought. . . . Discover that my Hingham ticket was a Needham one, get bag and cloak and we go to the Old Colony station and so to Hingham. Glad to see Martha and she to see me. Rest and dress, she giving me a white sack to replace my hot & dusty dress. Kind & thoughtful. Letter from Walter. Dear heart! Ballad with Martha. Mr. Lane comes. Also glad to see me. Supper. Talk. Martha & I read in "Tale of Two Cities" to him. Bed ere 11.

Thurs. June 14th. 1883

. . . Dress and go for Grace Channing, and we call on Walter. She was much pleased with him and his work. Which pleased me much, as I value her, & any favorable criticism is an agreeable change. . . .

Tues. June 19th. 1883 —

. . . Mothers birthday. Thomas sent her two Mormon books. Read in one of them. Letter from Walter. May he be happy! . . . Go to Jackson's but find Eddie wants no more lessons now. A little talk with Mrs. Jackson, & she shows me my room. Large, third floor, double window, like it much. . . .

Sun. 24th June. 1883.

. . . Walter. Talk a good deal, and come much nearer to each other. Goes at 11.

Wed. June 27th. 1883

. . . Walter comes. Happy evening. Goes ere 11. I love him.

Sat. June 30th. 1883.

5. Pack. . . . Off in 9.20 train. . . . Ogunquit ere 6. Supper. Rocks. Write to Walter. Bed. Glad to be here.

Tues. July 3rd. 1883.

. . . I am 23. Paint cliff from hole. . . . Letter from Walter. Supper. Read letter on rocks. Talk to the newcomers, Mr., Mrs., & Conway Brown. . . . Retire at 8.15 or so, & write to Walter.

Wed. July 4th. 1883.

6 or so. Finish letter to Cassie. Paint from 9 till 12, finishing view of cliff. Spend afternoon on rocks toward Pebbly Beach. A thunder shower. Get wet and enjoy it. The first storm I ever was so out in. Come up & change dress and shoes. Sketch and am sketched after supper. More thunder shower. Am reading slections [*sic*] from the thoughts of Marcus Aurelius Antoninus.[22] That is the kind of man I admire. Retire at 9.

Thurs. July 5th. 1883.

7. Sit around a [*sic*] talk to Mr. Brown. Go to Pebbly Beach and fix the little spring, enjoying it like a child. Wash feet and hands and face in cold sea water. Dine. Nap on the rocks. Another thunder shower. Come up to the house and find three letters from Walter & a card from Lu Hill. Not coming. Read them in my room while it pours and lightens [*sic*] outside. (It does now somewhat.) Go down and entertain the little Littles until supper. Will and Conway have been out in a boat all day and only just missed the shower. Home late, and eat thin supper like dinnerless boys as they are. Some of them fish, I read Marcus etc. and watch sunset, cloud, & mist effects. Music later, dancing of Patience, and general gymnastics. I feel hilarious as they do. Retire at ere 9. (I think) Write to Walter.

Fri. July 6th. 1883 —

. . . Walk down to Ogunquit with Will, and row nearly all the way back. First time I ever rowed on salt water. Like it. . . . Come up and talk with Conway after a little season of Marcus Aurelius. Sup. Then Conway and I take a bit of a walk and have some genuine talk. It does me good to feel that I do some good. . . .

Sun. July 8th. 1883.

. . . The boys brought me a great bunch of wildflowers today and arranged them beautifully in my room while I was out. Wrote some — *thoughts,* for Conway.

Mon. July 9th. 1883

. . . Conway & I . . . take a walk. He lets me try his revolver, and I hit with 4 shots out of 10. First experience too. Then we both have a nap on a sunny moss-&-grass-grown rock. Talk & recite poetry. Back, supper, and then watch the others fish and talk. Give him what I wrote, and he takes it *rightly*. Letter from Walter. . . .

Sat. July 14th. 1883.

5. Pack in a leisurely and masterful manner. . . . Start at 8 or so, with general handshaking. . . . Wait about . . . for the belated train, & then doze and rest till we get to Boston . . . and take horsecar for Providence Station. 5.30 train home. Walter to meet me, and laboriously carries both bag & bundle all the way home. . . .

Mon. July 16th. 1883.

. . . Go down to Mrs. Jackson's for a few moments. . . . Become a hireling as I phrase it for the admiration of my friends, at 5.35. Mrs. J[ackson]'s sister here. Arrange things in my room somewhat. Supper. Sit and talk with the family on the piazza. Retire at 9.40 & bed.

Tues. July 17th. 1883.

. . . Open & partly unback box to Eddie's great interest & amusement. Sew a little. Go out and see his garden, play battledore with him, & ball. Mend one of his balls, & give him a button, which *he* sews on his shirt. Dine. Talk a little with Mrs. J.[ackson], write a short letter to Walter, . . .

Sat. July 21st. 1883.

? Write to Walter. Lesson with Eddie, assisted by "Mauranny" his youthful friend. Letter from Walter. . . . Assist in entertaining Eddie's playmates. "Eddie says you're such a good catcher he's going to have you on his baseball nine!" And E. told me one of them wished I was *his* governess! Good thing. . . .

Tues. Aug. 7th. 1883.

. . . Call on Walter. Mr. Dorrance there. Hear that Sidney Putnam is drowned.[23] His poor mother! . . .

Wed. Aug. 8th. 1883

. . . 3 letters from Walter & one from Mr. Lane, Martha has a 9¼ [lb.] boy, born at 10 A.M. Aug. 6th.

Thurs. Aug. 9th. 1883.

. . . Go fishing with E. & M[auranny]., are joined by the little Allen's. Start at Red Bridge, & then go on to Ten Mile River Bridge, where E. catches two baby bluefish. . . . E. catches 6 in the afternoon and, after "Mauranny" had gone home, had the coolness to get me to take them off the hook because forsooth he didn't like the dirty work! Manly, that! He wont come home either till I leave him, and as punishment is allowed no battledore nor billiards nor reading in the evening. And his mother *says* he must go to bed at 8, but lets him play come-as-you-come & sit up till almost nine! I sewed in the evening. Bed by 9.35.

Sat. Aug. 11th. 1883.

. . . Drive to the Park . . . and stay there from 10 A.M. to 5 P.M! . . . See a miserable semi-furless cat, skinny, bare-legged, and am instrumental in having the poor beast slain. Sketch during concert, thereby attracting considerable attention. Should think they had never seen a pencil used before. A fire in a muck heap, engines, etc. Attend in person, but have to leave, with my reluctant charge, and take 5.10 car home. Read Mrs. Carlyle's letters[24] at intervals all day. . . . Left Mr. J[ackson]. reading "Ran Away to Sea" with every appearance of interest. Can't say I love these folk.

Wed. Aug. 29th. 1883—

. . . Read Mark Twain's "Prince & Pauper" during the day, and thoroughly *enjoy* it. . . . More or less billiards all day, and finally Eddie says to me "You lie!" over a disputed point. I leave immediately, tell his mother after a few moments reflection, and she forbids all games between us until Xmas! And seems to inwardly blame me for not attending to it by myself. A letter from Walter in the afternoon that made governessing a quick dream, and one from Mrs. Smith. E. & his father play billiards during the evening.

[*Charlotte left with the Jackson family on Friday, August 31, 1883, for an extended stay at Moosehead Lake, Maine. She returned to Providence on Tuesday, October 2, 1883.*]

Fri. Aug. 31st. 1883—

. . . we are off to Maine at 7 P.M. Had stateroom in sleeping car! My first experience of berths.—Don't like em. Had upper one & open ventilators, but didn't sleep much. Reach Bangor at 5 A.M. & breakfast. Walk about in the chill fogginess and see Bangor a little. Loaf. 7.20 train for Blan[-]*

Sat. Sept. 1st. 1883.

See last entry! —chard at 11.30 or so. . . . Arrive here at 2.30 or 40. Eveleth House, Greenville, Moosehead Lake, Maine. . . .

Tues. Sept. 4th. 1883.

6.30. Spend all day fishing at West Cove, I reading sketching and writing while they fish. Rowed 5 or 6 miles. A very happy day, thanks to wood & water, sky & wind. Wrote to Walter, & get letter from him.

Sun. Sept. 9th. 1883.

. . . Eddie rather ruder than usual to me. Can I stand it all winter? 'M-m-m! Write to Walter.

Fri. Sept 14th. 1883.

Two letters from Walter. E[ddie]. goes hunting with father & father's friend, and I tie worsted with Mrs. J[ackson]. & Mrs. H. Eddie back, and we row till dinner time. Then more rowing, dig worms, row. Supper. Tell him stories for a [*sic*] hour nearly. Mrs. J. thinks he had better have school this winter. Hurrah!

Sat. Sept. 22nd. 1883.

Morning in the boat with Eddie. Afternoon paint a little & then more boat with Eddie. A despicable boy. Short letter from Walter. . . .

Fri. Sept. 28th. 1883.

Up the lake to get the gentlemen at Lily Bay. Then back again as it was too rough to fish. I steered nearly all the time, and enjoyed being alone in the pilot house with the boat plunging like a horse. Am cold & tired in the afternoon; got wet in the morning going with E. after his trap, in a rowboat; combination of causes.

Sunday. Sept. 30th. 1883.

A snow flurry yesterday & this morning and inch or two on the ground! Dismal, cold, cheerless. I am blue and unreasonable, don't even know what I want. Play with E[ddie]. reluctantly; have a chance to talk somewhat with Mr. Smith, but find little to attract. Dinner. Swathe myself in shawls and try to pack. Bah! I'd like to have a fierce racking pain shoot through & through and all over me for a few moments, so that it leave me clearer. Pack all I can; and "amuse Eddie." Grand musical in the parlor in the evening. Hymns.

Tuesday, Oct. 2nd. 1883.

Breakfast at B. & P. station. Mrs. Jackson pays me $15.00 and off I set with the Hopkinses. Reach Prov[idence]. at 9.35 or so. . . . Leave bundles & go straight to Walter. A happy morning. . . .

Sat. Oct. 6th. 1883

. . . Call for Walter talk with him a little, & walk to Gilmore st. with him. He means to give up his Art! Because he cannot make it "pay," and because he must have money to marry, and he must marry. Well————. . . .

Wed. Oct. 10th. 1883.

. . . Go with Florrie to our first French lesson at the Berlitz. A delightful lady teacher, pretty and pleasant, sweetvoiced and kind. Enjoy it much. Stop and tell Walter I'll go to the A[rt]. C[lub]. Reception. . . . My picture well mounted and placed, looks well. I'm as proud as the hen with one chicken. . . .

Mon. Oct. 15th. 1883. Fire in Parlor Stove.

. . . First hour with gymnastic class. Great fun; they like it. Home. Sup & read, enjoying it much. Write to Walter, Cassie, & send "In Duty, Bound." [25] to the Century. Letters from Walter & Carrie Hazard.

Tues. Oct. 23rd. 1883.

. . . Letter from Century returning poem. Not a printed form at any rate. . . .

Sat. Nov. 3rd. 1883.

. . . Write "A Word to Myself." [26] & verse in L. Diman's A[utograph] album. Paint howling wolf on frozen lake at night.[27] Bed ere 12.

Sun. Nov. 4th. 1883.

. . . Walter from 7.30 to 10. He brings me a letter. Wishes me to be gentler.

Mon. Nov. 5th. 1883.

. . . Carrie Hazard calls, bless her heart, and gives me orders for some 16 dollars worth more cards, and wants to buy my moosehead sketch for $50.00! I won't have it; say $20.00. . . .

Fri. Nov. 9th. 1883.

. . . French. I do enjoy learning a language. . . . Ride home. Sup. Write. And paint lugubrious picture of "The Woman Against The Wall." [28]

Fri. Nov. 16th. 1883.

? Letter from Christian Register declining "In Duty Bound," only because they don't pay for poems unless ordered. Encouraging. . . . First meeting of a girl's club as yet nameless at the chapel. Younger girls of the S. S. 14 to 20 say, for reading & music etc. I am chosen president. Think it will be a good thing. See Mrs. Slicer home, then come myself & find Sam here. He stays till 11.45 nearly, talking Woman's Rights with me. A man far from broad. Bed bathless.

Sun. Nov. 18th. 1883.

. . . Walter. He is undecided on a question of right & wrong, but finally settles it. I wish we were well married — [29]

Sat. Nov. 24th. 1883 —

. . . Copy "One Girl" poem and send it to the "Alpha." [30] . . .

Sun. Nov. 25th. 1883 —

. . . Walter. I read him the letter I wrote Friday night. One of my turns of affectional paralysis.

Wed. Nov. 28th. 1883

. . . Call on Mrs. Williams, the colored woman our class are going to help. She is partially paralyzed, and has a little 9 year old boy. Lives in two little *holes* in an attic, & pays $4.00 a month for them! And there are four of these "suites" in that attic, $16.00. And our beautiful home with yard & fruit, is $15.00! Leave her 67 cts. of the class money. . . .

Fri. Dec. 14th. 1883

7.30. nearly. Housework, some. Two letters from Walter & one from Woman's Journal accepting "In Duty Bound." The first step, the entering wedge. No pay, but it's a beginning. . . .

Sun. Dec. 16th.

. . . Walter from 7.35 or 40 to 10. He brings me three pomegranates. I feel better; have been miserable in divers ways for weeks.

Thurs. Dec. 20th. 1883.

7.20. Letter from Martha with ticket & photo of Chester.[31] Miss Alden sent a Hingham's & Boston ticket. Pleasant to be wanted. . . . Gym. It is delightful, the affection those little girls have for me. . . .

Sun. Dec. 23rd. 1883.

7.50. *Awfully* cold, 10 below zero. . . . Walter brought me George Eliot's Poems, a delightful fat little account book, and some sable w[ater]. color brushes. He has also purchased for me lots of old Canton blue china—teacup, bowls, etc. I gave him a bundle of paint rags, a bottle of violet extract, a little thermometer on a beribboned card, and a tiny wisp of my hair in a sheath pin box.

Tues. Dec. 25th. 1883
Christmas Day.

7.30 or somewhere about there. Arrange presents & receive 'em from divers small pupils. Phebe Campbell brings me a pretty china box of finest bonbons and all the rest of the gym. class, cards. Kate Bucklin presents another silk umbrella & a book of Hawthorne. Mother gave me a photo. album, a Jap. nest of boxes, one cover & many boxes; a little black shopping bag, an ivory paper cutter, a little French set of finger nail beautifiers, an album for cards, & other things. Anna a black Spanish lace fichu. Aunt C. a new purse & a little Jap box. Lots of things. Lizzie six little silver pins. Henrietta a pretty box of candy. Aunt C. had her soap, Ray his stocking of small duds; & Clarence *his* stocking with the inimitable Mormon family. We had all the family to dinner, including Mary & the baby! The tree in Aunt C's parlor. Everybody more than satisfied, and Anna well tired of presents. A box from Thomas, with teaset of lovely *China*, frosted fruit cake, writing paper, h'k'f's, card, & bulb for mother, neckerchief & card for Aunt C., & card, box, h'k'f's, writing paper & Chinese baby for me. Jim came over between five & six & stayed till 10.30 or so.

Brought me a little fishwife statuette, from him & Sam, more soap for Aunt C. & a tiny bust for mother. Tired.

Wed. Dec. 26th. 1883.

Rise unconernedly [*sic*] when I get ready, leisurely pack and prepare. . . . Get boots and bundles & take train which was belated nearly half an hour. Read "The Mystery of Orcival" on the train & enjoy it much. Post card to mother in the B. & P. station, & take Herdic to Old Colony. Train just ready. Ride serenely to Hingham. Met by Martha. All serene and cosy. Lovely baby. All glad to see me.

Thurs. Dec. 27th. 1883.

Go out with M. Letter from Walter. Sent him one by Mr. Lane. . . . Enjoy being with Martha much. . . . Read and enjoy myself, sitting up in lonely state after they go to bed. After 11 when I go.

Fri. Dec. 28th. 1883.

Write to Walter to say when I'm coming home. Get letter from him. Sweep and dust to help Martha who has a sickheadache, or did in the night, and whose present "girl" is——*obtuse*. . . .

Sunday. Dec. 30th; 1883—

8. S. S. See Conway Brown. . . . Walter. Happy evening.

Monday. Dec. 31st. 1883.
. . . Almost Midnight

It is late. I am alone. The wind howls and sighs outside, the clock ticks loudly, and I sit waiting for the new year.

And this year gone?

Weakly begun, ill lived, little regarded.

Some things have I done and learned, but nothing to what I would have.

My clear life-governing will is dead or sleeping. I live on circumstances, and waves of misery sweep over me, resistless, unaccountable; or pale sunshine of happiness comes, as mysteriously.

I would more gladly die than ever yet; saving for the bitter agony I should leave in the heart of him who loves me. And mother's pain.

But O! God knows I am tired, tired, tired of life!

If I could only know that I was doing right————!

[1883 —— —— 1884]

Midnight————Morning—

The clocks ring 12.

With no pride, with little hope, with uncertain occasional happiness, with no glad energy and living power; with no faith or nearly none, but still, thank God! with firm belief in what is right and wrong; I begin the new year.

Let me recognize fully that I do not look forward to happiness; that I have no decided hope of success. So long must I live.

One does not die young who so desires it.

Perhaps it was not meant for me to work as I intended. Perhaps I am not to be of use to others.

I am weak.

I anticipate a future of failure and suffering. Children sickly and unhappy. Husband miserable because of my distress; and I———!

I think sometimes that it *may* be the other way; bright and happy; but this comes oftenest; holds longest. But this life is marked for me, I will not withdraw; and let me at least learn to be uncomplaining and unselfish. Let me do my work and not fling my pain on others.

Let me keep at least this ambition; to be a good and a pleasure to *some* one, to some others, no matter what I feel myself. Remembering always that the harder I work and more I bear and the better I bear it, sooner comes rest. Is it rest I wonder? I think if I woke, dead, and found myself unchanged——still adrift, still at the mercy of passing waves of feeling; I should go mad.

Can the dead so lose themselves I wonder?

And now to bed.

And let me not forget to be grateful for what I have. Some strength, some purpose, some design, some progress, some esteem, respect and affection.

And some Love. Which I can neither feel see nor believe in when the darkness comes.

I mean this year to try hard for somewhat of my former force and courage. As I remember it was got by practice.

January 1st. 1883—{sic}
Tuesday.

. . . *Conway Brown shot himself yesterday*; at Mrs. Maurans. A bright-faced boy of 20 or 21, an only child, loved, cared for, the idol of his parents; with no known grief or trouble.

He told me last summer that he had times of horrible depression. And had often thought of shooting himself. What mental misery it must have been to make him forget his parents and all the other ties that bound him to earth! I can sympathize with him; mental misery is real; and in a season of physical depression might well grow unbearable.

How needful to live so that in such times there is enough real work to look back upon to preserve one's self-respect! The only safety is within.

Wed. Jan. 2nd. 1884.

8. or a trifle before. Begin a course of diet, by means of which, and other changes I trust to regain my old force and vigor. . . . Mrs. Brown desired to see us—at the funeral. She waits me, I join her, and we go. Services at 12:30. The dear boy looked little like himself. His father seemed calm, his mother aged and worn already. Poor things! Poor things! . . . First evening at the gymnasium. Delightful to be there again. . . . I have not lost so much strength as I feared, can still go up the rope and on the rings, &c. Off on vaulting of course. Hour from 6.45 to 8 or so. Walk home. Finish "Prince and Page." Have eaten today, an orange & cup of hulled corn & milk at 8.40 about, a cup of oatmeal and milk and two biscuit at 11.30 or so, two more biscuit with a cup of milk at 3., and two oranges at about 9.

Feel well and contented.

Thurs. Jan. 3rd. 1884.

. . . Go to see Mr. Brown to carry a sketch of Conway which I made last summer when we were together; and to tell him of certain things he told me. Glad I went. He says it seems to *prove* his insanity, and that is of course what they most want to do. Home. Write to Walter a little, copy a poem and then this. . . .

Fri. Jan. 4th. 1884.

. . . Get a few flowers for Mrs. Stetson (25 cts.) and go to see her. Walter walks down with me, both silent. He was hurt at the gaiety in one of my letters. I shouldn't have sent it. . . . Write to Walter. Bed after 12, trying to forget personal misery in thought for others.

Sat. Jan. 5th. 1884.

. . . Two letters from Walter, and one from "Alpha"; accepting my poem with thanks, and saying they would be glad to hear from me again. . . . Go to gym. Take delicious shower bath, and am measured. 5 ft. 5 in. barefooted,[32] & naked weight 118 lbs. . . .

Sun. Jan. 6th. 1884.

. . . Walter after 8, and can only stay till 9.30. Glad, *glad* to see him. He brings me some thin paper. Write to him a little thereon & then here.

Fri. Jan. 11th. 1884

. . . Go to the studio and stay with Walter two hours. Happy & safe . . . Then to gym with Florrie. Feel *exceptionally hilarious* and cavort wildly. Pick up a 118 lb. girl, and *run* with her as easily as could be. Delightful shower bath afterwards. Ride home gaily. Write to Walter. Bed.

Sat. Jan. 19th. 1884.

. . . Find "Woman's Journal" with "In Duty, Bound"[33] in it. . . .

Wed. Feb. 6th. 1884.

. . . Get printed refusal from Century. . . . Go to see Dr. Wilcox about his house. Meet his wife & walk a little way with her. . . . Go to Dr. Wilcox office & after waiting & writing awhile, see him. I suggest alterations & improvements to his house, and he says he'll consider it. . . . Letter from Walter P.M.

Feb. 7th. Thurs. 1884.

. . . Go & look at another house down there, a new tenement house, *very* new, and garishly modern & ugly in many ways. . . . Write to Dr. Wilcox about tenement, and to Walter, bless him!

Wed. Feb. 13th. 1884.

. . . French. Am reprimanded by Madame for translating, and feel badly that I should need speaking to again. It's because of my mania for teaching.

Sun. Feb. 24th. 1884.

. . . Read, finishing [Mill's] "Liberty"[34] and beginning "On the Subjection of women." Walter comes and we go look at the house. He likes it but rather dampens my ardor by seeing drawbacks here and there. . . .

Tues. March 4th. 1884.

. . . Go to Kelly's for yellow flowers. Had none, so try Butcher and get some nice little ones, & a few violets. . . . Home & dress for Walters reception. Carrie's black silk, white Spanish tie, ruching, & lace in sleeves, yellow ribbon, yellow beads, gold comb, amber bracelet; yellow breast on bonnet, yellow flowers. Many people there, and all seemed pleased . . .

Sun. March 9th. 1884.

. . . Walter. Am lachrymose. Heaven send that my forebodings of future pain for both be untrue. Lent Walter $5.oo to get Irving[35] tickets.

Tues. March. 11th. 1884.

. . . Mother dolorous. Sew. Grow dolorous myself. Write here. Am *miserable.* Write a piece of biography and some verses.

Sat. March 22nd. 1884.

7 to 7.30. A fair clear warm beautiful Spring day. Wake early, lie happy and still, & sleep again conscience-free. Breakfast deliciously on eggs milk and fruit. A dear love-letter from my darling to add to the joyousness of the morning. . . . Found note from Eddie Jackson on reaching home.

"March 20 1884
Miss Pirkens
i am verry sick and would like to have you make me sum funny rimes and
pictures on square pieces of paper the way we did when we were down to
Maine if you please
There is a anser
  when can i
    have them

          Yours Truly
          Eddie Jackson
          204 Angell St."

Mon. March 24. 1884.

. . . [G]ym., enjoying it *intensely* and doing more than usual. Carried of [*sic*] a
girl on *one arm* and hip—easily!* . . .

Sunday, April 6th. 1884.

. . . Carrie Hazard and Margie stop and leave linen, Carrie an elegant white
cloth and dozen napkins; Helen a heavy rich bedspread, Margie a lovely gold-
and-silver fruit set, very lovely. . . . Walter comes for me and we go to measure
house, and enjoy it. . . .

Wed. April 16th. 1884.

. . . Get a few violets & go to see Walter. Stop a little while, and then we go
look at mattings. Then get the Ring. Inside "Walter" "Charlotte," the date,
and "Ich liebe dich." [36] . . .

Sat. April 19th. 1884.

6.30. Sew, breakfast, and betake myself to the house, where I remain from 9
till 12, while gas men, stove men, other men and a boy bring divers things to
our domicile. Walter arrives and remains with me. I sweep up the parlor. The
stove is magnificent and color of paint and paper highly satisfactory. We exult
in the prospect before us. . . .

Mon. April 21st. 1884.

. . . Get ring, my wedding ring! . . . [G]et my wedding dress, and Walter's
chiton. Also divers small wares. . . . Go for Walter, (after much shopping) give
him ring to keep till it is put on by him on our wedding night; & we trot
about. . . .

(May 3rd.) *Wed. April 30th. 1884.*

Omitted my journal on these last 3 days owing to much busy-ness. This and
the next were occupied in fixing things at the house almost wholly. All my
things brought over to the house. Big morning's work. Walter over. Wed P.M.
I went down st. for some last shopping

THREE

~~~

"By reason of ill health"

May 2, 1884–April 19, 1887

IN THE EARLY EVENING hours of May 2, 1884, Charlotte and Walter Stetson were married. Charlotte's fears about wedlock were temporarily suspended as she reveled in the unfamiliar ecstasy of her wedding night. While Walter waited in another room, Charlotte joyfully decorated their bed with lace, silk, and flowers, made herself a crown of white roses, slipped into a sheer white gown, and emerged, seductively, to greet her new husband. Walter placed Charlotte's wedding ring upon her finger and then rapturously undressed his new bride. The thrill that Charlotte felt toward the initiation of sexual intimacy is almost palpable in her simple description of the moment: "He lifts the crown, loosens the snood, unfastens the girdle, and then—and then," she wrote.

The next morning, Charlotte was still enthralled with what was ultimately just the illusion of wedded bliss: "Lie on the lounge in the soft spring sunshine and am happy. Happy. Happy. Walter stays quietly at home with me; and we rest and love each other." Predictably, however, the tranquillity was short-lived. Within a week, Charlotte was resisting her forced dependence on Walter: "I suggest that he pay me for my services; and he much dislikes the idea. I am grieved at offending him, mutual misery. Bed and cry." Whether the services for which Charlotte sought compensation included sexual as well as domestic duties is ambiguous, but in any event, the power struggle had begun.

During the next several weeks, both Charlotte and Walter tried to adjust to the new demands of marriage. There were, in fact, many happy hours spent reading together, drawing, and entertaining friends. There was also occasional heartache. Within weeks after the wedding, Charlotte reproached herself for being too "affectionately expressive," and Walter was forced to reaffirm his love whenever she grew insecure. In the early weeks of their marriage, however, the pleasure seemed to outweigh the pain.

By the end of July, Charlotte suspected that she might be pregnant. She apparently dismissed it, however, because a few days later, on August 5, she attributed her sickness to "inter-susception of the intestine." The symptoms, however, continued.

By the time Charlotte left Providence on August 18 for a visit to Martha Lane in Hingham, her pregnancy had been confirmed. During her two-week stay with Martha, Charlotte neglected her diary. When she resumed her writing on September 1, however, Charlotte made clear how annoyed she was by comments about her "condition."

As her pregnancy progressed, Charlotte filled her days with housework, reading, and going downtown whenever she felt up to it. Some days found her decidedly testy when "impudent" inquiries were made about her weight gain. In mid-September, Mary Perkins left for an extended visit to Thomas, who was now in Utah, and since Charlotte frequently felt ill, Walter began assuming many of the household chores.

Occasionally, Charlotte would feel "uncommonly well and brisk," but more often, she felt "tired," "feeble," and "weak." Her susceptibility to sickness during her second trimester caused Charlotte to neglect her daily routines, including her diary writing, with increasing frequency. After a particularly rough period in mid-October, Charlotte stopped writing altogether, citing ill health as the primary factor. She resumed her diary again about ten weeks later, on January 1, 1885.

The entry of January 1 is a tangled mass of contradictions. "I am a happy wife," she wrote. "I bear a child. . . . Ambition sleeps. I make no motion but just live. And I am Happy? Every day almost finds me saying so, and truly. And yet—and yet—'call no man happy until he is dead.'"

Charlotte's ambivalence likely stemmed from her growing realization that despite all of her reservations, despite all of her misgivings, despite all of her various attempts to end her relationship with Walter because she "love[d] WORK better," she had nevertheless found herself entrapped in a marriage that left her feeling suffocated and incomplete. The arrival of the baby would mark yet another setback in her long-stated desire to enter public service. All of the doubts and fears that she had expressed during her courtship were being realized, and Charlotte grew increasingly apprehensive as her due date approached. Five weeks before the baby was born, Charlotte reported becoming "so hysterical" that Walter felt compelled to stay home with her. And a couple of days later, on February 19, she reported a "wellnigh sleepless night. Hot, cold, hot; restless nervous hysterical. Walter is love and patience personified; gets up over and over, gets me warm winter-green, bromide, hot foot bath, more bromide—all to no purpose."

The unrest that Charlotte felt during her pregnancy was likely exacerbated by the dichotomy between the direction that her life was taking when compared to Walter's. After struggling against chronic poverty for years, Walter was at last enjoying at least a brief period of financial prosperity as he finally began to establish a reputation. He was, in fact, basking in the glory of newfound fame after a review in the September 1884 issue of *Art Amateur* offered highly favorable praise of his artistic talent. "The young man went home to Providence . . and in a few days awoke famous, with the great guns of a fervor over his little things booming in the Boston newspapers," the review read (*Endure*, p. 265). "Young Stetson gave proof of a natural productive genius," it continued. Walter had finally established his career.

Charlotte, in the meantime, was still dealing with the loss of her independence and trying to fight off the attendant depression. "She is . . . easily fatigued both physically & mentally & at times despondent, especially when she has fears that all that dreamed of life of great usefulness, may be past or beyond her reach," Walter remarked in his diary in September (*Endure*, p. 264). But most of the time, Walter seemed to believe that Charlotte was content. In reality, Charlotte continued to wrestle with despondency throughout her pregnancy. Perhaps because he was finally gaining a sense of security in his own life, Walter tended to romanticize Charlotte's pregnancy. Perhaps it was easy for Walter to deny the severity of Charlotte's depression by simply attributing it to her "condition." Or, perhaps he was subconsciously avoiding a painful truth. Whatever the reason, he was able to deny that anything serious was wrong with their relationship. Again and again, in fact, Walter's diaries allude to Charlotte's utter happiness—and to his own. Only occasionally does Walter complain about having to do housework, which was "wasting [the] energy, power that should be applied to [his] art" (p. 276). Charlotte doubtless felt the same way about her own work, but for the most part, she remained silent.

In early March, during the final weeks of Charlotte's pregnancy, the Stetsons hired one Mrs. Russell to serve as a temporary housekeeper for the young couple. The last two weeks before the baby was born were difficult ones. Charlotte felt "weak, draggy, [and] nervous," owing to the "unreasonable activity of the infant."

On March 20, 1885, a young nurse, Maria Pease, arrived at the Stetson household to relieve Mrs. Russell, the housekeeper, of her responsibilities. She and Charlotte fast became friends, and Charlotte seemed calmer under her care. They spent the final days before the baby's arrival engaged in long and enjoyable conversations.

Just before 9:00 a.m. on the morning of March 23, 1885, Charlotte gave birth to a daughter, Katharine Beecher Stetson. Her diary comments reporting the birth of her child are sparse, but telling:

> Brief ecstasy. Long pain.
> Then years of joy again.
>
> Motherhood means——Giving.

The weeks following Katharine's birth were difficult ones, particularly after Maria Pease departed in late April, when her month-long contract was up. For the first time Charlotte was left alone to care for the baby. Her diary entries for May reveal the extent of her anxiety as she tried to cope with the demands of new motherhood. "I wonder what people do who know even less than we about babies! And what women do whose husbands are less—sufficient," she dubiously remarked.

Many years later in her autobiography, Charlotte described in detail the misery she experienced following the birth of Katharine. "I, the ceaselessly industrious, could do no work of any kind. I was so weak that the knife and fork sank from my hands—too tired to eat. I could not read nor write nor paint nor sew nor talk nor listen to talking, nor anything. I lay on that lounge and wept all day. The tears ran down into my ears on either side. I went to bed crying, woke in the night crying, sat on the edge of the bed in the morning and cried—from sheer continuous pain" (*Living*, p. 91). That pain, "a constant dragging weariness" (p. 91), eventually would lead to a nervous breakdown. As the days passed into months, the depression began to consume her.

May 2, the first anniversary of Charlotte and Walter's wedding, was a monumental letdown. "I am tired with long sleeplessness and disappointed at being unable to celebrate the day. So I cry," Charlotte wrote plaintively. Certainly both Charlotte and Walter must have been struck by the difference that a year had made in their relationship. Gone was the thrill of their newfound intimacy. Gone, too, was the innocence of their youthful illusions.

Within a few weeks after Maria Pease's departure, fatigue and depression had taken their toll on Charlotte's nerves. On May 8 she recorded just the latest in a series of adversities: "A fine scare with Miss Baby. She slips off my hand and gets her face under water a moment. Frightens her and me too. Hard day in consequence, she restless and cryful, I tired." The next day, Charlotte awoke very tired and depressed. To her utter relief Mary Perkins arrived back from her long trip to Utah in the afternoon. Her return, however, was a mixed blessing.

Charlotte welcomed her mother's help with Katharine, but at the same time the old wounds of never feeling loved by Mary must have resurfaced in full force. The pattern from her own childhood, and the unresolved conflicts, seemed to be mercilessly repeating: "I would hold her close—that lovely child—and instead of love and happiness, feel only pain. The tears ran down on my breast. . . . Nothing was more utterly bitter than this, that even motherhood brought no joy" (*Living*, pp. 91–92).

Mary's apparent ease with the baby also seemed to exacerbate Charlotte's fears of maternal incompetence. "Mother over early," she wrote on May 10. "She takes all the care of the baby day times; washes her today with infinite delight. I fear I shall forget how to take care of the baby." Two days later Charlotte inscribed the date, "Tues. May 12th," but she never wrote the entry that she had apparently intended.

Tuesday, May 12, in fact, marked the beginning of another significant break of nearly three months in Charlotte's diary writing. She attempted again on August 5 to resume her writing, but it wasn't until the end of August that she was able to do so with some regularity. Charlotte had become increasingly depressed during the summer months. Her frustration at not being able to write is evident on August 5 when she lamented that she had "long been ill; weak, nerveless, forced to be idle and let things drift."

Over the next several months, Charlotte's depression continued to deepen. On August 28 she reported feeling "highly excited, hysterical; seeming to myself wellnigh insane." The extent of Charlotte's "hysteria" on that August day is apparent in her misspelling of young Katharine's name, an error that she repeated numerous times over the next several weeks. On other days her entries were disjointed or incoherent (see September 2, for example). By August 30, 1885, Charlotte faced "every morning [with] the same hopeless waking." The depth of her despair is stark and haunting: "Retreat impossible, escape impossible. . . . [Walter] offers to let me go free, . . . but he cannot see how irrevocably bound I am, for life, for life. No, unless he die and the baby die, or he change or I change there is no way out."

Even Martha Lane, to whom Charlotte confided her pain, seemed unusually unsympathetic. Complained Charlotte to her diary, "I wrote her my heart and she answers with not overwise head."

During these months Charlotte's depression became so acute that she occasionally shirked even her maternal responsibilities, perhaps as a way to avoid yet another failed relationship. Her preference to "go down street and do errands . . . to staying at home alone with [the] care of [the] baby" seems to have been a futile attempt to reclaim at least some of the independence that she had surrendered. Most of the days when she was alone with Katharine were passed miserably. On September 14, for example, Charlotte's depression was considerable. After a particularly difficult morning, she reported feeling "an oppressive pain that sees no outlet." As she came closer to the edge of emotional collapse, her rejection of domestic responsibilities became more pronounced. On September 17, while preparing dinner, Charlotte reported "giv[ing] out," so "Walter makes the bread." That same evening, however, she mustered the energy to play whist, an activity that she enjoyed immensely during the independent years before her marriage.

By late September, Charlotte was close to the breaking point. Even the arrival of Katharine's new nursemaid, Elisa Gärtner, did little to alleviate Charlotte's pain. "Dreary days these," she wrote. "Only feel well about half an hour in all day." In early October, Charlotte, Walter, and Mary finally concluded that Charlotte should journey west to rest her frazzled nerves. Her diary entry reflecting the decision is unusually optimistic. "We propound discuss and decide the question of shall I travel? Yes, I shall. I contemplate wintering in California. Hope dawns. To come back *well*!"

In late October, Charlotte left Mary and the new nursemaid in care of Katharine and headed west, first to visit her brother Thomas in Utah, next to see her father briefly in San Francisco, and then to her final destination: Pasadena, California, where she would spend the winter with her friends the Channings.

Although Charlotte suspended her journal writing during her visit west, her autobiography reflects the dramatic transformation that took place in her spirits when she was out of reach of the demands of matrimony and motherhood. "From the moment the wheels began to turn, the train to move, I felt better," she wrote (*Living*, p. 94). In California, Charlotte thrived. "This place . . . was paradise. Kind and congenial friends, pleasant society, amusement, out-door sports, the blessed mountains, the long, unbroken sweep of the valley, with snow-peaks at the far eastern end—with such surroundings I recovered so fast, to outward appearance at least, that I was taken for a vigorous young girl" (p. 94).

Almost immediately after Charlotte returned home in the spring of 1886, however, she experienced a major relapse. Her autobiography depicts her loss of hope: "I reached home with a heavy bronchial cold, which hung on long, the dark fog rose again in my mind, the miserable weakness—within a month I was as low as before leaving. . . ." (*Living*, p. 95)

In addition to having to confront the severity of her emotional illness, Charlotte also had to cope with the reality of her entrapment. "Am trying to get accustomed to life here," she wrote upon her return. "It will take some time." No amount of time, however, would prepare Charlotte for the pain that was still ahead.

For several months after her return, Charlotte abandoned her journal; she resumed it on August 27, 1886. She managed to experience some good days during that autumn; as always, her spirits soared during periods of productivity. Whether it be the reward of payment for her first publication, the pleasure of designing hand-painted stationery for friends, or the exhilaration of rowing Walter home from a moonlight visit to Pawtucket, Charlotte's "good days" followed a distinct and predictable pattern. When she was confined to the house or unable to work, the likelihood of her "great misery" returning rose significantly. Increasingly, Walter was called upon to intervene when Charlotte's depression became acute. The entry for September 19 describes a typical scene: "Get hysterical in the evening while putting K. to sleep. Walter finishes the undertaking and sleeps with her."

The autumn of 1886 also saw a dramatic rise in Charlotte's activism on behalf of women's rights. She began to write a series of articles and poems including

"Why Women Do Not Reform Their Dress" and "The Answer" for publication in the *Woman's Journal*, and she was incensed by an article written by English writer Ouida on female suffrage. "A *contemptible* piece of writing, bad in aim and execution," she complained in her diary. More significantly, Charlotte attended her first Women's Suffrage Convention in October and became friends with women's right activist Alice Stone Blackwell. As Charlotte expanded her awareness of women's issues, she also became more assertive in her views. On October 9, for example, Charlotte stopped by Walter's studio and criticized one of his paintings. She judged it "so harshly from a moral point of view that he smashes & burns it. I feel badly; and after some tears he comes home with me." At the same time tensions outside of the household also escalated with a new intensity. On October 22 Charlotte noted an encounter with her cousin Robert Brown. "Robert makes an ass of himself by his loudmouthed contempt of women's rights and other justice. It is hard to be despised by such men as that."

Along with her increasing activism, another event that affected Charlotte during this period was the unexpected death of her brother Thomas's young wife, Julia, who died very suddenly from complications associated with heart disease. Charlotte had stayed with them during her trip out west the previous winter, and the news of Julia's tragic death was a shock. Charlotte always became more reflective about her own life following the deaths of relatives, friends, and acquaintances. For the moment, Julia's death seemed to draw Charlotte and Walter closer together, if only briefly. They collaborated together on writing a play—a comedy—which they tried to sell to American actor William Gillette. While Gillette was "favorably impressed" by the play, he was not inclined to buy it.

Undeterred by Gillette's rejection, however, Charlotte was determined to continue to write. For the first time in her marriage, she was managing, however precariously, to balance the demands of marriage and motherhood with her desire to work. As 1886 drew to a close, in fact, Charlotte was finally beginning to gain a sense of accomplishment from her writing. "Get a paper from Walton, N.Y. with [my poem] 'The Answer' in it," she wrote on November 1. "Getting famous! . . . Read Women's Journal and Century in the evening, the latter to Walter. I am very happy."

As Charlotte and Walter immersed themselves into the frenzy of the holiday season, they did, indeed, seem to be very happy. Ultimately, however, they were avoiding, rather than confronting, the issues that would eventually end their marriage. Even though Charlotte continued to experience fatigue, disappointment, and gloomy days, the two were somehow lulled into a false sense of security. They peacefully coexisted over the next several weeks, with Walter often attending Art Club meetings in the evenings while Charlotte stole whatever quiet moments she could to write or to paint—or to express her growing contempt for domesticity. "Dress and go to Annie Rawson Vaughns tea," Charlotte wrote on December 8. "Very gorgeous indeed, wish I hadn't gone. I despise the whole business," she wrote derisively.

If afternoon teas were not to her taste, neither was any other activity that wasted precious time. "Accomplish nothing in all day, owing to late rising; baby tending, and putting her to sleep in the evening," she protested on December 12. But the next evening was spent more productively, and, consequently, more happily. "Do ink dinner cards in the evening—Walter and I are very happy together." Christmas Day was also spent happily with Walter: "Mother puts the baby to sleep; and Walter goes home with her. Then he and I have a little more chocolate and sandwich, and go happily to bed." And on December 26: "Up late, and pass a lazy happy day." But in her New Year's Eve retrospective of the year just passed, Charlotte was considerably more ambivalent in her views of both her relationship with Walter and the status of her "world's work."

> I have become a person more in harmony with my surroundings; better fitted to live peacefully among my friends; and yet have not lost a keen interest in the world's work. I can write and paint better than before; and think as well when I am strong enough.
>
> But I certainly have lost much of my self abandoning enthusiasm and fierce determination in the cause of right. Perhaps it is as well for the ultimate work done. I do not feel so. I feel in some ways lowered—degraded—traitor to my cause. But I am not sure, it may be a lingering trace of the disordered period just passed. When I know myself to be *well* in all ways I can better judge.

Within a few weeks, Charlotte would be sure; "the disordered period just passed" would be minor compared to the misery that lay ahead. Indeed, Charlotte was about to confront the most difficult trial of her life.

Charlotte began 1887 with a mission: "Have started on a course of reading about women," she asserted on January 5. Some of the reading she dismissed as too "scriptural and solemn"; the works she preferred were those which allowed "duties to Society as well as husband and child." As had always been the case with Charlotte, self-education through reading would inform her life's philosophy; it would help to shape her plan of "serving humanity." Conversely, however, it would also amplify her discontent over her limited roles of wife and mother. On January 6 Charlotte began to draft an article "on the distinction between the sexes," a theme that would influence most of her writing from that point onward. Walter attempted to be supportive, reading aloud to her Margaret Fuller's book, *Woman in the Nineteenth Century*, but he was clearly threatened by Charlotte's intellectual growth. He quickly imposed a two-week moratorium on her reading anything about "the woman question." She continued to write, however, sending off an article titled "A Protest Against Petticoats" because, she insisted, "it is well to keep the ball rolling."

Charlotte did, however, try to maintain a balance between indulging her own needs for intellectual stimulation and fulfilling her domestic responsibilities. She wasn't always successful. Sunday, January 9: "A wearying day. . . . Fall with K[atharine]. in my arms; bumping her head and lamming my knees. Then she tires me out in the sleepgoing; and I get real nervous and shaky. Walter gives me a warm bath and puts me to bed." Although Walter tried to console Charlotte when she became weepy, his patience began to wane and subconsciously, perhaps, he began to retaliate. Undermining her confidence where she was most vulnerable, Walter criticized her maternal competence: "Begin to give Kate her bath before breakfast, but get discouraged by Walter, who thinks eating directly afterward is injudicious. Accomplish little all day."

Walter's insecurity about Charlotte's renewed interest in women's issues was undoubtedly exacerbated by their latest financial setback—after a period of brief prosperity from the sale of some artwork—which reached a crisis in mid-February. "No coal, no money," Charlotte reported succinctly. "I tell Walter he *must* get it, or I will; and he does." Just four days later Alice Stone Blackwell asked Charlotte to manage a women's suffrage column in the Providence newspaper, which Charlotte agreed to do. She also resumed her reading about women's issues with renewed vigor and commiserated with "another victim" whose husband used his "'marital rights' at her vital expense." Significantly, a few days later Charlotte reported feeling "desperately out of place among a lot of young mothers" at a birthday party that she attended with Katharine. Charlotte was, perhaps unwittingly, beginning to more clearly articulate her growing conviction: the conventional roles of wife and mother made her feel desperately ill at ease and "out of place." This sense of displacement was at the center of her conflict. Her first priority was, and would always remain, her commitment to helping humanity.

A visit to Martha Lane and her newborn daughter, Margaret, in late February likely contributed to Charlotte's growing unrest. While she was buoyed by the appearance of her women's suffrage column in the *People*, she seems to have never fully recovered from the exhaustion that resulted from a cold she suffered during her visit to Martha and which she passed to Katharine. By March 9 Charlotte was feeling the effects of Katharine's illness: "I give out completely in the morning, crying with weariness." But even when Katharine seemed to recover, Charlotte never completely regained her strength. March 11: "When [Walter] gets back I am asleep on the bed, exhausted." And on March 13: "I have a crying fit while trying to make Kate go to sleep, and am all used up. . . . I put the baby to bed and collapse therein myself." Charlotte's depression had reached a dangerous new stage. The months of physical exhaustion and constant worry over their most recent financial troubles, added to the years of unresolved conflicts and resentment toward Walter, took their toll. "Get chilly and have a crying fit. Sleep ill, and am utterly useless the next day." Even Maria Pease, the nurse who had offered Charlotte kindness and sympathy just before and after Katharine's birth, seemed not to understand the extent of Charlotte's depression. "I love her, but she doesn't sooth me at all," Charlotte complained. Charlotte was still seeking to be soothed, supported, loved; she was a conflicted young mother still desperately in need of mothering herself.

During the spring months Charlotte had resumed her exercise regimen at the Providence Ladies Gymnasium. Although the workouts provided stress reduction and time away from Walter and Katharine, she soon started skipping time at the gymnasium in favor of her writing. When Charlotte initially resumed her routine in mid-January, she could barely contain her joy. "Find myself happy to the verge of idiocy at being there again," she confessed. "Am as light apparently but not as strong as of old." By March 18, however, Charlotte simply could not accommodate both activities into her schedule. Something had to go. Exercising was dispensable; writing was not: "I dont' go to gym., because I want to write some paragraphs for 'The Amendment.'" Within a couple of days, however, Charlotte was once again in the throes of despair: "Getting back to the edge of insanity again," she wrote somberly. "Write my 'column' though."

Over the next several weeks, Charlotte reported feeling increasingly anxious and on the verge of insanity. The combination of Katharine's frequent illnesses, Charlotte's subsequent exhaustion, increasing friction between her and Walter, and the defeat of the amendment supporting women's suffrage, which was a profound disappointment to Charlotte, all contributed to her "hysteria." On April 5 she was saved from a "hysterical" fit by the timely arrival of her longtime friend Jim Simmons, who managed to calm her. Walter, however, unable to cope with Charlotte's mood swing or to accept Simmons's ability to soothe Charlotte, stormed out of the house. When Walter returned, he broke down, and Charlotte had to suppress her own misery in order to attend to his.

During the following week Charlotte's depression deepened, and she began to make inquiries of her physician, Dr. Knight, about treatment in a sanitarium. On April 13 Charlotte began a week's "rest" at her mother's house, while Walter slept alone in the home that they had shared for nearly three years. By April 18 a decision had been made to send Charlotte to Philadelphia to seek the "rest cure" from Dr. Silas Weir Mitchell. Her longtime friend Mrs. J. Lewis Diman generously donated the $100 that would cover the cost of the treatment. Charlotte wanted to get well, but she also wanted Walter to accept at least some blame for her condition. Her unrestrained hostility toward Walter peppers the pages of her April 18, 1887, entry. In a rare departure from her usual practice, she used the diary entry to damn Walter directly, accusing him of broken promises, holding him accountable for her pain, and insisting that he bear sole responsibility for his misguided and destructive judgment, "before it seeks to mould another life as it has mine."

The next day, Tuesday, April 19, was Charlotte's last diary entry before she left to seek treatment from Mitchell. The entry is an ironic and chilling metaphorical depiction of Charlotte's condition as she describes being "locked out" of her home and "struggling" to find her way back in "with much effort." Her final words for 1887 are stark and ominous: "Begin to write an account of myself for the doctor."

Friday, May 2nd. 1884
My Wedding Day.

Am up betimes and finish my chemiloom. Down to the house betimes. Sew— Walter over. He goes between 2 & 3. I finish wedding dress; trim bonnet, arrange great stacks of flowers, and fly around generally. Home just after Mr. & Mrs. Stetson arrive. Bathe. Dress. Am ready at or near 6.30, and we are straightway wedded by Mr. S. Senior. Aunt C. hearty in her congratulations, his parents kind and affectionate, but mother declines to kiss me and merely says "goodbye." A splendid supper; for which I am well prepared; having forgotten to eat any lunch. Take many boxes, baskets, and bundles, and go——*H O M E !*

Mary & Ray congratulate us out of the window.[1] Come in, drop our baggage, and I install Walter in the parlor & dining room while I retire to the bed chamber and finish it's decoration. The bed looks like a fairy bower with lace, white silk, and flowers. Make my self a crown of white roses. Wash again, and put on a thin drift of white mull fastened with a rosebud and velvet and pearl civeture. My little white velvet slippers* and a white snood. Go in to my husband. He meets me joyfully; we promise to be true to each other; and he puts on the ring and the crown. Then he lifts the crown, loosens the snood, unfastens the girdle, and then—and then.

> O my God! I thank thee
> for this heavenly happiness!
> O make me one with thy
> great life that I may best
> fulfill my duties to my love!
> to my Husband!
> And if I am a mother
> ——let it be according
> to thy will!
> O guide me! teach me,
> help me to do right!

Sat. May 3rd. 1884.

Up at 8.20 or so. Get a nice little breakfast of omelette and chocolate. Lie on the lounge in the soft spring sunshine and am happy. Happy. Happy. Walter stays quietly at home with me; and we rest and love each other. Get johnny-cakes & frizzled beef for dinner; wash dishes, Walter wiping; and go down st. together. Get divers things, come home, have some supper; fix room, put my boy to bed, (he is well worn out with a long winter's work,) and essay to make bread; but can't find my yeastcake. Give it up in no ill humor; and write here.

O I am happy!
May I do right enough
to merit and deserve!

Thank God.

Mon. May 5th. 1884.

About 8 or less. Prodigious breakfast of oatmeal, chocolate, hot biscuit and salmon. Walter goes to work, and I go to sleep; and have a good three hour's nap with one wakeup. The young man returns at about 2; and I get him a little dinner. Then loaf a bit, wash dishes and fix bedroom. He feels dizzy; and I put him snugly to bed and then write. Am happy.

Tues. May 6th. 1884.

. . . Go down street and shop extensively. . . . Stop for Walter; and he comes home with me. Get a most delectable dinner of veal fried in batter and new potatoes. Very very delicious. Am tired later and am put tenderly to bed.

Thurs. May. 8th. 1884.*

7.10 or 15) Feel badly because Walter doesn't like the open windows; and because he casually drank the top of the milk that was to have been cream for him this morning; and because I broke the handle off a little Chinese tea cup. But he stays at home with me all day and I am consoled. Have a bit nap while he writes a reply to a Boston art critic who accused him of copying Monticelli. Get a most delectable dinner; including a dish of applesauce with egg top of peculiar deliciousness, which I bestow on the Arnold children after we've had some, as t'wouldn't keep. It was *good*! Clear the table, my dear boy helping as he did all day; light our new lamp; and sit down to sew and knit while he reads, aloud to me; out of Maclise and Dana. Quiet happiness. Write. Bed. O I am happy!

Fri. May 9th. 1884.

As usual.) Walter gone all day, and I do a good day's work; writing 7 notes of thanks, drawing some things for mother, arranging things in bureau drawers, etc. etc. Walter home a little after 6. He brings me an exquisite gauzy white

Turkish scarf. Get a nice little dinner. I suggest that he pay me for my services; and he much dislikes the idea. I am grieved at offending him, mutual misery. Bed and cry.

Sat. May 24th. 1884.

. . . Am disgusted with myself—numb—helpless. Tomorrow God helping me I will begin anew!

Wed. May 28th. 1884.

. . . Wash kitchen floor, sweep bedroom, etc. Walter home P.M. & helps me. Also fixes things in the house. Dinner. Dishes. Dress. He reads me an adulatory article sent by some Boston literary lady. Amusing. We don't *feel* famous in spite of the papers.

Sat. June 7th. 1884.

8.30. A long lazy day. Go down st. with Walter and shop. Get "Phantastes".² Ride home together. Read to him in Phan. He enjoys it. Lunch or dinner. More reading. A beautiful evening. Enjoyable operations in petty surgery. Supper. Talk earnestly on foreordination and free will. Does me good. Lie down alone awhile and think. . . .

Fri. June 13th. 1884

About 6. Feel sick and remain so all day. Walter stays at home and does everything for me. Bless him! Feel better late P.M. & get some mush & potatoes for dinner. Eat some myself. . . .

Sun. June 15th. 1884.

8 about. (Am sad: Last night & this morning. Because I find myself too—affectionately expressive. I must keep more to myself and be asked—not borne with.) Begin to make snowpudding. Little corncakes for breakfast. Sleep about three hours on mattress in garret. . . .

20th.

? Not much of anything but go down and get a little lunch and some books and take the 12.10 car for Pawtucket. A long lovely happy afternoon on the river. I row mostly to my much content; we linger under shady trees, dip our feet in the cool water and are very happy. Home by 9.20 or so. Eat. Bed.

Wed. June 25th. 1884.

. . . Walter home. Get miserable over my old woe—conviction* of being to outwardly expressive of affection. . . .

Thurs. June 26th. 1884.

. . . Still miserable and feel tired. . . . Walter home. Am miserable some more but he persuades me to believe that he never tires of me. . . .

Sun. July 6th. 1884.

. . . Loaf all day, getting through the housework late and lazy. Made ginger-bread; drew, and painted some. When shall I learn that the best way to get rid of work is to *do* it!

Mon. 21st July. 1884.

? Feel tired and discouraged. Get work done after a while and go out to take a walk. Take the pistol in my bag. Go some five miles I should judge. Write a little, sketch a little more; bring home flowers. Nap. Walter home, half sick, has spoiled the Couture plate.[3] Too bad. Bed early.

Mon. July 28th. 1884.

. . . Feel sick. Spend all the morning on the lounge. . . . Walter home. Brings peaches, corn, "tropical fruit laxative", benzine, etc. . . .

Thurs. July 31st. 1884.

. . . Walter gets breakfast. Eat the same—lose mine—eat another or fruit solely. . . . Go up to mothers with Walter. He rides down town and I stay and get flowers and talk with mother. Tell her my expectation.[4] . . .

Tues. Aug. 5th. 1884.

A really sick day, the worst I remember for years. "Inter-susception of the intestine" we conclude. Walter tries hot cloths with success in relief, but I retain nothing in all day but a piece of watermelon and a fig. Mother and Aunt C. call in the afternoon. I was asleep while Walter had been down town to get some prunes, etc. Begin with "Sal Muscatelle" at bedtime.

Thurs. Aug. 7th 1884.

3.45 and wander disconsolate. Walter gets up too, but can do no good and slumbers again. Return to bed at about 6 and sleep till 9 or so. Mother calls while I'm dressing, and brings flowers. Eat two bananas. She goes soon, and Walter and I soon after.

Stop at Dr. Olive Herrick's.

a female physician, lately from New York. My first visit to a doctor, caused by real distress. I am ashamed. I tell her all the symptoms, and how we suspect "intersusception" etc. She makes digital examination and explains that the uterus is displaced, has fallen backwards. Not severe or dangerous. She fixes it with an instrument, inserts cotton, and gives me "bitter medesin." . . . Go to Walter's and tell him. He comes home with me. Afternoon of weariness and shame. . . .

Fri. Aug. 8th. 1884.

Sick still. A small breakfast. Infest the lounge continuously. Walter goes off but returns early, bringing pears, peaches, etc; also much money. 25 for me,

25 for he, and 50 for *we*.* I eat, but Lo! it remaineth not within me but returneth to upper air. Mother and Aunt appear and I "spruce up" and appear amiable. Harry Manchester calls in the evening, but I must needs be excused. He'll tell his mother! And she—O woe is me!

Fri. Aug. 15th. 1884

Wash my dishes! Take car and meet Walter down st. Go to Silver Spring. Was sick twice before leaving home, am sick on boat. We wait for the second dinner. Don't eat much. Watermelon good. We shoot, Walter with magnificent success, winning congratulations from an excitable onlooker. Meet Aunt C. and return on same boat. Excitable onlooker is late, and clambers and clambers [*sic*] on boat with his hat in his hand. Comes and offers us wild cherries, exclaiming to Walter, "That's for your shot!" Go to café and have cream, ice, & cookies. Walter buys me Jean Ingelow's poems and I go and get weighed. Only 113![5] Home, stopping at mother's, both of us. Get supper mostly. Have tea and toast. Feel better thereafter and make bed etc. Dress up a bit. Read Jean while Walter sketches. Bed.

Sun. Aug. 17th. 1884

Am sick before breakfast, but have recourse to my beloved tea and eat a good meal. Lie down awhile and Walter looks over my old letters to pick out the poetry for me to put in the pretty Russia leather book he gave me. . . . Wash the dishes. Rest some more. Comb and wash my hair, and am much wearied thereby. Rest & have some more tea. . . .

Sept. 1st. 1884.
Monday—

near 8. Get breakfast. Am not actively sick. A glorious day. . . . Meet Mother and Miss Bullock. Go with them a little and then wait for mother at Gregory's, reading "Dr. Zay".[6] Go with Mother to Sutton's, meet Aunt C. there, and dine. . . . Stop at Walters for fashion book and take Brook St. car to Miss Murphy's. See her about dress, and leave braid, silk, etc. Walk home, *angry*. Bessie Peck has been inquiring if I am growing large! Confound her impudence! Walter in soon. Good dinner. Haven't been sick today! Arrange photographs and Accts.* Bed.

Thurs. Sept. 4th. 1884.

Up ere dawn, back again, up at 8 or so. Clear up the attic, Walter helping. . . . Fix parlor some, enema, chamberwork, bath. Make some white biscuit. Mother comes with flowers and pears. Lie and doze. Get mashed potatoes for dinner. Walter brings lobster home. Eat little, mostly biscuit. Read Nation. Walter deep in "A Perilous Secret."[7] Dismal evening, for I feel unable to do anything and am mortally tired of doing nothing. Get out on roof. Humbly ask if I can sleep there tonight and am told "No you cannot!" Serves me right for asking. Bed? I guess so.

Thurs. Sept. 18th. 1884.

. . . I go up to Mother's for the last time.[8] Walter says goodbye to her. . . .

Sun. Sept. 21st. 1884.

6.15. Arise betimes. Make fire for first time. Does not "draw" very well. Get breakfast ready, hot biscuit, baked sweet potatoes, oatmeal, coffee—fine. (and cold bluefish!) Take bath and dress. Sick twice. Had Great Expectations of much work today, baking of bread and cake, dinner (no joke, with my first chicken) dishwashing, etc. etc. Give out completely at breakfast! Try hot ginger. Lose it. Try claret. Lose that. Do nothing all day, and am sicker than I've been since the worst part of it. Walter gets the dinner, dear boy, and does everything. . . . I tried iced milk P.M. and lost that. Kept however some "dew-drops," which seemed beneficial. Eat about an ounce or 2 of dinner. To bed, still prone.

Mon. Sept. 29th. 1884.

7–8. Rained tremendously in the night and Perfect day thereafter. I *long* for the country, but we are short of money and can't go. . . . Get dinner. Very tired thereafter. Walter reads to me.

Tues. Sept. 30th. 1884.

after 8. Am enjoying café au lait breakfasts very much. . . . Note from Miss Pease accepting full engagement at $12.00 a week. Glad. . . . Feel uncommonly well and brisk. Put clothes on horse, do chamberwork, make bed, etc. etc. quite as of old. How nice it seems! . . .

Sun. Oct. 5th. 1884.

Lazy and comfortable. Good breakfast. Accts. Start to trim bonnet. Get tired, and cry bitterly for shame at my feebleness. Get up fiercely and go to work. . . . Have lunch. Am unable to wash dishes so Walter does it. Bless him! Good dinner, fricasseed chicken, potatoes both, and spinach all of which I eat. Write to mother. Bed.

Fri. Oct. 10th. 1884.

Glorious weather now. I have coffee in bed mornings while Walter briskly makes the fires and gets breakfast. O dear! That I should come to this! Another letter from Mr. Tewksbury, (To Walter), with draft for $25.00. Surely a practical admirer. Accts. Call on Lu Manchester. Go shopping. Stop for Walter and home with him.

[*1885.*]

January. 1st. Thurs.

My journal has been long neglected, by reason of ill health. I am now better, and hope to keep it regularly and to some purpose. This day has not been a successful one, as I was sicker than for some weeks. Walter also was not very well, and stayed at home; primarily on my account. He has worked for me and for us both, waited on me in every tenderest way, played to me, read to me, done all for me as he always does. God be thanked for my husband! I have done nothing today in way of work. Have slept and idled and read a little. No one has been here but Carl to wish us A Happy New Year.

This last year has been short. I have done little, read little, written little, felt and thought——little to what I should have.

I am a happy wife. I bear a child. I have been far from well. I do not know that I am better in any way. Unless it be better to be wider in sensation and experience, and, perhaps, humbler. Ambition sleeps. I make no motion but just live.

And I am Happy? Every day almost finds me saying so, and truly. And yet— and yet—"call no man happy until he is dead." I will see what my life counts when I am old. I do harm to no one that I know of; and one soul at least is much the happier by me. Another soul is coming. Much depends on that. If it and possible others are world helpers then indeed I shall hope.

God knows. I should not be afraid to die now; but should hate to leave my own happiness and cause fierce pain.

Yes. I am happy.

Sat. Jan. 3rd. 1885—

8–8.20. Make popovers for breakfast. Eat rather unsatisfactorily. Feel sick. Leave dishes and dress. Aunt C. calls. Read her letters of mothers and show her baby things. Postman brings Walter an admonitory letter from a friend of his at which he is much incensed.[9] Reads it to Aunt C. & I, *sans* signature. Answers. Aunt departing presently we walk down st. together. He goes to see his careful friend and I go marketing & shopping. . . . Buy almost $30.00 worth of baby things. Dress goods, etc. Call for Walter and find him reeking in horrible odors. Gus[10] there serene. . . .

Mon. Jan. 12th. 1885.

8–8.30. Was sick last night, owing to dinner and weariness. My darling cared for me with ineffable tenderness. A stormy night but slept well after I did sleep. He was up rather earlier than usual to carry Gus'es picture down as agreed; but didn't as it rained hard. We neither of us feel very well. Sew some on red sack; and he reads to me, Poe, & Keats. He goes down st. on errands, taking picture; and I take a nap. Then lunch and wash most of the dishes. He returns and I sew a little more. Then he dresses; we have a sad little supper, and he very reluctantly goes to New York. It is to see the Watts Exhibition; Mr. Whitaker goes with him. Says he never will leave me again unless he *has* to! Dear dear love. I am now going in to the Westcott's, to spend the night.

Wed. Jan 14th. 1885.

7.40. Went serenely in to play chess with Mr. Westcott last night; and were well in the first game; when lo! Walter! He went home and awoke the fires while I stayed and was beaten—not ignominiously. Then home, and glad to be there. We had a little supper and a little talk and so to bed. This morning *I* got up while he slept on; and did all the work but coal & ashes! (and bed). Finished letter to Martha, and then walked down st. with Walter. Shopped a little. . . .

Thurs. Jan. 15th. 1885.

9.15 –20. Not very well. Walter does things. I just make some buckwheats (Hecker's) and after breakfast collapse. A bad wet dreary day. I get so tremulous and teary that my boy stays with me. A long nap does me good. He gets some oysters and milk, I make milk-toast, and we have a good little dinner. . . .

Thurs. Jan. 22nd. 1885—

About 9. Not well yet. Lie around all day. Very cold weather. Walter stays at home with me. I manage to get a little dinner, and wash some of the dishes. Injection with unsatisfying result. Walter makes Parchesi board on paper and beats me *seven* games! A swallow of tea, slice of toast & cup of prune juice for supper.

Thurs. Jan. 29th. 1885.

8.45 or so. . . . Miserable night. Do nothing whatever but clean up the parlor somewhat, and put clothes on horse. My boy gets home early, and goes straight out again to get me things—oranges—oysters—medicine. I eat some raw oysters & an orange. Very hot and nervous evening. He gives me a hot footbath, hot "Dew-drops", and puts me to bed in a blanket.

Friday. Jan. 30th. 1885—

? Slept warm—dripping, and well. Much better this morning. Wash dishes during the day and cook some rice for supper. Worse in afternoon and evening, but not so bad as yesterday. Bed in blanket. Get frantically hot and nervous and kick out of it. Bad night, lame all over.

Monday, Feb. 2nd. 1885.

About 9. Took my bromide last night and slept much better; quieter in nerves even when awake and uneasy. Still weak today. Sew the least bit; read a very little. Feel so downcast that I take out my comforter, Walter's journal, and get new strength and courage thence, learning how good and brave he is. I *must* be strong and not hinder him. Eat good breakfast, dinner, lunch & supper. Have beef-tea again. That and sleep will fix me I know. Walter home well welcome. He settles all my monthly accounts. Dear dear love! I cleaned up somewhat, but did not wash dishes. Weak yet.

Tues. Feb. 3rd. 1885.

9 or so. Downhearted and woebegone. A poor night and feel no better; that is, no stronger. Letter from Martha, and brief note from Uncle Edward, asking Thomas' address. . . . Walter, rather late. He makes me some lemonade, and gets supper; Steak & peas. Eat quite well. Parchesi. Try hop tea but can't drink it—stomach won't have it. Bromide. Bed.

Wed. Feb. 4th. 1885.

? Slept pretty well; and feel *lots* better. Eat real good breakfast. . . . Am very very tired and lame at night; which displeaseth and grieveth my Walter. "I didn't *mean* to!"

Mon. Feb. 9th. 1885.

9 or so. A long day, very bright and warm in the morning. Sit out on the roof in the sun. Wash the dishes. Make a little custard and have nice dinner ready. Nap in the afternoon. Sew on diapers in the evening. Bathe by parlor fire. Bed.

Tues. Feb. 17th. 1885.

? Not well in the morning; so hysterical indeed that Walter decides to stay with me; but after having a slight chill, some sherry, beeftea & toast, I feel better; and he goes later. . . .

Thurs. Feb. 19th. 1885.

9.25. A wellnigh sleepless night. Hot, cold, hot; restless nervous hysterical. Walter is love and patience personified; gets up over and over, gets me warm winter-green, bromide, hot foot bath, more bromide—all to no purpose. About 2 or 3 I get up despairing, and go into the parlor. Fix fire and sleep some after a while, on lounge. Back to bed towards morning & sleep more. We rise late. . . .

Mon. March 2nd. 1885.

About 8. Breakfast and loaf about awhile. . . . Mrs. Russel arrives, with small baggage. She sits about and I work. Work considerable. She helps some. . . .

Wed. March 4th. 1885.

About 8. Mrs. R. after 9. She washes the breakfast dishes & I go out. Call on Mary. Get "Babyhood" which she has read enjoyed & profited by. . . . Home. . . . Mrs. Russell, adorned in my circular (!) goes out to call on some wealthy friends. I was glad to see her so pleased, and *intensely* amused at the effect. Dr. Tomlinson calls, prescribes for cold, insomnia, and night sweats. I like her much. . . .

Thurs. March 12th. 1885.

8.35. Can't stand or walk much on account of the muscular force and unreasonable activity of the infant. Do breakfast dishes, which were but few. Lie down mostly. . . .

Sun. March 15th. 1885.

8.30 or 40. Bad night, miserable morning. Weak, draggy, nervous. Lie around. Write some to Mother. Get bed made up with the mattress from upstairs. Mrs. R. does about all the work. Better in the evening. . . .

Fri. March 20th. 1885

. . . Up gaily and get good breakfast—chocolate, codfish à la crème, hot biscuit. Get Mrs. Russell over to partake. Eat heartily. Try to sleep afterward but can't, expecting Miss Pease. . . . Miss P. at somewhere near 1. Talk much and get dinner. Good. Mrs. R. washes dishes while I show all my things to Miss P. Try to sleep again but can't. Mrs. R. departs in peace at about 4. Have a real good talk with Miss P. and enjoy it. Like her *very* much. . . .

Sun. March 22nd. 1885.

7.10 or so. A pleasant day. Enjoy Miss Pease more and more. Sleep some. Read to her. Pale dinner of veal and things. Read some of my things to Miss Pease. Feel weak and sleepy. Write to mother.

March 23rd. 1885.

This day, at about five minuts
to nine in the morning, was born
my child, Katharine.

Brief ecstasy. Long pain.
Then years of joy again.

Motherhood means——Giving.

[*After the birth of Katharine, Charlotte neglected her diary for three weeks.*]

Sunday. April 12th. 1885.

First entry in three weeks. Am "up" but not vigorous. Retta Clarke called. Wrote to Mother.

Thurs. April 16th. 1885.

Go to ride with Walter—does me *good*. Horrify Miss P. by jumping from the buggy step. Lunch. Nurse baby. Sleep. Get up. . . . Dinner, good appetite.

Sat. April 18th. 1885.

Get up and take a bath. Breakfast. Baby for nearly two hours. Then a long nap. Then dinner. Then Baby. Then supper.

[*Another break occurs in the diaries between April 19 and May 1, 1885.*]

May 1885.
Fri. May 1st.

Am pretty well used up by loss of sleep. Walter stays at home in the morning and lets me have a nap. We begin to take ice. Katharine is better; sleeps from 11 till 3, is asleep again before 5 without pain and crying and now remains so at about 7. She has been troubled with indigestion and "wind"; I took some ginger today and think that helped. Mean to leave off cocoa for a while; as we fear it is too rich. She also has a cold. I wonder what people do who know even less than we about babies! And what women do whose husbands are less— sufficient.

Sat. May 2nd. 1885.

The first anniversary of my wedding day. I am tired with long sleeplessness and disappointed at being unable to celebrate the day. So I cry. Walter stays till 12. Belle comes and cleans up for me as usual. I send her for flowers to beautify our little house, and dress myself in black silk, jersey, and yellow crape kerchief. Haven't been "dressed" before in months. . . . Walter brings me lovely roses.

Mon. May. 4th. 1885.

A good night; baby slept till 3. Get her washed before Walter goes; and after she is asleep proceed to lunch and do housework. Seems good to be at it again. . . . Telegram from mother. She starts today. O I shall be glad to see her! [11]

Wed. May. 6th. 1885.

Katharine develops an unseemly inclination to wake and rise at two o'clock at night or so and remain awake for some hour and a half or two hours. She has a hard day, with considerable cry, very little sleep, and bad "diaper." I am very tired, very. Am starving for fear of giving her the colic. Guess I'd better eat more freely, as she has it anyway.

Fri. May. 8th. 1885.

A fine scare with Miss Baby. She slips off my hand and gets her face under water a moment. Frightens her and me too. Hard day in consequence, she restless and cryful, I tired. Mrs. Westcott comes in at nightfall and revives me much.

Sat. May 9th. 1885.

Another good* night—but am very tired and depressed in the morning. Walter shakes me up, sets me to eating, sends me out. I call on Mary and get flowers at Butcher's for mother. Come home with them and then take them up into her room. Home and get things ready to wash baby. At about noon mother comes, bless her, and thereafter all goes well. She worships the baby of course; and to my great relief and joy declares her perfectly well. We have a happy afternoon. . . .

Sun. May. 10th. 1885.

Not very good night. Mother over early. She takes all the care of the baby day times; washes her today with infinite delight. I fear I shall forget how to take care of the baby. . . .

Mon. May. 11th. 1885.

Fair night's sleep. Good day. So nice to have mother here. . . .

August. 5th. 1885 ——

5.30 Yesterday I arranged my books once more; hoping to be able to keep account of my life and expenses again. I have long been ill; weak, nerveless, forced to be idle and let things drift. Perhaps now I can pick up the broken threads again and make out some kind of a career after all.

Arose this morning at 5.30 and nursed the baby. Took my Mellin's Food as usual and got breakfast. Mine consisted of cocoa and a little bread. Nurse again at 8.45. Then write.

Fri. Aug. 28th. 1885.

It is vain to expect regularity at present. Any entry is better than nothing. On *Wed. the 26th* Katherine first put on short clothes. We have a girl. Daffney Lynch by name. She came *Mon. the 17th*. I paid her last Sat. She is eminently satisfactory. I am having a doctor. Dr. Knight. He came first I think on *Fri. the 14th*. Again, having considered the case on Sun. 16th. I had had one of my bad times when he was first sent for. The next day was bad too; highly excited, hysterical; seeming to myself wellnigh insane. Sun. when he came some better. Mon. (17th.) much better, walking down street with Walter, well all day. Tues. rode down, growing ill feelings in afternoon; ill turn at night, with pain and vomiting. Bad Wed. morning, better in afternoon when he came.

Very well *Thurs.* 20th. Painted a little, wrote verses for long neglected albums, tended baby while mother went out; began article on "The Inutility of Sporadic Reform." Felt clear headed and strong. Fri. not so well, but worked hard getting backroom in order; "baby's room." Very much used up Sat. when he came again; but read essay for him and talked glibly. Sun. felt pretty well and "dressed up." Put desk in order in the morning. Began to write P.M. but guests arrived. Mon. 24th. *miserable*, but so far better than I have been that I was able to write it down. Tues. Walter came home at noon and we took the baby to ride. Heavy showers. Wed. I rode down about noon, met Mr. Stetson Sen. and went home with him to dinner. Walter joined me there and so home. *Cold* The weather is *very* cold just now. Nurse baby, ginger tea, long nap. Thurs. still cold. Darn and mend pretty much all day. . . . Today have embroidered some on Katherines flannel petticoat, and now write. We began to read "Hard Times" last night.

Sun. Aug. 30th. 1885 —

Every morning the same hopeless waking. Every day the same weary drag. To die mere cowardice. Retreat impossible, escape impossible. I let Walter read a letter to Martha in which I tell my grief as strongly as I can. He offers to let me go free, he would do everything in the world for me; but he cannot see how irrevocably bound I am, for life, for life. No, unless he die and the baby die, or he change or I change there is no way out. Well.

1885. Tues. September 1st.

The first reasonably happy day for a long time. . . . Went down town, did a bit of shopping, stopped for Walter and rode home with him. Dinner. Read and sew. *Babyhood* and *Century* came. Began James' "The Bostonians."[12]

Wed. Sept. 2nd. 1885.

The eventful day on which we earnestly Mr. Tewkbury's uncle and other relatives will Buy.[13] As we are low in funds. I still feel pretty well.

Sat. Sept. 5th. 1885.

Not very well yet. . . . Letter from Martha. I wrote her my heart and she answers with not overwise head. We all go to the Brown's for supper and have a game of whist afterward. Baked beans the "piece de resistance." I enjoy it until after the baby wakes up and cries. They sing and play, and the poor little baby is well nigh crazed. Leave at 9. "Daphne" in the car. We hate to lose her.[14] Home tired. Sit up and talk and cry till near 12. Better so than in bed.

Thurs. Sept. 10th. 1885 —

Don't feel very well. Go down street and do errands preferably to staying at home alone with care of baby. . . . Very tired. Twitching and nervous. . . .

Fri. Sept. 11th. 1885—

A dear letter from Martha. Mother goes out & I tend baby. Dr. comes. More phosphorous & prescribes elixer coca. Show him my paintings. Read a little in the evening. Walter tired and we get into a quarrel over the windows, open vs. shut. I have a bad time; get out of bed and come down stairs in the dark.

Mon. Sept. 14th. 1885.

Go down and roll out bread. Back to bed a few moments. 8 o'clock! No time for bath! Cry and whimper, all upset. Feel badly. Cry more after breakfast. An oppressive pain that sees no outlet. Bathe and feel better. . . .

Thurs. Sept. 17th. 1885.

. . . We get supper. I give out and Walter makes the bread.

Sun. Sept. 20th. 1885

Walter makes fire. Our new girl, Elisa Gärtner and her father arrive about 9.30. Nice old gentleman. Takes snuff! Seems to think his daughter well situated. She sets to work in fine style. . . .

Mon. Sept. 21st. 1885.

Up at 5 with baby and small sleep after. Show Elisa about breakfast and set table. Clear it, and wash dishes as mother feels sick. Dead tired and lie down till afternoon. . . . Mrs. Tewksbury called on Walter today and bought "A Fool's Errand"[15] & "Morning Measure"—$650.00.

Fri. Sept. 25th. 1885.

Dreary days these. Only feel well about half an hour in all day. . . .

Mon. Sept. 28th. 1885

Arise and go to Boston; or rather to Jamaica Plain, and see Dr. Keller. Carry on the whole journey in a peculiarly lame and injudicious way—showing my illness. Am examined and speculumed and told that I am all right. Great is my satisfaction and relief. Home late but not very tired. Feel as if I should get well.

October. Thurs. 1st. 1885.

We are beginning to feed the baby once or twice a day, on Mellin's food. I don't mind since it's better for her. . . .

Thurs. Oct. 8th. 1885—

We propound discuss and decide the question of shall I travel? Yes, I shall. I contemplate wintering in California. Hope dawns. To come back *well*! . . .

Sat. Oct. 10th. 1885—

. . . Walter brings me $320.00 to travel with. John Mason's mother lent it. Also brings "Ramona"[16] and begins to read it.*

Sun. Oct. 11th. 1885.

Went to walk with Walter and the baby. Walter bathes me at night as I am much exhausted and my breasts trouble me some. They have to resort to the baby before morning. I had bound them up in accordance with Miss Pease's theory and practice. But disapprove of the effects and let 'em down.

Mon. Oct. 12th. 1885.

I don't remember this day —

[*Charlotte suspended her journal writing during her months in California.*]

[1886]

April. {1} 1886.
Thurs.

1st. Went down town with mother and Julia. Visited Reim's exhibition and Walter's Studio—"An Fleur de Lys." A beautiful place. His father's birthday. Went over there in the evening.

Sat. April 3rd.

Up betimes. Ordered things to eat. Breakfast late. Am trying to get accustomed to life here. It will take some time. I must systematize things some how.

[*Charlotte discontinued her journal writing until August 27, 1886.*]

Fri. August. 27th. 1886.

Begin to feel myself again. Am taking Buckland's Essence of Oats, with infinite good effect. Katharine and all are well. Am doing some note paper for Mrs. C. in pen and ink. Ate a good dinner today. Baby exasperating about her nap. Have just finished a letter to Julia. Have just received a letter from Atlantic Monthly actually praising my [poem] "Nevada"! But not accepting.

Sat. Aug. 28th. 1886.

A good day. Work more on Mrs. C's note paper. Go rowing with Eliza and baby later, and enjoy it. Paint in the evening —

Tues. 31st.

Poor day again. Manage to paint two sheets of note paper, under great disadvantages from Miss Katharine.

September 1886.

. . . Go to gym. Mr. Smith not in. Shop. . . . Go to gym. again. Am horrified to find that Mr. S. don't mean to have a ladies class till the new building is open! I reason with him. Go to Walter's. We go to Mr. Chas. Smith the broker

& auctioneer; and I talk to him about my "property." He says I can't do anything but wait. A mere business man, patronizing and contemptuous to a "woman." Ride home. Walter reads Century.

Sat. Sept. 4th. 1886.

Baby did not sleep well so I slept late. Walter returns about eleven! Recieve three dollars from the Journal for my poem "On the Pawtuxet."[17] My first payment for Mss! May it not be the last! . . .

Tues. Sept. 7th. 1886.

About 7. Walter slept with the baby to rest me; so I took her when she woke. A poor day. Accomplish nothing to speak of; only read a little in the geology book. Mother over to supper. Nice letter from Grace, which I answer immediately. Note from Mr. Smith of the gym. There are to be no ladies admitted till the new building is opened. I am much disappointed.

Sat. Sept. 11th. 1886.

Near 9. Feel dismal. . . . Home and fix lunch. Walter and I go rowing on the See-Konk. A splendid night. Full moon, no wind, warm. Go up to Pawtucket. . . . I row home, in fifty minutes, Four minutes. Enjoyed it very much, and it did me good. Bath, bed, and good sleep.

Sun. Sept. 12th. 1886

. . . I finish Aurora Leigh to Walter. It brings up my grief. Anything does. My four mile row did not tire or lame me *at all*, did me good. Washing my hair today utterly exhausted me! Tired back and brain. Write poem "O sick and miserable heart be still!"

Mon. Sept. 13th. 1886.

. . . Walter sends me one of the new Postal Sheets, just to show it me and say "I love you." Dear tender heart! . . . A fairly good day. But always the pain underneath.

Wed. Sept. 15th. 1886.

9. Slept well. Feel well. . . . I begin to feel like living. . . . Write to William Gillette.[18]

Sun. Sept. 19th. 1886.

9. Do not feel well during the day. Sew some on dress. Cold and windy. Good dinner. Get hysterical in the evening while putting K. to sleep. Walter finishes the undertaking, and sleeps with her. When I am nervous she never does sleep easily—what wonder.

Tues. Sept. 21st. 1886.

. . . . Letter from Thomas. Julia is going to have a baby in May '87. . . .

Sat. Sept. 25th. 1886.

. . . The Womans Journal comes. Bed early. Write to Alice Stone Blackwell,[19] & write "A Use of Memory." . . .

Sun. Sept. 26th. 1886.

8.30 or so. Sunday is usually a hard day for us both; Walter tries to do nothing but help me, and I get dinner and get tired. Today we both industriously bathed before breakfast. Then I cut his hair.[20] Tried to paint, but couldn't. . . . Got elaborate fricasee dinner. Good. Then I succumbed utterly; but aroused myself and took Kate up to Mrs. Diman's. . . . Walter met me, and home on the run, as it sprinkled. He is now putting K. to sleep. Write long letter to Martha.

Tues. Sept. 28th. 1886.

. . . Feel pretty well all day. Kate is too good to believe. She plays about all day, with me or Eliza, with little rags and pins and divers toys; busy, sweet, and patient. Bless her little heart! I love her. Good dinner. Read to Walter in the evening, while he cleans etchings.

Wed. Sept. 29th. 1886.

. . . Stop at Walter's and we go to the Public Library and read Ouida's article on Female Suffrage.[21] A *contemptible* piece of writing, bad in aim and execution. Read more after he goes. . . .

Sat. Oct. 2nd. 1886.

. . . (Woman's Journal comes with my poem in the *first* place.) . . .

Sun. Oct. 3rd. 1886. *

9.15. Write up herein since Wed. last. Do not feel very well and accomplish little. Walter takes the baby out, and I start a little article—"Why Women do not Reform Their Dress." A telegram comes here for mother. Send it up to her unopened. Presently she comes back with it—"Julia died this morning." . . . O my poor brother! . . .

Wed. Oct. 6th. 1886.

. . . Stop at Mother's. She was drearily washing dishes. She got a letter from Julia yesterday! Written last Wednesday. It is a dreadful blow to mother. . . . Then to my first Woman Suffrage Convention. A good audience. Mrs. Stone was the first speaker, then her husband, Mr. Blackwell, then Miss Haggart of Indiana. I left during her address, as her voice, high and monotonous, affected my nerves painfully. . . . Mrs. Stone is a lovely motherly sweet little woman with a soft quiet voice. Mr. B. spoke well and briefly. . . .

Sat. Oct. 9th. 1886.

. . . Stop at Walter's. Criticize his pictures, one so harshly from a moral point of view that he smashes & burns it. I feel badly; and after some tears he comes home with me. Find a letter from Mrs. Dun with check for twenty dollars, and two orders! Rejoice thereat. . . .

Mon. Oct. 11th. 1886.

. . . Take K. and go to mother's. She had had a letter from Bill, telling how Julia died. Heart disease. Only sick four hours. I am glad it was that instead of what we thought. Go to studio and leave K. while I cash check and do a few errands. . . .

Tues. Oct. 12th. 1886.

. . . A letter comes from Thomas to mother . . . and mother reads the letter aloud. My poor poor brother! He was not with her; but gone hunting as we all feared. He has taken the great sorrow in a noble way; and means to live well for his orphan boy's sake.————Letter from Alice Stone Blackwell today, very kind, says "The Answer" covers a year's subscription. The Boston Sunday Herald copied it! . . .

Fri. Oct. 15th. 1886.

9. A very hard night with baby; who has a head cold. Two hours sleep after she's up. Walter very much objects to going, (16th.), says he has a prejudice against the Hazards. Natheless we take the 12.50 train for Peace Dale, and spend the night at Oakwoods. A very very pleasant time. . . .

Sat. Oct. 16th. 1886.

But O the "billowy bed" they gave us! What is called a "wire mattrass." Too soft is as bad as too hard. But we sleep happily, and wake refreshed. Start at ten for Mrs. Cresson's, and stay there till 4 o'clock; when I return solus, leaving Walter for over Sunday. Safe home, walk up, and find all well and flourishing. Mother here, and the dining room fire made. Time too, it is real cold. Write note to Walter and to landlord; and put Kate to sleep. Tired, but not unpleasantly so.

Fri. Oct. 22nd. 1886.

. . . Go down to the Browns in the evening. Pleasant games of cards. . . . Robert makes an ass of himself by his loudmouthed contempt of women's rights and other justice. It is hard to be despised by such men as that.

Sat. Oct. 23rd. 1886.

9.15. Up till 1 again last night with K. Not sick but awake. . . . Get a full mail, three copies of W. J. with my article "Why women do not reform their dress" in it. . . .

Wed. Oct. 27th. 1886.

The great day. Succeed in getting everything well arranged and myself dressed by three o'clock. Shortly after Mr. Gillette appears. A very pleasant afternoon with him. Mother comes over to supper, radiant in her best black silk. A good supper. Read play thereafter. He is favorably impressed, but does not stop to give a full opinion, having to catch train. But he liked it. Gave us pass for three to his play now being given here.

Mon. November 1st

. . . Get a paper from Walton N.Y. with "The Answer" in it. Getting famous! Read Women's Journal and Century in the evening, the latter to Walter. I am very happy.*

Tues. Nov. 2nd. 1886.

. . . Walter goes to his Art Club; and I go and call on Dr. Mary Walker. Like her; but am not converted. She has no feeling for beauty in costume; thinks it beneath intelligent beings. She wears heels; and was put to it for a reason when I attacked them. Her costume was old-fashioned, very. Short hair of course.

Mon. Nov. 8th. 1886.

8. Paint on cushion all the morning; Telegram saying Mr. Tewksbury is coming, comes with wife. To lunch and dinner. He and Walter go off together; and I try to get acquainted with Mrs. T. but don't get far. She is shy. A large woman with a fearfully small waist, an absolute deformity. Have great difficulty in not talking to her about it. Mr. T. brought me a great basket of fruit, very nice. Also a box of good candy in the afternoon. Two good meals anyway I gave 'em. Pleasant time.

Sat. Nov. 13th 1886.

. . . Read Womans Journal. Walter goes to the Art Club Jury and I write an article and a half in the evening: "Necessary Steps" & "The Dress of Women etc."

Thurs. Nov. 25th. 1886.

THANKSGIVING DAY. An extremely disappointing day. Prepare to have dinner at two, and get everything well underway when Walter arrives and says they wont come till late. Eat a lunch, and have dinner at five, but don't enjoy it. Mother S. brought me over a huckleberry pie and a jar of quince. . . .

Wed. Dec. 8th. 1886.

. . . Dress and go to Annie Rawson Vaughns tea. Very gorgeous indeed, wish I hadn't gone. I despise the whole business. . . .

Sun. Dec. 12th. 1886.

Accomplish nothing in all day, owing to late rising; baby tending, and putting her to sleep in the evening—

Mon. Dec. 13th. 1886.

. . . Do ink dinner cards in the evening—Walter and I are very happy together.

Christmas Day. 1886.

Up first and give Walter his violets and a bit of a verse. Finish fixing tree and presents in the morning while Walter goes down town. Bathe and dress in good season. Anna, etc. first arrivals; then Mary etc. Walter has to go at the last moment and borrow mother's teaspoons. Clarence dessicates the turkey carcase. Stetsons, en masse at a little before five; all but Mr. Gilmore, who comes later. Get the repast ready about 5.15, the two families fraternizing meanwhile. A delightful supper, which I enjoy as much as anybody. Chopped turkey sandwiches, delicate, small, and crustless, hot coffee and chocolate, some of mothers nice rusk and Eliza's sponge cake and cookies, fruit and candy. Enough and *good*. I ate for six myself. Then our tree, gorgeous with candles. An immensity of presents, the floor and table full. Universal satisfaction. Our folks go first on account of children; all of whom behaved admirably. All depart by about eight. Mother puts the baby to sleep; and Walter goes home with her. Then he and I have a little more chocolate and sandwich, and go happily to bed.

*Sun. Dec. 26th. 1886.**

Up late, and pass a lazy happy day. Walter has to go to studio and do some plates. While he is gone I rearrange tree as well as I can, and recandle it. Also finish large card for Sophie while Katharine plays about with her new toys. . . .

Fri. Dec. 31st. 1886.

Up about 8. Sew some, tend baby, read a little in "Century." Arrange Mss. and Journal's in the evening.

I leave behind me tonight a year of much happiness, growth, and progress; also of great misery. But the happiness and progress are real and well founded; and the misery was owing mainly to a diseased condition of the nervous system. It is past, I hope forever.

I have become a person more in harmony with my surroundings; better fitted to live peacefully among my friends; and yet have not lost a keen interest in the world's work. I can write and paint better than before; and think as well when I am strong enough.

But I certainly have lost much of my self abandoning enthusiasm and fierce determination in the cause of right. Perhaps it is as well for the ultimate work done. I do not feel so. I feel in some ways lowered—degraded—traitor to my cause. But I am not sure, it may be a lingering trace of the disordered period just passed. When I know myself to be *well* in all ways I can better judge.

I have written half a play this year and a little good poetry. Also some painting and drawing which has been very profitable to me as work. This is an immense gain on last year and that before. At any rate, I feel happy and contented with my home and family; and have hope and courage for the New Year.

May it be fruitful of good!

[1887]

January 1st. 1887

. . . Go to Pub. Lib. and get new card. Fill it with books on Women. Read article in the Forum on Woman Suffrage by Higginson. . . . Stop at Walter's and he gives me his Xmas present as a New Year's gift; an exquisite Calendar on parchment; full of his sweetest thoughts in color and verse.[22] A dainty lovely thing. Bless his dear heart! Home together in the awful slop and slush and ice. Dine well on roast chicken. Then I christen my new sketch book and pencils. Then here.

Sun. Jan 1st. 1887.*

8 and after. A far better Sunday than usual. I am busy all day; mending, writing, arranging. Good dinner. I find I get tired and cross — i.e. used up, at about 5 P.M. Put Kate to sleep and then finish "Ode to A Fool." Mother came over at dusk, in spite of the terrible icyness just to see how I was. Dear mother!

Tues. Jan. 4th. 1887.

. . . Write. Our refractory student lamp takes fire, and Eliza and I have a lively time. Scorch the rugs and the table, ruin the lamp, spill the ink, and Eliza cuts her hand and breaks a pane of glass trying to open a window. I put the fire out with rugs, and don't get burnt at all.

Wed. Jan. 5th. 1887.

. . . Go to Pub. Lib. and read Howell's "Mouse trap." Rather poor for him; too exaggerated to be funny.[23] Get "Women of France" by Julia Kavanagh. Have started on a course of reading about women. 1st Monod's "Life & Mission of Women." Very scriptural and solemn, the rib theory at its utmost. 2nd. "Women in America." A little better than Monod; allowing duties to Society as well as husband and child. This third is historical and promises well. . . .

Thurs. Jan. 6th. 1887.

. . . Make buttonholes in Katharine's skirt. Bathe that bewitching damsel and put her to sleep. Begin article on the distinction of the sexes. . . .

Sun. Jan. 9th. 1887.

9 or so. A wearying day. Mend some. Get supper as usual. Fall with K. in my arms; bumping her head and lamming my knees. Then she tires me out in

the sleepgoing; and I get real nervous and shaky. Walter gives me a warm bath and puts me to bed.

Mon. Jan. 17th. 1887.

Still feel poorly. Arrange items of dress, and depart at 6 for the gymnasium. Speedily make friends; and resume my old position. Find myself happy to the verge of idiocy at being there again. Am as light apparently but not as strong as of old. Miss a car in returning and have to wait half an hour on the bridge, but there are several of us so we do not mind. Home happy. Chocolate and bread and butter.

Wed. Jan. 19th. 1887.

. . . Go up to mother Stetson's with Walter for dinner and stay there most of the afternoon. Shop a little and stop for Walter. Home. Feel very tired. He reads to me, "Women of the 19th Century," by Margaret Fuller.[24]

Sat. Jan. 22nd. 1887.

8. Feel very mean, but gradually recover. Woman's Journal comes, always welcome. Write part of "A Protest Against Petticoats," answering a plea for them. It is well to keep the ball rolling. . . .

Sun. Jan. 23rd. 1887.

9.5. Finish letter to Martha and article against petticoats. . . . Finish Margaret Fuller's book; Fine! . . .

Sat. Feb. 5th. 1887.

Paint all day and go over to see mother towards night. Walter brings home "The History of Womankind in Western Europe." I had left off my course of reading for two weeks, to oblige him. This is a very useful book.

Mon. Feb. 7th. 1887.

Begin to give Kate her bath before breakfast, but get discouraged by Walter, who thinks eating directly afterward is injudicious. Accomplish little all day, but have a very jolly time at the gym. in the evening. I seem to slip into my old position of inspirer very easily. And the girls like it. . . .

Sun. Feb. 13th. 1887.

10! Get Kate attended to and go over to Carrie's to dinner. Start in 3 o'clock car. Nice time. Home ere 8. Katharine very good indeed, as usual.[25] Eliza comes and puts her to sleep.

Mon. Feb. 14th. 1887.[26]

A dreary and useless day. Attend to Kate and wash dishes. Dr. Knight comes to see about K: says her liver is not working right, and to give her meat. Leaves medicine. Mother in a little while. Carry up to see Mrs. Cotton; and she (K.)

makes herself disagreeable as usual. But the children are angelic and get on with her very well. . . .

Tues. Feb. 15th. 1887.

A Financial Crisis. No coal, no money. I tell Walter he *must* get it, or I will; and he does. Sit doleful a little, then manage to eat something, and get to work. . . .

Sun. Feb. 20th. 1887.

Read. S. Journal while Walter sleeps; loaf till 11.30, wash Kate and nap her, write to Alice Stone Blackwell, accepting offer; feed K, dress, read some poetry, cry some over our incompatibility. Mr. & Mrs. Smythe call, and we get them to stay to some dinner. Have a good talk with Mrs. S. She is "another victim". Young, girlish, inexperienced, sickly; with a sickly child, and no servant; and now very sick herself. Ignorant both, and he using his "marital rights" at her vital expense. Ah well!

Tues. Feb. 22nd. 1887.

. . . Take Kate to Nannie Cotton's birthday party. She enjoys herself in a stately and solemn fashion. I feel desperately out of place among a lot of young mothers. . . .

Thurs. Feb. 24th. 1887.

8.30. train to Boston. . . . 2.35 train to Hingham; meet Mr. Lane at station. He is not enthusiastic; Chester being sick. But I go out, meaning to return. Stay however; and make myself agreeable to Chester & the baby.

Mon. March. 7th. 1887.

A very hard night. Katharine down with my cold, way down. Walter sends for doctor and tells mother, who arrives speedily. But it don't do me much good, for Kate will go to no one but me. I hold her all day, as I did about all night. My cold getting better. Dr. comes about noon.

Wed. March. 9th. 1887.

Bad night again, (colder room,) and baby worse in the morning. Diarrhoea sets in. I give out completely in the morning, crying with weariness. But Kate seems better in the afternoon, we both getting some noon sleep; . . .

Thurs. March. 10th. 1887.

No better. Mother again and doctor again. He says it is only the "cold" that makes the diarrhoea. A dismal rain and snow. I take coca, but do not feel brilliant. . . .

Friday, March. 11th. 1887.

. . . Put K. to sleep while Walter goes out. . . . When he gets back I am asleep on the bed, exhausted.

Sun. March. 13th. 1887.

A very hard day. I have a crying fit while trying to make Kate go to sleep, and am all used up. Miss Pease comes in the afternoon, and cheers us somewhat. Stays to dinner. Clarence drops in for a few moments. Then I put the baby to bed and collapse therein myself.

Tues. March. 15th. 1887.

Bad day. A cold snow storm. I rose early and felt pretty well, but got tired of couse [*sic*] later. . . . Put K. to sleep and sleep in the rocking chair myself. Get chilly and have a crying fit. Sleep ill, and am utterly useless the next day . . .

Thurs. March. 17th.

Sleep miserably and then lie in bed till noon. Feel better. . . . Miss Pease calls. I love her, but she doesn't soothe me at all.

Fri. March. 18th. 1887.

. . . I dont' go to gym, because I want to write some paragraphs for "The Amendment." . . .

Sun. March. 20th. 1887.

Bathe. Bad day. Getting back to the edge of insanity again. Anna and Aunt C. call. Put K. to sleep and feel desperate. Write my "column" though

Monday. March. 21st. 1887.

Slept in the spare room last night, and feel much better. Take K. out in the morning, . . . Call for Effie Rathbone and she walks with me to Miss Austin's on Congdon St, wheeling baby by special request on her part. But Miss Kate weeps and wails when we get there, and makes me carry her back to Effie's gate in my arms. Wheel her home from there, feed her a little, eat a bit myself, and start out in 2 o'clock car. . . .

Tues. March 22nd. 1887.

Try the spare room again, but Miss Kate howls for me in the night, won't let her father touch her. Up late, but feel pretty well. . . .

Wed. March. 23rd. 1887.

Baby's [2d] birthday. Mother gave her a dress & petticoat, mother Stetson a wee napkin & bib, Jennie a bib. Kate Bucklin gave me ten dollars for her. . . .

Fri. March. 25th. 1887.*

Baby sick. Wakeful night for us both, but don't seem sick till she gets up. Goes to sleep in my arms, and won't leave me in all day. Mother over, and doctor comes. Says it may be measles. Left medicine. Administer it, and she recovers with great speed, eating supper, and seeming as well as ever.

Tues. April 5th. 1887.

A miserable night and day. . . . Evening approaching to frenzy, but Jim Simmons arrives just as I get hysterical and calms me down finely. Walter rushes out for a walk and Jim drawls and talks and is as pleasant as can be. After he goes Walter breaks down, and I soothe him and love him and get him to sleep.

Wed. April 6th. 1887.

Good night. Good day. Take baby out to Susie's. Have a nice time. Mother over to supper, and Miss Brown calls. We all ride down town to get the election returns. *Woman suffrage defeated* as I expected. . . .

Sat. April 9th. 1887.

Worse. Take Kate over to mothers and leave her there, while I go see Dr. Knight. Explain my condition and he gives me two medicines. Wearily return, bring Kate back, and lie down. More physical exhaustion than I've felt yet.

Sun. April 10th. 1887.

Don't feel so much active misery, but am in a pitiful condition nervously. The least irritation upsets me quite. Walter takes baby out. I call on Mrs. Diman. Have some dinner there. . . .

Mon. April 11th. 1887.

. . . Mrs. Diman proposes to give me a hundred dollars! That is to send me away to get well. . . .

Tues. April 12th. 1887

Ride over to Dr. Knights to inquire about sanitarium, sea voyages etc. Find it hard to walk. Come back to Mrs. Diman's, rest, dine, come home. . . .

Wed. April 13th. 1887.

. . . Begin my week at mother's to rest Eliza. Walter sups with us and sleeps & breakfasts alone in the house.

Mon. April 18th. 1887.

Take baby to Mrs. Vaughn's during school. Back very tired. Egg nogg. doze. dine. Come over home, and am here now. Have made bed, made fire, washed dishes, write two notes. Am very tired.

I have kept a journal since I was fifteen, the only blanks being in these last years of sickness and pain. I have done it because it was useful. Now I am to go away for my health, and shall not try to take any responsibilites with me, even this old friend.

I am very sick with nervous prostration, and I think with some brain disease as well. No one can ever know what I have suffered in these last five years.

Pain pain pain, till my mind has given way.

O blind and cruel! Can *Love* hurt like this?

You found me—you remember what.

I leave you—O remember what, and learn to doubt your judgement before it seeks to mould another life as it has mine.

I asked you a few days only before our marriage if you would take the responsibility entirely on yourself. You said yes. Bear it then.

Tues. April 19th. 1887.

Snowed yesterday. Cold night. Wintry this morning. . . . Take baby to Mary's. Back and lunch. Come over home. Doors locked. No key to be found. Struggle in at bay window with much effort. Clear up and write here. Begin to write an account of myself for the doctor.

[*This entry was Charlotte's last before she went to seek treatment from Dr. S. Weir Mitchell. She abandoned her diary writing until 1890.*]

FOUR

"You are getting to be a famous woman my dear!"

January 8, 1890–July 15, 1893

T HE NEXT TWO AND A half years marked a major turning point in Charlotte's life. During the spring of 1887, at the age of twenty-six, Charlotte had sought the rest cure as treatment for neurasthenia from Dr. S. Weir Mitchell of Philadelphia. Designed to treat depression by focusing on its symptoms, rather than its causes, the "cure" included enforced bed rest and removed all liberties and freedom from the patient. "I was put to bed and kept there," Charlotte explained in her autobiography (*Living*, p. 96). "As far as [Dr. Mitchell] could see there was nothing the matter with me, so after a month of this agreeable treatment he sent me home, with this prescription: 'Live as domestic a life as possible. Have your child with you all the time. . . . Lie down an hour after each meal. Have but two hours' intellectual life a day. And never touch pen, brush or pencil as long as you live'" (p. 96).

The "prescription" nearly cost Charlotte what remained of her sanity: "I went home, followed those directions rigidly for months, and came perilously near to losing my mind" (*Living*, p. 96). Walter's diaries report that by June 1887 Charlotte was suicidal. She "was in the depths of melancholia again, with talk of pistols & chloroform" (*Endure*, p. 342). By early that fall it was apparent that a separation was inevitable. "In a moment of clear vision, we agreed to separate, to get a divorce," she wrote in the autobiography. "There was no quarrel, no blame for either one, never an unkind word between us, unbroken mutual affection— but it seemed plain that if I went crazy it would do my husband no good, and be a deadly injury to my child" (*Living*, p. 96). Because of the financial impossibility of maintaining separate households, however, the formal separation was postponed. Still, Charlotte spent long periods of time away from Walter, who was devastated by the breakup. "What this meant to the young artist, the devoted husband, the loving father, was so bitter a grief and loss that nothing would have justified breaking the marriage save this worse loss which threatened. . . .

If I had been of the slightest use to him or to the child, I would have 'stuck it [out]'. . . . But this progressive weakening of the mind made a horror unnecessary to face; better for that dear child to have separated parents than a lunatic mother," Charlotte wrote (pp. 96–97).

During much of the summer of 1888, Charlotte and Katharine spent time with Grace Channing in Bristol, Rhode Island. In a letter to Walter, Charlotte wrote with stinging candor about how much better she felt when she was away from him. "I'm not homesick a bit, don't think of missing you and am getting well so fast. I am astonished at myself," she wrote. "I haven't felt *unhappy* once since I left. The fogs and mists are rolling away; I begin to feel alive and self-respecting. Oh the difference! You are very dear to me my love; but there is no disguising the fact that my health and work lie not with you but away from you" (*Endure*, pp. 363–64).

After returning to Providence in September, Charlotte raised enough money, through the sale of property that she had been left to her by an aunt in Hartford, for her and Katharine to accompany Grace back to Pasadena. They left for California in early October. During her first few months in Pasadena, Charlotte's primary source of income was from teaching drawing. In December, Walter joined Charlotte in Pasadena, hoping for a reconciliation. His efforts proved futile. As Charlotte explains in *Living*, "a dragging year followed, and in January, 1890, he finally left me, called suddenly to the bedside of his dying mother. This was the definite open separation, following the decision of the fall of 1887" (p. 109).

It was during this period that Charlotte began keeping a diary once again. Because it had been more than two and a half years, however, and because of the lingering effects of the breakdown, it took some time for her to reestablish the habit of making daily entries. The diary itself, which was physically tiny compared to her early journals (it measured only 2⅛ by 5⅜ inches), was not particularly conducive to writing lengthy notes; hence, the brevity of many of the 1890 entries.

Charlotte wrote sporadically in her diary in 1890; large gaps appear throughout. At the same time, however, the 1890 diary is a remarkable document because it chronicles the transformation that took place in Charlotte's intellectual life. The year, in fact, marked the beginning of one of the most productive periods of her life. The early entries continue to reflect despondency, despair, dullness; by the end of the year, however, they bear witness to incredible growth and stability as her confidence was gradually restored.

One of the most significant events in 1890 was Charlotte's introduction to Nationalism, a reform movement that would influence her activism over the next several years. The Nationalist movement advocated an end to capitalistic greed and class distinctions and promoted the peaceful, progressive, ethical, and democratic improvement of the human race. Charlotte was quickly drawn into the movement, which seemed to be compatible with her own emerging values. Her poem "Similar Cases," a witty and biting satire ridiculing the conservatives who resisted social change, was published in the *Nationalist* magazine and won her instant acclaim. Among those applauding the poem was William Dean Howells, who wrote that he had "read it many times with unfailing joy" (*Living*, p. 113). With Howells's endorsement, Charlotte "felt like a real 'author' at last" (p. 113).

As the year progressed, in fact, Charlotte gained momentum. In June she was approached by a woman who asked her to speak to the Nationalist Club of Pasadena; Charlotte agreed, and her lecturing career was launched. In August she produced her single most famous work of fiction, "The Yellow Wallpaper," and in the month of September alone, she produced fifteen separate works: essays, poems, and the start of a novella. By the end of December, Charlotte was able to look retrospectively at the year as one of "great growth & gain. My whole literary reputation dates within it—mainly from 'Similar Cases'. Also the dawn of my work as lecturer." At last, Charlotte was earning an income doing what she had always wanted to do.

In 1891, although her popularity as a writer and lecturer was increasing and her activism on behalf of the Nationalist movement was flourishing, Charlotte still experienced periods of depression, owing in part to "the sense of responsibility of various kinds." At other times, however, she seemed to be invigorated and thrilled by her success as a lecturer, even staying up late to engage in discussions with friends and acquaintances. On Sunday, February 8, for example, she wrote: "Lecture to 1st Nat[ionalist]. Club in L. A. on 'Nationalism & Love.' Great enthusiasm. . . . Sit up till 2.30 talking to Mary—she to me mostly!" And then the next day, "Am kept up, talking, till 3 A.M.! On February 21 Charlotte was undoubtedly delighted when her uncle, the prominent Unitarian clergyman Edward Everett Hale, acknowledged her growing fame, as she recorded his remark in her diary: "You are getting to be a famous woman my dear!" And the next day, following a lecture on Nationalism and religion, "Graybeards come up afterwards, to shake hands and pay their compliments. I rejoice in the respect of men—old men—for my sexes sake."

Because of the growing demands for Charlotte's services as a public speaker, care for Katharine became a growing concern. (Charlotte would write extensively on the subject of child care in later years.) Friends were usually willing to help out, however, so Charlotte was often able to accept lecture engagements, which became her primary source of income. Along with her growing reputation came the power to negotiate the terms of her compensation. On May 12, for example, she wrote: "Go meet Mr. Ray at his office. I demand prepayment for the lecture Saturday or else I don't give it." And she kept her word. On Saturday, May 16, she reported the following: "Go to Alameda with Mrs. Prescott, meet Mr. Ray and his wife, but come back without speaking. He does not pay me the fifty dollars in advance as agreed and I will not speak without [it]."

As Charlotte's popularity increased, so did her circle of friends. In January 1891 Charlotte met Harriet ("Hattie") Howe, a feminist activist and member of the Los Angeles Nationalist Club program committee. In April 1891 Charlotte made the acquaintance of poet Ina Coolbrith, and on May 11 she was introduced to Adeline E. ("Delle") Knapp, a journalist for the *San Francisco Call* with whom she would share a significant, if volatile, two-year relationship. Over the next few days, Delle Knapp called on Charlotte several times, and on Thursday, May 21, Charlotte confided to her diary: "Go and lunch with Miss Knapp. I love her ————" By Saturday, May 23, 1891, the relationship was intensifying even more: "Miss Knapp . . . stays here all night." On Monday, June 1, Delle Knapp spent the night with Charlotte again, and the next day, June 2, Charlotte reported having passed a "wretched night, only made bearable by Miss Knapps tender helpfulness. She is a dear woman." Charlotte's language describing the time she shared with Delle grew increasingly sensual as their relationship developed. On June 4, for example, after dining out together, Charlotte described the mood during the boat ride home. "A calm delicious night, warm, starlit, with the light-engirdled bay all smooth, and we two happy together. She spends the night."

Charlotte and Delle (or "Delight," as Charlotte affectionately called her) grew even closer during the second half of 1891. Delle shared her interest in Nationalism, and Charlotte reported being "very happy together." During periods when they were separated because of conflicting schedules, they would write to one another almost daily. On Monday, June 15: "I write to my love," Charlotte remarked. On Friday, June 19, "Walk up to the P.O. before dinner, & get three letters from Miss Knapp. . . . Another letter from Delle in the evening, and the blessed photographs. Letter in that too—five in one day!" On July 3, Charlotte's thirty-first birthday, she received four letters from Delle, and on the fourteenth, when Delle returned to Pasadena, Charlotte was delighted: "My girl comes," she wrote simply, invoking language that she hadn't used in her diary since her days with Martha. A few days later, "Take a moonlight ride, first with Kate, then only each other."

Whatever affection Charlotte seemed to feel toward Delle, it was neither as intense nor as loyal as was her love for Martha. As lonesome as Charlotte was for Delle during periods of separation, she managed to find ways to fill the void. During one separation in late June, Charlotte recorded: "Read poetry to Hattie in the evening and makelove to her." Charlotte's allusion to making love to Hattie is curious, particularly when it is considered in conjunction with her comment two days later that she had passed a "very well behaved day." Charlotte's autobiography refers to Hattie simply as a "warmly devoted friend," but in her essay "Charlotte Perkins Gilman—As I Knew Her," Harriet Howe admits to being enthralled with Charlotte and characterized her as a "scintillating soul." Since Delle was away on business, Charlotte may very well have turned to Hattie, as the entry suggests, for the love that she had been missing since Delle's departure.

The summer of 1891 was significant in other ways as well. Charlotte's crusade on behalf of Nationalism was intensifying, as was her activism on feminist issues. Charlotte also began her divorce proceedings against Walter, although nearly three years would pass before the divorce would be final. But concerns about the divorce in no way impeded Charlotte's productivity. On the contrary, the promise of freedom seemed to fuel her energy; in July alone she wrote over twenty essays, articles, and poems.

The greatest difficulties Charlotte faced in 1891 were coming to terms with her mother's persistent illness, which was later diagnosed as cancer, and struggling to meet the various demands on her time and emotional resources. When Thomas could no longer afford to keep his mother with him in Utah, Charlotte reluctantly left her "little cottage" in Pasadena and moved north to Oakland, where Mary Perkins joined Charlotte, Katharine, and Delle Knapp in September. While Charlotte's autobiography suggests that the move to Oakland was undertaken because the work opportunity was better (*Living*, p. 132), it seems likely that Charlotte also wanted to preserve her relationship with Delle, whose home base was San Francisco, just across the bay. In Oakland, they set up household: "Arrive . . . at 9.15 A.M. Delight waiting on the wharf. All come over together to this nice boarding home—1673 Grove St., Mrs. Barrows. Very pleasant. I have a lovely room with Delle, and mother one with Kate."

The strain of balancing relationships, meeting demands, and attempting to be productive, however, quickly took its toll. On Thursday, October 29, Charlotte assessed the situation: "Still very tired. . . . Go to Dr. Kellogg's P.M. She says I put myself back 3 weeks by my exhaustion of yesterday."

By Christmas, Charlotte's fatigue and anxiety about Mary's illness was acute. She celebrated Christmas "by a fit of hysterics." When her physician and friend Dr. Kellog Lane advised Charlotte that she probably could not stand the strain of the "present family relationship" much longer, she and Delle decided that a move to the country would be advantageous for all of them. At year's end she tried to be optimistic in the face of great uncertainty about the future: "It is the anxiety etc. about mother that is wearing me now. That must be borne. May next year help more!"

In spite of Charlotte's hope that 1892 would be a better year, it was marked by "poverty, illness, [and] heartache." The first ten days of January saw Charlotte, Mary, and Katharine all seeking treatment from Dr. Kellog Lane for various maladies. As Mary's cancer caused her increasing pain, Charlotte's sense of helplessness grew proportionately. Her method of coping with the strain was to distract herself with work. Much of her work centered around her Nationalist concerns and the promotion of her socialist philosophies. She regularly attended meetings of the Pacific Coast Women's Press Association, the Woman's Club, the Ethical Society, and the New Nation Club, where she was elected corresponding secretary.

In early February, Charlotte, Delle, and Katharine moved to a boardinghouse at 1258 Webster Street in Oakland, while Mary stayed temporarily with Dr. Kellog Lane. When the woman who ran the Webster Street boardinghouse left to attend a sick brother, Charlotte took over the management of the house—and the cooking. "9 people in the house—8 to cook for!" she wrote on February 29. "I can't have mother yet!" Within a couple of weeks, Katharine came down with a bad case of the measles, but Charlotte seemed to handle it well. Through all of the turmoil—the cooking, the housekeeping, the measles—she continued to write and to lecture. And then on April 2, Mary Perkins moved back in.

By the middle of April, the demands on Charlotte's time had become so consuming that she could no longer maintain her diary with any kind of regularity. During the summer of 1892, Charlotte managed only a handful of entries. In September, however, after Hattie Howe arrived as a boarder and assumed some of the responsibilities, Charlotte resumed her journal. The enormous strain of the preceding weeks was captured on September 13, when Charlotte wrote: "See Dr. K. She concludes to do nothing for me at present. Says I had better break down honestly now than be bolstered up and break more extensively later. A wise physician."

Still, Charlotte managed to keep writing; it seemed, in fact, to help bolster her spirits. October 25: "Am feeling first rate these days—full of plans to write, sew, build, etc. The creative instinct rising and promising well for work when the strain is off." At the same time her relationship with Delle was beginning quietly to erode. References to her in the diary are sparse and nebulous. "Delle goes off on some trip," Charlotte wrote indifferently on October 3.

By the end of the year, Charlotte had to work hard to keep up her spirits. Mary was nearing the final stages of her battle with cancer, and throughout November and December there was a veritable parade of incompetent helpers traipsing through the boardinghouse. Charlotte tried to look at the humorous side. November 15: "Mrs. Haydon goes, praise the Lord! Mrs. Moore and small daughter appear in her stead—praise the Lord again! (might as well do it always)." December 10: "Mrs. Moore & daughter depart—praise the Lord again! She was either drugged or cracked—a lunatic. I have now secured a nurse for

Monday—and am to do my own work for a while." Later that day: "Miss Bennett comes from S.F.—to nurse mother. I experience a great sense of relief and go out to ride on the cable car." December 11: "Mrs. Bennet proves totally inadequate, and has a sick headache which induces her to sit in the kitchen all day." And finally, on December 12: "Mrs. Bennett departs, Mrs. Alban comes, and proves a delight—kind, willing, helpful, pleasant—we all like her. I am cook and the others help."

When a fellow socialist called on Christmas Eve to offer assistance because he had been told that Charlotte was "destitute," she took his visit with good humor as well. But by Christmas Day, the effects of the chronic strain were obvious: "We have a fine Xmas dinner but I am unable to cook it. Delle & Hattie do it all. I am very weak. Mother is low too, just now."

Charlotte's end-of-the-year retrospective poignantly reflects her despair. "Care, anxiety, grief, and shame for many many failures. My last love proves even as others. Out of it all I ought surely to learn final detachment from all personal concerns. . . . There is only to go on."

Facing tremendous odds as 1893 began—wrestling with poverty, with the final stages of Mary's illness, and with her troubled relationship with Delle— Charlotte tried to rouse herself to meet the various challenges: "Joy in life—Get up! It is time to begin! Plenty of time ahead—glorious world—let's start," she commanded herself on January 4.

Her self-directive seemed to work, at least temporarily. Charlotte produced numerous short articles, a short story, and several poems during the month of January, despite frequent altercations with Delle. As it often did, the tension in the household manifested itself physically in Charlotte: she complained on January 19 of experiencing "a tired miserable day, [with] increasing weariness and irritability," and the next day, she added, "My back is worse again—the recent trouble."

The end of January found Charlotte reflective: "Have done about fifteen pieces of salable work this month—three lectures, three poems, nine articles of one sort or another. Received $40.00 therefor so far. Fair work for an overworked invalid." The quantity of work was, indeed, impressive considering the various obstacles confronting Charlotte. The news that Delle was to be sent to Hawaii in early February to cover the proposed annexation was undoubtedly welcomed by Charlotte: the demands of caring for Mary during the final phase of her battle with cancer were difficult enough without having to worry about her floundering relationship with Delle.

Charlotte was as concerned about Mary's emotional well-being as she was about her physical comfort. She was particularly determined that Mary not worry about her impending divorce from Walter. Having already encountered

journalists who had made a circus out of the "circumstances" surrounding the
divorce, Charlotte was guarded when a reporter showed up just two weeks before
Mary's death to interview her about her position on marriage:

> The Examiner sends a man, Mr. Tod, to interview me on my views on the
> Marriage Question—the decrease of marriage. I refuse on the ground of the
> Examiner's reputation—will not write for the paper. He begs, he tries to
> fool me into conversation, he argues, he offers to pay me, he threatens cov-
> ertly—I succeed in getting rid of him.
>   Am exhausted by the contest, however.

Charlotte's exhaustion intensified as she spent long nights sitting up with
Mary. Friday, March 3: "Sit up till near 2 with mother—The nurse gets 4 hours
sleep. Write short powerful paper—"The Sex Question Answered" for the
World's Congress. Nothing seems to seriously affect my power to write. This
paper has been done in short laborious efforts during these wretched days, and
finished last night by mother's deathbed." Early on the morning of Tuesday,
March 7, Mary Perkins quietly passed away.

Charlotte's father, Frederick Perkins, from whom Mary had been divorced for
years, accompanied Mary's body to Los Angeles, where it was cremated. Charac-
teristically, Charlotte had little to say in her diary concerning her feelings about
Mary's death. She matter-of-factly reported washing and dressing her mother's
body, gathering people to attend the "short and scant" funeral service, and cleaning her mother's room in the days following her death. Still, the cumulative effect of losses of various kinds—the death of her mother, the end of her marriage,
her rapidly eroding relationship with Delle—caused Charlotte enormous pain.
Her response, as usual, was to immerse herself in work. Although she managed
to keep busy, Charlotte still had to prepare for yet another potentially painful
transition: Delle's imminent return from Hawaii.

Although Charlotte was "absurdly glad to see" Delle when she returned to
Oakland on April 5, their relationship was in jeopardy. On May 3 Charlotte
wrote: "Trouble with Delle over the yard—and other things." May 11: "All
along lately hard times with Delle. Am to exhausted to attend committee
meeting to arrange constitution for State Council of Women. Delle goes without me. . . . Dreadful time with Delle." And the next day: "Home utterly exhausted—scene with Delle all the way up from ferry to house, in the car." By
May 14 they had decided to part company: Delle "decides to leave the house.
I have so desired since last August—and often asked her to." Delle remained,
however, for another two months, and it was July before she packed her belongings.

In the meantime, Charlotte stayed busy. As always, occupying herself with
work was a way to avoid confronting the pain of yet another loss. Charlotte be-

came active in a number of reformist organizations—the Pacific Coast Women's Press Association (PCWPA), the Woman's Alliance, the Economic Club, the Ebell Society, the Parents Association, the State Council of Women—reading papers, organizing meetings, recruiting members. She also became involved in writing for and in editing the *Bulletin*, the official journal of the PCWPA. And as always, she was preoccupied with her precarious financial situation. On June 28 she wrote succinctly: "Miss White calls and lends me ten dollars. I go down & [pay] gas bill—shut off this noon if I did not."

In the midst of this latest financial crisis, Charlotte came perilously close to making a decision that almost certainly would have proved disastrous. After the wife of an acquaintance was brutally murdered, Charlotte considered taking in the motherless child at the request of the bereaved widower, J. Griffes of the *San Francisco Call*. After discussing it with her friend Dr. Kellog Lane, however, Charlotte thought better of it. "Dr. K. advises me not to take the Griffes[.] Wise woman. I had best keep clear of men."

Charlotte, in fact, seemed to think that she best keep clear of any intimate involvements as her relationship with Delle came finally, and unceremoniously, to an end in mid-July: "Her behavior has been such as to gradually alienate my affection and turn it to indifference," she wrote on July 15. "It is a great relief to have her go."

[1890]

January, 1890
Wed. 8.

Went to Dr. Gleason's. Like her very much. She talks to me.

Thur. 9.

Rode on a burro, first time. Liked it.

Sat. 11.

Walter gets a telegram. "Come at once, quickest way, your mother is very low.

Sun. 12.

Grace to dinner. Pack. Walter goes by two thirty or so. . . .

Mon. 20.

Began writing with Grace, retouching "Pretty Idiot,"

Sat. 25.

Wrote with Grace all day. Dr. Gleason to dinner.

Fri. 31st.

Still tired, weak and sad. I haven't much strength. Rode with Dr. Channing. The girls to tea.

February.
Sat. 1st February.
Finished Pretty Idiot alterations. Tea at the Senters. Made blue Jean skirt.

Sun. 2.
A weary day. Very miserable. Grace in twice. . . .

Fri. 7.
Rest mostly, feel a little lame. Gymnastics in the evening.

Tues. 11.
"Colonial Tea" at Mrs. Grangers. Very pleasant. Grace spend the morning here talking with me.

Sat. 22.
Am pretty miserable just along here. Mrs. Plank to clean.*

*Sun. 23.**
Dine at Mrs. Mitchells. Good morning's work with Grace. Am really miserable.

Thur. 27.
Feel better, arrange mss. to send off. . . . Grace P.M.

March.
Tues. 4.
Wash my hair. Work on "Wistaria"

Wed. 5.
Work with Grace on new play.

Sat. 8.
A fine busy day. Am feeling better. Write by myself in the evening.

Tues. 11.
Finish copying "The Giant Wistaria" [1] & send of tomorrow. Play whist at Mrs. Kimball's.

Sat. 15.
Sweep violently. Write "Jilt" story.

Tues. 18.
Work with Grace A.M. Whist at Mrs. Grangers P.M. Go to bed with Kate. I'm so tired!

Wed. 19.
Write on play *alone*! . . .

Mon. 31.

Sent Walter Graces $25.00 to go to N. Y.

June.

Sun. 15.

Lecture on "Human Nature" at Nationalist Club. Great Success.

Mon. 16.

Letter from W. D. Howells, praising "Similar Cases" & Women of Today."[2]

Wed. 18.

Read two ghost stories at Mrs. Mitchells. . . .

August.

Fri. 8.

Lecture in S[anta]. M[onica]. on "Unnecessary Evils." Full house.

Sat. 9.

Return to Pasadena. Second meeting of girls class. Check for $10.00 from Kate Field.

Sun. 24.

Work hard & achieve nothing! A walk with Kate towards night. Finish copy of Yellow Wallpaper in the evening.[3]

Mon. 25.

5.50. Wash dishes. . . . Try to write all day—without success. Dr. C. in twice.

Tues. 26.

. . . Begin rocking chair story. Delia for drawing. Miss Cole takes me to ride. Tea with Mrs. Senter. Dr. Channing in the evening.

Wed. 27.

. . . Go to see a Miss Orton about teaching drawing in her school. Dr. C. gives me some acid phosphate & tea. Take both with good effect. Write. . . .

Thur. 28.

Tramp to breakfast. . . . Send "Yellow Wallpaper" to Howells. Write two brief essays on Maternal Instinct etc. . . .

Fri. 29.

. . . Copy "Maternal Instinct." Write on "Inanimate?," and copy "The Divine right of Mothers." . . .

September.

Mon. 1.

. . . *Miserable* night—over dose of acid phosphate gives *terror.* . . .

Sun. 7.

7.45. Poor day. Arrange for work but do little. Little walk with Kate. Dr. Channing in the evening. Brings me an old lecture of his to read.

Tues. 9.

5.20. Write, to no purpose. Spend the afternoon walking with Kate in the Arroyo—nap there. Mrs. Carr in the evening. Nice talk.

Wed. 10.

7. Good day. Write "The Illogical Mind" in the morning, "The Body & Dress" in the afternoon. Dine and spend an hour or two with the Clarks. Dr. Channing.

Sat. 13.

8. Bad night. Feel very weak and faint but not blue. . . .

Mon. 15.

Kate and I spend the day at Long Beach—Dr. Channing's treat. A good time. Awfully tired.

Sun. 21.

7. Begin novelette "A Fallen Sister." Walk in arroyo with Kate. Dr. C. in.

Mon. 22.

6.15. Wash dishes; Begin large essay "Are Women Normal." Write 3600 words. Call at Mrs. Mitchells with Kate. Stay to tea. . . .

Tues. 23.

7. Letter from Mr. Henry Austin,[4] "Traveller Literary Syndicated." Copy and arrange mss. to send him. . . .

Thur. 25.

6.40. Wrote "Are Men Better Than Women?" and finished "Society and the Philosopher." Walk & run with Kate. Dr. C.

Sat. 27.

7.20. Write letters, and send off all this week's mss. to Mr. Austin. Go to S. P. S. leaving Kate with Mrs. Clarke. . . .

Sun. 28.

Rest mostly and write letters. Dr. C. Copy some poems.

October.
Wed. 1.

Wash dishes. Mend. Go in the afternoon to meet a Miss Oakley who wants to teach literature here. Dr. C. Borrow a dollar as I've had not one cent for three days.

Sat. 4.

6.45. Feel well. Call from Miss Shoemaker. Write "A Daughter's Duty." Go down street with Kate, and to see Mrs. Plank in her new house. She gives me a pie.

Mon. 6.

. . . Letter with check from K[ate]. F[ield's]. W[ashington]. Go down st to cash it, and have Photo taken. . . .

Sat. 11.

Clean out stove, etc. etc. Mrs. Carr calls & Mrs. Rust. Go to S. P. C. Leaving Kate at Mrs. Clarkes. *Coal fire*! thanks to Dr. Channing. Get photographs to send Mrs. Atherton. *Splendid.*

Mon. 13.

Not feeling well this month.

Mon. 20.

Wrote to Grace and Walter. . . . I am exhausted. Dr. C. in the evening, and I go to Dramatic meeting.

Sun. 26.

Copy & send off all Mer-Songs etc. to E. E. Hale. Also send "Yellow Wallpaper" to Mr. Austin. Very tired & weak. Call on Mrs. Mitchell & Mrs. McCaudlish. go to walk with Miss Lyman. She offers to loan me $25.00.

Fri. 31.

Mrs. Hill takes me home to arrange for costume tonight. Am a fortunetelling witch-gypsy at a Halloween Party—eminently successful. Also tiresome.

November.
Sat. 1.

Write a long letter to Grace. Rest. Miss Picher pays $7.50 for six small cards.

Sun. 2.

Dr. C. solders tub. Wash Kate. Lecture to Nationalist Club. 3.50! . . .

Thur. 6.

Still fixing for my "school." Helen Hill calls. Is enthusiastic and admiring, but fails to appear at night! A rainy day & evening, but our performance was a success. We are to repeat it—Sarah Dexter *fine!*

Mon. 10.

Arrange for that school exhibition again and give it in the evening. Walk down with Mr. Masters. Great crowd. *Awfully* tired!

Tues. 11.

Pretty much used up. Paint on teatray. Ladies call to talk Nationalism. Go to Colonial teaparty as Madame de Remusat in the evening—at Mrs. Dexters.

Thur. 20.

In town. Call on Miss White, artist, Miss Anthony, lunching with her. Go to Pub. Li. and see Dr. Follansbee. Bad case of retroversion and uterine catarrh. Buy Fountain [?] syringe & medicine.

Sun. 23.

Rehearse at Opera House P.M. taking Kate

Tues. 25.

Go in town, lunch with Miss Anthony. . . . Read Kipling & enjoy him mightily. Read his "Drunes of the Fore & Aft" to another patient. . . .

Fri. 28.

Work hard again and up later. Rehearse in the evening.

Sat. 29.

Work awfully hard. Miss Anthony out to tea. Have to dress in haste, & get no supper. Play a great success as far as acting goes. No profits however. Retire at 1.30 or 2.

Sun. 30.

Up late in the morning. Miss A. washes dishes. All dine at Mrs. Mitchells. Then we have a "shooting party" in the Arroyo. Not much shooting. Read to Miss A. in the evening. tired—awfully.

December.
Thur. 11.

omitted—too weak—too busy.

Fri. 19.

Write paper on The Economic Side of the Social Question. Call at Miss Lyman's.

Sat. 20.

Write on Nationalist lecture. Read paper at Socialist Purity Society. Mrs. Carr for a moment in the evening.

Sun. 21.

Lecture to Pasadena Nationalists on "Nationalism & Love.

Tues. 23.

Sew on a new crimson dress for Kate. Miss Allen for her lesson—50 cts.

Thur. 25.

Xmas Day. Stockings. Mrs. Master's tree. Dine at Mrs. Rust's. Tired out.

Sat. 27.

Write lecture for Los Angeles Nationalists—"Our Opportunity." . . .

Sun. 28.

Lecture in town, great success. Am to give three more.

Wed. 31.

Sew—wash dishes. Tea at Mrs. Rusts.
A very quick, but very hard year; cruelly hard since Grace went. A year of great growth and gain. My whole literary reputation dates within it—mainly from "Similar Cases." Also the dawn of my work as lecturer.

[1891]

Thursday, Jan. 1, 1891

Pasadena, California. I watched the old year out and New Year in as before these many years—alone.—writing a letter to Grace. I sewed all day, varying the afternoon with a call on Mrs. McCaudliss. Wrote to Walter in the morning.

Sunday, Jan. 4, 1891

Write 24 double pages of lecture "Nationalism & Religion." Deliver the same in the afternoon. . . . Very successful. Got $4.30 cts.—Mrs. Carr put in a whole dollar! Awfully tired with the days work.

Monday, Jan. 5, 1891

Wash dishes and arrange parlor. 1 P.M. train in town[.] Dr. Follansbee says I am 90 per cent better, and I'm sure I feel so. . . .

Wednesday, Jan. 7, 1891

Write a cheering letter to Walter, who is blue under adverse criticism. . . .

Friday, Jan. 9, 1891

. . . Letter from Walter stating that his show is a complete failure financially! Poor boy! It is so hard for him. But these days of money rule are drawing to a close. I write him a letter and a wee child's poem—"The Bad Little Coo-Bird." A lady calls, friend of Mrs. Carr's, wants to read my "Nationalism and Religion, so I lend it. Also I talk to her, a lot. A moment's call on Mrs. Rust, walk with Kate, supper with "Woman's Journal," read to Kate, put her to bed, and now to write.

Sunday, Jan. 11, 1891

. . . Go in town on 11 A.M. train. . . . I give "Nationalism & The Virtues" in Temperance Temple. Splendidly received. Get 7.50 for the two addresses so far. Am engaged for a week from Wednesday to speak to the Woman's Club there—$5.00. Rode back with Mrs. Johnson, have a bite, and then to the train again. Pleasant ride home with a very thin young moon in the afterglow. Letters from Walter & Grace. Answer several letters.

Monday, Jan. 12, 1891

. . . Write to Walter and send things in to the Nationalist man and Mrs. Howe.⁵ Call on Miss Lyman and Mrs. Walker. Read them "The Unexpected." Home all serene. Write in the evening—send copies of poems to Current Literature by Mrs. Athertons request. . . .

Tuesday, Jan. 13, 1891

. . . Kate Field today with a story of mine, and I understand the thing has come out in the Christian Register.

Wednesday Jan. 14, 1891

I am beginning to feel *well*. . . . Take two P.M. train to the Raymond and rehearse for "Popping the Question."

Friday, Jan. 16, 1891

Arrange costume for our performance this evening. Mrs. Mitchell invites me to a lecture on Oxford by a Bostonian lady, but I don't go. Leave Kate to supper at Mrs. Rust's. Dr. Channing undertakes to put her to bed and spend the evening here. Take the 5.25 for the Raymond with enormous bundles. Have a gorgeous dinner there, and the play passes off very well indeed. My costume still brings down the house. Home early and comfortable in a carriage[.]

Sunday, Jan. 18, 1891

. . . [G]ive "Our Opportunity" to the Nationalists. It seemed to me to fall rather flat; but that was because of the enthusiastic reception in town. They don't applaud much out here. . . .

Wednesday, Jan. 21, 1891

6.45. Finish lecture in good season. . . . It was a great success. Some of the women cried, and they actually clapped at times! Then an attempt at organizing—lots of enthusiasm, and introductions without number. Also an engagement there for the next Wednesday fortnight, and one in Rosedale to be arranged. Also $6.20 in cash! That is worthwhile. And money more fairly earned I never saw—free gift for well-appreciated [*msm*]est work. It does me good.

Monday, Jan. 26, 1891

. . . Mrs. Kunst calls, brings back two Mss. and begs for more. I give her several. She also asks an autograph. Three letters from Walter with good news after all about the N. Y. Ex. Write to him. . . . I'm tired; but happy, owing to my increasing prospects and Walter's new success.

Sunday, Feb. 1, 1891

. . . Mrs. Carr ran in and borrowed a lot of my mss. to read to her people— said she would have a "Stetson afternoon."

Monday, Feb. 2, 1891

Clean up a little & bathe. Miss Knight calls, leaves papers, and calmly deposits five dollars—as if it was in the hat she said! Very lucky too, for Mrs. Rum appeared in the morning and took 75 cts I owed her, so I had but one quarter left! . . .

Sunday, Feb. 8, 1891

. . . Lecture to 1st Nat. Club in L. A. on "Nationalism & Love." Great enthusiasm. . . . Sit up till 2.30 talking to Mary. . . .

Monday, Feb. 9, 1891

. . . Am kept up talking, until 3 A.M.!

Tues. Feb. 17, 1891

. . . Take 4 P.M. train in town with Kate. go to Mrs. Howe's, 1216 San Pedro St. Good diner & good bed. Speak in the evening, after several others, at an entertainment in honor of Susan B. Anthony's birthday. They kept me till the last because they said "people will wait for *her*!" Rainy & unpleasant. . . .

Saturday, Feb. 21, 1891

Scurry about and get in town by 10 o'clock train. . . . Home on 4 P.M. with Dr. Channing. Find that Uncle Edward and Nellie have arrived at the Dexters. Go there and an enthusiastically received. It does me *good* to see them. Stay to dinner, with Kate.
Uncle Edward says—"You are getting to be a famous woman my dear! Says "Similar Cases" is a great "campaign document." Kate has an earache . . . .

Sunday, Feb. 22, 1891

Bad night owing to poor Kate. Wash dishes, etc, go to the Channings. Uncle Edward holds a service there, as it storms hard. I skip off to . . . lecture in Los Angeles leaving Kate to go to the Masters later. A horridly wet day, but a very good time none the less. Give them "Nationalism & Religion," with a good reception. Graybeards come up afterwards, to shake hands and pay their compliments. I rejoice in the respect of men—old men—for my sexes sake. . . .

Tuesday, Feb. 24, 1891

. . . I am feeling miserably since Sat. night—Kate's earache! Then the wet Sunday in town, and the sense of responsibility of various kinds.

Saturday, Feb. 28, 1891

. . . The mail has come—a whole week of it! Walter has been sick—at Dr. Knights. Much better off so than had I been there.

Sunday, Mar. 1, 1891

Hurry and go in town to hear Uncle Edward preach. . . . Great crowd. . . . Uncle E. speaks splendidly. I am so *glad* to have him.

Tuesday, Mar. 3, 1891

Try to rest but am too tired. Lie about all day helplessly. . . . I am "lower" than I have been since before Xmas.

Thursday, Mar. 5, 1891

. . . [I]n the evening we drive to the temple and hear Uncle Edward speak to the Nationalists—and others. Also we hear Prof. Henri Fairweather—who insisted on thrusting himself in to gain the advantage of the crowd & advertisement. He speaks and sings without break—a good voice and no ideas. Uncle E. made a delightful address.

The Nationalists want to give me a "benefit," as they thought I was going away for good!

Friday, Mar. 6, 1891

. . . Reception P.M. I find myself quite a small lioness—*very* small. A pale tea. Then we carry Uncle E. to the church, where he has a reception. Am very tired.

Tuesday, Mar. 10, 1891

Read Olive Schreiner's "Heaven" and cry like a child.[6]

Am very wretched indeed—tired that is, weak and nervous. . . .

Monday Mar. 16, 1891

["]1st Semi-Annual Convention of the Pacific Coast Woman's Press Association." I attend in the morning, get enrolled, and then go with Kate and get a Turkish bath. Kate has a little one too. Attend in the afternoon, and in the evening, read my paper on "The Coming Woman." A very marked success. . . .

Tuesday, Mar. 17, 1891

Convention again. . . . Sit through the afternoon with much weariness. Again in the evening, and recite "The Obstacles" and "A Conservative." Much applause.

Friday, Mar. 20, 1891

Father calls. . . . Dr. gives me stryclinia and Maltine and cotton wool. Read "Yellow WallPaper" to the family in the evening.

Saturday, Mar. 21, 1891

Pack Kate's things and see various people. Begin to feel a very little better. . . . Go across the ferries with Kate in the afternoon and see her off—she goes to the ranch with Mrs. Swett and Mr. Parkhurst. I find myself really grieved to part with her—lonely at not finding the golden head on my pillow.

Wednesday, April 1, 1891

. . . Up at 6.30 and go with Mrs. Parkhurst to visit the Almshouse. Mr. and Mrs. Weaver, the superintendant and his wife, meet us with buggies, and we are well fed and entertained all day. 800 paupers in that asylum. All was neat and well-kept, every reasonable measure taken, but O————! a man without legs, a monkey-man—brainless but happy—an idiot girl of thirteen helpless as in [*sic*] infant, an old woman dying alone in a "ward" unconscious, and with no one even to brush the flies from her face; a girl blind, dumb, deaf, and an idiot; a parchment-faced old man, tied in a chair and moaning endlessly—lunatic; and without, the steady fresh [*msm*] wind, great hills, trees, [*msm*]ers clear blue sky and green [*msm*].

Sun. April 12, 1891

A long quiet restful day in the great outdoors, with Mr. Parkhurst and Kate. Such glorious beauty and peace! It did me years of good.

Thurs. April 16, 1891

Meet father at Mrs. Parkhurst's at about 10 A.M. He brings Kate various small things, once his and some candy. I consult with him about the manager and the contract. Mrs. Waterman arrives with that paper, and with father's approval I sign it. Lunch there. Arrange further with Mrs. Waterman and then come to Mrs. Prescotts again. Sit down peacefully and write long letters to Grace and Walter as to my new and brilliant prospects. My contract is for less than a month, and gives me fifty dollars a lecture.

Tuesday, April 21, 1891

Feel pretty well. Write to Walter, and a note to Mr. Ray. . . . Then go down town on a few errands, and lo! A lithograph in all the windows "The Eminent Lecturess"! A fine portrait too, from the Cosmopolitan photograph. . . .

Sun. April 26, 1891

Bathe Kate and self. Mr. & Mrs. Lemmon come to dinner. They are botanists, very interesting. Miss Ina Coolbrith comes also.[7] Talk and read to them all the afternoon. Then take a walk with Kate, very beautiful, down to the grass-grown willowshaded banks of "the lake" so called, and along wellkept streets of elegant houses.

Tues. April 28, 1891

Am sick all day, with nausea. Lecture in the evening, my first under Mr. Ray's management. I was very weak and had to sit mostly, and leave the stage once. A very thin cold uninterested audience.

I gave about the same reading which met such applause on Fri. April 10th in S. F. But it fell flat. Get twenty dollars, with promise of more.

Wed. April 29, 1891

. . . Go to see Bernhardt in "Cleopatra,"[8] a theatre party invited by Mr. Gaden—the "Feminine Vanity" man. I give him a autograph copy of that poem, illustrated in pen-and-ink.

Am much impressed with the power of the great actress, and surprised by her appearance of youth, and the *cleanness* of her acting. It gave me the impression of a singlehearted deep and ardent love—more love than passion in our disparted sense.

I noticed with all her passionate freedom of gesture that all movement was *above the waist. . . .*

Tuesday, May 12, 1891

. . . Call from A Miss Knapp, newspaper woman, also from Madam Wendte and Mrs. Moffat[9] (sister of "Mark Twain") I go to S. F. with Kate, call on father at the Bohemian Club, and go meet Mr. Ray at his office. I demand prepayment for the lecture Saturday or else I don't give it. . . .

Saturday, May 16, 1891

Go to Pub. Library and arrange for tonights readings. . . . Go to Alameda with Mrs. Prescott, meet Mr. Ray and his wife, but come back without speaking. He does not pay me the fifty dollars in advance as agreed and I will not speak without.

Sunday, May 17, 1891

Miss Knapp calls for me early, and I go with her (and Kate) to Irvington to spend the day. We drive, deliciously, dining at Sunol. Home late and very tired.

Thursday, May 21, 1891

. . . Go and lunch with Miss Knapp. I love her————. . . . 4 P.M. boat home. Go to Mrs. McChesneys to dinner and meet three friends of hers, teachers. I feel better—thanks to Miss Knapp.

Saturday, May 23, 1891

In town early. See about my printing. Call on Miss Knapp, wait, leave note. . . . Do some shopping. Meet Miss Knapp and lunch with her. . . . Go read proof at printers. Take a Turkish bath. Get circulars and tickets and 5.30 boat, Miss Knapp also. She stays here all night.

Sunday, May 31, 1891

Talk and read with Miss Knapp. She goes on the 3.30. Kate & I walk over with her to E. Oakland—Train back. Then I leave Kate and call on Miss Ina Coolbrith and the McChesneys. Go to bed with Kate and sleep well.

Monday, June 1, 1891

Go in town on 8.30 boat with Miss Knapp. Go to her office, breakfast with her, then get tickets for Thursday—steamer, Pomona. Back late to lunch. Dr. Kellogg has been to see Kate, who got badly poisoned Saturday. She and her husband and sister come to dinner, also Miss Knapp who stays all night.

Tuesday, June 2, 1891

A wretched night, only made bearable by Miss Knapps tender helpfulness. She is a dear woman. A dreary day, write some letters. Go to Dr. Kelloggs with Kate P.M. & get more sugar pills. Get Kate a pair of shoes & a whirligig. Go over to meet Miss Knapp & cross the bay with her—Dear heart! Go to bed with Kate, and sleep some, thanks to Dr. K.

Wednesday, June 3, 1891

A good night. Feel tolerably well. write a little. Go over and lunch with Miss Knapp, and take a cable ride. Come back feeling well, and write part of an article on "The Dressmaker." Miss Knapp suddenly reappears, just a call. . . .

Thursday, June 4, 1891

Another good night. Write solid essay on "The Reaction of Work."—2500 words. Feel well. Go over at night and meet Miss Knapp—after a long talk with Dr. Kellogg in the forenoon—and bring her here to dinner. Then we go over the bay again, meet Mrs. L. H. Smith, and call on Mrs. Sperry. Then a little spree at Swain's. Then home on the 10.45 narrow gauge boat—a calm delicious night, warm, starlit, with the light-engirdled bay all smooth, and we two happy together. She spends the night.

Friday, June 5, 1891

Go over on early boat with Miss Knapp. . . . Call on Miss Ballard, a girl sick with rheumatic gout, typewriting the whilst most bravely. Meet Miss Knapp again, and lunch. Take cable ride. Come home on 2.30 boat and have a nice nap. Miss Knapp calls just before supper—for a few moments.

Sunday, June 7, 1891

Pack! Hard days work. . . . Miss Knapp near supper time. We are very happy together.

Monday, June 8, 1891

Miss K. off on the 8.30. . . . Miss Knapp comes down to the boat—after all—to my joy. Kate and I stand proudly in the bow till we clear the gate. Then she falls sick and I also, and we "seek the seclusion that a cabin grants." Keep comfortable by lying still. No lunch but some lovely cherries Miss K. brought us ere starting. No supper but some hard tack & cheese.

Begin divorce proceeding
Thursday, June 11, 1891

. . . Call on Dr. Lummis and ask advice about divorce. Get it. Get letter of introduction to nice lawyer and go to him. He undertakes the case. It is to cost only fifty dollars, and take about three months. Then go to Dr. Follansbee's. Am not at all badly off inside. . . .

Monday, June 15, 1891

. . . Go in town on the 8 A.M. See lawyer. Case looks bad. Manifest collusion, fear of the judges quashing the case, etc. Call on Dr. Lummis—twice. She is to see the prohabate judge and sound him. Go to Dr. Follansbees. . . . Home tired. Rest. Mrs. Mitchell & Mrs. Wotkyns call after supper and Dr. Channing also. Then I write to my love.

Friday, June 19, 1891

. . . Walk up to the P.O. before dinner, & get three letters from Miss Knapp, one from Grace, and the negatives for Kate. Spend most of the afternoon on the beach with the children, and get *awfully* used up. Another letter from Delle in the evening, and the blessed photographs. Letter in that too—five in one day! Write to her in the evening.

Tuesday, June 23, 1891

Up betimes, and go to L. A. & Pasadena on numerous erands. Successful day though rather hard. Read poetry to Hattie in the evening and makelove to her.

Thursday, June 25, 1891

A very well behaved day. Write some 18 pages "copy," bathe with Kate, Nap P.M. Talk to Hattie, go fishing with Kate, write to Walter and Delle. tired, rather.

Friday, June 26, 1891

Up at 6 or so. In town on 7.25. Call on Mr. Davis; he returned *all* the money I paid & am introduced to Mr. Swanwicke who is to take my case. He seems an able man. Go to the "Friday morning Club," and read my paper on "The Real Woman" with much effect. $5.00. Go to lunch with Dr. Lummis, and home with her for a hasty toilet. Then to see Mr. Swanwicke, and an interesting talk we had. His opinion is favorable but not assured. Pay him $25.00 on acct—the same sum due at my convenience later. Also ten dollars for "costs." . . . *Very* tired—to tired to write to Delle.

Thursday, July 2, 1891

Up at 5 nearly. Work hard all the morning, with a few rests, fixing the house for Miss Knapp. Arrange bedroom, dining room, and kitchen; transferring all Kate's playthings, and putting a cot bed in the kitchen for her. . . . Rest P.M. & go down town with Kate to get fireworks. Feel rather badly at night, and take a cup of tea. . . .

Friday, July 3, 1891

My 31st birthday. Do a good mornings work housecleaning. 4 letters from Miss Knapp. She cannot come till the 13th or 14th. I am rather relieved because there was so much work to be done in these few days. Rest and write to her in the afternoon and evening. . . .

Thursday, July 9, 1891

A good day. Write article "Masculine Feminine and Human" for Kate Field's W. . . . Copy article and make ready to send. Rest some. . . .

Friday, July 10, 1891

Another good day. Write two short articles, "Time to Read for the House-keeper," and "The Home"—some 3000 words. Go downt [*sic*] street in the afternoon, after resting and writing to Delle—last letters before she leaves. . . .

Tuesday, July 14, 1891*

My girl comes. Up fairly early. Arrange things, clean and nice and take 1 P.M. train in. Miss Knapp arrives by the 2.20. We go to the Hollanbec to dine and out on the 4 P.M. Have a simple banquet and I go to the tableaux. They are a success. Home a little after eleven. We have a bite and go to bed.

Saturday, July 18, 1891

Delle not well. Stays in bed nearly all day. Take a moonlight ride, first with Kate, then only each other.

Thurs. July 23, 1891

A good day. Write some 1800 words on "The Sense of Duty in Women," copy "How Human are we" and part of the other. Hot day. Lunch and dine at the Dexters as usual. Letter from Delle.

Friday, July 24, 1891

103 in my parlor, 130 out on the path in the sun. Hottest day known in years. I like it. Write short article on "The Shape of Her Dress," and copy about 1000 words I guess. . . . Two dear letters from Delle. Write to her in the morning, also now. 97 here on my table at 9 P.M.—tisn't the lamp either. Horse car rail *curved up from the ground* by the heat! Car went over it and then it curved up again!

Saturday, Aug. 15, 1891

. . . . Ask Mrs. Scoville to lend me fifty dollars for three months on a seventy five dollar security in lace—she wouldn't!

Sunday, Sept. 6, 1891

Write on "The Human Ideal" for first lecture. Awfully hot. letter from Delle. . . .
Last evening in the little cottage. I have lived much here.
I love the place—Pasadena, and mean earnestly to return, build, and live.[10]
We will see.
But this home I shall probably not see again—it will be torn down.

Monday, Sept. 7, 1891

Burn letters etc. Wash dishes, clear out kitchen closet, etc. etc. Pack two boxes of books. Go in to rehearsal in the evening. Out 9.25.
Go over to Mrs. Dexter's to stay till I go.

Friday, Sept. 18, 1891

Arrive in San Francisco at 9.15 A.M. Delight [11] waiting on the wharf. All come over together to this nice boarding home—1673 Grove St., Mrs. Barrows. Very pleasant. I have a lovely room with Delle, and mother one with Kate. . . .

Wednesday, Sept. 23, 1891

Write verses—"We, as Women" in the morning, sew lace in Delle's gown, etc. Nap. All hands go over in the evening to the open meeting of P.C.W.P.A. I give one poem, Hand in Hand, and Delle closes the evening with a fine speech.

Thursday, Sept. 24, 1891

Unpack all my boxes & get bookcase and desk fixed before Delle comes— room looks lovely.

Sunday, Sept. 27, 1891

A very pleasant day. Arrange pictures in our room in the morning, and then Delight, Kate, & I, with Puss [12] the lovely mare, go out in the country and ride—all of us, taking turns. . . .

Friday, Oct. 2, 1891

Take my first ride, alone, on Puss. She takes me swiftly back to the stable, and I have no objections to it! . . . Glad to get back to Delight.

Wednesday, Oct. 7, 1891

A bad night. Delle not feeling well. Arrange Mss., trying to get hold of the situation, write "A Mercantile Skunk"! Also "The War-Skunk.", apropos of Ambrose Bierce of the Examiner.

Thursday, Oct. 29, 1891

Still very tired. Have nap after breakfast & feel better. Write letters. Go to Dr. Kellogg's P.M. She says I put myself back 3 weeks by my exhaustion of yesterday. . . . A lovely evening with Delle. God bless her!

Friday, Nov. 13, 1891

. . . Mother & Mrs. Barrows go to a "recital," Delle and I to a People's party Ratification meeting. Some fine speaking. I am incensed by the "we, as women" assumptiom, and being requested to speak, give them the poem of that name. Tremendous applause, and a determined encore. [*msm*] Enjoyed the evening much.

Tuesday, Nov. 17, 1891

. . . . Delle and I spend a happy evening over a constitution for the new Nationalist Club, or, as I have called it "The New Nation Club"; she gave me "Roberts Rules of Order," and we work hard.

Wednesday, Nov. 25, 1891

. . . Mr. & Mrs. Salzer (Nationalists) call, and invite me to preach, Sunday evenings, a little group guaranteeing $5.00, and the Gilson's willing to let Hamilton Hall for half that. I agree to try it for a few Sundays, for that assured $2.50.

I am called to the Ministry

Thursday, Nov. 26, 1891
{Thanksgiving Day.}

I am exceeding thankful. For Delle, mother here, Kate, improved health, outlook in work—and last night's honor. . . .

Thursday, Dec. 10, 1891

Go to lunch with Kate at Mrs. Percy's. An awful experience. Like climbing a greased pole. I grew nervous, tired, incapable of formulating an idea save such as I knew were unpleasant to her. Button holes were my only satisfaction—I made seven I think. Home exhausted, wretched. Letter from Walter enclosing one from Grace—reproaches at the delayed case. Delle cheers and comforts me [*msm*]

Thursday, Dec. 17, 1891

All sick in the house—dismal enough. Get letters off & my picture for Walter[.] Go over and lunch with Delle & get things in Chinatown—she does. . . .

Tuesday, Dec. 22, 1891

Down town with Kate and shop. Home tired [*msm*] Finish Besant's "St. Katharine by The Tower," a most miserable book—utterly without excuse for being that I can see.

Mr. Ernest Himes comes for me in great distress to go with him—help him—try to see his wife—she has left him. I go to court with him—he had got her there on writ of *habeas corpus*—but he could not prove she was detained against her will. Ride a little with him and try to brace him up.
He and his brother come up in the evening.

Christmas Day —
Friday, Dec. 25, 1891

Celebrate by a fit of hysterics in the morning, and am laid up thereby. Delle arranges room. Mr. White and Miss Diezmann to dinner—good dinner. Afterward the distribution of gifts. Kate much impressed by her first handsome doll, procurred by grandma from grandpa—a beauty.
All amused by their small [*msm*]kes. Play whist.
Delle gave me a beautiful seal leather sermon holder, with paper cut to match, a new journal like this and various other things. Dear loving heart!

Saturday, Dec. 26, 1891

Stay in bed late. Dr. Kellogg in. She doubts if I can stand the strain of our present family arrangement much longer.
Write some sermon on "Pain."

Sunday, Dec. 27, 1891

Still pretty weak. Delle nurses me all day. Write entire new sermon—"The Human Will." Give it in the evening.

Thursday, Dec. 31, 1891 [13]

Delle not well, and I have another hysterical attack and sleep ill. Feel wretchedly in the morning. Go with Delle way over to the Park, & see the elephants and things. Did us good. Get splendid dinner at New York Kitchen. Delle takes papers and comes home. She has a nap. Play chess with her. Then she works in the evening. We figure on the advantages of moving into the country and conclude to do it. I am by no means well. Two fits of wretchedness in a week is bad. Still the year shows much gain. It is the anxiety etc. about mother that is wearing me now. That must be borne. May next year help more!
God help me!

[1892]

Friday, Jan. 1, 1892

Noise and fireworks celebrate the birth of the New Year. I have waited for it as usual and hope to do right in this coming more than in that past. . . . Delle home early. A splendid dinner at 4. Then a pleasant sleepy evening *en famille*. Bed ere 10.

Monday, Jan. 4, 1892

Mother has an attack like incipient paralysis. Is much frightened. Dr. K. gives us all medicine, including Kate! I go to the city. Mrs. McChesney on boat. Get Delle and go to special meeting of P.C.W.P.A. Very amusing. Home, dinner, mother some better, go to 1st semi-annual meeting of New Nation Club. Elect officers. . . .

Friday, Jan. 8, 1892*

Kate not very well. Go to see Dr. K. about her. We must arrange to get mother to the Hospital soon. Home & write, "The Cart Before The Horse," copy poems to send Bellamy[14] etc.

Saturday, Jan. 16, 1892

Write some on address for the Churches. Call for Mrs. Dewey and go with her to a Farmers Alliance meeting in our hall. A basket lunch, and pleasant time generally. Am introduced to ever so many, and make a few remarks. Take a cableride. Go again with Delle in the evening and speak a little. The first time I have spoken—not read. Do not make a success of it, nor enjoy it, but mean to try again.

Monday, Jan. 18, 1892

. . . Write all the afternoon—"How our surroundings Affect Us." Go with Delle to the reception given to the visiting delegates of the International Leauge [*sic*] by the P.C.W.P.A. . . . Kate Field is very nice to me, and we sup together. A pleasant evening. See Mrs. Frank Leslie Wilde and her husband. He is a brother of Oscar Wilde.

Friday, Jan. 29, 1892

Call on Dr. Coyle P.M. to see about addressing his church. Found furnished rooms on Webster st.—like 'em. . . .

Monday, Feb. 1, 1892

Feel pretty well. Begin paper on "The Economic Side of Marriage." Get used up over Kate. . . .

Friday, Feb. 5, 1892

Up early and finish packing. Mat comes at 9.15 or so. Move over to 1258 Webster St., three furnished rooms. A very pleasant change. . . . Have a *lovely* nap. Meet Delle, and get a good little supper. . . .

Monday, Feb. 8, 1892

Delle sick, stays at home. I take Kate to her first school—Miss Wyman's on Alice St. A lovely girl, the teacher, and just a pleasant little home school. Kate likes it. . . .

Monday, Feb. 29, 1892

. . . 9 people in the house—8 to cook for! I can't have mother yet!

Wednesday, Mar. 2, 1892

Am now doing finely with the cooking. Have a splendid appetite and feel well. . . . Delle rather uncomfortable, but able to stand the crowd for a season.

Friday, March 11, 1892

Kate comes down with Measles! . . .

Sunday, Mar. 13, 1892

Universalist Church 11 A.M. My first real church service. I did the whole thing, and enjoyed it. Only the prayer seemed a little difficult—I don't believe in regular public prayer. Good attendance, very. They were pleased I think.

Monday, Mar. 14, 1892

Wrote, today and tomorrow, lecture for Unity Club. long, good. Measles galore, no sleep, no regular meals, housework allee samee.

Tuesday, Mar. 15, 1892

. . . Delle's birthday!
   trimmed a hat for her, and a few small etcs

Wednesday, Mar. 16, 1892

Just work and

Thursday, Mar. 17, 1892

Measles.

Friday, Mar. 18, 1892

The chick makes

Saturday, Mar. 19, 1892

a good recovery.

Wednesday, Mar. 23, 1892

Kate's [7th] birthday. Go shopping with her in the morning, and take an excursion on Merrit Lake and its willow-hung banks in the afternoon.

Saturday, April 2, 1892

Mother moves in. She likes her room and bed and board, seems very comfortable. . . .
A servant was to have come, but fortunately got a better place—*much* to my relief.

Friday, May 27, 1892

Signed contract with Mrs. Palmer for stove & carpets. Have paid her up to May 15th—$70.00 in full to date & have her receipt. Am to pay her the rest—$175 before Dec. 31st 1892 or forfeit all.

Letter from Grace.
Saturday, May 28, 1892

Have been unable to keep this. Am unable now, but must get to work.

Tuesday, Aug. 2, 1892

Mrs. Howe arrives from Los Angeles. Got her a room on Franklin St.

Monday, Sept. 5, 1892

Labor Day. Kate, Mrs. Howe & I ride in carriage with the President of the Day in the labor procession. P.M. We go the park (Shellmound) where there is a picnic, and I read the essay on labor. Get a medal therefor—said to be 40.00 worth. . . .

Tuesday, Sept. 13, 1892

See Dr. K. She concludes to do nothing for me at present. Says I had better break down honestly now than be bolstered up and break more extensively later. A wise physician.
Delle is not well. . . .

Friday, Sept. 16, 1892

Hattie moves in. Bless her heart! We all love her and wear her out with many services.

Friday, Sept. 23, 1892

Convention, lots of work these three days, but good effect in all ways.

Monday, Sept. 26, 1892

Hattie has to go back for a week or so to pack her furniture.
We miss her.

Friday, Sept. 30, 1892

Up till 12.30 watching mother & writing in my room.
Doctor—
Mother's last day down stairs—I *think*. About now anyway.[15]

Monday, Oct. 3, 1892

Doctor. Mother still very weak and low.
Delle goes off on some trip.
Mother has paid my milkbill, & Kate's school bill.

Tuesday, Oct. 18, 1892

Mrs. Haydon, of Missouri, comes on a weeks trial to do our work.

Tuesday, Oct. 25, 1892

. . . Am feeling first rate these days—full of plans to write, sew, build, etc.
The creative instinct rising and promising well for work when the strain
is off.

Sunday, Nov. 6, 1892

Mr. Edmund Russell calls in the evening—stays till 11.30 and we send him
off for his last boat. Very enjoyable evening. I made a lovely robe out of an old
shawl for the occasion—worn over a slim pongee.*

Tuesday, Nov. 15, 1892

Mrs. Haydon goes, praise the Lord!
Mrs. Moore and small daughter appear in her stead—praise the Lord again!
(might as well do it always)

Thursday, Nov. 17, 1892

Hattie comes back, bless her heart. Looks pretty well. The Moores do well.

Thursday, Nov. 24, 1892

Mrs. McChesney gives us a turkey—they being invited out. Splendid turkey.
The day all goes wrong however, no porridge, breakfast unsatisfactory, mother
very wretched. . . .
Ina Coolbrith our guest of honor. A dear woman.

Thursday, Dec. 1, 1892

Ina Coolbrith brings Joaquin Miller[16] to see me.
   I don't think him great.

Saturday, Dec. 10, 1892

Mrs. Moore & daughter depart—praise the Lord again! She was either drugged
or cracked—a lunatic. I have now secured a nurse for Monday—and am to
do my own work for a while.

Miss Bennett comes from S.F.—to nurse mother. I experience a great sense of relief and go out to ride on the cable car.

Sunday, Dec. 11, 1892

Mrs. Bennet proves totally inadequate, and has a sick headache which induces her to sit in the kitchen all day.

Monday, Dec. 12, 1892

Mrs. Bennett departs, Mrs. Alban comes, and proves a delight—kind, willing, helpful, pleasant—we all like her.

I am cook and the others help.
I go over to the business meeting of W. P. A.

Tuesday, Dec. 13, 1892

Go with Delle, Mr. Tod & the Press Club, and James Whitcomb Riley, to visit Joaquin Miller.—or else it was—today* [Wednesday, Dec. 14].
Joaquin Miller called again the night before.

Sunday, Dec. 18, 1892

News in the Chronicle of Walter's application for divorce.

Examiner man comes for an interview and makes a mess of it of course,[17]

Call man comes too, and does it well.

Tuesday, Dec. 20, 1892

I meet Hamlin Garland at a club lecture in S. F.[18] He speaks, well. I read a poem.
Mrs. Alban has to go home, and her sister Mrs. Wright takes her place. Another jewel. These women are the first I have had who were wholly helpful.
Editor of the Stockton Mail heard me last night and wrote for the paper to print whole. [*msm*] Did so.

Wednesday, Dec. 21, 1892

It appears that I am sicker than I thought. The doctor says "Scrofula." That name strikes very cold.

Saturday, Dec. 24, 1892

Mr. Andrews, Socialist, calls, as a committee. He had heard that I was "destitute," and was sent to offer assistance[.] Good for my people!

Sunday, Dec. 25, 1892

We have a fine Xmas dinner but I am unable to cook it. Delle & Hattie do it all.
I am very weak.

Mother is low too, just now.

Tree at 5. Miss Coolbrith in for a while. A pleasant Xmas after all. I faring best of all under my many gifts.

Wednesday, Dec. 28, 1892

Gave out in the morning. Rode on cable car with Hattie. All mixed up this week.

Sick—sicker.

Saturday, Dec. 31, 1892

Toil about the house, "doing with painful industry what others scorn to do with ease." Very weak. Nap in the afternoon—little one. Endeavor to arrange acct. books for the year.

It has been a year of great and constantly increasing trouble. Poverty, illness, heartache, household irritation amounting to agony, Care, anxiety, grief, and shame for many many failures [*msm*]. My last love proves even [*msm*] as others. Out of it all I ought surely [*msm*] to learn final detachment [*msm*] from all personal concerns [*msm*].

The divorce is pending [*msm*] undeclared. Mother [*msm*]. . . . There is only to [*msm*]. . . .*

[1893]

Sunday, Jan. 1, 1893

12. The bells and horns, the steady booming of one big whistle, the scattering explosions, announce the new year. Hattie & Delle and I are sitting up in Delle's room. We have just had a rere-supper with delicious coffee. D. has gone outside I think. Both have gone now.

> May last year's misery be less
> And new strength through me flow,
> More power to see and to express
> The blessed truths I know.

And—a little less pain if you please! I can do more work if I suffer less. . . .

Wednesday, Jan. 4, 1893

. . . Joy in life—Get up! It is time to begin! Plenty of time ahead—glorious world—let's start

Sunday, Jan. 8, 1893

. . . Begin lecture on Socialism and Morality. . . . Mr. Griffies[1] of The Call, with wife and child visit us in the afternoon. An earnest genuine little man—something like Walter in build. Plump calm pleasant wife, sturdy

little girl. I get desperate tired with the conflicting voices—He—she—
Delle—Kate—their baby & I. . . .

Monday, Jan. 16, 1893

. . . Spent most of the day writing and arranging for address on city politics.
Mr. Hough comes for me and we all go. Hattie, Delle, & I, after a grand row
with Delle. She is in a wretched condition of health[.]

The evening was strange—a crooked hall over a saloon, mixed audience from
babies to greybeards, mixed program, and a long one.

I was nominated as school director, but found to be unqualified on account of
limited residence.

Thursday, Jan. 19, 1893

. . . Write and send off some stuff to the Stockton Mail. A tired miserable day,
increasing weariness and irritability. . . .

Friday, Jan. 20, 1893

. . . My back is worse again—the recent trouble.

Saturday, Jan. 21, 1893

. . . Miss Coolbrith, the Griffies, & Mr. Russell spend the evening. Mrs. Dar-
row and her grandson call, with mother's burial robe.

Monday, Jan. 23, 1893

Write *"Through This."* [19] . . .

Sunday, Jan. 29, 1893

Up at three with Kate, who has whooping cough it appears. This too!
Delle gets me some coffee and breakfast for all of us. I write "The Modern
Mother"—18 pages of it. Mrs. Alban in. Miss Coolbrith also. I take Kate to
the doctors to announce the complaint.

Tuesday, Jan. 31, 1893

Write a little. . . . Hattie & I go out with Puss. Delle returns in high feather.
Is detailed to go to Hawaii and interview the Queen—apropos of proposed
annexation to U. S. She and I go to see "The Old Homestead." Good.

Have done about fifteen pieces of salable work this month—three lectures,
three poems, nine articles of one sort or another. Received $40.00 therefor so
far. Fair work for an overworked invalid.

Friday, Feb. 3, 1893

Go over to see Delle off, Hattie & I. Dine together at Wilson's. Lots of folk, at
the boat, P. A. women and Call men. Then Hattie & I trot about, and I buy
shoes—$5.00 beauties. Almost a year now I've worn shoes that hurt.

Sunday, Feb. 5, 1893

Write letters and such. Go to hear Cyrus Feed with Hattie—teacher of Kore-shanitz. An ordinary person, unimpressive, illogical. How pitifully it speaks our unhappy condition that we are so ready to hear such persons!

Mrs. Durfee gives me a hot bath & massage—fine.

Unless I learn my desired virtues *now* I never shall. Difficulties are nothing. The power to live rightly is outside of these difficulties. . . .

Monday, Feb. 6, 1893

Get letter from Carrie Hazard with 25.00 & check from K. F. W. for 5.50. . . .

Tuesday, Feb. 7, 1893

Feel pretty well considering—mother had a fairly comfortable night. The work drags however, and by afternoon I am very tired. Call on Ina Coolbrith. Hattie comes there and we go to the Pub. Li. Very tired.

Friday, Feb. 10, 1893

Finish "Steps in Civilization," good. Sit with mother. Must stay in now to help her in and out of bed—Mrs. Wright is no longer able to manage alone.
*Get notification of appointment on Advisory Council of Woman's Branch of World's Congress at the World's Fair. I wish I could go personally. Write answer.

Wednesday, Feb. 22, 1893

Begin article on "The California Beauty Contest."

Thursday, Feb. 23, 1893

. . . The Examiner sends me a man, Mr. Tod, to interview me on my views on the Marriage Question—the decrease of marriage. I refuse on the ground of the Examiner's reputation—will not write for the paper. He begs, he tries to fool me into conversation, he argues, he offers to pay me, he threatens co-vertly—I succeed in getting rid of him.

Am exhausted by the contest, however.

Tuesday, Feb. 28, 1893

Mother comfortable but very weak & low. . . .

Sit up till 1, and then sleep in clothes.

Warm bath in the morning. . . .

Friday, Mar. 3, 1893

Am hard set by this "cold." The ominous eruption on my back has "gone in," to try the lungs perhaps. Sit up till near 2 with mother—The nurse gets 4 hours sleep. Write short powerful paper—"The Sex Question Answered" for the World's Congress. Nothing seems to seriously affect my power to write. This paper has been done in short laborious efforts during these wretched days, and finished last night by mother's deathbed.

She is very low now—going fast. . . .

Saturday, Mar. 4, 1893

A little broken sleep—I cough wakefully and the constant moving overhead is arousing. Get letter asking me to give a lecture to 1st Xtian Church in S. F. Of course. . . .

Either today or tomorrow write short paper for Mrs. Prescott, giving reasons for assuming woman's dependence to be conducive to sexual immorality. I close by saying "The essential indecency of the dependence of one sex upon the other for a living is in itself sexual immorality."

Monday, Mar. 6, 1893

Mother sinking all day. The laudanum ceases to take effect by nightfall and her cough grows worse. Dr. Kellogg in about 7.30 can find no pulse. Orders chloroform to quiet the cough. I go out with Hattie & get it. Give it to her till after 11. Every time she rouses it is only to cough terribly. Try and rest a little then but am soon up again.

She passed away at 2.10, very quietly. The nurse and I wash and dress her and clear up the room—all done before 5. Then we try to eat—try to sleep. I don't succeed.

Tuesday, Mar. 7, 1893*

Mother died this morning at 2.10. I lie down at 5.20 & rise at seven—I could not sleep. Get the breakfast and then go the city, stopping at Dr. Kelloggs, an undertakers, & the Enquirer Office. Go to father, to Mr. Worcester, lunch at Mrs. Morses, father again, and home. Mrs. Paulson calls in the evening with migonette.

Father over in the afternoon.

Wednesday, Mar. 8, 1893

. . . Hattie and I go out with Pussie and ask friends to the funeral services. Very scant and short, merely a little reading and less speaking by Mr. Worcester. Some 20 people. . . . The body went away at 7.30. Father was to go south with it—to Los Angeles for cremation.

Tuesday, Mar. 14, 1893

Go to Dr. Kellogg's in the morning. Arrange things in my room in the afternoon. Sleep with Hattie.

Letter from Worthington, took three short essays
"Likes & Dislikes,"
"The Modern Mother,"
"Matters of Opinion"
20.00 for the lot. Wants paper on Crinoline—wants short stories.

Tuesday, Mar. 21, 1893
Spend the morning among the lawyers to no great purpose. . . .

Kate's Birthday.
Thursday, Mar. 23, 1893
Toil and labor for and in Kates party, all day. She has five little girls out of
eight invited and a banquet—cake with candles, etc.
In the evening, Hattie & I go to Reform Conference Meeting. Very interesting
indeed, no nonsense, much good and brief speaking. . . .

Dumbells!
Monday, Mar. 27, 1893
Write powerfully on economic paper. Go to see Dr. Kellogg & read it to her.
Feel *well*. Get patterns of leggings and cut and baste them. Am going to have
a suit of dark green ladies cloth with trousers and leggings and belted tunic.
Go to Economic Section in the evening and "answer questions. Such ques-
tions! Was not as great as I should have been—as wise, as calm, as patient, as
loving. Let my irritation show.
  Such paltry people!
  Such feeble minds!
  Such ignorance!

Sunday, April 2, 1893
Kate is hilarious over Easter. She decorates the table with flowers, and presents
us all with eggs of various sorts. I have a good day. Make up my bed at last,
and arrange linen.

Tuesday, April 4, 1893
Put Delle's room a little in order; and work hard cleaning the north one. Wash
the window! sweep and wipe the floor!! Carry rags to the hospital. Send of
mother's ashes to Cousin Ray, for burial. 1.90 for the little foot-square box, to
Providence. Feel well.
  And tomorrow Delle comes back.—I wonder.
Take hot bath and sleep splendidly. Up once with Miss Sherman however.

Wednesday, April 5, 1893
Up betimes, get breakfast, and off to meet Delle. Steamer in at about 9.20.
The dear girl looks splendidly, and I am absurdly glad to see her. Go with her

to Call office and she with me to see Mrs. Pendleton & Selina Solomons about the Woman's Alliance. Then home. A hasty dinner and she returns to the city. I write a little on tomorrow's paper. Sleep with Delle.

She has been to Hawaii, as special correspondent, apropos of proposed annexation. Has done fine work.

Sunday, April 16, 1893

. . . Kate spends the day alone, for scaring people—startled Hattie most injuriously this morning. . . .

Wednesday, May 3, 1893

Trouble with Delle over the yard—and other things. . . .

Friday, May 5, 1893

Finish Socialist paper. Good. Lunch with Mrs. Morse & read her *"The Socialist Question Answered"* and this last one. Enjoyable afternoon. She gives me a dress, a beautiful Challie, and agrees to have my black silk made at her dressmakers. Dr. Buckle, Dr. Shuey & a Mrs. Cheek come in the evening to hear my sex paper. Read it gladly.

Tuesday, May 9, 1893

Dined with Dr. Kellogg-Lane, discussed the Pschopathic book she lent me, my "case," and, more especially, my paper for the W. C. T. U. S. P. Convention "The Social Question Answered." She arranged to have me read it there. . . .

Thursday, May 11, 1893

All along lately hard times with Delle. Am to exhausted to attend committee meeting to arrange constitution for State Council of Women. Delle goes without me.

. . . Dreadful time with Delle.

Friday, May 12, 1893

. . . Home utterly exhausted—scene with Delle all the way up from ferry to house, in the car.

Sunday, May 14, 1893

. . . Delle comes home. She decides to leave the house. I have so desired since last August—and often asked her to.

Tuesday, May 16, 1893

Delle departs, to stay a week at Dr. Kellogg's preparatory to further settlement elsewhere. . . .

Tuesday, May 23, 1893

Am really sick—worse than for a long time. Read "The Social Question Answered" before Social Purity Convention of W. C. T. U. Fair success. Went to

see Mansfeldt in "Beau Brummel" [20] with Delle, Hattie & Miss Coolbrith.
Fine—a real pleasure. Most delicate yet powerful art.

Wednesday, May 24, 1893

. . . Delle takes me to see Mansfeldt again in "A Parisian Romance." Splendid
acting—long applause. After a dozen bows, he makes a little speech.*

Saturday, May 27, 1893

Somewhere along here go to see Dr. Kellogg. Am pretty low.

Wednesday, May 31, 1893

Arrange for a year & a half's work to clear off debts. [21] Write all down clearly
and stick in my glass. . . .
Ina Coolbrith in in the evening to be cheered up. I do it.

Friday, June 9, 1893

. . . Write "What the People's Party Means." Mrs. Wright goes with me to
Berkeley, where I read the paper written this morning. Small audience, but
good, highschool graduating exercises take the crowd. They were much
pleased and give me ten dollars, greatly to my surprise. It was welcome . . . .

Friday, June 16, 1893.

. . . Mr. Will Clemens [22] calls while I'm out—& goes over to Miss Coolbrith's.
I go over there. Most interesting evening—most interesting man. He speaks
of lodging here.

Saturday, June 17, 1893

. . . Wrote "An Unnatural Mother—2200 wds. Populist convention P.M. See
Delle.

Wednesday, June 28, 1893

Miss White calls and lends me ten dollars. I go down & [pay] gas bill—shut
off this noon if I did not. . . .

Thursday, June 29, 1893

Dreadful news in the paper. The woman murdered in a low saloon in S. F. was
Mrs. Griffes—he of the Call. And he never knew it up to last night—thought
she was visiting friends! [23] Delle and I go over to see him—not there—leave
note. . . .

Saturday, July 1, 1893

. . . Mr. Griffes comes to supper and stays a little. He bears his sorrow most
nobly—wonderfully beyond my widest hopes. It is good to know a man can
be like that. His whole desire is to clear her of all possible blame. There is
none but an inherited taste for liquor and a democratic disposition. He asks
me to say a few words at the funeral tomorrow. I am but too glad.

Sunday, July 2, 1893

Go to funeral by 9.45 train. Undertaker's parlors in S. F. 11 A.M. About 20 there. We get a lot of bright sweet peas—Delle's treat, and cover the coffin with them. A friend plays a little. I speak for some fifteen minutes. Go with party to the Cypress lawn cemetery, and leave the body in the vault until the crematory is done. Mr. Griffes does all he can to keep up the spirits of the party and I help. He wants me to take the child. I wont without him. I am to consider it. Home on 3.15—nothing to eat since 7 save some apricots I got at ferry. Pleasantest funeral I ever attended—more noble spirit in it. Mr. G. is fine. Am very tired. Ina over a little.

Monday, July 3, 1893

. . . $20.00 from father this morning, and there will be no more now. Write to Mary Johnson about Mr. G.'s baby. Joaquin Miller calls. Go out with Kate P.M. . . . Call on Dr. Kellogg. . . . Dr. K. advises me not to take the Griffes[.] Wise woman. I had best keep clear of men.

Wednesday, July 5, 1893

. . . Delle kept little Frances over night. A dear child. I have her to dress. Her father calls for her early. Mrs. Collins daughter for the rent—can't pay. . . . Scribner's Mag. send back "The Wolf at the Door" [*msm*] asking that it be made less fierce and gory. I alter according to suggestion—fairly well too. Mrs. Poulson to see Delle.

Thursday, July 6, 1893.

. . . Delle comes up and spoils the rest of my evening. She and her affection! . . .

Wednesday, July 12, 1893

General disturbance with Delle. She undertakes* to be out within a week—& that Mr. Wetmore [*msm*] shall not come here at all. A Mr. May of Berkeley (Box 468) comes to engage me for a speech on the Nationalization of The Liquor [*msm*] Traffic for Sunday. Miss Coolbrith in. . . .

Thursday, July 13, 1893

. . . Much perturbation in the family owing to Delle. . . . Hattie is become a mere rag because of it all.

Saturday, July 15, 1893

A mighty cleaning day. Chinaman cleans parlor, the two closets, etc. etc. Delle is in and out, departing with her things.
Her behavior has been such as to gradually alienate my affection and turn it to indifference. It is a great relief to have her go. . . .

FIVE

"A prayer of thankfulness for all good things"

July 20, 1893–June 30, 1897

E XCEPT FOR OCCASIONAL bickering, Charlotte and Delle managed to remain
cordial after their parting of the ways. Both were involved in local socialist
organizations, and their paths frequently crossed. Clearly, however, their relationship was over. Delle became involved with a Mr. Wetmore, and Charlotte
threw herself into her work. Throughout the summer of 1893, she wrote poems
for inclusion in her book *In This Our World*, which was published in the fall. She
also sponsored a series of "at home" evenings, to which she invited a number of
guests who would engage in lively discussions about various social, economic,
and ethical issues.

In addition to seeing her poetry in print, another significant event in
Charlotte's life during 1893 was her increased involvement in the Pacific Coast
Women's Press Association. She attended the PCWPA Convention in September,
and on the twenty-second she recorded: "Election morning. I am made President—wear black silk. Mrs. Carr takes Delle & me to lunch, and then me to
have my photograph taken at Tabers. Bless her dear heart!" By October, Charlotte had taken over the management of the *Impress* (formerly the *Bulletin*), a small
literary weekly to which Charlotte contributed articles, poems, editorials, reviews,
and short stories. Her involvement with the *Impress* would consume much of her
time and energy throughout the twenty weeks that it was in print. As usual,
however, Charlotte thrived when she was engaged in work that she found to be
meaningful. Her emotional highs throughout this period resulted from her sense
of accomplishment: "Home happy," the diary routinely notes. And despite reporting that she was "not at all well," on October 16, Charlotte was still left
feeling optimistic after a "Populist parlor meeting" was held at her home. "Sixteen in all. . . . Some good talk and planning done. A feeling of purpose and hope."

In February 1894 Grace Channing arrived from the East for a visit. Charlotte was profoundly happy to see her again. February 7: "Up and arrange for Grace's coming. Go down with Kate to meet her at 16th Station. Am very very glad to see her. Home—talk etc." February 10: "A wonderful pleasure to be with Grace again—dear queen!" And when Grace left to return home on February 16: "Grace goes away. Leaves an awful hole," Charlotte wrote sadly.

One of the things that the two apparently discussed was Charlotte's desire to send Katharine east to live with Grace and Walter, who were planning to be married in June. The difficulty in providing adequate care for Katharine, both from a financial perspective and from an emotional one, may well have been one of the factors in Charlotte's decision. Charlotte and Grace had been friends for years; Charlotte trusted Grace and knew that Katharine would be well loved under Walter and Grace's care. Even so, she addressed the issue defensively in her autobiography, arguing that her actions in relinquishing custody were clearly in Katharine's best interest: "Since her second mother was fully as good as the first, better in some ways perhaps; since the father longed for his child and had a right to some of her society; and since the child had a right to know and love her father—I did not mean her to suffer the losses of my youth—this seemed the right thing to do. No one suffered from it but myself. This, however, was entirely overlooked in the furious condemnation which followed. I had 'given up my child'" (*Living*, p. 163).

The financial burden of single motherhood, coupled with the demands of Charlotte's work—which left little time for Katharine—was a reality that Charlotte had to face. Her decision to take work in San Francisco, in "a place unsuitable for a child" (*Living*, p. 162), was by no means an easy one. The autobiography poignantly captures the pain that Charlotte felt in being without her daughter: "There were years, years, when I could never see a mother and child together without crying," she wrote (pp. 163–64). The elusiveness of love of any kind seemed to be a recurring pattern.

Shortly before Katharine left, the final decree dissolving Charlotte's marriage to Walter was granted. As she attempted to fill the void inevitably left by the divorce, by Grace's departure, and by Katharine's imminent return to the East, Charlotte apparently felt the need to reaffirm her attractiveness by alluding in the diary to various "suitors" (none very serious) who were, she believed, vying for her affection. On Wednesday, March 7, she wrote:

Mr. Hough spends the evening.

For the first time in my life I am conscious—faintly—of what I take to be the standing condition of "lovely woman."
A recognition of the possession of sex attraction.
But this is no place to use it.

A couple of weeks later, on March 20, Charlotte once again commented, somewhat humorously, on the unsolicited attention being cast her way:

> My Fate seems turned.
> Within two days I receive
> two declarations of love!!!
> > Rather late change—
> > rather hopeless.
> > Gratifying none the less.
> One brings hope strength and
> joy. I needed it, and
> thank God for it.

Charlotte's reaction to the male attention followed a similar pattern to that which followed her loss of Martha, years earlier. At that time, when her self-confidence was quite naturally shaken, Charlotte claimed that it was "a new thing to be admired" after receiving attention from Walter Stetson. Similarly, as the marriage to Walter finally broke up (not long after her relationship with Delle Knapp had ended), Charlotte may have subconsciously been attempting to restore her self-confidence by documenting the attention from others.

In any event, it was sometime in May that Katharine went east to live with Walter and Grace. On June 9 Charlotte was pleased to receive a "nice letter from Grace about Kate." Whatever misgivings she may have entertained about her decision, Grace's letter seemed to offer reassurance. Still struggling against constant poverty, Charlotte found that Katharine's departure at least lessened the financial strain. The day she received Grace's letter, Charlotte went shopping for a few needed items. Even if her financial situation was not substantially improved, at least it somehow seemed less onerous: "Come home 'broke' but happy," she remarked contentedly.

Charlotte relocated to San Francisco in June 1894 to take over the management of the new *Impress*. There she was joined by her much-older friend and mentor Helen Campbell. Freed from the sole responsibility of caring for Katharine, Charlotte could devote unlimited time to the newly revamped paper. Indeed, the months that she worked on the *Impress* with Campbell (whom Charlotte regarded as a second mother) were as rewarding as they were demanding. Campbell not only provided Charlotte with a sense of purpose, but her nurturing affection also filled some of Charlotte's long-unmet needs. Campbell, as a maternal figure, made Charlotte feel more secure than she had in some time, particularly considering all of the trauma that she had endured in recent months. Finally, life seemed happy.

On June 18 Charlotte arrived home to find a letter from Walter announcing his marriage to Grace. "I feel so glad I put on my terracotta robe and a 'coiffure,'" she remarked cheerfully. Even a reporter who attempted to interview Charlotte about her reaction to Walter's wedding could not spoil her happiness; the diary reports that she succeeded in passing a pleasant evening after his departure.

Just a week earlier Charlotte had learned that her father had married Frankie Johnson Beecher, the woman to whom he had been engaged before he met Mary Perkins. Rather than feeling blue over either her father's remarriage or Walter's, the news seemed to reinforce Charlotte's desire for the freedom that allowed her to write. She reported feeling proud when she completed work on her second edition of *In This Our World*, and a few days later she seemed intoxicated by life itself. "Walk home up the windy hills, and feel merry and mischievous when I get there. That's *good.*" And the next day, "Feel fine! Go for Mrs. McRoberts & get her to swim with me. Good time—feel glorious after it."

Charlotte's glory, however, was fleeting. Within the next two weeks, that old persistent enemy—poverty—returned with a vengeance. Charlotte had borrowed money to buy Katharine's ticket back east, and since her income was so irregular, depending upon speaking engagements and the sale of poems and articles, she was constantly beset with financial difficulties. While she maintained her composure, and even her humor, during many of her economic trials, the situation in July hit her particularly hard. On July 13 she wrote, "Hunt desperately for money and can't get it. Feel miserably and can't work." The next day was even worse: "Am feeling badly. Go down town to try to borrow that money. People mostly out. . . . Mr. Sargent is coldly rude to me when I ask him (for advance only). Not insolent but utterly cold and haughty. 'I know of no one whom I could approach with such a proposition' was all he said." Luckily, July 16 brought good news when Mrs. William Booth, the mother of one of Charlotte's acquaintances, generously provided a loan of $100.

Throughout August, Charlotte worked on the *Impress*, wrote poetry, and gave public lectures. And in late August she attended the Woman's Congress in Golden Gate Hall; in September she presided over the opening of the fourth annual convention of the Pacific Coast Women's Press Association. The convention was a great success, and Charlotte was pleased by the tribute she received at the end of the convention: "The P. A. gives me a great basket of flowers—gorgeous— amaryllis & ferns & sweet peas." She was finally receiving—and enjoying—the recognition she had always sought. Her "prayer of thankfulness for all good things" was, it seemed, finally paying off.

Charlotte abandoned her diary in September 1894, and there is no extant diary for 1895, but the year marked another significant turning point in Charlotte's life. She left California during the summer of 1895, after the *Impress*—the literary weekly that she managed—folded. Charlotte's goal had been to remake the *Impress* into a "good family weekly" which would be "varied and interesting" (*Living*, pp. 171, 173). Unfortunately, it lasted for only twenty weeks. According to Charlotte's account in *The Living of Charlotte Perkins Gilman*, the paper's demise was the result of the bias against her by "the San Francisco mind" that found her reputation as a divorcee and as an "unnatural" mother intolerable, particularly after she published a poem by Grace Channing Stetson in the first issue.

"This fiasco was what showed me my standing in that city," she wrote (*Living*, p. 173). The public outrage was the last straw. "I had put in five years of most earnest work [in California] with voice and pen, and registered complete failure. . . . I had warm personal friends, to be sure, but the public verdict [of my work] was utter condemnation" (p. 176). Charlotte decided to go east. Without knowing when, or where, or how, Charlotte resolved that it was time to take her message in favor of social reform on the road, where she hoped it would be better received. "I planned programs for the world, seeing clearly the gradual steps by which we might advance to an assured health, a growing happiness. If they did not see it, would not do do it, that was not my fault; my job, my one preëminent work, was to 'see' and to 'say,' and I did it" (p. 183).

For the next five years, Charlotte was on the road—"lecturing and preaching" (*Living*, p. 183)—with "no address in my little book to which to send 'the remains' in case of accident" (p. 181). The years during which Charlotte was "at large" marked the beginning of the major phase of her career.

At the invitation of Jane Addams, Charlotte traveled to Chicago where she spent several months at Hull House, the social settlement house founded by Addams and Ellen Gates Starr. Hull House offered strong community support services and was "widely known and honored" as a place that attracted "distinguished people, humanitarian thinkers from all over the country and from other countries, too" (*Living*, p. 184). There Charlotte enjoyed "companionship, fellow feeling, [and] friendly society" (p. 184). When she was asked to head a settlement house on the North Side, "in a place called 'Little Hell,'" Charlotte declined (p. 184), citing chronic health problems as the reason. She promptly recommended her old friend and mentor Helen Campbell, however, who accepted the position.

At the end of January 1896, Charlotte attended the annual Women's Suffrage Convention in Washington, D.C. It was there that she met the prominent sociologist and professor Lester F. Ward, the country's leading Reform Darwininst, whom she referred to in her autobiography as "quite the greatest man" she had ever known (p. 187). Charlotte reported dining and spending the evening with Ward on January 26, the culmination of a "beautiful rich day," and on January 28 Ward hosted a reception in Charlotte's honor. At the close of the convention, she returned to Chicago to recover from the mumps before leaving on an extended lecture tour which would take her to dozens of cities including Milwaukee, Detroit, Philadelphia, Boston, Kansas City, and Topeka.

In early March, Charlotte reported experiencing "Glorious days—the Work

very clear." But by the middle of the month, the optimism was waning, and
Charlotte experienced a temporary relapse of the old melancholia. On March 15:
"Am so bad that mother [Helen Campbell] sends me over to Dr. McCracken's.
They take me in joyfully and keep me. Also they recognize that I am in a serious
condition." The next day, "Sit down in office to talk to Dr. and weep dismally. It
is really the beginning of melancholia. Am very weak—can hardly sit up—low
appetite—mind a heavy dark grey." And on March 17: "Wake dully. Feel no
better. . . . Have hourly medicine."

The demands of her new career, and the attendant depression and anxiety,
likely triggered the old feelings of loss that often resurfaced during particularly
stressful periods. Perhaps being under the care of a mother figure recalled for
Charlotte the loss she had experienced on a number of levels: the death of her
own mother, the loss of various loves, the giving up of Katharine, and now the
literal loss of a place to call home.

Charlotte managed to pull herself out of the depression, however, and by
March 20 she had reclaimed her health and resumed her activities. Despite a
schedule which included "fifty-seven or more sermons and addresses, average of
more than two a week" between January 2 and July 3 (*Living*, p. 190), Charlotte
still made time to visit her new stepfamily in New York City which had resulted
from Frederick Perkins's remarriage in 1894. Happily, she found her stepmother
and stepsisters to be perfectly charming, and they maintained a close relationship over the years.

One of the highlights during the spring of 1896 was Charlotte's return to
Providence for the first time in eight years. In two separate trips, one at the end
of April and another in early May, Charlotte became reacquainted with numerous friends and relatives—the Dimans, "Old Mr. Stetson" (Walter's father), the
Browns, the Phelons, and others. Many of them went to hear her lecture, and
Charlotte seemed genuinely surprised by the reception she enjoyed. As she remarked in a letter to Walter (see Appendix B), "Everybody seemed glad to see
me. How pleasant it is. I had no idea they'd be so glad."

Charlotte was also pleased when at the end of May, Martha Lane came to hear
her speak to the Massachusetts Women's Suffrage Association. As always, the two
of them fell quickly back into a comfortable friendship, sharing lunches and teas
and sailing together "on the blue Atlantic" with Martha's young son, Chester.

Another significant relationship that Charlotte formed during the first half
of 1896 was with George O. Virtue, a friend of Helen Campbell's whom Charlotte had met in California. The two, in fact, may have been romantically involved. References to Virtue in the diary for 1896 are cryptic but suggestive.
For example, on March 22: "All go out but Mr. Virtue & I. We have a long talk.
Strange, interesting, touching, superhumanly absurd. Supper up stairs. Bit of
walk in evening, with G. V." Virtue also presented Charlotte with a book on

women's rights, saw her off at the train station when she left town, and spent several evenings alone with her. When Virtue became seriously ill in February, Charlotte nursed him back to health. But regardless of whether there was romantic involvement (or whether they simply shared similar beliefs and concerns), Charlotte's heavy schedule between mid-April and late June made it exceedingly difficult to conduct a relationship of any kind. In early July, however, the two spent some "happy" days together at George's home in Iowa, where Charlotte celebrated her thirty-sixth birthday.

On Wednesday, July 8, 1896, Charlotte sailed for England to attend the International Socialist and Labor Congress as a delegate from California. Charlotte stayed first with her friend Alfred Hicks and his wife, Amie, who served as her English hosts. The Hickses introduced Charlotte to scores of people and took her sightseeing in and around London. "Go with A[lfred]. to Richmond & row to Hampton Court—up the beautiful Thames. 8 hours on the river, with lunch. A most satisfying day," she wrote on July 24.

A couple of days later, on July 26, Charlotte attended the Great Peace Demonstration in Hyde Park where she spoke before an enormous crowd. The next day, the congress opened. Charlotte was in her element: speaking, lobbying, debating, and in general having a pleasant time. She met a number of prominent figures, including future prime minister Ramsey MacDonald, poet and artist William Morris, and playwright George Bernard Shaw, with whom she discussed "literary work" and received "very friendly and useful criticism." And, to her delight, the Fabian Society, a "group of intelligent, scientific, practical and efficient English socialists" (*Living*, p. 203) devoted to democratic ideals who counted Shaw and MacDonald among their ranks, honored Charlotte with a membership. She was also thrilled to meet author Alfred Russel Wallace, who originated independently the idea of natural selection, and writer and socialist Edward Carpenter.

Perhaps because of the excitement of the congress, or perhaps because of the strain of the trip itself, Charlotte experienced yet another period of acute depression, which began in mid-August. She report feeling "really very low again," "miserable," and "ghastly tired." By the end of the month, Charlotte believed she was seriously ill. "This illness seems more physical than usual. Doubtless a sympathetic collapse internally," she wrote on August 22. And on the twenty-eighth, "Try to write—can not. Brain will not work. I notice, gradually in the past month or two, a loss of my ready control of words.—aphasia?"

Once Charlotte hit the British lecture circuit for a three-week tour, however, her recuperation was rapid, with the exception of chronic fatigue. She was pampered by her British friends and "luxuriat[ed] in bed breakfasts and late rising," while being treated "like a sick princess!" By September 22, she had apparently recovered: "Third day of feeling well. I believe the tide has turned."

Much of the rest of the trip Charlotte spent visiting, lecturing, reading, writing, shopping, and sightseeing—Westminster Abbey, the Tower of London, the National Gallery, the British Museum. She also traveled to Camden, Liverpool, Shields, Edinburgh, and Glasgow, where she spent the last week of her trip lecturing to very small audiences, which left her reflective: "A week of foregone failure, hard work and 'heavy sledding' in general. Pay $16.25!!! Stood it fairly well."

On November 19 Charlotte sailed for the United States. Despite a rough voyage which left her seasick, she maintained her sense of humor. Thursday, November 26: "Thanksgiving Day. I give thanks earnestly, for a good world, a good God, and to be able to eat dinner again!"

On Monday, November 30, 1896, Charlotte arrived in New York and immediately took up residence in the boarding house at 20 W. 32d street where her stepmother and stepsisters resided. It was there that she learned that her father, Frederick Perkins, was seriously ill and had been placed in the Delaware Water Gap Sanitarium because of failing health. With Mary deceased, her father's health declining, and Kate living with Walter and Grace, Charlotte reestablished a sense of familial intimacy by quickly bonding with her new stepfamily, whom she described affectionately in a letter to Walter (see Appendix B). She found her stepmother to be "a dear little lady and I like her much. Also she likes me. With her I inherit stepsisters . . . sweet little blond damsels, twins, very like, and looking sixteen though twenty-two."

In addition to getting to know her new family, Charlotte spent much of December sewing, relaxing, and spending time with her friend activist Harriot Stanton-Blatch, a daughter of Elizabeth Cady Stanton, whom Charlotte had met in England. She also spent time that month Christmas shopping, lecturing, and trying to sell copies of *In This Our World*, with moderate success. On December 10 she agreed to contribute articles to the socialist magazine the *American Fabian*.

The week following Christmas, Charlotte resumed her writing with renewed vigor. But although she reported feeling "serene, strong, [and] happy" on January 1, her entry the previous evening betrays a sense of loneliness: "Upstairs at 11.50 and received The New Year Alone as usual."

Lonely or not, Charlotte was certainly busy. In January she left New York to attend a suffrage convention in Des Moines, Iowa, stopping in Rochester to visit Susan B. Anthony and her sister, Mary. After the Iowa convention, Charlotte hit the lecture circuit again, speaking in Nebraska, Illinois, Michigan, and Washington, D.C., where she attended the Mother's Congress and met Mrs. Grover Cleveland. Upon her return to New York, Charlotte grew alarmed by her father's rapidly declining health. "He looks old and uncared for," she noted on February 20. And on March 3 she began shopping around for a new "home" in which to place him. "Take Kathie [Charlotte's stepsister] & go to Fordham 'Home for Incurables'. Won't do to my mind. Lunch & go to Morristown, N. J. to see Dr. Wright's place. Just the thing." Fortunately, Charlotte was able to get her father settled in Morristown almost immediately. March 11: "Go to see father in Morristown P.M. He is real *happy* and comfortable and likes the folks & place. I am so glad."

Monday, March 8, marked a day that would prove propitious. Charlotte noted casually that she had looked up her first cousin Houghton Gilman, a Wall Street attorney, whom she had not seen in over fifteen years. Two days later, on March 10, she noted simply: "Houghton Gilman calls. Like him." By the sixteenth of the month, Charlotte Perkins Stetson and George Houghton Gilman were courting.

In addition to the thrill of new romance, Charlotte was delighted when on Saturday, March 20, the prominent and influential American writer William Dean Howells attended a meeting of the Single Tax Club to hear her speak. "Wm. Dean Howells came to hear me! Was introduced—says he is coming to see me!!!" she wrote euphorically. "A very jolly & exciting discussion. Houghton there and came home with me," she continued. Howells did, in fact, call on Charlotte the next day, and the two quickly became friends, socializing and corresponding frequently from that point on.

During the spring of 1897, Charlotte enjoyed remarkable health and productivity. "Feel very happy & strong," she wrote on April 5. Indeed, for the first time in a long time, Charlotte not only felt well, but she also enjoyed a new sense of self-confidence, which was undoubtedly reinforced both by Howells's encouragement and a series of offers that came her way. English writer and illustrator Oliver Herford, for example, asked to meet Charlotte and offered to design a new cover for the third edition of *In This Our World*. She was also flattered to receive an offer to chair a department at the Kansas Agricultural College for $1,400 a year, which, although she declined it, was certainly a boost to her non-college-educated ego. Invitations to return for "repeat engagements" on the lecture circuit also helped to bolster her spirits during the spring.

The four-month lecture tour commencing on April 21 was highly successful. Audiences were receptive, and Charlotte spoke well. She was also enormously productive, often writing on the train between destinations. One major project was a manuscript for a novel, "A Different Thing," which apparently was never completed. The other more significant enterprise was still in the planning stages; actually, the origins were just beginning to germinate in Charlotte's mind for the project that would become *Women and Economics*.

Also adding to Charlotte's sense of well-being during the spring of 1897 was her growing relationship with Houghton Gilman. The two exchanged letters frequently while she was on tour, and before her departure they spent countless

hours together. March 31: "Houghton comes, rather late, and spends the evening up stairs with me. Delightful time. Get very friendly." April 4: "Houghton
at about 10. Go to Bedloe's Island and ascend inside of the Statue of Liberty—
look out of her crown. Then see the aquarium. Then go to Staten Island. Dine at
South Beach. . . . Tired but happy." By April 11, Houghton's charm was scoring
points with Charlotte's stepmother: "Houghton comes & we go to Brooklyn together. I speak on the Economic Basis of the Woman Question to the Brooklyn
Philosophical Assn. . . . Mother comes, late, & we go back with her. Houghton
delightfully polite to her—wins her completely. Stays to supper and spends the
evening with me in my little room."

On the day that Charlotte departed for her big lecture tour, it was Houghton
who was there to bid her adieu: "Houghton meets me & sees me off. He has been
a great pleasure."

Thursday, July 20, 1893

Am so much moved by the needs of the women that I write a new paper.
Speak in the evening. A very trying occasion—so much to say and so much
I must not say—to them.

Friday, July 21, 1893

Go with Kate to the Del Monte Baths, and she tastes the bliss of warm water
in a great greenhouse.
Rocks in the afternoon. Mr. Bamford with us. Read "Girls of Today" in the
evening meeting. Then take a walk with Hattie & Mr. Bamford, & have my
head examined by a little itinerant phrenologist—Sedgcomb or some such
thing; at his request for the privilege.

His reading compares well with Fowler's and was very satisfactory to me.

Monday, July 24, 1893

. . . Delle and Mrs. Poulson call in the evening. Delle asks that I explain to
Mrs. P. why I will not give her back the paper she gave me owing the reasons
for her leaving. Very painful experience—O very.

Bed late and much depressed

Wednesday, July 26, 1893

Check from Scribner's for "Wolf"—$25.00! . . .

Thursday, July 27, 1893

. . . Talk with Hattie; seeing newly and with great clearness what abnegation
and sacrifice stand for in moral evolution.
What we call Self-Personality (the personal inclination)—is the echoing fading force of the Great Life in its Material Limitations. The fresh life force
must come direct, (through the mind?) not through inherited inclinations.

Therefore to hold personality in abeyance and act *direct* from God is to help evolution.

Monday, July 31, 1893

. . . First day since June 1st that I sat to write and couldn't! A poor poem to be sure, and several starts—no good. Send off Heaven & Pioneers again. Go with Kate to see Miss Stempel P.M. Delle there!!! Asks to drive us home! Mrs. S. thinks she will join assn. at once—Home rather late. Ina to supper. Nice letter from Grace today. Answer it.

Friday, Aug. 4, 1893

. . . Go to Delle's rooms very reluctantly to a meeting called by her to arrange program for convention—she being chairman of that committee. Meeting called at 7 . . . but no Delle till near 8. Riding with Mr. Wetmore. He sends up note asking her to walk home with me, I am forced to allow it and to stop at Ina's with her. Am introduced to him in half darkness.

Monday, Aug. 7, 1893

Delle calls early and is offensive. Says my behavior to Mr. Wetmore was "like a servant girl's." Says she will never enter my house again. Wrote on "The Importance of The Period of Youth." & "The Holy Stove." . . . Father comes also, stays to tea and till 9.30. Ina over also.

Tuesday, Aug. 8, 1893

. . . Go with Kate to meet Margaret & Basil.[1] A mere girl she, he a lovely little thing, solemn and bright. Mr. Griffes calls. Let him take my poems to read—those prepared to publish.

Wednesday, Aug. 16, 1893

. . . Go to Call office and get mss. Delle attaches herself to me there. Great difficulty in getting home alone—she sticks so!

Saturday, Aug. 19, 1893

Margaret and Hattie Kate and Basil, set forth for Cliff House, with lunch Basket. I stay at home alone, sleep long P.M. get rested.
Write "The Collective Conscience" with temperance moral, for Berkeley gospel meeting.

Thursday, Aug. 24, 1893

Up early and see Margaret & Basil off on the 8.6 train. Fine race to expressman for her trunk. Home very limp and weak. Accomplish naught. . . .

Saturday, Aug. 26, 1893

. . . Feel wretchedly. Do nothing. Revive my spirits by reading Longfellow. He should be called "The perfect poet" like what's his name "the perfect painter." Also read Elliots grand Hymn "O May I join the choir invisible!" Read "Barbara Dering"[2] later—a singularly pointless book it seems to me [msm]. Go to the park with Hattie P.M. Try "the maze" and swing.

Thursday, Aug. 31, 1893

. . . Go to Golden Gate Hall—Testimonial to Miss Coolbrith under auspices of Bohemian Club. Joaquin Miller makes a fool of himself. We all come back to my house and have a little supper—ham omelet & cocoa—and whatever else could be found. Ina & Joaquin—Mr. Markham,[3] Mr. Griffes, Hattie & I—and Mrs. Porter, who arrived late.

Tuesday, Sept. 5, 1893

Feel Bad yet.
Hattie gets me a bottle of Fellow's Compound Syrup of Hypophosphates and I seem to feel it at once. . . .

Sunday, Sept. 17, 1893

Mrs. Shuey comes early, she and Mr. Markham stay to breakfast—fine breakfast. . . . We go up to see Joaquin Miller. Mrs. Darling meets us & I ride with her—Mr. M. & Mrs. S. walk. He goes to his house & we women call on Miller who receives us in bed. Dirty person that he is! All cigar ashes on the floor beside him. I try to arouse him on the S. P. question, dubious success. Climb the Hills behind. Dine with the Darlings. Home very tired.

Tuesday, Sept. 19. 1893

Wrote my convention paper—"Voices of The World," short. . . .

Wednesday, Sept. 20, 1893

Convention opens—P.C.W.P.A. General business and some papers P.M. A social meeting in the evening. Good many there during day.
Had refreshments—fruit—crackers—cheese $11.20—enough for 200 people. 5.00 would feed our meetings well. . . .

Friday, Sept. 22, 1893

Election morning. I am made President—wear black silk. Mrs. Carr takes Delle & me to lunch, and then me to have my photograph taken at Tabers. Bless her dear heart! Journalists afternoon—very interesting. Evening in the hall—public meeting—good audience, good program. . . . The [*sic*] give me a floral tribute!

Saturday, Sept. 23, 1893

Mrs. Darling[4] over night. Joaquin calls early. Go to drive with Delle, Mrs. S. P. Carr, and Miss Carr. Very pleasant drive. Lunch at Snell Seminary with them. Talk earnestly to Mrs Carr, an earnest receptive woman, full of enthusiasm for good.

Nap afterward and begin to feel good.

Sunday, Sept. 24, 1893

. . . Delle calls. . . . Eat a bit and set forth up to Mr. Markham's where we ate of books talk and dinner—very enjoyable. Delle & Mr. Wetmore appeared on horse back at the car end, and reappeared as we finished dinner. We left them there. Later they call, spick and span. A pleasant evening. . . . I like Mr. W. very much indeed. He wants a room here—or perhaps she wants him to have it!——dubious, very.

Friday, Sept. 29, 1893

Write poem "I went to look for Love." A Lodger appears, takes me by storm, and engages the front room for tomorrow. We all toil to arrange it, moving Miss Coolbrith's manifold belongings into the north room.

Monday, Oct. 16, 1893

Not at all well. . . . Populist parlor meeting here. Father to tea. Sixteen in all—seventeen counting Mr. Denison who called briefly beforehand. Some good talk and planning done. A feeling of purpose and hope. . . .

Friday, Oct. 27, 1893

Up at 6.15. Get a nice breakfast. Delle & Mr. Wetmore come. No Griffes. He arrives very late—very much ashamed.

We get started at 8.30 or so. Unfortunate outfit—a stiff pole to the wagon, a "green team"—Nellie just in from pasture and in foal—never driven double before, no breeding, no brake. A twenty two mile drive—forty four in all! The last four mountain road. We have to walk up the hills and the gentlemen hold back the wagon going down. Father Agapius well worth the trip; also his place—caves, springs, relics, honey & water, and "metheglin." Tea and bread at four.* That with an apple, all. Walk about seven miles. Dine at Haywards at 7. Telegraph to Kate. Home at 10.15 or so, by moonlight. Very pleasant day, but [*msm*] all of us missed engagements.

Saturday, Nov. 4, 1893

. . . . Go to notary public, & to P. O. & arrange about Impress. . . . Sample & select paper for my book cover. See Mr. Cheney at Pub. Lib. about Impress. Go to printers to get contracts. . . .

Saturday, Nov. 11, 1893

Work on Impress.

Saturday, Nov. 18, 1893

My book begins to come in.[5] looks fine. 124 pages. About 5½ by 6½ paper cover. 150 copies. Cost me selling at 25 cts.

Go to city & read proof on Impress.

Socialist Labor Party Entertainment in the evening.

[1894]

Mon. Jan. 1, 1894

. . . Went to bed this morning at about 2.30 or 3. Mrs. Johnson, Mr. Griffes, and Mr. Webster last night—sort of Spook-party. Oyster supper at 12. . . .

Desired for this year.
Less words and better.
More love for people, with concomitant
Health.

Sun. Jan. 7, 1894

7.50 Try all day to work on Impress and succeed not at all.

Sat. Jan. 20, 1894

. . . Jane Addams is coming, wants to start some organization for working women. . . .

Wed. Jan. 24, 1894

Mrs. Webster and three children come. Take three bedrooms furnished and use of kitchen—$30.00 a month. Not bad. . . . Essay Club P.M. . . .

Thur. Jan. 25, 1894

. . . Kate goes to walk with the Webster children and is not home till after six and after dark. Mrs. Webster wild. Hattie and I run about wildly, I go to Snells, and then return to look again. Take Mrs. W. to police station and give the alarm. They return however before Mr. Webster is telephoned for. Then I dine, and then we all go to hear Delle's paper on "What Working Women Want." I answer questions afterward. Splendid time.

Friday, Jan. 26, 1894

. . . I am utterly used up by the worry and exertion about the children.

Keep Kate in bed all day, where she is a miracle of goodness. Go in evening, with Hattie and Mary to see "Held By The Enemy," *by the Charity Company for the benefit of Unemployed Women
Fine acting.

Sun. Feb. 4, 1894

. . . . My little book [*In This Our World*] is going off splendidly—about 130 left here, and some of course unsold. Splendid reviews of it, appreciative personal letters, orders from individuals, telegram for fifty copies from Woman's Journal; general enthusiasm.

I must have a new edition.

Wed. Feb. 7, 1894

Up and arrange for Grace's coming. Go down with Kate to meet her at 16th Station. Am very very glad to see her. Home—talk etc.

Fri. Feb. 9, 1894

Still rather wretched in health I find. Try to write letters.

Sat. Feb. 10, 1894

Nice long day in the city with Grace. Do various errands. Carry in report and cash for unemployed women to Mr. Bowen of the Associated Charities. Call on father twice—2nd time to get name of lawyer to undertake divorce if possible.

A wonderful pleasure to be with Grace again—dear queen! . . .

Mon. Feb. 12, 1894

Go to see the lawyer, Mr. Philbrook and talk over the case. Says it can be done on "wilful neglect." Undertakes it. . . .

Tues. Feb. 13, 1894

Reception to Miss Addams at Mrs. Howards in evening. Grace and I go. Very enjoyable and interesting. . . .

Fri. Feb. 16, 1894

Grace goes away.

Leaves an awful hole.

Mon. Feb. 19. 1894

Some where along here get a fine letter from Mr. W[illiam]. D[ean]. Howells, about my book.

Thur. Feb. 22, 1894

. . .

The Websters all move out
—*Glory Be!* . . .

Tues. Feb. 27, 1894

. . . Saw Mr. Philbrook. Signed complaint and go [*sic*] notary's affidavit— a most light oath—gave Mr. P. another Payment 35 in all now (this was yesterday[.] He is to urge care.

Impress mailed. . . .

Wed. Feb. 28, 1894

Wash dishes, etc. Go to Dr. Kelloggs. Am *very* low in all ways—mentally morally & physically. . . .

Sun. Mar. 4, 1894

A reporter from the Call—Mr. Howell, brings me an Examiner with the whole story about Grace Walter and me. . . . Write to Grace.

Mon. Mar. 5, 1894

. . . Mrs. McRoberts goes with me to call on Mrs. Hearst, to ask who wrote yesterday's outrage in the *Examiner*.[6] She is much moved, and will find out if she can. Then I go to the Mercantile Library, & then to see Philbrook. He says all this will not hurt the case at all.

Mr. Markham calls and stays to supper and later.

Wed. Mar. 7, 1894

Don't feel able to go to town and work. Stay at home and arrange Impress accts.

Go to Dr. Kelloggs.

Mr. Hough spends the evening.

For the first time in my life I am conscious—faintly—of what I take to be the standing condition of "lovely woman."

A recognition of the possession of sex attraction.

But this is no place to use it.

Thur. Mar. 8, 1894

. . . Go to see Proofs at *Thors*. Fine. he says I look like George Sand—that makes another. George Elliot, Rachel, Christina Rossetti; a noble list.[7] . . .

Fri. Mar. 16, 1894

In the morning I go with Mrs. Barnes to hear Prof. Ross on the Economic Basis of Morals. Good. I talk to him some. Drop in on Presdt. Jordan {of Stanford University}. He invites me to lecture there—third Tuesday in April. I am much pleased. . . . Then an afternoon tea is given in my honor—ladies tea—lots of nice women.

Tues. Mar. 20, 1894

. . .

My Fate seems turned.
Within two days I receive
two declarations of love!!!
    Rather late change—
    rather hopeless.
Gratifying none the less.

One brings hope strength and
joy. I needed it, and
thank God for it.

Fri. Apr. 13, 1894

. . . Lunch with Winifred Black—"Annie Laurie." [8] Just she and I and her two year old. Very plesant time; strong pleasant interesting woman. . . .

Wed. Apr. 18, 1894

. . . . (Decree of divorce granted me today.)

Thur. Apr. 19, 1894

. . . . Find in the papers the announcement of the granting of my divorce. A slight matter now its done.

Sat. June 9, 1894

. . . Nice letter from Grace about Kate.[9] . . . Go down town and shop—get groceries, meat, veg., underwear, & black skirt. Come home "broke" but happy. No callers. Bed at ten. . . .

Mon. June 11, 1894

. . . Learn that my father has remarried, the lady that he was engaged to before he met my mother.

Tues. June 12, 1894

. . . Receive proposal to publish my book & verse from T. Maxwell & Son, *Dumfries* [Scotland].

Wed. June 13, 1894

Work on Impress all the morning—the New Impress, arranging for prospectus, etc. Write some letters also. Go to . . . talk business with Mr. Murdock about printing the paper for us. . . .

Fri. June 15, 1894

. . . Go to Dr. Kelloggs. She says *I am all right*. This on top of all I've done lately is remarkable, and most encouraging for entire recovery and establishment of my former health! Please God it shall be so. . . .

Mon. June 18, 1894

Arrange for Impress prospective. Go to see Murdock and have talk with him. . . . Home. Find letter from Walter—telling about his wedding with Grace. I feel so glad I put on my terracotta robe and a "coiffure."
Reporter from *The Call* seeks to interview me on the above theme, in vain [10]. . . .

Sun. June 24, 1894

Work on paper all day mostly & finish it. Prepare copy of "In This Our World" and send to W. & R. Chambers, 339 High St., Edinburg, Scotland—as per order received through Scribners. Feel very proud of the same. Write to Scrib. & to Francis Gilman.[11]

Thur. June 28, 1894

. . . Call on Mr. Johnson—he buys 50 copies of *The Impress* for his ad. therein. Said I was the only one who had been shrewd enough to make him buy anything!? Walk home up the windy hills, and feel merry and mischievous when I get there. That's *good*. Read some Browning to the folks. Write letters.

Fri. June 29, 1894

Feel fine! Go for Mrs. McRoberts & get her to swim with me. Good time— feel glorious after it. . . .

Read Bierce's last Sunday abomination. That man ought not to go unwhipped[.][12]

Mon. July 2, 1894

. . . Call to see Mr. Barry and enrage him over Bierce's last outrage. Agree to let him have something for this weeks Star. Come home and write it—"A Reproach to San Francisco." . . .

Tues. July 3, 1894

Go swimming with Mrs. Gaden. Splendid time. Lunch with her. . . . Am 34 years old today.

Wed. July 4, 1894

Stay peacefully at home. Write
The great Railroad Strike[13] is of more importance than the 4th in most minds.
Write things about Bierce for the Call & The Woman's Journal.

Sun. July 8, 1894

. . . We are all wild over the strike.

Fri. July 13, 1894

Hunt desperately for money and can't get it. Feel miserably and can't work. Committee meeting at Mrs. Gaden's. Go settle Mrs. Stacorn's acct. about those chairs.
Miss Knapp—I think—has sent me a marked copy of The Impress with corrections. Anonymous.

Sat. July 14, 1894

Am feeling badly. Go down town to try to borrow that money. People mostly out. . . . Mr. Sargent is coldly rude to me when I ask him (for advance only). Not insolent but utterly cold and haughty.

"I know of no one whom I could approach with such a proposition" was all he said.

Mr. Bunker of the Report is cordial and helpful. Call on Mrs. Gaden—go to bath with them—too ill to go in. Back to lunch, and rest. Get to feel all right again by talking to Mrs. G. about their troubles. . . .

Mon. July 16, 1894

Sit to write Impress. Mrs. Bunker calls and says her mother can let me have that money. Joy. . . . Mrs. Bunker with the $100.00. It is from her mother, Mrs. Wm. Booth, and wishing to have no note or acknowledgement—is glad to do it.
The dear woman! . . .

Thur. July 19, 1894

Went to bed with a prayer of thankfulness for all good things. Slept well. . . .

Sun. July 29, 1894

Hurrah! My puzzle in Ethics is solved. It *is* the duty of the individual to react; we are the environment of each other and we must establish causation by our action and reaction.
    Write it out briefly. . . .

Mon. July 30, 1894

Go to grocers P. O., and to Mrs. Morse's to lunch. . . . Home happy. Find a delightful letter from Paul.[14] Write a little and talk with Mrs. C[ampbell].

Wed. Aug. 8, 1894

. . . Lecture in evening—best yet—hall half full, cleared about four dollars.
    House joyous. . . .

Wed. Aug. 22, 1894

Woman's Congress meeting in Golden Gate Hall. Attend both sessions. . . .
Lecture on Improvement of People.

Fri. Aug. 24, 1894

Begin to feel very greatly appalled at the work before me with the paper.

Tues. Sept. 4, 1894

Preside A.M. over opening sessions of fourth annual convention of P. C. W. P. A. . . .
    Good crowd, very successful, one atrocious woman with poem—an ass— Dr. Newlands by name.

Thur. Sept. 6, 1894

. . . Preside at election . . .
A great success.
The P. A. gives me a great basket of lowers—gorgeous—amaryllis & ferns & sweet peas. . . .

Sun. Sept. 9, 1894

Arrange desk and write letters—many. Dine at Mrs. Morses at 4.30. Sleep calmly there from 6 to 8.25! Home & arrange for lecture, etc.
Our mother[15] went over to Alameda, & Mrs. Hough with her.

Sat. Sept. 22, 1894

Hot hot O Hot!

[*Except for Xs marking the beginning of her menstrual cycle each month, the rest of Charlotte's diary for 1894 is blank; there is no extant diary for 1895. The diaries resume on January 1, 1896.*]

[1896]

Wed. Jan. 1, 1896

At 80 Elm st. Chicago, Ills. Wrote plans and possibilities. . . . Good talk with Mr. Virtue last night.

Friday 3

Milwauke Woman's Club. 10 below. Mrs. Robertson calls for me at 8.30 A.M. Go to Girls College & speak ten minutes to them. . . .

Thurs. Jan. 16, 1896

. . . [S]peak on "What Life is For"—("Child question") in Unitarian Church. $25.00. 11.30 train Detroit—Historical Society.

Friday 17

Small sleep. Chicago at 8. Breakfast in Central Station. Home. rest some; dress, lunch early, go to Evanston, speak before "The Friday Teacup." $10.00. Mother very miserable. Mr. Virtue gives me "The Rights of Women." . . .

Thursday 23

Bad night. Car-sick in morning, no breakfast, no lunch. Changed at Harrisburg. Wash. at 1.15 or so. Come to Hotel Arno. lunch & sleep. Prof. Lester Ward calls. enjoyed seeing him. Miss Anthony more than kind & Miss Shaw and all. Convention in evening. I came last—a substitute—and read poems. Great applause.

Friday 24

Convention A.M. Introduced as W. C. A. delegate. Am liked. Lunch. Nap. Write. Introduced in evening session as other delegates. Speak ten minutes— not very well, but much applause. A nice talk with Alice Stone Blackwell; books are selling and being asked for. All well.

Sunday 26

Preach A.M. in People's Church. Prof. Ward & wife came to hear me. Preach P.M. in Convention— (Church of Our Father) in Rev. Anna Garlin Spencer's place. Sup and spend evening with Prof. Ward. Beautiful rich day.

Monday 27

So I have the mumps! Or something like it. Drag dutifully throug [*sic*] the sessions. Am crowded off in the evening. Really feel sick—lay down all day when I didn't have to go out. Was too weak and used up to speak when my time did come—just time to excuse myself was allowed me. My father called on me!

Tues. Jan. 28, 1896

Speak before the Judiciary Committee of the House of Rep. Attend afternoon session and fight the resolution disavowing the "Woman's Bible." It went though [*sic*], hotly and closely contested. Go to a reception given me by Prof. & Mrs. Ward. Speak at Convention at 10. Am seen home by Dr. Eaton and put to bed. Says its Grip.

Fri. Jan 31, 1896

. . . Mumps still present but am not so weak and ill since Thur.

Saturday, Feb. 1

Loaf, pack, and write. Start for Chicago on the 4.30 train. Day coach to Harrisburg. Sleeper to Columbus.

Sunday 2

Long tedious day. Reach Chicago at 5.15 very much exhausted. Miss car and get home late, a mere rag. No one here but Mr. White. Miss Vogel sick with mumps, Mr. Virtue with mumps & a carbuncle. I go over with Mr. White to see him. Bath and bed.

Friday 7

Make cards for bulletin board. Mr. V. comes over to lunch. Nice talk P.M. I go out in evening to Springfield. Mr. White went down and saw me off—I was exceeding grateful for I felt very weak and ill.

Good boys, both.

Wed. Feb. 12, 1896

A very heavy snow storm. Go to Hull House P.M. with great difficulty, and am disgusted to find it was only a reception! Home tired.

Make delicious Valentine for Mr. White.

Thursday 13

Short time with Mr. V. A.M. Lunch with Dr. McCracken. Speak at Mrs. Scribners on "The New Motherhood." Pleasant and well received. $10.00. part of evening with Mr. V. in place of mother whom I put to bed.

Sunday 23

Write to Walter & Kate. Talk with Mr. Virtue. . . . Mr. White and I act Pyramus and Thisbe[16] with two napkins and four chairs. Sing hymns and talk.

Sun. Mar. 1, 1896

. . . Glorious days—the Work very clear.

Sat. Mar. 7, 1896

Sit to write and do several business letters. Am pretty miserable with bad cold & nervous exhaustion. Lie down some. . . .

Saturday 14

Very bad day. Mother feels very badly about my behavior. I know that my behavior is my condition—that I am not well. . . .

Sunday 15

Am so bad that mother sends me over to Dr. McCracken's. They take me in joyfully and keep me. Also they recognize that I am in a serious condition. . . . Sit up pretty late and talk with Dr. Mac.

Mon. Mar. 16, 1896

Sit down in office to talk to Dr. and weep dismally. It is really the beginning of melancholia. Am very weak—can hardly sit up—low appetite—mind a heavy dark grey. Ride with Dr. A.M. & a bit at noon too. Nap P.M. . . .

Tuesday 17

Wake dully. Feel no better. Ride as before and sleep P.M. Have hourly medicine. Mother comes over. (Bit of note from her and from G[eorge]. O. V[irtue]. in the morning mail). Bed early.

Thurs. Mar. 19, 1896

Feel better on waking. Today—or it may been yesterday*—one faint touch of a feeling of happiness—normality. . . .

Friday 20

Feel better. All symptoms steadily good now. Dr. is astonished to see how fast and steadily I gain.

Sun. Mar. 22, 1896

Hot bath. Sing. Breakfast. All sing. Arrange letters & do some work and much talk with mother. P.M. all go out but Mr. Virtue & I. We have a long talk. Strange, interesting, touching, superhumanly absurd. Supper up stairs. Bit of walk in evening, with G[eorge]. V[irtue]. Mother & I talk late.

Wed. Mar. 25, 1896

A bad day—nervous physically—intensely so toward night. Cannot bear the children even.

Thurs. April 9, 1896

Just sleeping at Mrs. Dow's & doing what I can at Settlement days. Write "The People" for Woman's Congress.

Sat. April 18, 1896

Up betimes & pack. Farewells etc. Mr. Virtue goes down with me, leaving oranges. Very pleasant journey. Eat two square meals out of lunch box. *Beautiful* spring weather. Enjoy every mile. Read "Mehalah" by S. Baring-Gould [17] in the evening. Poor book—poor author.

Sunday 19

(At father's—first experience!) Slept well. Woke happy. Coffee & rolls at Albany at 9. *Good.* Enjoy the Hudson. Reach N.Y. at 1.45. Mama meets me & I go to her house. Father in Washington. Have a nice talk with mother.

Tues. April 21, 1896

. . . Am to go to Providence as substitute for Mrs. C. C. Catt. Miss boat and go by midnight train, after dinner and long nap at home.

Wednesday 22

Providence.[18] Pleasant trip. In early. Go to breakfast with the Phelons—great surprise and joy. See the lady who expected me—Mrs. Bowles. Call on the Browns, back to Mary's and have a bit of lunch, Address the Com. of Senate & House in the State house. Call on Mrs. Diman, nap at Mary's, she and Anna go with me to reception & banquet. Speak again. $20.00.

Fri. April 24, 1896

Brooklyn. Go to drive with Mrs. Cary in Park, Greenwood Cemetery, etc. Nap—or effort at one. Write a little. Go over to the city, meet Mr. Sanders, sup with him, and go call on Miss Prestonia Mann, soon to edit "The American Fabian." Arrange to go to "Summerbrook." Mr. S. comes all the way home with me. . . .

Wed. May 6, 1896

Go to see relatives & friends. See Grandma, now 91 and very well and bright, Uncle Charles, Mrs. Arthur Perkins, Mrs. C. D. Warner, Mrs. George Warner, Mrs. Day and the Stowe girls. Lunch with Mrs. Day, and talk. Back to Aunt J.'s & have a nap. . . . Lots of good talk.

Fri. May 15, 1896

Call on Mr. Stetson sen. Poor old soul! He tells me much family trouble. Poor family! Call on Millie Cooley. Delighted to see me. All look just the same. . . .

Saturday 23

Up betimes. Pack. 8.20 train to Boston. . . .

Monday 25

Out to Hingham by 9.30 train. Glad to see Martha. Lunch & some supper. Go to Lynn and lecture on The New Motherhood. . . .

Tuesday 26

Come in to the Mass W. S. Assn. meeting at Park st. church. Am well received. Speak variously. Martha in P.M. & hears me. Meet Helen Gardener in evening meeting. Go home with Mr. Blackwell. Beautiful home, good night's sleep. . . .

Wed. May 27, 1896

Glorious spring morning. Sit out doors and write. Such sweet spring air! Go to lunch with Helen Gardener & her husband.—Col. Stuart & wife. Interesting time. They tell me Arena news. Go to W. S. festival. Dine to music. Speak in evening, among others. Julia Ward Howe there—77th birthday. Meet Mrs. Lloyd Garrison. Home with Mr. Blackwell.

Monday, June 1

Buy nice book in Boston and other things. Meet Martha, lunch with her, go to Hingham by boat. Nice trip. . . .

Tuesday, June 2, 1896

Go with Martha and Chester to Marshfield, and go sailing on the blue Atlantic. With Dana Blackman, friend of M.'s, a born sailor.

Thursday 4

Reach Chic[ago]. at 2.40. Mr. White meets me, and goes about with me while I do errands. Get str. ticket for England. Buy linen travelling dress—$5.00 etc etc. . . .

Tuesday 9

Sleep fairly well. Another restful day, with a little riding in beautiful Topeka. Speak on "Production and Distribution" in a small hall to a small audience. Good lecture—folks pleasant.

The newspapers are very pleasant and fair. Spoke in High School A.M.— ten minutes on Educated Bodies.

Saturday 13

Parlor meeting at Mrs. Wheelers, women & girls. Spoke on "The New Motherhood. Successful. Stayed to dinner. Stupid evening—the men afraid of me.

Sunday 21

Preach in Methodist Church on "Whoso loseth his life for my sake"—Very well received. A Mr. Barretman—Co. Supt. put into Mrs. McKey's hand

$5.00 for me, and said "God bless her, and tell her to keep on preaching that gospel." . . .

Monday 22.

Stormy night, Up at five. 6 A.M. train to Winfield. Breakfast in hotel. Am left in delicious peace and loneliness at Mrs. Albright's home. Write. Winfield Assembly P.M. Hear part of Gov. Hubbards address on "Japan." A Bombastic egotistical long winded fat man.

Fri. June 26, 1896

Chair car to Strong City, common car to Manchester. Chair car to Concordia. Hour & 40 minutes wait at Strong City. Stood the night first rate. Concordia at 8. Two good rooms at boarding house, *alone.* Nap. Write. Say a few words at Institute. Dine well. Sleep three hours. Speak in evening on "The Royal Road to Learning."

Tuesday 30

Rest and loaf. Ascertain about train. People call. Speak again in evening on "Kingdom Come." A little better but not much. Leave on the 1.30 train—night. Dont want to see this place again. A person (*presumably* here) printed on the white satin lining of my hat—"Better get your face plated!" [19]

Wednesday, July 1

Kansas City at 7 A.M. Coffee & rolls in depot. . . . take 5.25 train for Bedford Iowa. Met by George Virtue. Drive to his house in buggy. Thunderstorm—partial breakdown—various vicissitudes. Very glad to be here.

Friday 3

Thirty-six years old. George gives me Sill's poems.[20] Rest in hammock write letters, eat sleep and am happy. We go in after mail again, no, go in to lecture on "The Heroes we Need Now." Presbeterian Church. George & his sister go with me. Fairly good.

Saturday 4

Celebrate by falling down the cellar stairs—or was it yesterday? Bump my elbow badly.
Go in town towards night.

!Start to England!
Wed. July 8, 1896

Come down to Settlement & pack. Go & have tooth filled, and shop. Back to lunch, finish packing, off on 3 P.M. train, Mr. White & Mr. Sweezey attending to the last second. Nice brothers both. Pleasant journey on sleeper. Feel calm and happy. Cash low however down to 100.00 [21] in envelope & inside 20.00 in purse. Never mind.

Thursday 9

Reach Toronto at 8 A.M. or so. . . . Boat leaves at 2 P.M. Str. *Spartan* Richelieu & Ontario Line. Very rough on Lake—most everyone sick. I'm not, but can eat little supper.

Friday 10

Good nights sleep. Wake among the Thousand Islands. Fine, but rather monotonous—prosaic—and, in the "resort" part too populous and fashionable. But the Rapids are glorious. Montreal about 7. . . .

Tues. July 14, 1896

Icebergs! Yes, lots of them. Just like the pictures & descriptions. Finally get past the straits & out to sea. Still foggy—men at the masthead. Read & write.

Fri. July 17, 1896

Up barely in time for breakfast; and to my surprise, part with some of it! Eat some more, and retire to the deck. Lie down all day, along the steampipe thing around the cabin. Am warm cheerful and not at all sick if I keep still. Beef tea & biscuit cracker for lunch. Nap in berth. Deck again. Biscuit & orange juice for supper. But am serene and comfortable. Nearly all sick.

Mon. July 20, 1896

Sight land towards night.

Tuesday 21

Str. lands cable at Birkenhead, we go over to Liverpool in a tender. Alfred Hicks meets me there. Spend night with Mrs. Worrall—Sefton Park. She is "Julia Dawson" of the Clarion. Nice people.

Thurs. July 23, 1896

Set forth with Alfred. Call on T. Fisher Unwin.[22] Very polite. Shows me my book reviews—many & good. . . .

Friday 24

Letter from Mother. Go with A[lfred]. to Richmond & row to Hampton Court—up the beautiful Thames. 8 hours on the river, with lunch. A most satisfying day. Much good talk.

Sun. July 26, 1896

The Great Peace Demonstration. Go out rather early. Attend service in St. Margerets (near W. Abbey.) Get a *good* lunch. See the fathering of the

Unions etc. on the Embankment. Speak from platform 3. in Hyde Park— with Bebel Burroughs, etc. A *drenching rain*. I was the last speaker on the last platform to stay it out.

Monday 27

The great "International Socialist and Labor Congress" begins. I went first to meet the other American Delegates (as yesterday A.M.) then to Queen's Hall— the largest in London. Meet the Fabians, long honored. Bebel, Singer, Lieb-necht, Jaures, Lafargue, Eleanor Mark Aveling, etc.—lots of great names there. Lunch with Mrs. Hicks & Alfred.

Wed. July 29, 1896

Congress. (Tues.) went home to lunch after serving on commissions. Everyone very polite & kind.
Tea at Mrs. Sydney Webbs. Meet Prince Borghesi[,] Graham Wallace and other interesting people.

Wednesday {Aug.} 5

Write letters in tent. Some talk with Bernard Shaw [23] on literary work—very friendly and useful criticism. . . .

Mon. Aug. 10, 1896

Go to Mrs. Stanton Blatch [24] 3.10 train for Basingtoke[?]-Waterloo Station. Pleasant evening talking with Mrs. S.-B. Very advanced indeed.

Wednesday 12

Find that I am really very low again. O dear! It is so long.—Try to write something on Social Evolution to rest my brain. . . .

Friday 14

Another miserable day. I'm really very low. Some letters. Get one from mother; (H[elen]. C[ampbell].) Go to Hampstead [?] Heath with Claire & Fanny. A glorious sunset. And the whole place so big beautiful happy and— *Free*! A foretaste of the new time. . . .

Saturday 15

J. R. McDonald calls,[25] interviews me on the American Situation. Am to write something for their new magazine—The Progressive Review." Begin it. Feel quite fine to be at work. . . .

Wed. Aug. 19, 1896

Still forlorn.
Go with Fannie and Harriet (our maid!) to the Zoo. Harriet had never been. Great fun. Rode on the elephant and fed everything.
Ghastly tired.

Sat. Aug. 22, 1896

The Hickses all set off for the country. I am very comfortable at Fan's, but not able to work.

This illness seems more physical than usual. Doubtless a sympathetic collapse internally.

Tues. Aug. 25, 1896

Go to visit Mrs. Jacob Bright (sister in law of Mrs. John Bright) at "The Chestnuts," Woolburn near Maidenhead Bourne End Sta!!! Mrs. Stanton-Blatch & her brother Theodore; old Dr. Bird & his sister, Grant Allen [26] & his wife. Walk in garden—lunch—steam launch trip on Thames. Very lovely, very. Talk a good deal with Mr. Allen, attack him on his ethics. . . .

Fri. Aug. 28, 1896

Up at 8.20 or so. Answer notes. Try to write—can not. Brain will not work. I notice, gradually in the past month or two, a loss of my ready control of words.—aphasia?

Sunday 30

Delightfully high up room, looking on the Thames. Mr. Steele to breakfast. We go a rowing. Nice dinner, nap. Some people call—Mr. Fry, artist, a Frenchman, etc. See Wm. Morris for a moment—he is very ill.[27] See Mrs. Morris & Rossetti's famous portrait of her. Speak in to H. Socialist Society on "Socialism in America." Went well. Speak in Hammersmith.

Saturday {Sept.} 5

Go to Newcastle. A young comrade, going also to the "Van" goes with me. Talk—more than I ought. Arrive very tired. Am in a wretched condition truly. Alfred Hicks meets me—takes me to Miss Roecliff's—a nice little lady—school mistress—charming. She treats me like a sick princess!

Sun. Sept. 6, 1896

Loaf about. Alfred in and out. Go in evening with Miss Roecliff to see a bit of English fashionable society. Very amusing but also tiresome to a degree.

Sat. Sept. 12, 1896

Shop and go to see "The New Castle up on the Tyne" again—1000 years old! Alfred to lunch & sees me to train at 3.47. Reach Glasgow at 8.30—very tired. Go to hotel. Don't like it. Try another—won't stop, make cabman take me to a third. Cranston Waverly Temperance fairly good.

Tues. Sept. 15, 1896

Pleasant time, quiet and good. Look up infant mortality statistics. Tea at Mrs. Glasier's. . . . Speak on The New Motherhood to Woman's Labour Party. Crowded hall. Made an impression.

Wednesday 16

Off for Edinburgh on 11 A.M. train. . . . Nice trip. Feel well. Met by Mrs. Dowie—glad to see me. Quiet house delightful old lady. Go out alone between showers and see beautiful Edinburgh from Castle hill—sunset & moonrise—buglenotes—all glamour & loveliness. People in evening.

Thursday 17

Wet day. Write, read, rest, have good time—. Get very friendly with my hostess and "Struey" a shaggy waggy little doggie.

Fri. Sept. 18, 1896

Mrs. D. shows me over the Castle—herself a living guide book. Enjoy it much. Am still bed-breakfasted and lunch-napped, most luxuriously. *Am improving.*
Welcome batch of letters in morning.

Sunday 20

. . . Speak P.M., for Labor Church on "The New Religion." Enthusiastically received. . . .

Tuesday 22

. . . Third day of feeling well. I believe the tide has turned.

Sun. Sept. 27, 1896

Waked at 8.30. Fine night. No coffee for breakfast however! Alas! Write letters. Bit of a walk. Dinner. Speak P.M. for Labour Church, on "Thou Shalt Love." Well received. Ben Gillett home to supper with us. He spoke morning & evening in same place.

Sat. Oct. 3, 1896*

William Morris died today. . . .

Fri. Oct. 9, 1896

. . . Go in evening to my first Fabian meeting. Very exciting.

Tuesday 13

. . . Go to memorial meeting for Wm. Morris. A thoroughly good and genuine affair.

Sun. Oct. 18, 1896

Go to see Miss Jane Hume Clapperton,[28] and Mrs. Calhoun, a travelling American. Enjoy Miss Clapperton. Home very jolly.
Am having much mild fun with Tiddliwinks—with Claire.

Monday 19

Go with Claire to see Tower of London.
Interesting, but wearying.

Sat. Oct. 24, 1896

Go to Dorsetshire—Parkstone, to visit Alfred Russell Wallace.[29] Speak in evening on "Our Brains and What Ails Them." Small hall & audience, but successful lecture, very.

Fri. Oct. 30, 1896

Speak for Woman's Industrial Council at Mrs. Stapley's P.M. on "Women and Work." Herbert Burrows there. Go with him to Socialist Club to tea, *very* jolly. Then go to Fabian Society with Mr. Pease. Very nice.

Tuesday {Nov.} 3

Went to Westminster Abbey and prowled awhile. Go [*sic*] Edward VI's inscription for Kate. A quiet evening.

Wednesday 4

Went to National Gallery of paintings and saw more than I could hold.

Monday 16

Fog and headache. Do some shopping. Speak in evening on "Woman and Man"—first good feeling one—went well.
Small house though.

Wednesday 18

Last night thank goodness. "Woman and Child." Well received all; and appreciated by a few.
A week of foregone failure, hard work and "heavy sledding" in general. Pay $16.25!!! Stood it fairly well.

Thursday 19

Furnessia sails. . . . Have a nice large stateroom, sit near the captain, feel fine.

Few passengers. Room to myself.
Starts about 9.30 P.M.

Fri. Nov. 20, 1896

Wake up cheerfully and start to dress. Give it up and tumble back to berth. Sea sick! She stops at Moville & I come on deck. Succumb when she starts again, and drop into berth with clothes on. Stay there till Tues. P.M.!!!

Saturday 21

Seasickness not so bad as stated. I lie peaceful and alone—a blessed rest—eat nothing, drink nothing—suffer nothing. Nausea is not painful. Do some wide pleasant thinking.

Sunday 22

White grapes are good when you're seasick. The Stewardess brings me what I need and more than I can take, "appearing at intervals."
Still serene.

Tuesday 24

Up again, and stick it out till night, when I get my clothes off—what joy!—and tumble in.

Get the Stewardess to bring me a big glass of hot milk with brandy in it. After slight resistance my stomach surrenders to the stuff. Sleep well thereon. And knit. And feel serene.

Thurs. Nov. 26, 1896

Thanksgiving Day. I give thanks earnestly, for a good world, a good God, and to be able to eat dinner again! Enjoyed my lunch—think of it! and ate a course dinner!

Some of this last left me later, and I demanded hot brandy & water on retiring. Good stuff.

Monday 30

Arrive—about 2 P.M. Drive up to my mamas—20–W. 32nd st. They are glad to see me. Letters waiting. Little up stairs room. Will be $7.00 a week. Visit awhile first. Go out & take a walk. All comfy.

Tuesday, Dec. 1

Slept beautifully. Splendid breakfast. Take a bit of walk. Nice neighborhood. Write & rip. Go shopping after lunch—small stuff to make over red dress.

Feel real well. Good appetite for breakfast. sleep well—all serene.

Wed. Dec. 2, 1896

Sew on red dress A.M. Nap after lunch. Sew more. Dine with Mrs. Stanton-Blatch at her mothers.[30] Charming old lady. Pleasant evening.

Thursday 3

Mother gets letter saying father is worse. . . . Call on Mrs. Stanton-Blatch to say I can't go with her tonight. Go down to see father at sanitarium, Delaware Water Gap. He is much better, and seems glad to see me. Good food, nice place.

Wednesday 9

. . . Special delivery letter from Mrs. Stanton-Blatch asking me to go with her to reception at the Waldorf—Washington grandees—about a Motherhood Congress. Poor meeting, but a good sign.

Sunday 13

Call for Mrs. Stanton-Blatch and she takes me to hear Felix Adler. Not great. On the Parental Relation.—poor. Talk with Mrs. Stanton thereon. Home to dinner. Mr. Pelton, friend of Mary's, brings me "The Damnation of Theron Ware"[31] to read. Write to Kate.

Friday 18

Don't feel quite as well as I did. Send off Kate's things. Go to see Miss Mann. Ask her to lend me $25.00—she makes it fifty! Orders 100 books which will nearly pay it. Lunch there. Have photo taken at Bloomingdale's—$1.50 a doz. cabinets!! . . .

Friday 25

A dear little box from Kate—five dainty gifts. A tie from Kathie, two little silver duds from Mary. Feel very serene. . . . .

Thursday 31

Nice day. Wrote "First Class in Sociology" for Jan. Fabian. Took a walk. Good lunch. *Heavenly* nap. Call on Miss Mann with mss. She likes 'em. Home. Letters. Dinner. Letters. New Years eve party in evening. Pleasant talk with Mr. Shelby the lawyer. Upstairs at 11.50 and received The New Year Alone as usual.

Health and Work!

[1897]

Fri. Jan. 1, 1897

The midnight hours and bells tell of the New Year. Down stairs they dance. I am in my fourth floor back, serene, strong, happy. For the year I ask Health, and to do my Work.

Quiet day. Finished letters. Took a walk. Lunch. Nap. Read & write. Evening down stairs—One word game etc.

Saturday 2*

. . . William Gillette calls. A hopless [*sic*] pessimist.[32] Stay down in evening. Antonio Apache calls on the family. A splendid Indian—six feet four, and broad in proportion, and a polished courteous man of the world.

Fri. Jan. 15, 1897

Sleep ill—waking often to see time. Up at 6.30, bathe, dress, & finish packing. Down by 7.45. Mr. Lemercier goes to station with me—carries bags. "Fastest train in the World". Leave at 8.30, Rochester at 3.25. Miss Anthony—sister of Susan—meets me. We go to a Unitarian Woman's meeting—I read "The Lesson of Death". Meet various people. Eat a good supper and am in bed by 9 o'clock.

Mon. Feb. 1

Start for Omah [*sic*] on 8.25 train. Arrive near 2. Dine at restaurant with Mrs. Ford. Speak at Woman's Club on "Women & Politics". Read "Mother to

Child" by request. Make an impression. Receive $10.00 — (trip cost $9.00!) Return on 4.50 train—arrive 9.30 or so. Walk up to Sabin House.

Tues. Feb. 2, 1897

Up betimes. Breakfast. Go to the Capitol with Mrs. Johnston & Representative Bird and at 9 sharp open the House with prayer!!! Prayed five minutes. Receive five dollars!!!! Then to High School & speak[;] not very well received. Lunch, rest, Miss Gillette calls for me, visit her mother, dine there & visit some people, called for by Mrs. Scott & go to Highland Park College. Lecture on Our Brains & What Ails Them. 25.00. They didn't like it much I think. Pack.

Sunday 7

Dine with the Marshalls— (went over on the steamer with me) at 48 Groveland Park. Back here. Mr. White here. Telephone from Mrs. Coonley, & I meet her at Mrs. M. T. Wynne's, with Dr. Bedell and Ruth McEnery Stuart,[33] and we talk on Man & Woman. Mrs. Yale there too—fine old lady. Good talk.

Wed. Feb. 10. 1897

Off betimes to Mrs. Dow's to get things and say goodbye & thankyou. Get *"The Yellow Wallpaper"* of Mrs. Furness— (in her absence!) to read here. Read it, to Mrs. Coonly, Sarah and Avery, and Ruth McEnery Stuart. . . .

Wednesday 17

Slept well. Go to opening of Mother Congress in Arlington Hotel. Awful jam. Don't get in. Go to the White House Reception given in honor of the M. C. & shake hands with Mrs. Cleveland—nice woman. Another jam. Home eat rest a bit & to go Congress again. Moved to church. Big crowd. Enjoy it—it means much though little enough is yet said or known. Two visitors to dinner. Tired, very.

Sat. Feb. 20, 1897

Talk and pack. Early lunch. 12.15 train to Water Tap Pa. Change at Phila. & Manunka Chu[illeg.]. Arrive at 7 P.M. pretty tired. Father very glad to see me. He looks old and uncared for.

Wednesday {March} 3

Take Kathie & go to Fordham "Home for Incurables." Won't do to my mind. Lunch & go to Morristown, N. J. to see Dr. Wright's place. Just the thing. Home late and very tired. Something to eat and bed. . . .

Sat. March 6, 1897

Alfred Hicks arrives—to breakfast. Go down town with him. Call on Mrs. Catt. A. & I go up in tower of World Bldg. and view N. Y. Look for Ypsilanti underwear—in vain. Lunch. Good nap. Read Kipling's "Seven Seas" to Alf—lots of 'em—a real happiness. We go to Fabian Study Club in evening. I don't take to Marx as an economist.

Mon. March 8, 1897*
Go down town with Alfred. Look up Houghton Gilman.³⁴ Hunt for under wear again, & find the Ypsilanti underwear agency. Home to lunch. Nap. . . . Sit in A's. room all evening, eat oranges, read, and talk.

Wed. March 10, 1897
. . . Houghton Gilman calls. Like him.

Thursday 11
Feel fine. Arrange plans of work. Write a bit. Buy Whitely exerciser for father, patterns, shoes, etc. for me. Go to see father in Morristown p.m. He is real *happy* and comfortable and likes the folks & place. I am so glad. Back on 5.25. Talk a little with folks in evening. Bed rather early.

Tues. March 16, 1897
Go down cellar and get things out of trunk. Go through all my things and arrange what to make, what to keep, what to throw away. Very tired. Hough-ton comes about six. Dine gorgeously at the Imperial. Then go to see the 7th Regiment perform. He is a member of Company B—the "Old Second" that used to be first. . . .

Friday 19
. . . Go to Jersey City and dine at Dr. Florence De Hart's. Then speak at Mrs. Mary Philbrooks—parlor meeting. Very dull and difficult. Sleep ill thereafter—also for the first time in life I rise and slay bedbugs—four fat conspicuous tame bedbugs!

Sat. March 20, 1897
Go to Hoboken and take 9 A.M. train to Morristown. Spend an hour and a quarter or so with father. He is very contented there. Home late to lunch. Then nap—good one, dress, dine, and to speak on "Why We Work" to Single Tax Club. They are horrid as usual, but Wm. Dean Howells came to hear me! Was introduced—says he is coming to see me!!! A very jolly & exciting dis-cussion. Houghton there and came home with me.

Sunday 21
Lovely day. . . . Mr. Howells calls on me! Brings his daughter—they are just as nice as can be. Asks me—and mother—to call on Mrs. Howells & go to meeting of Pub. Ownership League and am put on committee. No harm.

Sun. March 28, 1897

Houghton comes at 9.40 or so. We set forth to go and see father. Walk to ferry. Go to Hoboken. Find no trains run on Sunday (D. L. & W.—"Delay, Linger & Wait" Mary says.) We serenely go to Bronx Park, and dine at the Hermitage—in a green arbor out of doors. *Delightful time.* Nice talk. I call on Mrs. Howells. See daughter also. Very nice time. Pleasant talk here in evening with Mrs. Mitchell & "Peter."

Tues. March 30, 1897

. . . My health is certainly better. I have been really working for two weeks, and feel no worse for it! . . .

Wednesday 31

. . . Houghton comes, rather late, and spends the evening up stairs with me. Delightful time. Get very friendly.

Sunday {April} 4

Another fair day. Feel well— (and look well, in the blue suit!) Houghton at about 10. Go to Bedloe's Island and ascend inside of the Statue of Liberty— look out of her crown. Then see the aquarium. Then go to Staten Island. Dine at South Beach. Walk around a bit, see fort Wadsworth—from without— etc. Tired but happy. Home at near six. Some talk down stairs and bed early.

Mon. April 5, 1897

Long good sleep, and feel well. Write to Kate and lot of others. Feel very happy & strong. . . .
Messenger with note from Mrs. Howells asking me to lunch. Oliver Herford to meet me!!![35]

Wed. April 7, 1897

Finish off striped waist. Go to lunch with the Howells and Oliver Herford who wished much to meet me. Delightful time. Mr. Herford walks home with me, buys two books, wants to make design for cover—very cordial. . . .

Sun. April 11, 1897

. . . Houghton comes & we go to Brooklyn together. I speak on the Economic Basis of the Woman Question to the Brooklyn Philosophical Assn. Not very good—nor bad. Mother comes, late, & we go back with her. Houghton delightfully polite to her—wins her completely. Stays to supper and spends the evening with me in my little room. . . .

Wed. April 21, 1897

Up betimes & feel well. Get off all smooth and lovely. Houghton meets me & sees me off. He has been a great pleasure. Join Mrs. Blankenburg at Phil. at 12.20 or so & arrive at Harrisburg at 3.25 or so. . . . A number of Indian girls from Carlisle School come and sing for us in our Suffrage meeting in the Legislative Chambers. I speak—not at all successfully.

Monday 26

Nice day. Feel fine. Get lot of letters including invitation to chair in Kansas Agricultural College—$1400.00 a year! Cookery & Hygiene preferred! . . .

Thur. May 13, 1897

Am feeling rather dull along now. Write letters. Read lot of poems to Mrs. Dow as she sews. I guess I have twenty or thirty good ones for my next edition—twenty or so brand new. . . .

Wed. May 19, 1897

Am really feeling dismal again, and can't say why.[36] Write to Houghton. Copy poems. Lie down after lunch. . . .

Wednesday 26

A suddenly arranged excursion. Mrs. Lee mounts her wheel and collects eight ladies & a team & driver. Go to Sister Lakes, some twelve miles; row, dine, loaf about, go to Magician Lake & it's island cottages—home about six. Lovely day and very pleasant time. A beautiful world and lots of nice people on it!

Am to stay over and speak tomorrow night.

Saturday {June} 5

. . . Lester F. Ward sends me "Collective Telesis" with reference to "Similar Cases."

Read and enjoy it.

Sunday 27

Lazy day. All these days lazy. Speak in evening at Congregational Church on Social Settlements. Was presented with the collection—$3.96!

Tuesday 29

Loaf and wait. Try to write letters.

Hot weather.

Feel weak.

Get letter from Howells about book.

Wed. June 30, 1897

Send letter & some new poems to Ripley Hitchcock, reader for Appleton's, at Mr. Howell's suggestion. . . .

SIX

"The splendid truths I know"

July 1, 1897—March 12, 1935

STILL FUELED BY THE energy and confidence that she enjoyed during the spring of 1897, Charlotte continued strong throughout the early summer. On July 1 she began drafting an article about the "economic basis of [the] woman question." At some point during the day, Charlotte realized the magnitude and philosophical import of the connection between economic dependence and female subjugation. "Get hold of a new branch of my theory on above subject—the biggest since I saw it. Now I can write the book," she remarked decisively.

"The book" that Charlotte envisioned that hot July day evolved into *Women and Economics*, the magnum opus of her long career. A major feminist polemic addressing the relationship between sexual oppression and economic dependence on men, *Women and Economics* eventually was translated into seven languages and won Charlotte international acclaim when it was published in 1898.

Although it was July 1 when Charlotte realized she was onto something big, it wasn't until August 31 that she actually began drafting the book. In the interim, however, she discussed her economic theory with several people, including Jane Addams, who was "really impressed—with the new big idea. To have her see it is a great help," Charlotte reported in her diary.

The first two weeks of August 1897 Charlotte spent at Summer Brook Farm in the Adirondack Mountains of upstate New York, a commune of sorts, to which the owner, Prestonia Mann, invited "numbers of interesting people of a progressive tendency" (*Living*, p. 230). The household work was divided among the guests, and Charlotte relished the experience. "All hands do the washing—great fun," she declared cheerfully on August 2. While Charlotte managed to produce a bit of writing during her stay, she also spent time relaxing and seemed to especially enjoy berry-picking trips and a climb up Mount Hurricane. But for part of that summer she also experienced profound loneliness, particularly since she hadn't seen Houghton in several months. July 22 was a markedly difficult day: "A bad day. Heart ache—promiscuous lonesomeness." Finally, on August 14, she arrived back in New York. At the train station Charlotte was reunited not only with Houghton but with Katharine as well, who would stay with Charlotte briefly before departing for Europe with Walter and Grace.

The few days with Katharine were happy ones. On Sunday, August 15, Charlotte and Houghton took Katharine to see the Statue of Liberty, and the next day mother and daughter went shopping. August 17 was particularly delightful: "A fine long day in the Park with Kate. We do everything pretty much, and she has a very good time. Is especially delighted to learn to row—which she does in astonishingly quick time." After seeing Katharine off the following day, Charlotte spent some happy time with Houghton before departing again, this time for Greenacre, Maine. On August 22 the two spent the entire day together: "Houghton comes early and we set off for the day. Lovely time . . . walk to Palisades—beautiful! Dine in Englewood. . . . He is a dear boy."

On August 31, in Laconia, New Hampshire, Charlotte began *Women and Economics*. The first 356-page draft was completed just thirty-nine days later, on October 8. Even more remarkable, however, is that Charlotte worked on the book for just seventeen of those thirty-nine days in "five different houses" (*Living*, p. 237). One of those houses was Martha Luther Lane's, where Charlotte visited in September. By September 25, Charlotte had made enough progress on the book to interest Small, Maynard and Co. who had already contracted to publish the 1898 expanded edition of Charlotte's volume of poems, *In This Our World*.

Throughout the fall of 1897, as Charlotte revised her *Women and Economics* manuscript, Houghton Gilman was exceedingly supportive, reading her revisions and offering encouragement. On December 16 Charlotte submitted the revised draft to Herbert Small, who accepted the manuscript on December 19, and *Women and Economics* appeared in print the following June.

New Year's Eve, 1897, proved to be happier than New Year's Eve, 1896, which Charlotte had lamented spending "alone as usual." This time she and Houghton shared the evening, and their relationship seemed comfortable and secure. "Houghton comes. . . . A good talk and we see the old year out *together*," she wrote contentedly. But even with the incredible accomplishments of the year behind her, Charlotte was careful not to take her good fortune for granted. Her "Notes for 1898" were tentative and reserved: "Health pretty fair now. Am able to work. Literary reputation steadily increasing. Things look bright."

Early in 1898 Charlotte submitted the final manuscript of *Women and Economics* to her publisher, Small, Maynard and Co. Soon after, she started to search for other means of income. *Illustrated American* wrote to solicit articles at the rate of a penny per word, and she was still a regular contributor to the *American Fabian*. Still, the financial outlook for her immediate future was bleak, even though Small and Maynard issued her a $25 advance in late April.

In early February, Charlotte briefly had her hopes raised that her financial worries might be assuaged when English stage actress Annie Russell asked to see the script of "A Pretty Idiot," a play on which Charlotte and Grace had collaborated back in 1890. On February 5 Charlotte read the play to Russell and others, who liked it only "fairly." Even though Russell declined the play, Charlotte was persistent, approaching her a couple of days later with an idea for another comedy, tentatively titled "The Price of Love." Once again, although Russell reportedly liked the idea, it too fell by the wayside. During the writing of her autobiography nearly twenty-seven years later, Charlotte still expressed disappointment that her dramatic aspirations never materialized.

As a result, Charlotte spent much of the winter and spring of 1898 concentrating on other means of securing a steady income. She wrote numerous short articles, which she submitted to *New Nation*, *Criterion*, and *Scribner's*. She also wrote some poetry and short fiction and was pleased when in mid-April an English publisher wrote to solicit some manuscripts. Lecturing engagements in April and May also brought in some much-needed money.

By the time June arrived, Charlotte was ready for a vacation and decided to spend the summer at Cold Spring Harbor, Long Island. It was "such a blessed cool sweet still place!" she remarked in her diary late in the summer. And, in fact, despite the chronic depression that resurfaced temporarily in July, Charlotte did enjoy herself immensely at her "summer home." Katharine, now thirteen, arrived with Houghton in mid-June. She "is tall and lovely, sweetmannered and strong. It is good to see her," Charlotte wrote. She and Katharine spent peaceful, happy days that summer, swimming, berrying, catching turtles. "She is so good to be with," Charlotte remarked on June 19, and the next day: "Kate hunts frogs and is as good as gold. We play games after supper." June 27: "We skip stones in the harbor, find some strawberries—generally enjoy ourselves." The two also picked wild mushrooms, walked together, read together, and played card games. Houghton, who was becoming a fairly steady companion, often joined their activities. And although Charlotte had to borrow money to remain in Cold Spring Harbor through the summer, she reveled in the tranquillity.

At the end of August, Charlotte returned to New York with Katharine, who was to rejoin Walter and Grace on their way back to Pasadena. After seeing Katharine off at the train station, Charlotte went home and "collapsed." A week in the city was enough: Charlotte headed back to Cold Spring Harbor for another two weeks. "Have lovely bath in *pond—starlight*," she wrote the first night back. And the next day, "Delightful night. Feels good after the city. Have a swim on rising." On September 25, however, Charlotte packed her belongings and returned to New York. The summer was over, and as restful as her time away had been, there was work to be done: the reality of Charlotte's financially precarious position had, inevitably, to be addressed.

Back in New York City, Charlotte quickly resumed her work schedule and social activities. She continued to spend some "delightful" time with Houghton and with several acquaintances and friends. One frequent companion was Lillian Wald of the Henry Street Nurses Settlement, who was known for her tireless social work as the "Jane Addams of New York." Charlotte also made her last visit to her critically ill father in late September. "Go to see father—8.50 train. Carry grapes. Knew me for a while. Probably can not see him again.————"

In early October, Charlotte left for a trip to Boston where she visited, among others, her publishers, Small, Maynard & Co., Martha Lane, and Alice Stone Blackwell. She was also introduced in Boston to American author and Whitman literary executor Horace L. Traubel, who wrote a particularly fine review of *In This Our World*.

Following the Boston trip, Charlotte headed briefly to Michigan to lecture and then to Chicago where she remained for several weeks, lunching with Jane Addams, sharing a podium with Hamlin Garland, and collaborating on yet another play, this time with Hervey White, a young Harvard man "interested in sociology" (*Living*, p. 185), whom she had met through Helen Campbell several years earlier. Once again, however, the play was never produced.

Charlotte spent a "decidedly lonesome Xmas" in Chicago. By the time January 1 arrived, however, her outlook seemed to be brighter. In a note to herself on the frontispiece of the diary for 1899, Charlotte reflected on one's duty in life. One of those duties, she believed, was "to tell and tell forever Humanitie's great secret—That each one *is all the rest*—and each 'can *do*' himself, the world's work, so made easier for all, a calmness, born of the immeasurable Power which moves us." With that philosophy in mind, Charlotte began another lecture tour in early January, stopping first in Chicago and then in Toledo and Wauseon, Ohio, where her address on socialism was well received. "Mr. Jones gave me twenty five dollars and offered a lot more—but I thought best not to indulge," Charlotte wrote solemnly. The next leg of her trip took her to Missouri and then to Tennessee, during a particularly brutal cold spell. February 9: "Gas frozen last night. No heat in my room. Ink froze inside my bag! Water pitcher of course." And on February 12: "Water freezes in my room—Still cold. This is preternatural weather. We all sit stranded and hug the fire."

From Tennessee, Charlotte traveled to Alabama where she spoke to a Students' Club whose audience was "most cordial and enthusiastic." The next day, the audience at a Women's Club meeting was packed. "Tremendous crowd-standing, lots couldn't get in. Went well, very. Great enthusiasm. . . . (People fainted—went out, recovered—*and returned*!)" Charlotte was delighted by the show of support. Her next stops were in North Carolina and then on to Washington, New York, Boston, and Cambridge, Massachusetts.

Contemporaneous with Charlotte's extensive travels and growing international reputation was the growing relationship with Houghton Gilman, seven years her junior. Separated for long periods because of Charlotte's travel schedule, the two seemed to have built their relationship largely through the exchange of correspondence that took place over a three-year period, from shortly after Charlotte renewed her acquaintance with Houghton back in 1897 until their marriage in 1900.

The extant correspondence is in the form of Charlotte's letters to Houghton; she apparently did not keep his letters to her. The letters that survive have been collected by Mary A. Hill and published in *A Journey from Within: The Love Letters of Charlotte Perkins Gilman, 1897–1900* (Lewisburg, Pa., 1995). The letters are remarkable for what they reveal about the nature and complexity of the relationship that evolved between the two. Still searching for love, yet fearing the consequences of commitment, Charlotte was determined from the start not to repeat the mistakes of her earlier marriage to Walter. In a letter dated September 16, 1898, she outlined her priorities, insisting that if they should marry, she be free to work and travel as she saw fit: "As you value my life, my sanity, my love . . . you will have to give up a certain ideal of home . . . . I *must not* focus on 'home duties'; and entangle myself in them. Remember it is not an external problem with me—a mere matter of material labor and time. However vague and absurd my talk may seem to you; it is practical enough to be a question of life and death with me," she wrote (*Journey*, p. 75).

Houghton not only agreed that Charlotte should not concern herself with domestic responsibilities, but he also encouraged her to write and to lecture, often accompanying her to speaking engagements and reading and responding constructively to her works in progress. Charlotte seemed comfortable enough to confide to Houghton, on the pages of her letters, her most intimate feelings. Her letters candidly reveal her desire for physical affection, describe the severity of her chronic depression, confess the pain and guilt she felt over her maternal failure. Into letter after letter Charlotte poured her heart. But then, suddenly, often without warning, Charlotte would withdraw: her guard would go up, and she would express reservations about the sincerity of Houghton's love. At other times she would voice distress that her emotional vacillations would cause him pain. In a letter dated November 3, 1897, for example, Charlotte wrote: "You see all my life I haven't had what I wanted in the way of being loved. . . . And I'd *much* rather not have you at all than to hurt your feelings and make you angry perhaps" (*Journey*, p. 114). Because love had proved so elusive in the past, Charlotte was probably terrified that it would end badly again. She was as afraid of being with Houghton as she was of being without him.

Gradually, however, Houghton began to win Charlotte's trust. On May 22, 1898, she wrote: "I am going to marry you just because I love you and so I can't help it" (*Journey*, p. 146). But she was also discovering how compatible she was with Houghton. Houghton was vastly different from Walter; he was not threatened by Charlotte's work, and he seemed to take her occasional outbursts in stride, recognizing the insecurity and vulnerability that underlay them. And as Charlotte's trust grew, so did her love. "You are more to me than my child," she wrote on March 12, 1899 (p. 249).

Charlotte and Houghton discussed at length the possibilities of having children together. "O I want a new baby so! I want to begin again and have a fairer chance," she wrote" (*Journey*, p. 335). But in less romantic moments, Charlotte realized clearly that another baby likely would imperil her mental health and ultimately would prove unwise.

In late April and early May, shortly before she left on another trip to England, Charlotte and Houghton spent a few happy days together in New York. When she set sail on May 4, 1899, Houghton was on hand to see her off.

Charlotte's main purpose in traveling to England during the spring and summer of 1899 was to attend the Congress of the International Council of Women. Since the congress did not open until June 26, however, she had several free weeks during which she renewed acquaintances from her trip in 1896, composed some articles, and called on her English publisher, T. Fisher Unwin.

On the evening that the congress opened, Charlotte attended a "grand reception in Stafford House in [the] evening," hosted by the duchess of Sutherland. She was also a guest at Lady Battesea's reception at Surrey House and at the Rothschild garden party at Gunnersbury Park. As a delegate to the congress, Charlotte was invited to Windsor Castle to take tea with Queen Victoria. Although her account of her decision to forgo the invitation is quite humorous in *The Living of Charlotte Perkins Gilman* (pp. 264–65), the diary entry betrays regret: "Think I made a mistake in not going to Winsor to see the Queen,—a concession to the Congress," she lamented on July 7. One invitation she did accept, however, came in a sixty-three-word telegram from the countess of Warwick asking her to speak before a group of four hundred laborers from Birmingham. The engagement became one of the highlights of her trip.

The congress itself was highly successful, providing an opportunity for women affiliated with organizations from all over the world to share their political views and experiences. Charlotte's own presentation, "Equal Pay for Equal Work," in the session on the "Ethics of Wage Earning," was exceptionally well received. "Overflow meeting in spite of rain," she reported in her diary. As she often did when her confidence was high, Charlotte spoke extemporaneously on the topic, rather than reading the paper that she had prepared. She also produced some good articles during this trip, including an account of the congress, "The

Great Meeting of Women in London," for the *Saturday Evening Post* and "The Home without a Kitchen" for the *Puritan*.

One other highlight during this visit was Houghton's decision to join Charlotte in England for a month. He arrived on July 13, and although they were separated by Charlotte's lecturing schedule and by his visit to an aunt, the time they did have together was happy. They continued to discuss their plans to be married, although Charlotte seemed to be vacillating just a bit. On July 26 she discussed her reservations about marriage and childbearing with a Dr. Kennedy, who offered support and encouragement. "Call on Dr. Kennedy and get medicine and advice. He says I should marry!" she remarked in her diary.

After Houghton left for New York in mid-August, Charlotte stayed another two weeks or so before setting sail herself. She arrived back in the States on September 11 after an "uneventful voyage" which was "rather dull and long." The trip had left her feeling a little out of sorts. "Not seasick," she reported, "but not in vigorous health either."

Within a week after her return to New York, Charlotte and Houghton began to make wedding plans and tried to project their future income and expenses. Although Houghton apparently felt "badly about business things," Charlotte was enjoying at least a temporary period of "prosperity." A few days after arriving home, she received her largest check to date—$125 for an article she had placed in *Ainslee's Magazine*.

That "windfall" was followed by another, more significant acknowledgment of Charlotte's influence, when Herbert Small of Small, Maynard and Co. approached her with a contract for another book. The terms he offered were generous for the time—a $500 advance and royalties of 15 percent for the first 5,000 copies sold, and 18 percent thereafter. In the same week, two lectures in Boston yielded Charlotte $87, and she received $48 a couple of days later from the *Saturday Evening Post* followed by $25 for a lecture to the Woman's Club.

While she was in the Boston area in early October, Charlotte made a trip to visit Martha Lane. Although she had attained celebrity status, Charlotte's sense of adventure, particularly as it pertained to matters of justice, continued to be displayed: "Talk with Martha, write a letter. Lie in wait for thieving boys and catch one—spraining my finger thereby! But 'it was a glorious victory.'"

Following the Boston trip, Charlotte headed west, finally ending up in California, where she would spend the winter writing the first draft of *Human Work*, the book which was under contract with Small, Maynard and Co. Along the way Charlotte stopped in more than a dozen cities to visit friends and to lecture. By the time she reached San Francisco in early December, Charlotte had amassed enough money to pay off some of her old debts, many of which were five or more years old. She was particularly proud when her old friend Hattie Howe accompanied her to pay rent that was owed to a previous landlord: Hattie "goes with me to Oakland & we find Mrs. Collins at 1258 Webster & pay the rent bill $140.00 —& 20 due on gas. She was paralyzed with astonishment," Charlotte gloated in the diary. And even after her falling out with Adeline Knapp, Charlotte still honored her obligation to repay money borrowed several years earlier: "See Mr. Bartnett and arrange about paying Miss Knap—leave 25.00 for first payment."

On December 23 Charlotte was reunited with Katharine. The next day, Christmas Eve, Charlotte spent with Walter, Grace, and Katharine in Pasadena. Christmas Day, however, was difficult for Charlotte. She found herself defending her choices—and particularly her lifestyle—when she went to call on her old friend Gussie Senter and her mother, who greeted her coldly. "See them both & Mrs. Masters. All cold—Gussie explains their views—I am an unnatural mother! Well!" It wasn't the first time Charlotte had had to defend herself against such charges, but it still saddened her. To Houghton she wrote, "I've just made a fool of myself. Went across the way to call on some old neighbors, and— I foolishly supposed—friends, and got violently slapped in the face. . . . It's the 'unnatural mother' racket—same old thing. . . . I haven't felt so uncomfortable inside for ever so long" (*Journey*, p. 334). Significantly, less than a month later arrangements were made to have Katharine go to live with Charlotte for a while.

As the year drew to a close, Charlotte looked ahead to the next century. In her "Notes for 1900," Charlotte issued a self-directive: "Get well—get well—get well. And do good work! Pay all debts if possible." A poem inscribed by Charlotte on the frontispiece for the diary for 1900, in which she enlists God's help, captures beautifully her views about her self, her life, her work. It reads, in part:

> Help me to grow!
> Help me to fill the days
> With deeds of loving praise
> For the splendid truths I know . . .
>
> Slowly so long—and dark!—
> Down at the lowest mark—.
>   The light grows now!
> God! I am seeking still
> To learn and do your will—
>   Still show me how!

At the height of her career, Charlotte Perkins Stetson, now a world-renowned lecturer, wanted more than ever to share with society "the splendid truths" that she had come to know.

Charlotte began the new century in Pasadena, California, where Katharine was living with Walter and Grace. Mother and daughter spent time together in the Las Casitas foothills where they "tramped . . . together, read, played games"(*Living*, p. 276). It was also there that Charlotte completed the first draft of her next substantial book, *Human Work*, the work she regarded as "the greatest book [she had] ever done, and the poorest . . . the least adequately done" (p. 275).

Early in 1900 Charlotte's diary reports that she, Walter, and Grace engaged in serious discussions about the possibility of Katharine living with Charlotte for awhile. "I guess she will come to me for a year with mutual satisfaction all around," Charlotte reported on January 20. If Charlotte had shown a poor sense of timing in sending Katharine to live with Grace and Walter at the start of their marriage in 1894, it was time for fair play on Walter's part: Katharine arrived on Charlotte's doorstep the month following her June wedding to Houghton Gilman.

It was early in February 1900 that Charlotte broke to Katharine the news of her impending marriage to Houghton. Charlotte recorded Katharine's reaction in her diary. She "takes it very sweetly—but [is] not overpleased I fancy." Charlotte, however, seemed ecstatically happy, particularly during the honeymoon that followed her June 11 wedding in Detroit. She and Houghton traveled first to Canada and then to the lakes and mountains of upstate New York. They spent peaceful, lazy days, reading, walking, conversing, and playing croquet. Upon their return to New York, the marital bliss continued.

At the end of July, Katharine joined her mother and new stepfather in New York. They searched endlessly for a flat that would accommodate all three of them comfortably, and Charlotte tirelessly investigated schools in which she might enroll the fifteen-year-old Katharine. Still, Charlotte made time to write, and on August 25 she completed her next book, *Concerning Children*, in which she discussed her theories of child rearing.

In early November, when Charlotte left for an extended lecture tour, Katharine stayed behind in New York with Houghton and Helen Campbell, whom Charlotte recruited to serve as Katharine's substitute mother (*Living*, p. 287). Charlotte returned to New York on December 15, after a six-week absence, with a much-needed profit of about $130.

Most of 1901 was happy and productive. Charlotte worked on revising *Human Work* and drew crowds at numerous lectures. In the autumn of 1901, she learned how to ride a bicycle and began attending college football games with Houghton. The old fatigue and depression, however, would occasionally resurface, and in December, Charlotte received, as an experimental treatment, a mild form of electric shock therapy from Dr. Mary Putnam Jacobi, who took a particular interest in Charlotte's "case." [1]

One method of alleviating depression that Charlotte had found effective from her adolescence was physical exercise. As a supplement, perhaps, to Jacobi's treatment, Charlotte in January 1902 joined a women's basketball team. It was an experience which she found to be "great fun." "Enjoy it hugely & am not tired," she wrote with obvious satisfaction. For several weeks she and Katharine spent Saturdays at the gymnasium, playing basketball with several other women. By the end of February, however, Katharine had grown suddenly and danger-ously ill. In March she was diagnosed with scarlet fever. Despite the relapse in her own health, Charlotte attended Katharine, with the help of a nurse, and kept a close watch until the doctor pronounced her well in May. Katharine's recovery was complete enough that she was able to join Grace and Walter in Italy in September.

With Katharine away and Houghton often spending evenings at the armory because of his membership in the National Guard, Charlotte often experienced acute loneliness. On November 6, 1902, for example, Charlotte complained: "Ho. goes to armory. I am reduced to solitaire again, and then doze unhappily all the evening." On December 11: "Buy half a pint of scallops for my lonely supper—Ho. not home." Within a few weeks, however, there was little time for loneliness. Charlotte departed on yet another lecture tour, and upon her return she launched into another remarkably productive writing marathon.

On May 3, 1903, Charlotte suspended her diary writing. She explained her rea-sons in *The Living of Charlotte Perkins Gilman*: "These diaries are a nuisance. Page after page of those dismal 'downs' with the cheerfully welcomed 'ups.' . . . After 1903 I gave up the fat three-by-six kind, . . . and took to thinner ones" (p. 294). Those thinner "diaries," begun in 1904, are not diaries in the traditional sense at all: they are, instead, a record of Charlotte's financial accounts, appointments, speaking engagements, travel plans, and shopping lists. Only occasionally after 1903 did Charlotte include remarks that are noteworthy.

Although Charlotte ended her diary writing in 1903, a comment inscribed in the inside front cover of the diary for 1900 seems to have aptly summarized Charlotte's agenda for the twentieth century: "Because God, manifesting himself in Society, calls for ever fuller and more perfect forms of expression; therefore I, as part of Society and part of God owe my whole service to the Social develop-ment." For the remainder of her life, Charlotte Perkins Gilman worked hard at devoting her service to that very cause.

It was, of course, the publication of *Women and Economics* in 1898 that won Charlotte Gilman international acclaim, but it was in the postdiary years of the early twentieth century that Charlotte was most prolific. Over the course of her long career, she produced nearly two hundred short stories, approximately five hundred poems, seven nonfiction books, eight novels and novellas, a handful of plays, hundreds of essays, an autobiography, dozens of diaries and journals, and close to a thousand lectures. By her own estimate she also produced "no end of stuff not good enough to keep" (*Living*, p. 100).

One of Charlotte's major accomplishments in the early years of the twentieth century was her critically acclaimed book *The Home: Its Work and Influence*, published in 1903. "The most heretical—and the most amusing" of her works (*Living*, p. 286), *The Home* expanded many of her earlier arguments in *Women and Economics*, most notably that the home was the source of oppression for many women and that it needed to undergo major modifications in order to promote a healthier environment for all of its inhabitants. It was a work that showcased Charlotte's caustic wit.

In between writing projects Charlotte continued to lecture. In 1904 she traveled to the International Congress of Women in Berlin, Germany, which was attended by some three thousand delegates. Following the congress, Charlotte spent ten days with Katharine in Italy, who was living in Rome with Walter and Grace. The next year, 1905, brought more international travel—to England, Holland, Germany, Austria, and Hungary, where Charlotte lectured extensively (*Living*, p. 301). She completed numerous stateside lecture tours over the next several years. In 1911 Charlotte's next significant single work, *The Man-Made World*, was published, in which she outlined the destructive effects of artificially imposed gender distinctions. In 1913 Charlotte traveled to Europe for the last time to attend the International Woman's Suffrage Convention in Budapest, Hungary. When Charlotte wasn't traveling, she was writing, although she found her work increasingly difficult to market. "Social philosophy, however ingeniously presented, does not command wide popular interest," she reflected in her autobiography. "I wrote more and sold less" (*Living*, p. 304). Not easy discouraged, Charlotte decided to market her own material, and in 1909 she launched the *Forerunner*.

Perhaps the greatest literary accomplishment of her long career, the *Forerunner*, a small monthly magazine, was in circulation for seven years (1909–16). Every month Charlotte single-handedly wrote, edited, and published the magazine, which had about fifteen hundred subscribers from all over the United States and as far away as India and Australia (*Living*, p. 305). Each issue of the *Forerunner* offered readers at least one short story, some verses, a serialized novel, several essays, a sermon or two, a satirical piece, and comments and reviews. Its purpose, Charlotte wrote in the November 1909 premier issue, was to "stimulate thought; to arouse hope, courage and impatience; to offer practical suggestions and solutions, to voice the strong assurance of better living" (p. 32).

The unique blend of socialism and feminism featured on the pages of the *Forerunner* reflected Charlotte's belief in the potential of every human being to contribute to society through productive thought and work. The topics that Charlotte addressed ranged from the need for women's dress reform to a call for adequate child care to an appeal for women to enjoy reproductive and economic freedom.

Although the readership of the *Forerunner* never reached the three thousand needed to make it self-sustaining, Charlotte was nevertheless pleased by its reception. "I [was] most agreeably surprised by the acceptance of so much of what I had to offer," she wrote in her autobiography (p. 308). Among the reasons Charlotte cited in the February 1916 edition of the *Forerunner* for ending its publication was that writing the equivalent of twenty-eight books in seven years had "relieved the pressure" of what she had to say (p. 56).

As it turned out, Charlotte Gilman had plenty more to say. In 1919 and 1920 she contributed over three hundred articles to various *New York Tribune* syndicates, including the *Louisville Herald*, the *Baltimore Sun*, and the *Buffalo Evening News*. In 1923 she published *His Religion and Hers: A Study of the Faith of Our Fathers and the Work of Our Mothers*, an examination of the androcentric basis of traditional religions, which focused too heavily, she felt, on the fear of death and the anticipation of an afterlife. In 1925 she commenced work on her autobiography. She also published articles in several magazines and newspapers until 1932.

Through all of these years, Charlotte enjoyed a close relationship with Houghton Gilman. The two resided in New York City from just after their marriage in 1900 until 1922, when they moved to Norwich Town, Connecticut. Charlotte's second marriage was nothing like her first; the trials that she had endured with Walter Stetson—and the fact that she had managed to survive— somehow gave her the strength and courage to love again. She gradually learned to trust Houghton, who was wholly supportive of her career. He was, in fact, a strong and ardent champion of her work. Charlotte notes with some amusement in *The Living* that she and Houghton were regarded by fellow neighbors "as a model couple" (p. 296), a reputation they apparently earned from the frequent walks they took together.

The only really difficult times that Charlotte and Houghton seemed to face was during the years they shared their house in Norwich Town with Houghton's brother, Francis, and his wife, Emily. Emily, in particular, seems to have been the cause of considerable tension in the household (see the entry in this chapter dated July 29, 1925, for example, and the entry dated June 25, 1930, in Appendix A for Charlotte's account of some of their run-ins). But Charlotte and Houghton weathered the bad times, and Charlotte's autobiography reports that after their marriage they "lived happy ever after" (*Living*, p. 281). In 1934, when Charlotte was seventy-three, Houghton died very suddenly after suffering a cerebral hemorrhage. "Whatever I felt of loss and pain was outweighed by gratitude for an instant, painless death for him," she wrote in her autobiography (p. 334).

Two years earlier, in January 1932, Charlotte learned that she had inoperable breast cancer. Within a short time after Houghton's death, Charlotte began planning her suicide. A proponent of euthanasia, Charlotte explained her decision in *The Living of Charlotte Perkins Gilman*. "I had not the least objection to dying," she wrote. "But I did not propose to die of this, so I promptly bought sufficient chloroform as a substitute" (*Living*, p. 333). Since Charlotte felt that she no longer had "any power of service" to contribute to society, she decided to exercise her right "to choose a quick and easy death in place of a slow and horrible one" (p. 333). In late 1934 she moved back to Pasadena, California, where Katharine, long married and the mother of two children, lived with her husband, Frank Chamberlin. There she was joined and comforted by her lifelong friend, Grace Channing Stetson, who had herself been widowed for over twenty-three years. On the evening of August 17, 1935, Charlotte ended her life, preferring "chloroform to cancer" (p. 334). She died quickly and quietly.

Nearly sixty-five years after her death, the words of Charlotte Perkins Gilman are still making an impact. In a 1993 survey conducted by the Siena Research Institute, she ranked sixth among the ten most influential American women of the twentieth century. In 1994 she was inducted into the National Women's Hall of Fame in Seneca Falls, New York. The legacy of Charlotte Perkins Gilman lives on.

Thur. July 1 {1897}

Still weak, but fall to work in sheer despite [*sic*] on article about economic basis of woman question.

Get hold of a new branch of my theory on above subject—the biggest since I saw it.

Now I can write the book.[2]

Fri. July 2, 1897

Talk with Mr. A. on Economic Basis of W. S. Feel somewhat bright. They have a party in the evening—neighbors—call it my birthday party. Icecream & cake. I "speak" & read some poems.

Sun. July 4, 1897

A little rain in the night, muggy. Noisy day in the bosom of the family. Storms heavily in the afternoon.

Saturday 17

Change at Salamanca. Change at—something else. Wyoming [N.Y.] by 11.30 or so. . . . Jane Addams & Miss Mary Smith here—to my delight. Pleasant evening.

Monday 19

A good morning. Talk with Miss Addams.[3] She is really impressed—with the new big idea. To have her see it is a great help. Pick raspberries—they have 'em black red & white! And great currants of the same three colors! Walk to the spring. A lovely place. . . .

Thur. July 22, 1897

A bad day. Heart ache—promiscuous lonesomeness. Physical cause I suspect. Try to write on story—housework one. Read "Gates Ajar"[4] out by the spring. Play games and do puzzles in the evening.

One small letter from Houghton—via Kansas & Chicago! . . .

Sun. Aug. 1, 1897

A fine morning, though not yet clear entirely. Hearty breakfast. A youth, horse and buggy, take me the twenty miles to Summer-Brook Farm,⁵ 10 A.M. to 2 P.M.—inside of 4 hours. All glad to see me. *Lovely* place, way up at the head of Keene Valley near the Willey house. Write to Kate. . . .
Most beautiful house, and glorious mountains. . . .

Monday 2

All bright and jolly, though still some clouds. All hands do the washing — great fun. Write & read. . . .

Thur. Aug. 5, 1897

Most of us go up Mt. Hurricane an all day trip—four hours up—two & a half down. Splendid time.

Friday 6

Go berrying—(blue) with Uncle George. Great fun. Get about three quarts or 4? Enjoy it *much*. Mr. Whitehead comes over. Talk with him and enjoy that much, too. . . .

Fri. Aug. 13, 1897

Talk with Mr. & Mrs. Radcliffe-Whitehead. Afternoon with Alfred Hicks who appears at this last minute. Lecture in evening on The Social organism, at The Casino—Small house. Load of Summer-brookers drove over to hear me—glad to see 'em.

Saturday 14

Set forth for N. Y. Alfred rides to Westport with me. Reach N. Y. at 9.30.— Katharine already there! and Houghton. Feel very mixed up and tired. . . .

Sun. Aug. 15, 1897

Houghton calls early & we take Kate to Bedloe's Island & up Liberty; and to the Aquarium after dinner, accompanied by mother & Mr. Lemercier, we go to ride in various cable cars to see High Bridge at Harlem.
A nice talk with H. after everyone is gone—.

Monday 16

Go shopping with Kate, getting many things. Lunch with Houghton at his club—very pleasant indeed. Shop more. Home late and tired. Houghton comes up to take us to something, but we only sit around & play the One Word Game. which Kate enjoys.

Tues. Aug. 17, 1897

A fine long day in the Park with Kate. We do everything pretty much, and she has a very good time. Is especially delighted to learn to row—which she does in astonishingly quick time.
Both go to bed early.

Wednesday 18

Put in a few stitches in Kate's pongee's, pack her valise, and take her down to Hotel Albert where are Grace and Mrs. Rudd. Go out to do an errand or two for Grace & meet Walter on Broadway—take him along to shop! . . .

Sat. Aug. 21, 1897

Pack and arrange. . . . Lunch early and go to see father on 1.20 boat. Houghton joins me & goes too. Father fails. A year or two at most the doctor says. . . .

Sunday 22

Houghton comes early and we set off for the day. Lovely time. 125th st. ferry—Englewood electric—walk to Palisades—beautiful! Dine in Englewood. Then go back as we came & out to Washington bridge—over it & return on High Bridge, & walk down to end of 6th Ave. El. & so home. Supper, a pleasant time with the folks; and then another good talk with Ho. He is a dear boy.

Tues. Aug. 31, 1897

Begin my book on The Economic Relation of The Sexes as a Factor in Social Development. Write only about 1700 words, but do some planning. All pleasant and quiet and nice here, but a rainy day.

Fri. Sept. 10, 1897

Hot—very hot. loaf around all day. Rewrote part of Wed's work & finished Chap. V. Mary and I go to the Brown's to tea. Uncle William grows rather feeble. . . . Robert & his bride to tea. Amusing—as of old.

Saturday 11

Don't feel up to work. Write letter instead. Hot—very. Sudden change P.M. with violent wind. . . . Go over to Dr. Knights & stay to dinner. Seems glad to see me. See a lot of Walters pictures there—*splendid.*

Monday 13

Go to . . . R. I. School of Design & Art Club—see Walter's pictures there and talk with a Mr. Kinyon . . . who admires Yellow Wallpaper. . . .

Wed. 15

. . . [T]ake 5.12 train for Hingham & Martha.

Friday 17

Write more—no good—haven't got the right handle. Read book to Martha, afternoon & evening. Feel better about it. . . .

Sat. Sept. 18, 1897

Write about 2000 words on Chap. VI. Goes better. . . . Beautiful afternoon. . . .

Wed. Sept. 22, 1897

To Boston with M. on 9.20 train. Leave bags at Park Sq. station & go to Doll & Richards where I meet Sylvester Baxter. He takes me to the Atlantic office & introduces me to Mr. Page. Very cordial. Also to New England Mag. office & Mr. Edwin D. Meade. Also to Maynard, Small, & Co. (Bliss Carman is the Co.!⁶ and was there!—they want to publish my poems.' All very friendly & polite. Call on Alice Stone Blackwell also. Good talk. Lunch, get bags, go to Aunt Emily's. Glad to see me.

Saturday 25

Call on "my publishers" at 11. Bliss Carmen has now read my poems and approves! Good. See only Mr. Small this time. They want to do the poems & also to look at the book.⁷ Good. . . .

Fri. Oct. 8, 1897

Finish book. 356 pages. That is finish first draught. Date and arrange the separate chapters as written in different houses & do it up.
Houghton in evening and we open box in cellar and bring up some mss.

Tues. Oct. 12, 1897

. . . Houghton in evening, with book. He has read it—likes it—says its good. Quiet evening.

Mon. Oct. 18, 1897

. . . Houghton takes me to see "The Little Minister—Maud Adams.⁸ She does well.

Wed. Oct. 20, 1897

. . . Work on dress and copy poems. Rather a low day—it does not agree with me to climb stairs with bundles!
Work on poems all evening.

Sun. Oct. 24, 1897

Bad day. Houghton comes early and spends the day. Corrects copy for me & looks over lectures and things. Also we play a game of chess which he beats. Goes home to tea but returns again and takes me to hear Ingersoll⁹— at my request. Very interesting. Poor argument, but good speaking and lots of fun.

Saturday {Nov.} 6

Sew some. Take mss. to Scribner—14 poems. Call on the McDonalds (English) at Mrs. Wald's¹⁰—nurses settlement—265 Henry st. Not in. Mr. Bates calls in P.M.—asks me to go to football watch next Sat. Mrs. Hardy calls in evening. Houghton later. Nice long talk. He is a great comfort.

Wednesday 10

. . . Call on publishers—(Small, Maynard, & Co. 6 Beacon st). They take book. Give me new Whitman! I feel fine over the Book. . . .

Sunday 14

Go for a walk with Houghton. He goes home to lunch, but returns P.M. & we talk and mark poems for publisher till six. . . . Cut my new Whitman and enjoy it.

Sun. Nov. 21, 1897

Nice day. Write to Kate. Houghton about 10.30. Play chess—one game—I beat. But O, I cannot *play*! Tires me much. Read him the new chapters in the book. He begins to be really impressed. Good! Nap after dinner. Walk. Write letters in evening—and talk to various borders.
Arrange old letters. A good day's work!

Thur. Nov. 25, 1897

Work on book. Walk a wee bit. Streets full of masquerading beggars—little boys mostly—a pity—in America! . . .

Friday 26

Work on book. Go to see Father P.M. He fades gradually. I find him sitting dully in his chair—alone. He gets very bright and interested when I talk and tell him things. But he can say very little now, connectedly. Houghton and Francis in evening. Read The Yellow Wall Paper at Francis urgent request.

Sunday 28

Houghton. A delightful day[.] He draws up my "will"—is to be executor. Give him list of my debts with notes thereon. I read him three chapters of book. He agrees with me that the V is fine. Mother hears one—is impressed. Write letters in evening.

Wed. Dec. 1, 1897

Work on book. Mrs. Annie L. Peck the mountain climber calls. . . .[11]

Fri. Dec. 3, 1897*

Houghton take me to see Ada Rehan[12] in "The Taming of The Shrew." Fine. Then we frequent the "Arena" as usual.
Did work on book, but draggy. . . .

Sun. Dec. 5, 1897

Feel fine. Houghton comes. Read least three chapters—10 done. Splendid time. He is more and more impressed. Read him some Whitman that he likes too. Good. . . .

Tues. Dec. 7, 1897

Work on book—goes well. Walk. lunch. Rest. Miss A. L. Peck calls with tickets for her lecture tonight. Write letters. Go to Social Reform Club in evening—Jane Addams speaks on Survivals of Ethics and Alderman—etc. A splendid paper—deep, thoughtful, suggestive. Walk home all by my lonely after eleven—no harm!

Sun. Dec. 19, 1897

Fine day. Mr. Small calls A.M. Is greatly impressed with the book and wants it as soon as possible—print in Jan. Take a fine walk after he goes—two miles in half an hour! That's the way it used to be. . . .

Sat. Dec. 25, 1897

A quiet Xmas enough. Mother & Kathie go out to see Margie. I write and sew and walk—no, it's a snowstorm. In the evening we play with my new ball in Dr. Shelby's room—great fun.

Fri. Dec. 31, 1897

Write, A.M. & P.M. all of IVth Chapter. Answer every letter I have on hand— so as to begin the New Year clear. . . . Houghton comes. Begins to read these IV chapters. A good talk and we see the old year out *together*.

Notes for 1898

Health pretty fair now. Am able to work. Literary reputation steadily increasing. Things look bright.

[1898]

Sat. Jan. 1, 1898

Houghton with me to see the New Year in. Feel well and happy. Bed after one. Up at 8.20. 10.15 train to see father. Houghton with me. Dine there at a hotel. Two hours with father. He seems about the same. Home to dinner and work some in evening. Dr. Shelby calls. Much impressed by book.
Letter from Illustrated American asking for articles—one cent a word. Good.

Sunday 2

Fine day. Feel well. Dust and arrange room. Copy V chap.—5000 wds. Also finish Fabian article—a page or two only. Houghton comes P.M. Reads V chap. In evening we go through the whole five & correct errors. A big day's work—mustn't do it again. Very tired.

Mon. Jan. 3, 1898

Too much work yesterday—very poor day—only 16 pp. of an easy chapter. Write to Kate P.M. . . .

Mon. Jan. 17, 1898

Ah! Feels like vacation. Loaf—just write ten letters cards & notes—that's nothing!

Feel happier too. Guess I shan't break down this time.

Write to Kate P.M. Loaf about—read, lie down—talk. Houghton in evening. Finish entirely & send off last chapters. H. brings me a nice net battledore set.

Monday 24

Fine day. Nice mail—note from Walter Page of the Atlantic & from Fred Peabody!!! [13] Wants to know me. Call on Mr. Page. Go to publishers & correct proofs. . . .

Thursday {Feb.} 3

. . . Mr. Hendricks calls for me and we spend the rest of the morning with Miss Annie Russell, the actress.[14] She wants to see "A Pretty Idiot." I stop on way home and get it, of Maude Addams. . . .

Saturday 5

Go to Mrs. Pomeroy's & meet Annie Russell & others—to read "A Pretty Idiot." They like it fairly. Houghton & I go out to see Father. He fails painfully; but seems comfortable enough and is still glad to see me. Dreadfully tired—the effort to amuse him. H. home with me to dinner & stays.

Monday 7

. . . Call on Miss Russell & tell her "The Price of Love" story with view to play. She likes it. . . .

Friday 25

. . . Miss Pearson, nursed me at Weir Mitchells—calls. Houghton in evening.

Saturday {March} 5

. . . Go to see father P.M. He is in bed—feeble—hardly talks at all. . . .

Thurs. March 10, 1898

. . . Francis takes me to dine at "Boulevard Café" on 2nd Ave. and we are there joined by Arthur Hale. All go to Hoyts Theatre, and see Miss Annie Russell in "Dangerfield '95" a one act curtain raiser. *Magnificent* acting. She is certainly great. Then "O Susannah!"—a wretched piece. . . .

Sunday 27

Houghton early to go to Long Island with me—rainy day—don't go. Three games of chess in the morning—I beat. Am a little better able to play then last fall—not much. Read "The Giant Wistaria" P.M. . . .

Saturday {April} 2

Write and arrange for work. Feel rather low. Go to see Father P.M. He still knows me and is glad to have me there. Recite Kipling to him. He likes it—really. Home tired. Sew in evening.

Thur. April 7, 1898

. . . Poems come—six copies.[15]
Very nice.

Sunday 10

Easter Sunday—feel very miserably—pretty nearly a headache! Loaf about. Dr. Shelby takes me to walk in The Park. Lovely—quiet—warm. Home much better. Eat good dinner. Sleep all P.M. & feel fine. . . .

Mon. April 11, 1898

Write on "The Upward Current"—not very good. Walk, lunch, nap, sew P.M. & learn more Kipling. Ho. in for a few minutes. Go to Miss Wald's to dinner. Mr. & Miss Howells & the Gilders there & Miss Mary Smith of Chicago. All to meet Mr. Rosenfeldt[16] the Yiddish Poet. In default of another victim I read the translations & he recites in the original. Very interesting. Strong good work. Nice time. Mr. Yoke comes home with me. Abraham Cahan[17] & wife there too.

Sun. April 17, 1898

Warm still lovely day. Ho. & I go to Cold Spring Harbor—(Philo. P. Jarvis) to look at boarding place. Charming place—very well satisfied with it. Nice people too. We walk about in woods & on beaches and down lovely road. Pick trailing arbutus! Little girl gives me white violets. Beautiful day. . . .

Sat. April 23, 1898

Sew. Take lovely trip with Ho., P.M. to Fort Washington Point on the Hudson. Find flowers, saxifrage, anemones, shadbush—even one adder's tongue. Heavenly day—warm, soft, hazy. Such a good time. . . .

Friday {May} 6

Rather a low day. Mrs. Borden takes me to see a strawberry farm in the morning. Eat all I want. Heavy storm in afternoon. Go to a Negro Lunatic Asylum—concert by Inmates—in evening! Mrs. Royall's aunt is a physician there. Very interesting.

Sat. May 21, 1898

Advance sheets of Book at last! Letter from Grace & one from Kate—very happy day.

Friday {June} 3

. . . Speak to "peace resolution" in afternoon meeting. Mrs. Fred. Douglass[18] speaks on "The Convict Lease System in the South." . . . Home with Mrs. Douglass.

Sun. June 12, 1898

Houghton comes for me and we set forth for my summer home, Cold Spring Harbor Long Island. Very pleasant. Sit about under trees. Walk in woods etc. He takes 5.01 home—or tries to!
Letters from Kate and Grace—they may be here any day.

Hot.

Monday 13 Hot.

. . . Two telegrams from Houghton, and at 7.45 he arrives with Kate. Has to stay all night too—dear boy. Katharine is tall and lovely, sweetmannered and strong. It is good to see her. . . .

Tues. June 14, 1898

Wake up Houghton at 5.30 & he takes the 6.35 train in town. Kate & I sleep later. Sew on bathing dress, and ramble around. Kate is delighted with the pond. . . .

Thur. June 16, 1898

Try to write. Bathe at 11.15. Kate picks wild strawberries, plays with her turtle, makes a fish net, and has a good time generally. Go around the pond. Go for mail after supper. . . .

Sunday 19 Warmer.

Walk down to meet noon train. No one comes. It rains a little P.M. Kate & I go into the wet bushes and cut some good sticks.
She is so good to be with.

Mon. June 20, 1898

Still cool. Write cat story for The Youth's Companion.
Feel very blue.
Kate hunts frogs and is as good as gold.
We play games after supper.
Have cut ourselves fine black birch stick.

Thursday 23

Feel better thank goodness. Write or try to. Get started towards a story. Starved by dinner time. But Mrs. J. is moved to have a good beef stew—after two days of bread & milk & strawberries. Eat, sleep, & feel well. Go rowing on lily pond—in spite of Mrs. Jones!

Fri. June 24, 1898

Write "The Lake of Mrs. Johnsmith." Good I guess. Good dinner too. Rest. Kate & I wash our hair in the pond. Then I mend her dress and so on. She cuts her toe in the pond. Do her up. Games, supper, games.

Saturday 25

Put pocket on blue skirt—very successful garment. Wash Kate's hair and mine, in the pond. Play cards under the trees and look out for Houghton, who arrives about 5.45 on wheel—such a sight! A bath & his fresh clothes revive him however. . . .

Monday 27

Very flat day. Can't write a bit. Sew on waist Kate made me—altering it. Bathe in pond. K. & I walk "down the street" by way of the woods, and get sodawater. No mail at all! We skip stones in the harbor, find some strawberries—generally enjoy ourselves. A new boarder—biologist—Mr. Sumner. Nice youth.

Thur. June 30, 1898

Mr. Sumner takes Kate & me out rowing by moonlight. Very lovely.

Sunday {July} 3

I am thirty-eight years old. Houghton sends me a pair of silversleeve links. Bathe and so on as usual. Hot. . . .

Mon. July 18, 1898

Letter from Criterion—they've taken "The Lake of Mrs. Johnsmith." Warm criticism of poems from "The American." . . .

Friday 29

First even partly clear day for nearly two weeks.
Bathe much in the clean warm pond.

Tuesday {Aug.} 2

A dip before breakfast. Go to the beach and have fine salt swim in morning. Spend afternoon—3 to 6—in the pond. Fine time.

Wednesday 10

Begin to read *The White Company*[19]—very interesting. Houghton arrives about 4. We all swim—cold. . . .

Thur. Aug. 11, 1898

Pleasant morning together in spite of the rain. H. & I prowl in the old mill while Kate writes a letter. My head very weak. Read to K. after H. goes at about 4 P.M. . . .

Monday, Aug. 15, 1898

Really feel pretty well. Write nice letter to Ho. Row & turtlechase with Kate. Finish *"White Co."*

Saturday 20

All bad days and nothing in 'em

Sunday 28

Houghton at 10. Kate & I go to meet him. He looks well after his vacation. Swim, catch turtles, tip over boat, good time generally. Give out in afternoon; very much down. Play games, row with both boys, walk with Houghton, talk and cry.

Wed. Aug 31, 1898

Up early. Take 8.06 train. Ho. meets us in city. Go to Hotel Albert. Wait till after one, then dine. They presently arrive. Go shopping with Grace & Kate. . . .

Thur. Sept. 1

. . . [S]ee Katharine off. . . . Go home & collapse. To weak to go out.

Tues. Sept. 6, 1898

. . . Ho. comes for me & we go back to Cold Spring together.
Such a blessed cool sweet still place! Have lovely bath in *pond—starlight*.

Wed. Sept. 7, 1898

Delightful night. Feels good after the city. Have a swim on rising. . . .

Wed. Sept. 14, 1898

These are long heavy days; head thick and weak, and body weak too.

Thursday 15

But I get through the time, sleep nearly twelve hours, and am in the air mostly.

Sat. Sept. 24, 1898

A beautiful morning. H. & I go after wild grapes—but don't get any. Then seek apples, & bring home two bags full. Good meals all day. Nap P.M. Go over letters and things with Ho. Make a sestina and do word squares in evening. Lovely day.

Fri. Sept. 30, 1898

. . . Go to see father—8.50 train. Carry grapes. Knew me for a while. Probably can not see him again. . . .

Sun. Oct. 2, 1898

Am greatly astonished by a call from Houghton at about 10.30. Thought he was in Norwich. We take long cable ride & he dines with me at home & stays, till we go to Miss Walds—till near 6; & then comes back for me at ten. Another delightful day. . . .

Thur. Oct. 6, 1898

Conseived the idea of rubbing capsicum vaseline into the roots of my hair, for dandruff & loss of hair! & tried it. Have lost nearly half this summer.

Wednesday 19

. . . Meet Mr. H. Traubel[20]—praises my poems, gives me his review. Fine. . . .

Mon. Nov. 7, 1898

Write letters, here & in town. Get mail. Call on . . . Dr. W. E. Morgan, 39 Huntington Ave, who examines eyes for nothing if you are poor! Did so for me. My eyes are "probably perfect," but muscles weak. Prescribes Strictnine pills. . . .

Mon. Nov. 21, 1898

Mr. White—work ahead on Play. Go down with him and I go to hear Mr. Herron. Great man. Go to lunch with Jane Addams & other guests. Talk. Home late and very tired. . . .

Thursday 24

. . . Hull House. Hamlin Garland . . . there. . . . Read some poems in evening, after Mr. Garland. Home early.

Wed. Dec. 7, 1898

The children are sick & I am to go nights to Hull House for a while. Write article for Woman's Journal on "The Causes and Uses of the Subjection of Woman"—2000 wds. . . .

Wed. Dec. 21, 1898

Write Chicago letter—pretty good, pleased with it; begin to get the place a little. Lunch & coffee—go down with Miss Dow to Woman's Club—am subspeaker on "Women Humorists." Fairly good. Write & read to Mrs. D. in evening, up here in the sky parlor of course.

Sun. Dec. 25, 1898

Snowstorm.
A decidedly lonesome Xmas! Open my little package from Kate. The Dows left remembrances—nice breakfast of orange, beans & brownbread, *good*. Mrs. Turner of Battle Creek sent me a pair of knit bedshoes, & Miss Turner of Boston a "Lend a Hand Calendar.

[1899][21]

Mon. Jan. 9, 1899

More talk, letters, etc. Take 2 P.M. train to Wauseon—met by Mr. Brown— rest a good while, nice supper and speak in evening, about Socialism. Went well. Collection, five dollars. Mr. Jones gave me twenty five dollars and offered a lot more—but I thought best not to indulge. . . .

Sunday 22

Preach on "The Heroes We Need Now" in Dr. Sunder's Unitarian Church. Rest P.M. Mr. Nelson here to dinner. Preach on "Whoso Loseth His Life" etc. at Congregational Church—Dr. Fisk. Not very good. Ten dollars from contributions.

Thursday 9

Gas frozen last night. *No* heat in my room. *Ink* froze inside my bag! Water pitcher of course. Mail comes—twenty or thirty letters at once (or by two mails). Answer some. Get tickets, send telegrams, etc. Address Peabody Normal Institute—girl's societies. . . .

water freezes in my room—
Sun. Feb. 12, 1899

Still cold. This is preternatural weather. We all sit shawled and hug the fire. I exult in my comfortable room—(considering) and write letters. . . .

Mon. Feb 20, 1899

Birmingham at 5.50. Slept little. Carsick in morning. Not much breakfast. Doze and write letter—train to Columbus Ga. at 9.30. Arrive at 3.30 or so. Try to eat lunch—do not try dinner. Milk & cracker at Mrs. L. H. K. Chappell's a good nap—hot bath—and lecture to the Students Club in Parlor on "What we Need to Know Today." Went splendidly—people most cordial and enthusiastic.

Tuesday 21

Up at 5.30—train 6.30—Atlanta at 11.15. Met by carriage—Mr. Lowe, young Mrs. Lowe, and Mrs. Ottley. Trunk comes promptly—put on red dress & go to a ladies lunch in my honor. Then a long nap & dress—supper and lecture for the Woman's Club on "Two Changes." Tremendous crowd-standing, lots couldn't get in. Went well, very. Great enthusiasm. Milk & bread—and bed. (People fainted—went out, recovered—*and returned*!)

Sunday {March} 19

. . . Letter from S. & M. about book—new edition coming. 2000 nearly gone. Letter of invitation to address Nat. Council of Women in London last of June. Cable "yes."

Thursday 23

. . . Sat. Phil. evening Post. asks me to write editorial articles.

Tues. March 28, 1899

Begin on some "editorials" for Phil. Sat. Eve. Post. Write three. "12 Best Women," "Automobils & Candy" & "Physical Culture." 5 or 6,000 wds. each. Very tired and limp P.M.

Sat. April 15, 1899

. . . Take 10.15 train. Houghton meets me. So glad to see him. Lunch together. . . .

Sunday 16

Houghton in awhile and sees me off for Irvington. Met by Mr. Walker—most polite—guest of honor etc. Wants me to send him all I write! That I won't. But we arrange for some work. Back on 4.01 & Ho meets me. Dine with Miss Wald & Ho calls for me & sees me home.

Wed. April 19, 1899

. . . Go to Newark P.M. and speak for Woman's Club there. $10.00 on "Work." Back in haste—dress, eat—and set forth with Ho. & the Shelbys to the "Dollar Dinner." Have a box. Mayor Jones of Toledo escorts me to the platform; W. J. Bryan gives me his seat, all very grand. Make brief speech on "What a Just Economic System would do for Women." A fine evening altogether.

Thursday {May} 4

Set sail at 10 A.M.—[illegible] 10.30 on S. S. *Furst-Bismark*,[22] Hamburg-American. Houghton takes me down & flees away. . . . I ensconse myself on deck chair—in NY. Go down & eat bouillon, bread, & prunes for lunch.
Some toast for dinner—and then am brought more on deck by amiable steward.
Room 71—with three German Jewesses—detached!
Best berth, mine, 3.

Fri. May 5, 1899

Aha! Now we get it. Cup of hot water A.M. The loan of two oranges P.M.—soon returned. Bed all day & sick as I have it—nothing painful or severe—just sick. Got partly dressed during A.M. & stay so.

Saturday 6

Get dress on and toddle up stairs, to lie dismally on bench all day. Cup of bouillon.
    Am inspired to take some hot water with a little whiskey in it—and morsel of cracker before sleeping.

Monday 8

Call for eggs, toast, & hot water for breakfast and eat 'em gladly. Take a bath in stateroom & dress clean. Try to write but find I cant. Eat lunch & dinner, but don't feel so well. Merry in evening however. My roommates keep me awake late.

Tues. May 9, 1899

Quite ill again, though not "sick," eat nothing but eggs for breakfast—not good ones—& a cup of bouillon for lunch. Have some more hot water & whisky for a night cap—& four crackers. feel better. . . .

Thur. May 11, 1899

Cold salt bath at 7:30. Gruel. Rest, dress, pack, sit about, watch landing at Cherboring 10 A.M. Write to Ho. Reach Southhampton at about four P.M. 5.10 train to London. . . . Feels very good to be here—a great relief to get off that boat.

Wed. May 17, 1899

Arrange things—rest. Write a little. Go out about 12. buy some oranges. Nap after lunch. Write to Houghton. Tea. Go to look up Mrs. Purdy, 27 Palace Court—who offers to "entertain me during Congress. It is where I gave a drawing room talk before—rich old lady. The "British Housemaid" suspects me of not being "a caller"—very funny.[23] . . .

Saturday 20

Write paper for Congress—on Equal pay for Equal work. . . .

Tuesday 30

Lot of letters—one from Houghton. I lie flat on the daisies & buttercups and weep—very low indeed. . . . Some whist in evening—does me good.

Mon. June 26, 1899

. . . 1st meeting of Congress P.M.—just the tail of it. Grand reception in Stafford House in evening—Duchess of Sutherland, Lady Aberdeen, & Countess of Warwick receiving.

Thursday 29

. . . Great Suffrage meeting in evening—very successful indeed. Sit on platform but don't speak. Miss Anthony cordially received.

Fri. June 30, 1899

. . . Evening on Ethics of Wageearning—my paper—Equal Pay for Equal Work. Talk instead of read. Overflow meeting in spite of rain.

Friday {July} 7

A note or two. Go to Elliott & Fry's & have photograph taken—as a "Celebrity!" . . . Think I made a mistake in not going to Winsor to see the Queen,—a concession to the Congress. . . .

Thursday 13

Houghton comes—go to St. Pauls with him. . . .

Fri. July 14, 1899

Wrote article on Congress for Arena.—over 3000 wds. lunch, Nap. telegram from the Countess of Warwick to come there & speak—63 wds.[24] . . .

Tues. July 18, 1899

I have three afflictions—my pivot tooth is loose! There are *things* in my Hair!! And a minor one.[25] Put on stuff to slay Things. Ho. calls. We go to the British Museum & to Kensington Gardens. . . .

Thur. July 20, 1899

. . . We two go to a reception at the Duchess of Sutherlands. She is very polite to me—says she has bought the book.

Wed. July 26, 1899

Wrote to Ho. Call on Dr. Kennedy and get medicine and advice. He says I should marry! Walk to Grov. Cres. Club, through Park, feeling much better. . . .

Sun. July 30, 1899

Bad days—I am exceedingly weak and dull.
Everything pleasant and restful here too.

Thur. Aug. 17, 1899

Go in to Mrs. Grant in Edinburgh by 12.10, bus & train. . . . Lecture on "The Social Organism" for Summer School of Languages. Went well. . . .

Tues. Aug. 29, 1899

Do some shopping—get steamer ticket—see publishers, etc. . . . Begin "Brushe's Remedy" for seasickness.

Thur. Aug. 31, 1899

. . . Start about 11.30. Room 8. Berth 4. Nice sofa bed under porthole. Am not sick.

Sun. Sept. 10, 1899

A day late. Bad weather most all the way.
Uneventful voyage—rather dull and long.
Not seasick, but not in vigorous health either. . . .

Friday 15

Good nights sleep. Good mail—lots of letters & the Ainslee check $125.00. . . .

Mon. Sept. 18, 1899

Write three eds. for Post—"Supply & Demand in Literature" "Ed. & Punish." "Ethics in Schools." . . . Meet Ho. in Park and take walk. . . . He is feeling badly about business things.

Tuesday Sept. 26, 1899

Go in town—meet Miss Wellington. Stop at W. J. office & get letters etc. Also S. & M. He wants another book. Offers 500.00 down, 15% to 5000 & then 18%. . . .

Tuesday {Oct.} 3

. . . Go to Martha Lanes. Glad to see me.

Wed. Oct. 4, 1899

. . . Talk with Martha, write a letter. Lie in wait for thieving boys and catch one—spraining my finger thereby! But "it was a glorious victory." Martha, Margaret and I go on a little picnic P.M. very nice—Read "The Gentleman from Indiana" in McClures—*Splendid*. That is America.

Thur. Oct. 12, 1899

. . . Mdme. Schwall of Paris wants to translate my book. Good. Stone of Chicago wants to publish one of mine—good too.

Wednesday 25

. . . Address Contemporary Club in evening on "What Work is." Rather hard sledding, but struck some kindred notes. Especially in a youth who turned out to be Booth Tarkington.[26]

Thur. Nov. 9, 1899

. . . Supper, dress, lecture on Mother Home & Child in Unitarian Church. Very good—house & lecture. Enjoyed in thoroughly. Ex. Gov. Altgett[27] called on me just before supper. Good man.

Tues. Nov. 21, 1899

Off on 10.40, Burlington Route for Denver. Quiet day. Write, read, talk to fellow traveler who said she "knew I must be something."

Mon. Nov. 27, 1899

. . . Lecture at Brigham Young Polysophical Academy in evening—"Our Brains & What Ails Them." Went very well.

Tuesday 28

Go over the Brigham Young Polysophical Academy with Mrs. Gates.[28] Write to Ho. After dinner & attempted nap, go off alone and ascend a tiny foot hill behind the State Insane Asylum. Lecture in evening on Women & Work. Not as good as last night—nor as well liked.

Sat. Dec. 9, 1899

Call on Dr. Van Orden & pay dentist bill—$50.00. (He says twas 40 & allows 10 on new work.) Call on Hattie Howe in Berkeley & get mail. She goes with me to Oakland & we find Mrs. Collins at 1258 Webster & pay the rent bill $140.00—& 20 due on gas. She was paralyzed with astonishment.[29] . . .

Saturday 16

. . . See Mr. Bartnett and arrange about paying Miss Knap—leave 25.00 for first payment.[30] Quiet evening reading & bed early.

Sat. Dec. 23, 1899

Hot dusty ride over Mojave desert. L. A. at 2.30 or so. Katharine to meet me—dear girl. Come to Pasadena, late. Meet Grace & Walter at the station coming in town. Mrs. Viall at the Channings—ride up to Las Casitas—lovely place. Glad to be here—Bed at 8.

Sunday 24

Slept well. Write. Do up things. Lunch. Nap. Go down to the Stetson family's Xmas. Get very tired. Especially from Dorothy's voice. Sleep in Kate's room— or try to. Almost no sleep. A smart Earthquake at about 4 A.M.

Mon. Dec. 25, 1899

Dreadfully tired. The Xmas excitement hard to meet. Call on Gussie Senter at her mothers. See them both & Mrs. Masters. All cold—Gussie explains their views—I am an unnatural mother![31]
Well! . . .

Sun. Dec. 31, 1899

Finish answering all letters on hand. Slept ill—feel badly. . . .

Notes for 1900

Get well—get well—get well. And do good work! Pay all debts if possible.

For 1900

For this New Year—and last
Of the century nearly passed—
Help me to grow!
Help me to fill the days
With deeds of loving praise
For the splendid truths I know.

Help me to finish clear
All claims of the old year—
And all behind
And to meet all duties new

With loving service due,
And a steadfast mind.

A clear and steadfast mind!
Help me, O God, to find
　　Such hold on you
As may dispel disease
That I may with speed and ease
　　Work deep, work true!

Slowly so long—and dark!—
Down at the lowest mark—.
　　The light grows now!
God! I am seeking still
To learn and do your will—
　　Still show me how!

New Years Day.

[1900]

Mon. Jan. 1, 1900

A late start for Pasadena. "The Tournament of Roses." A fine parade. Katharine in white on her wheel—very lovely. Lunch at the Channing-Stetsons. & see Kate. . . . Write to Ho.

Sat. Jan. 20, 1900

Write a letter, talk a bit, see some of Walter's work, more serious talk about Katharine. I guess she will come to me for a year with mutual satisfaction all around. . . .

Wed. Feb. 14, 1900

. . . Grace comes up, late to dinner. Nice afternoon with her on my little hill. Tell her about Houghton. She is impressed with the new book—I'm glad.

Fri. Feb. 16, 1900

. . . Loaf about P.M. Kate comes. Tell her about Houghton. Takes it very sweetly—but not overpleased I fancy. . . .

Sun. May 27, 1900

. . . Special delivery from Houghton. We can't be married in Ill[inoi]s. it appears.

Mon. June 11, 1900

Set forth to Detroit, the Dow's man carrying my bags to the train. Arrive at 6. Houghton in the station. We drive to Mrs. Corbett's. I make a rapid toilet.

Mr. Reed Stewart, Unitarian minister, arrives about 7.30, and we are married. A very short and reasonable service. Then [a] very nice little dinner—far [*msm*] long, and we go the [*msm*]ll H[*msm*].

Tues. June 12, 1900

Stay peacefully in Detroit. Call on Mrs. Corbett in the afternoon. Then to Belle Isle—a lovely Park, & have supper there, and a walk in the moonlight.

Sat. June 23, 1900

Quiet lovely days—stroll about—pick berries—play croquet—read & loaf.

Wed. July 4, 1900

Hot & pleasant. A nice day with Houghton. He brought me a croquet set for a birthday present, & we set it up & play.

Sun. July 8, 1900

. . . Read "Vesty of The Basins"[32] with Houghton, and am very happy, forgetting heat[,] weariness & toothache. . . .

Mon. July 16, 1900

. . . Very hot. Houghton pretty tired. Tries to fix his bicycle—no good. Stroll about a bit. I am "low" and he plays piquet with me to cheer my spirits. Does so!

Thurs. July 19, 1900

Feel so mizzerable that Ho. persuades me not to go in town.[33] Funny to have some one to care. Loaf about & have very quiet good day. Sew a little, write some letters—read and rest.

We talk and stroll and I read some ms. & we play piquet in evening.

Fri. July 27, 1900

Househunt vigorously, A.M.

Find some agreeable places. . . .

Tues. July 31, 1900

Ho. comes back. Calls on us. I go to office with him & get letters. Then I go up town & look at more houses. Fall in love with the "San Marino—" W. 112 close to colleges.

A *perfect* little flat—but only five rooms! Katharine arrives at 6. . . .

Wed. Aug. 1, 1900

Take a holiday (!) and go a turtleing with Katharine. Catch 27! Get awfully tired during the day somehow.

She is delighted with the croquet.

Thur. Aug. 23, 1900

. . . We are to have the top flat in The Avondale—76th & Amsterdam Ave. Good!

Sat. Aug. 25, 1900

Finish book [*Concerning Children*]—read, correct, & write the end of last chapter. Ho. home early. Croquet.

Mon. Nov. 5, 1900

Pack for six weeks in two bags. Off at 3.45. Ho at the Station. 4 P.M. train for Chicago. . . .

Sat. Nov. 24, 1900

Go down with Jennie Harvey to hear Jane Addams. Warmly greeted by the audience & make a few remarks "by request". . . .

Thurs. Dec. 13, 1900

Good sleep. Breakfast in Café at some distance. Write letters serenely and do accounts. I clear about $130.00 out of this trip— . . .

Tues. Dec. 25, 1900

We darken the room & light our tree at 10 A.M. All very jolly & nice. K. has some 57 presents! . . .

Mon. Dec. 31, 1900

I am happy & content.
Houghton—Katharine—
Home.

Notes for 1901

May I grow stronger and do good work in spite of my happiness!

[1901]

Sun. Jan. 13, 1901

Nice day at home. Read mss. to Ho. and sew while he reads Veblen. Get tired variously. Play hide & seek P.M. . . . Bed early.

Am not at all strong along now.

Sat. Mar. 23, 1901

Katharine's 16th birthday. Get her small "Lorna Doone" & pot of violets. . . .

Tues. Apr. 9, 1901

Bad news about Mrs. [Helen] Campbell—her mind is wandering again— & so is she. . . .

Tues. Apr. 16, 1901

Mrs. Campbell stops an hour on way through city—says she speaks in Bridgeport tonight. I see her off at station. She seemed excited but still rational.

Wed. Apr. 17, 1901

I lunch with Mrs. Mann Martin to meet Dr. Mary Putnam Jacobi. Call on Mrs. Campbell's mother at address she gave me—no such resident.

Fri. Sept. 6, 1901

President MacKinley shot by an assassin, Czolgosz (?) at Buffalo.

Sat. Sept. 14, 1901

. . . President McKinley died at 2 o'clock this morning.

Thurs. Sept. 19, 1901

President McKinley's funeral. Stores closed. City in mourning. Cars all stop at 3.30. . . . K. & I went down to Ho.'s office & came up all together. . . .

Mon. Sept. 23, 1901

Still fine weather. Various chores. Get at my letters. . . . Meet Kate in the Park & read "Forest Lovers"[34] to her. Canoe for half an hour. . . .

Tues. Sept. 24, 1901

Katharine developes tonsilitis—quite weak & ill.

Sat. Oct. 19, 1901

Begin the bicycle—practicing on a quiet block nearby. No [sic] difficult—only some nervous strain.

Sat. Nov. 9, 1901

. . . Ho takes me to my first football game. Columbia & Syracuse. Syr[acuse]. beats. Good game—like it.
Ho has acquired some necessary funds and we feel easier.
I begin to feel well again.

Sat. Dec. 7, 1901

. . . Dr. Jacobi writes offering to attempt something for my brain trouble.

Tues. Dec. 10, 1901

. . . Call on Dr. Jacobi & state my case. She is to undertake it—her own proposition.
Feel pretty well.

Thur. Dec. 12, 1901

Go to Dr. Jacobi & am "done to" variously. . . . Feel weak and poorly. . . .

Tues. Dec. 17, 1901

Feel very poorly. Shop all morning rather wearily. Dr. J. at 12. She puts electric plat [sic] on the solar plexus—and we do the other things. Sew some in afternoon & evening—but feel very badly. . . .
Dr. orders phospho-glycerates in wine—fine stuff.

Tues. Dec. 24, 1901

Down town late P.M. Got tree etc. A.M. & set it up.
K. goes to bed saying it was the first time she had ever gone without a stocking. So we fix one for her after she is asleep.

Wed. Dec. 25, 1901

Wet & warm. K. up early, hilarious over her stocking. . . . Many presents & much satisfaction. . . .

[1902]

Wed. Jan. 1, 1902

. . . A happy and hopeful New Year . . . . To get strong and clear-headed again, and then—To Work!

Thurs. Jan. 2, 1902

A hopeful New Year. Am improving under Dr. Jacobi's treatment. K. is well and happy—went to Boston yesterday. Ho. is well and happy. Sees his way clear for the year almost. He is to try 5.00 a week now for K[atherine']s new allowance of 1.00, mine equal, and the household expenses. . . . Do some writing . . . my Success article—10 swift easy pages. Not very good though. . . .

Tues. Jan. 7, 1902

. . . [C]all on Mr. Howells. He is most kind, and interested in my book. Feel rather tired in the evening. . . .

Mon. Jan. 13, 1902

Not well—querulous & depressed. . . . Quiet evening with Ho.

Tues. Jan. 14, 1902

Still feeble. Ride down to doctor. Get some electricity—the right kind—& feel much better. The doctor looks over some of my ms. and advises that I sail right in and write the book without striving for arrangement. Walk part way home. . . . Ho. & I go to library after supper.

Sat. Jan. 25, 1902

. . . K. & I set forth at ten to Barnard College, where we meet the others—seven in all, & play basketball. Great fun—enjoy it hugely & am not tired.

Sun. Feb. 2, 1902

Went to Boston on 10 A.M. train. Tea & night with Martha. . . .

Tues. Feb. 4, 1902

Come in to Boston early & call on Grace. She has to go out to a funeral. I . . . go to Pub. Library for a while. Talk with Grace—& lunch. See a few of Walter's pictures. . . .

Thurs. Feb. 13, 1902

Sweep & wash my room. Tired. Don't try to write. Walk part way to doctor. Can't read Cell book—brain won't hold it. Sew a little P.M. Very tired evening & can't do anything.

Sun. Feb. 16, 1902

Beautiful day—but still do not feel well. Ho. & I take a wee walk after breakfast. Accomplish nothing during morning. Francis to dinner. I hurry off & go to Brooklyn—Philosophical Assn. Long Island Business College. Speak on Social Inertia. Went very well. Home rather late near supper. . . . Dr. Shelby calls later. We begin to read [Shakespeare's] "Much Ado About Nothing"—taking parts.

Wed. Feb. 26, 1902

Work some—feeling rather dull but work through it, feeling better at the end! That is real progress. Walk down town gaily—join the League for Political Education. . . . Katharine ate no breakfast—no lunch—a little beeftea & cracker—high fever. Send for Doctor Shelby. Comes up in evening—no definite name given so far.

Thurs. Feb. 27, 1902

Slept in Ho.'s room, attending to K. Pretty good night—not lightheaded at all. Cough hurts some in morning however. Dr. S. P.M.—Pneumonia. . . .

Fri. Feb. 28, 1902

Good night for K.—feels much better. I slept pretty well too, but am not very lively. Doctor P.M. K doing well. telegraph Grace & W. Miss Addams calls.

Mon. Mar. 17, 1902

Sudden bad turn—severe nausea, vomits all day, in all ten times. Telephone for doctor & he comes up about 2. Sends nurse at night—a Miss McCarthy. K. has a rash.

Tues. Mar. 18, 1902

Miss McCarthy turns out to be futile—& not pleasing. Send her off. She kicks about loss of job—as it may prove a contagion case. Give her ten dollars.

I jokingly tell the doctor that K. has scarlet fever—and he fears it is!

Next nurse arrives—Miss Mendel—tall beautiful cheerful vigorous calm quiet agreeable capable—a treasure. So we settle down to contented quarantine.

Wed. Mar. 19, 1902

Health office comes. Scarlet fever & no mistake.
Here's a go!
I ask about my lecture tomorrow. Health Officer[,] Doctor & nurse all say I can go, with proper precautions.

Thurs. Mar. 20, 1902

Take cleansing bath—bichloride bath—wash hair in bichloride & comb it with new comb—put on entire different clothes even to garters & hairpins & disinfect watch, & walk across park to lecture. . . . Good little audience—fair lecture, not over good. They sent big bunch of roses to K. . . .

Wed. Apr. 16, 1902

Good day. Go downtown A.M. & get some things. Check from Truth— $66.oo[.] Ho, by special delivery, gets check for $6234.oo! (His Uncle Daniel's business.)

Sat. Sept. 27, 1902

Katharine sails for Italy. . . .

Wed. Oct. 1, 1902

Made cake & arranged for dinner. Sewed. Dentist after lunch. Am very weak & nervous & it is a severe operation—base of lower eye tooth—so I ask for chloroform & get it. A few whiffs—"Squibbs Chloroform"—& I'm off. The whole tedious jarring thing done at no loss of strength! Excellent. . . .

Thurs. Oct. 2, 1902
Begin Work!

. . . A letter or two, and really got at my work—looked things over and wrote a few pages on "Is The Home a Success" series. . . .

Sun. Oct. 5, 1902

. . . Rather a feeble day. *Paint* a bit in the afternoon—first time in many years; not a good picture, but hopeful sign. Write to K.

Sun. Nov. 2, 1902

. . . Car up to 18th st, examine beautiful apartment house where I want to live bye and bye. . . . Capt. VanderLoo calls—keep him to supper. He brings big stories of my fame abroad. . . .

Mon. Nov. 3, 1902

Began "[Human] Work" again! Wrote some 8 pages—arranged and planned. Not tired. . . .

Thurs. Nov. 6, 1902

Am feeling rather badly, but do some seven pages & arranging. . . . Get books from library.

Ho. goes to armory. I am reduced to solitaire again, and then doze unhappily all the evening.

Thurs. Nov. 13, 1902

Feel pretty well. Write 20 [pages] . . . . Go to bed early—leaving "pantoum" for Ho. He—dear boy—makes me one too, on finding it.

Tues. Nov. 18, 1902

Big day. Large leap ahead in grasp of book. Go to Brooklyn P.M. and speak a little to W.S.A. there on W[omen]. & E[conomics].—& poems. Nice time [$]10.00. Come home & get dinner gailly. Write good letter to K. . . .

Sun. Nov. 30, 1902

Quiet day. Letters. Walk. Nap. Preach in evening in Universalist Church— Rev. Mr. Bauer—on "The Highest Human Duty." Went very well indeed. . . .

Tues. Dec. 2, 1902

Go to Lyons. . . . Speak for Civic Club, in Town Hall, on "Public Ethics." Went well.

Took a lovely walk before lunch—out on the hills, & picked dandelions! saw many & picked one that is.

Very warm beautiful day. Another walk P.M. after my nap.

Thurs. Dec. 4, 1902

Go to Syracuse. . . . Take fine walk over the hills near by. Mother's World in evening. . . . Best lecture yet. An enthusiastic Mrs. Kennedy says it was just like Henry Ward Beecher.

Mon. Dec. 8, 1902

. . . Home & get dinner. Not tired! I cannot account for this continued high level. My trip seems to have done me good.

Thurs. Dec. 11, 1902

. . . Buy half a pint of scallops for my lonely supper—Ho. not home. Am ptomaine poisoned by them (I suppose) & have a bad night.

Mon. Dec. 15, 1902

Still unrecovered from those scallops! Indigestion forsooth! Ptomaine say I . . . I take a little whiskey in a glass of milk & some crackers. Some sweet oil at bedtime.

Wed. Dec. 17, 1902

Worse. Nauseated on rising—very weak. Go back to bed. Eat some rice & milk & presently throw it up. Alarmed. Send for Dr. Shelby who comes up before 10. Houghton waits. Guess it was ptomaine poison all right—though he will not directly admit it. Stay in bed til late P.M. on milk & lime water with some med. feel better in evening.

Thurs. Dec. 25, 1902

A quiet pleasant Christmas. Francis to dinner. Splendid little Turkey. Real good time. Katharine sends photographs. I have a lot of most gratifying presents—especially from Houghton.

Wed. Dec. 31, 1902

Consider the [*Human Work*] book done—practically—the first draught.

[1903]

Thur. Jan. 1, 1903

Quiet day at home with with Ho. We "figger" in the morning— . . . and see our way straight & clear to fall of 1904—with the European trip all in. Good. . . . Mr. Page—L. C. Page Pub. Co. spends the evening here—trying to secure my next book & others to come. Am well pleased with him. . . . Our New Years resolution—to get up at 7 o'clock! do it today.

Mon. Jan. 12, 1903

Arrange mss. for publishers, 4 chap. of H{uman]. W[ork]. & 1 of Home. . . . Home late and unusually tired out. Nice quiet evening with the patient Ho.

Fri. Jan. 23, 1903

Write good article 2500 wds. on "The Home As a Social Medium" for Success. . . . Feel well till mid-evening & then suddenly get tired out—

Sun. Jan. 25, 1903

Didn't sleep much. Get to Cincinnati on time. . . . [Go] to lecture in Odd Fellows Temple. Give 'em a good one, hour & a quarter about "Mother Home, & Child." . . .

Mon. Jan. 26, 1903

. . . Get off to Dayton on 8.30 breakfasting in station on grapefruit, coffee & crackers out of my box. Dayton at 9.53. Arrange to take 3.45 via Xenia, home. $4.00 excess fare, & 4.00 for sleeper—for one night! The villains! Then to the great N.C.R. works—evidently a feature of the town. Car labelled with 'em! Warmly received. Have my picture taken forthwith! Am shown about.

Go to lunch in the Men's Club House—a lovely place. . . . Talk in the girls dining room. Have to "holler." . . . Just make connection at Xenia. Sup on crackers & chocolate with icewater.

Tues. Jan. 27, 1903

Fairly good night. Extortionate fast train 2 hours late! No rebate however. Come home & get myself a nice lunch. . . . Feel pretty well. . . . Ho. about 6.10. So good to be home with him.
Quiet evening, bath & bed early.

Wed. Jan. 28, 1903

. . . Francis comes. We all suddenly go to the theatre—the new one at Columbus Circle—"The Majestic"—A *beautiful* theatre—very rich and noble—dark green moire & white marble—most satisfying. See "The Wizard of Oz"—funny & amusing, also a rich spectacular. . . .

Mon. Feb. 2, 1903

. . . I go down to see McClure. He is interested in *The Home*, think they'll take it & publish some chaps in the magazine. good—could hardly be better. . . .

Fri. Feb. 13, 1903

Write the Home as an Environment for Women for "Success." . . . We go out to dinner & then to see Annie Russell in Mice and Men.
The most painful play I ever saw—I sit and suffer and snivel & come very tired. . . .

Sat. Feb. 14, 1903

Wake weary & sad from that weepful play—Loaf. . . . Go to Susan B. Anthony dinner at Clarendon Hotel Bklyn. . . . Make brief speak [*sic*]—very warmly received.
Home late—or early—12.45. Houghton very much worried—no wonder.

[1905]

Tues. Feb. 7, 1905

Sail [for London]—10 AM—Fine weather—up, out, & eat, bed early.

Sun. Mar. 1905

Go to Hamburg. Write letters. Thin bed. Cotton quilt. No fire. Hotel del Europe. *Very Poor.*

April {?} 1905

. . . To help [Suffrage] is a clear duty. To oppose it is to stand ridiculous and wrong to future history.

[1907]

Sat. Sept. 7, 1907

Worked a little. . . . Wrote *Why Walk Backward* 2500 wd. *Gen'l Beauty & Local Pride* 1000 [words]. Planned for lectures & began to writes letters toward. Sent out ms.

[1909]

Thurs. May 27, 1909

Resolved: that The most urgent measure for the Welfare of the human race is the arousing of class consciousness in the working class!

[1910]

Fri. Sept. 2, 1910

Finish Diantha![35]

[1911]

Aug. 1911

One thing we can all be thankful for
   And thats good friends
You will always find others to serve your ends
   If your effort in life is to give
Theres none so poor that he has no friends
   Unless he's too mean to live.

[1914]

Notes
To Do This Year—

1. Get well.
2. Earn $3000.00
   A. Lecture
   B. Write—*make early arrangements.*
3. See friends—call—write

[1915]

Sat. July 10, 1915

Herland done.[36]

Sat. Nov. 27, 1915

Invited by Henry Ford to sail on Oscar II—to Peace conference in Europe. declined.

[1916]

Jan. 1916

> Get stronger: more exercise.
> Finish Forerunner in good shape.
> Get house in perfect order.
> Arrange all papers.
> Arrange satisfactory wardrobe.
> See more of people—have friends in
> once a week and go out once or twice.
> Keep accounts better.

Sat. Oct. 28, 1916

In hand—[$]138.57 (15 cts. ahead!)

[1917]

Feb. 1, 1917

. . . Am sure of enough [money] for T[homas]. et al, to May 1st. [$]765. Prob[ably] sure enough for K[ate]. 200.00 Poss[ibly] enogh [*sic*] for all summer, total of 1500.00.

[1918]

Tues. Jan. 1, 1918

. . . Since Sat. Phenomenal cold. Sunday coldest ever recorded in N.Y. 14 *below*. *No gas Sunday. No steam* by Tues. very little gas. Keep oven going in kitchen and sit in it—as it were.

Sat. Jan. 5, 1918

Sitting in K. close to stove can see breath! Wow! No hot water. 18° above Zero in parlor.

[1920]

Wed. May 19, 1920

Syracuse. W[omen's]. Congress. The World We Have to Make. Hotel Onondaga 12.30.

Sept. 5, 1920

Man—worshipping women—revere not sex—but what he vaguely recognizes as what humanity ought to be—the beauty, purity, tenderness, patience—he calls her "an angel"—and feels that he is not the type.

[1921]

{undated first page}

Begin in good health and happy. . . .

Thur. Feb. 24, 1921

Zona Gale [37] & Grace to dinner. . . .

Aug. 1921

"On the general count of getting themselves recognized as the intellectual equals of men, women have lost by their neglect of form. This is notably the case with one of the most original women thinkers, Charlotte Perkins Gilman. Mrs. Gilman is not without style, but it is the style of Mrs Gilman's mind, thin, vivid, and swift as a lightening streak, rather than the carefully finished instrument of communication. Only in her most ambitious and perhaps most deeply felt works, like "Women and Economics," does it produce organic literary form. Undoubtedly this has lead (!) to misappreciation and the neglect of Mrs. Gilman's contribution long before we have ceased to need it." Mary Austin, The Bookman, Aug. 1921.

Oct. 1921

The Children's Home—children for adoption—Look for little girl about four—

[1922]

Notes

In good health & spirits. Have begun taking Kepler's Malt & Cod Liver Oil—to get fatter. only weigh—ab[ou]t 115.

Thur. Feb. 16, 1922

reached Pasadena about 2.15 P.M. Met by Mrs. Park, cab to Katharine's.

Thur. Mar. 30, 1922

Houghton's father dies abt. 5 P.M.

Fri. Mar. 31, 1922

Wire from Ho. Go to bank. . . . Make black smock in evening—late up.

Sat. Apr. 1, 1922

Train late—car late—arrive too late for funeral. . . .

Wed. Apr. 2, 1922

Mrs. Stevens died. Fell from Window————. about 5 A.M. He heard her scream—

Houghton tells me of dreadful news——Impossible!

[*Charlotte appended the following note later*:]

Within a few days or weeks *another* of Mrs. Meserole's escaped victims also fell out of the window at the same hour!—

Long distance hypnotism?——?

Sun. July 9, 1922

Amy Wellington[38] taken ill—one of her attacks gets Dr. Shelby.

Sat. July 15, 1922

Miss W[allace]. gets in another dr. & they hustle Amy off to the Presbyterian Ho. Operate at 10 or 10.30. give no hope.

I was with Miss Wallace in the hospital from 10.30 to after 1.—Amy lived. May linger four days or so they think. Fibroid growth had strangulated intestine. Worst operation they ever saw! . . .

Mon. July 17, 1922

Amy still living.

Thur. July 20, 1922

She has survived the four days—& they are going to "put back" the section of intestine which was left outside! & which now looks healthy again!

Sat. July 22, 1922

Sent for to Norwich. Aunt L[ouise] very weak.

Mon. July 24, 1922

Aunt L. better—amazingly so.

Mon. Aug. 7, 1922

Dear Aunt Louise died today, Aug 7th.

Thur. Aug. 10, 1922 {?}

Will read to assembled cousins. Cousin Caroline, Francis, & Houghton executors. Can do as they please will all but the Lane money. Much excitement & "figgering."

Fri. Sept. 22, 1922

arr[ive]. Norwich to live.[39]

[1923]

Notes

Start with nothing in bank but $75. Houghton put in for me! . . .

Tues. Jan. 23, 1923

Century takes Book—*His Religion & Hers*.

Tues. July 3, 1923

Birfday! 63! Well and happy! Houghton here. Gave me "Golden Bough" & Ghent's book on "Reds."

Wed. Aug. 8, 1923

Ho's birthday. Many boxes of chocolate. Supper party. Boat to N.Y.

[1924]

Wed. July 25, 1924

Shall be, July 8, only $10.00 behind. save that soon.

Friday, June 27, 1924

If I manage on 2.50 a week to New Years, can save out of "tips"

Tues. July 22, 1924

Still 10. behind.

Sun. July 27, 1924

Sent Grace $50. Have now in bank, will give T[homas]. in Aug. & Sept.—if I can get along on $19.00!

Wed. Aug. 6, 1924

Have caught up on "tips" and am about 14.00 ahead.

Tues. Nov. 24, 1924

lunch with Martha. Night in Hingham.

[1925]

Wed. July 29, 1925

This was because of Emily's[40] objecting to my feeding her at meal times or from the icebox at night—she believing the cook as to what I gave her. To save myself continuous suffering, humiliation and anger I chloroformed my darling pussy cat. She died in my arms, peacefully buried by the Del. grape vi[*msm*]

[1926]

Mon. Aug. 9, 1925

Absurdly pleased with check for [$]20.00 from Jewish Daily Forward, for little article on "What is a Radical."

[1927]

Notes

Play less.
Work more.
Use God.

[1931]

Fri. Apr. 3, 1931

Dr. Freeman arrives. I have Pneumonia it seems. Consolidation in left lung. Says I must have a nurse. Don't. Get on all right with Ho. & kind Mary to bring trays.

[1934]

Fri. May 4, 1934

Houghton died.
about 11 P.M.

Thur. July 12, 1934

let Grace have $75.00.

Fri. Oct. 12, 1934

end of X ray for now.

Tues. Nov. 20, 1934

I am feeling thoroughly well, eat well—enjoy my meals, feel continuously cheerful.

Fri. Nov. 23, 1934

Bible class people called up, & Mr. Alley . . . speak for 'em Sunday.

Wed. Dec. 26, 1934

9.45 X ray
begin again!

Memoranda

Discovered very early in year 1932.
began X ray in Aug—
8 to 12 treatments—then 3 m[ore]. visit for examation [*sic*], in 1933, twice and dismissed until further trouble. Went again in Feb 34 & began treatment again Mch 1st, every day—12 or 14 I think.

[1935]

Fri. Jan. 4, 1935

Thomas in—lunched with me. Lamb stew—good!

Fri. Jan. 18, 1935

X ray, 2 P.M.
Just to look at it

Fri. Jan. 25, 1935

x ray—10.30?
last for the present

Tues. Mar. 12, 1935

dine—& discuss "How May Youth use its Heritage." Panel meeting.

[*With the exception of minor account information, the March 12 notation above, made just five months prior to her death, is the last entry in Charlotte's personal diaries. Even at the end Charlotte Perkins Gilman was still trying to raise social awareness—still trying to motivate people to think about issues affecting them and their world. These many years later, she is still succeeding.*]

APPENDIX A

From "Thoughts & Figgerings"

IN ADDITION to the diaries that Charlotte Perkins Gilman used to chronicle her activities and to express her thoughts about events as they occurred, she also often wrote her long-term plans, her philosophy, her objectives, and occasionally her grievances on various scraps of paper, which she collected and saved over the years. The odd assortment of papers that survives, written between 1883 and 1935, reveal much about the process by which Charlotte used her writing as a way to "think on paper"—both as a means of organizing her ideas and of exercising her intellect. Sometimes the thoughts were written in haste; other times Charlotte wrote meticulous and detailed accounts about what was on her mind. But they always served a therapeutic purpose: "All these loose pages, accumulating along the years, mark the incessant effort to drag that shaky mind back to its task, to cheer it, stimulate it, comfort it, through self-suggestion to make it go" (*Living*, p. 166). As Charlotte sorted through those odd little scraps of paper during her final years, she labeled the collection simply "Thoughts & Figgerings."

Following is a chronological sampling of some of the most revealing of her collected thoughts. (Other papers in the folders include shopping lists, account information, lists of illnesses, lists of friends, travel plans, ideas for articles, household inventories, etc.) Charlotte's contemplations in the selections below range from her love for Charles Walter Stetson, to her constant battle against poverty, to her feelings about her breast cancer—which she refers to simply as that troublesome "critter."

Nov. 3rd. 1883.

A Word to Myself.

Whereas I, Charlotte A. Perkins, am at this time 23 years old and not content, I desire to know *why* not!

What have I done so far to fulfill my duties as a member of the world? If I were dead tomorrow what were lost?

What do I mean to do and be? *Why am I unhappy now?*

[227]

I have *promised* to marry Charles Walter Stetson. I shall keep that promise if we both live and are not prevented.

I have agreed then to be his wife. Yes. I love him? Yes.

And by love I mean that I want him more than anyone else on earth? That and more. It should mean more. It should mean that if he loved not me I should still love him. Should I? As far as I can now know and foresee—Yes.

Now Love is more than *wanting*. *Love* is the infinite desire to benefit, a longing to *give*, not merely a hungry wish to take. Than [*sic*] if I love this man, and this man most of all the world, what do I *do* for him? How do I, shall I, benefit him? Of material comforts I can as yet give nothing. And of spiritual? Truly the best, the only thing to do is to sanctify and upbuild myself, and then, loving him, he can be bettered and made happy thereby. . . .

Unselfish, True, and Wise; Strong, Brave, and Pure——if I am these I do right by my husband, my children, my God, and Mankind.

This works comes first.

If I have Love and Happiness or lose them; if I suffer or enjoy, in any case this is my first life duty—ambition—work!

If I am these I have *lived* indeed. Having no lover it is my duty to God and man and myself.

Having a lover it is my first duty to him.

To be *Unselfish. True. Wise. Strong. Brave. Pure.*

Charlotte A. Perkins
Wed. May 31st, 1893 —
1258 Webster St. Oakland Cal.

Age—near 33 (July 3rd.)

Probably 40 years time before me.

Desired to accomplish in that time—the utmost attainable advance of the race.

Means of accomplishment—the perception and transmission of truth, applicable truth.

Most immediate necessity: the maintenance of self and child. . . .

[May 31, 1893].

If I earned $100.00 a month for 17 months—. . . . I should be out of debt.

A year and a half—by Dec. 1894 I should be out of debt.

A year and a half. Write 3 hours, five mornings a week.

Tomorrow is the first of June. I will begin.

March 26th. 1894.

There remains of my life, to set a large limit, as much again—34 years. I will say 40.

The usefulness of these rests on my power and goodwill; and these again rest on my health and happiness.

If it be that I may not have—as indeed I never have had, personal happiness; or rather, happiness in personal relation; it follows that I must ensure as far as may be, happiness in general relation.

Now this requires—first money. Then such material conditions as are called for by my special activities. Following and going with these is the ceaseless call for such behavior to all passing relations as shall produce the most good—those large and unremittingly demanded virtues, cheerfulness, courtesy, justice, patience, humility, truthfulness, loving kindness always.

Now as to material conditions. My most peremptory need is clothing, good, beautiful, sufficient.

I must make it a matter of honor to provide these.

April 8th. [1894?]

Help me to work! To really do the things I have in mind.

To write—write—write. A novel for next year? A play? A serious book? Help me to see the way and follow it. Whatever else may come or go this is my clear straight path —to work. What needs now is to place things. Keep my mind clear and my heart strong! pour in—pour in—give me more and more of the great stream of life. Let me feel it and give it out in all the ways I know. This means health and power and all good. Help me O God!

May 9, 1894

I am about to give up my home, send Kate to her father, and begin new; being now a free woman, legally and actually.

New Year's Day. 1896—

I am now thirty-five years and six months old.

As far as I can judge my work lies mainly in public speaking, in writing for a purpose, and in organizing.

With always the personal touch as highest of all.

For the professional uses I need; 1 vocal training, physical culture, and splendid thought and life: 2 the craft of writing developed by earnest use; 3 patient power, deep thought, wide knowledge, & parliamentary drill.

For the personal life I need————much.

Believing what I do I should have a steady calm and peace-disbursing power. I should stand for good will, sweetness, cheerfulness, and *peace*—like a great angel.

My personality still stands in my way somewhat.

I must not forget to apply to myself the truths I preach to others—

Knowing—seeing—feeling as I do my conduct should be nobler.

I must learn to hold more steadily my currents of great joy, and incorporate them. This I have long seen and not yet done.

Suppose now I look forward bravely, blinking nothing, and assume my full place ————: In the world's life of today I stand, greatly gifted, nobly trained, most strangely led, stepping forward now swwiftly into the full light of large usefulness.

I should assume to *be there*—no—not yet—I must not hurry—it is coming.

I must not try *too* hard, but take what comes.

Still—I may plan—may work.

Most of all should work at *being*. Seek steadiness.

A wise restful power.

Must get where nothing will disturb—upset. . . .

Jan. 1st. 1897—

Life lies strangely quiet now. All the wants are gone, and all the pains. I have but one idea—or a double idea—to get well and work. This month just passed promises well. Well. Except for not having the sea appetite I feel as well as when I landed, and am able to work a little. It isn't much, but I can write an hour or two a day without breaking down. I walk with pleasure, eat fairly, and keep happy. There seems no occasion to say anything here—it is a question of bearing ahead steadily—a long breath—a thirty years wind.

To write and speak—draw too when I can get to it—I think. Begin to feel a bit uncertain about that, but I guess I shall do it yet.

To lift and stir and stimulate—to help on women and the Race—Yes.

To be unceasingly true to what seems to me the Right Way. A full belief in God. A sensitive following and yielding to the development of life. . . . Health and Work—it all comes back to that. . . .

Mon. A.M. April 5th. 1897.

When I came to know Houghton—

> In a strange life—widespread—thin—,
> Full of great lights, and fresh with strong cold winds—
> Alive with sudden changes, rich and sweet
> With knowledge that the world is coming good,
> And this—for me—is the one way to go;
> But broken also with deep shuddering gulfs
> And robbed to nakedness—in such a life,
> Sudden, a little glade of level grass,
> Elm trees and robins, lilacs, and a swing—
> Old times—old faces—things I used to know,
> And things I knew not—, lovers—friends—a home—.
> It's good to look at. Thank you. And goodbye.

Charlotte Perkins Stetson

Jan. 18th. 1898

I see no reason why I should not grow into smooth clear headed practical life now. Whatever I think and feel, my value to others is in what I do—in social contact and expression.

Personally, to grow more kind, patient, courteous, true, just, cheerful—a pleasure and a help to all. *To all.*

See the good and help it. People *are*—help them.

As I count to the century depends on the two main channels—tongue and pen.

These open well—better and better.

As poet—as author—as orator—I am being given a recognized place.

To *fill* it—to win more and more.

This means the same method as before—to see clearly and think boldly and speak wisely and well. Better style also—will grow. The dreams and hopes and aspirations must focus in definite work. . . . This means health. A clear contented mind. Steady quiet easy work. And I don't see why not. No Kate yet awhile. No Houghton. Just work. Good. . . .

I want patience. A long sweeping peaceful range of vision—long health—to work *easily*—for three years. Health and comfort and peace of mind. Happiness.

Should I not be happy?————— . . .

I must come out forever from the feelings of shame and regret. Must leave off the past more fully than ever before.

Must feel and be a strong calm brave happy useful honorable woman. Must bloom and shine in the splendid joy of living and give the world the light and hope and strength, the clear simple pleasant commsense [*sic*] about life, which it so needs.

To see great lovely truths and teach them. O blessed blessed life! No matter *what* it costs—a blessed life.

And if with this may come the dear sweet joy of home and love————.

To be worthy. *Worthy*. From today to live as all women to live. So if this great happiness does come I shall not feel the weight of it too much.

And if it does not—I shall be able to live on nobly without it. . . .

May 9th
1900

I am here to serve the world. As a perceiver and transmitter of truth and love—an interpreter[,] a reconciler. This is as true now—in happiness, as it was in pain.

Through my happiness I can serve better. My marriage is not a wrong to Houghton. I bring him love and wisdom, help in his best ideals, a home life to his liking. He is not sure of wanting children—and I may have them. We will see. I can not give him all I would like to—but he loves me. To make him happy means a quiet beautiful, comfortable home, pleasant society and good living: for me to be there mostly, and to be well and happy. I must be well and happy—it is a clear duty.

And I ought to be. Such clear wide lovely work! Such endless work! Such good work. Now to write, this summer, beautiful things. Not for money. The money will come or not, as always. But because these things need to be told.

Oct. 5th. '03

Things I'm going to Have.

Big dark red desk & cane revolving chair.

Full stock of all kinds of needed stationery.

Work table—sewing things etc, perfect appointments.

Dressmaking form—good one—*my* figure.

Long mirrors.

Some good rockers.

Dressing cabinet for Houghton.

Shoe-dressing stool

Jewel case for bureau & small one for travelling.

A Globe.
Maps—many.
Billiard table.
Piano
Pianola for Houghton.
Hymnbook, college songs, etc.
Music box. Victrolla

July 3rd.
1920.

Sixty years old.

If I am to do my full duty must "cease to repine," pitch in, do at once the work that will set me going at best pitch.

If, in the rest of this year, I can do as planned; 2 co-plays & fine good spectacular scenarios, these should accomplish it. Still sixty:——— . . .

Here is planned a New Life.

Emergence, Achievement, Triumph.

All that I have meant to do, done, and more.

It means Joy, Peace, Health, and wide helpfulness to others.

It would fairly guarantee the accomplishment of further work; of my Weeks Summer School, and so on, ten or fifteen years.

It gives broader base to the Social Philosophy and makes more possible the poems.

It would give great joy to Houghton; and enable him to work as he best liked.

If this is necessary to my fulfillment of Social Duty—and that work is to come through me—this will happen.

May 7th—1924

I am 64 years old—practically.

I have done =

A shelf of books—some of the first importance.

A mass of magazine stuff—all tending upward.

Poems—many, some excellent, some useful, none deleterious.

Lectures; for 34 years.—thousands I guess—a thousand anyway—all tending upward.

I am now happy, comfortable, taken care of by Houghton. Ought to be at work ten more years.—to 75. . . .

But!——To reestablish my place and set the books going—must do some fresh, distinctive work—*now.* . . . . . .

July 23. 1925.
65 years old—

To do. Can work probably ten more years. *Personal.* Make Houghton happy as I can. That means keep well, keep cheerful; keep on good terms with the rest of the family—love and encourage him. take care of Thomas: Do for K. if I can—could make dresses for D. sometimes? Be neighborly and pleasant.

My work: to See and to Say:

Pull myself together: Face the world's present problem: write out my Standard and Programs: Make up my mind, clear and strong: as to what is to be done—should be done—& preach it. My job: get on to it. . . .

April 25th. '29 Come come!——As for past—drop it!
Have accomplished really a good deal—in the right direction. As for present—excellent. Nothing wrong but lack of funds and lack of social contacts.

As for future—Say I have but five more years of work—six. Ought to be able to get Ethics in shape—& Autobi—and write something powerful on sex. Would like—travel with Houghton.

Wed. June 25th 1930.

Yesterday I learned through Mary Baggat the cook, (my only communication with Emily [Gilman, wife of Houghton's brother Francis] is through the servants,) that she wanted pie,—"huckleberry pie, custard pie, pineapple pie."

I promptly ordered custard pie for today, and bought a can of shredded pineapple for another day.

While I was out she inquired of Mary what was for dessert, and learning that it was custard pie she refused it and asked for fruit. There was only a pineapple which I wanted for dinner tonight. Mary prepared it for her.

When I returned and found what she had done I refused to furnish the pineapple and had the pie served. Also I concealed the pineapple, judging that she would send Francis for it.

Failing to find it he came into the library where I lunch alone to accommodate Emily, and asked "Is there any reason why Emily cannot have pineapple for her dinner?"

I said there was, that I had arranged to have it for tonight and had provided her with the pie she had asked for yesterday. He said that they paid for everything fifty-fifty, and as a climax said with a sweeping gesture "Then strike that off the account."

(Half a pineapple is not very expensive.)

Dissatisfied with this rather lame conclusion he presently returned ans [sic] said "I am very glad you did this. Now I've got you where I want you, and I'll crack you between my fingers like a lobster!" (He told Houghton it was "louse"—not "lobster.")

To which I merely replied "I will tell your brother what you say." As I instantly repeated this over the telephone I am sure of the words.

August 11th
1930.

Seventy. What of it? . . .
Outlook: If all clear and progressing normally, what exercise for human faculties?

a. The usual economic necessities to be met.
b. All the higher processes carried on & developed as Art, Service, Education, Religion.

c. The "landscape gardening" of the world; conquest of vermin, conservation of resources, endless improvements. New energy & joy with each generation.

Wed.   1932   April 14th.

72. Seventy two in July.

Physically well; eyes, ears & innards.

A little heavier—125 or so.

Mind dull, slow, shunning responsibility, forgetful, no "urge to do."

But—given opportunity, the same power to reach and stir, amuse and stimulate, convey ideas.

And what I have written, of late—has been good—a few small things.

What I must face is lessening power.

What I *must* do is get my papers in order, to use—or destroy. . . .

Think I could still rise if fed—stimulated—in contact with thinkers & doers.

Dec. 26 [1932?]

For Heaven's Sake look forward a little!
This is splendidly worth doing
Nobody else can do it!!!
Poor though it is its the best offering: ought to stir some women.

One Girl.———
One girl reads this, and takes fire!
Her life is changed. She becomes
a power—a Mover of others—
I write for her.

July 31st 1933

Seventy three.

With hopes of, say, seven yrs. more. In that time:

'33 Get ethics in shape.

'34 Get all my "Gilmania" in shape.

'35 Of Her.??

'36 edit & revise for library edition

To Do—in Cal[ifornia].

1934—

Sept—If I live a year————

Work up the autobiography.

Do "Of Her."

Write 6 articles at 50.00 =   300.00

Give 10 lectures at 50.00 =   500.00

52 w[eeks]. Lectures do not count in time.
  Say, widest allowance, a month.
  Article, *plenty* of time, six weeks.

Autobi[ography]: two months & six w[eeks]   4 m[onths].
one for complete rest   1 m[onth].
                                                             5 m[onths].

  leaves 7 [months] for "Of Her":

  Good library to work in at times.

  My!
  That would be a good finish! . . .

          [1934.]

                                                 October 28th.

Well. . . .
Very comfortably situated, very.
Ought to be able to do some work.
What have I to offer?

          [1935]

I've just discovered why I'm so *hiddjus* tired — toxins! Can't expect to have this critter
3½ years & *no* trouble!
It is such below zero tiredness — 90° *below*

APPENDIX B

Verse, Letters, and Miscellany

CHARLOTTE tucked between the pages of her diaries numerous poems, letters, and miscellaneous notes that reveal much about her relationships with other people, most notably with Martha Luther and Walter Stetson. Included in this appendix are poems, letters, and miscellany that are still physically located within the diaries; also included are several poems and letters alluded to in the diaries but located elsewhere, primarily in Volumes 21 and 22 of the Gilman Papers or in the unprocessed addenda to the papers that were acquired by the Schlesinger Library after the bulk of the collection was purchased.

Preceding each document is a letter indicating its location, as listed below. Where dates were missing, I have attempted to locate the documents in the time period during which they were most likely written. I have indicated the speculative "placement" of the written work with a bracketed [?]. All entries have been placed chronologically based on actual or reconstructed dates. Unless otherwise noted, most of the following selections were hand inscribed by either Charlotte or Walter Stetson, as indicated.

Source Abbreviations

I   Insertions found in the diaries or dated comments inscribed in the front or back of a diary
P   Poems found primarily in volumes 21 and 22 of the Gilman Papers and mentioned in the diary text
U   Unprocessed addendum to the Gilman Papers

[*P. Composed Oct. 1879*]

> To May Diman. 1880.
> May! Dearest May!
> The sweetest brightest fairest May
> That ever folded a celestial wing

A radiant flood of heavenly light to bring,
And bless the cold earth with the breath of Spring.
Most fitting name!
What swift bright thoughted angel came
Darting from the wide realms of space
To where thy lovely baby face
Lay, smiling, at the christening place
And bade them call thee May?
So grandly fair!
The strong free beauty of the Huntess Queen,
And yet so innocently pure and sweet
That a worn man from the hot city street
Might follow humbly after thy white feet
Looking for lilies where the footsteps fell.

[*P. Valentine poem, composed Dec. 10, 1879*]

To Martha Luther. 1880.

O quaint young damsel with the large grey eyes,
And glossy hair that shineth like the Day
And Martha, thou who hast a form
Outrivalling in willowy grace
A weeping ash tree trimmed with lace:

Thou who desirest in a thoughtless mood
That I would number thee among the lost
Who find upon the day of mating birds
Greeting the postman in their hapless glee
An unsuspected Valentine from me:

List to the words of her who knoweth well
That thou, who art a chicken in her sight
Regardest her with feelings far from cold;
That unto her thy heart dost still incline
Like to the oak tree and the clinging vine:—

I love thee much! Thou hast in black and white
A fond confession that I well could wish
Had never met the garish light of day,
That I had ne'er been tempted to exhume
From the dark caverns of my deep hearts gloom.

But since the deed is done, why let it stay,
The *fact* is there, and though the lapse of time
May change the current of my heart, yet now,
As long as our ideas and tastes are such——
I love you much!

[*P. Following is Charlotte's first published poem. It appeared in the* New-England Journal of Education *on May 20, 1880, when she was nineteen.*]

To D——— G———

When first the days are warm and bright,
    When first the blue-birds sing,
When first the wind against the cheek
In subtle odors seems to speak
    Of Memory and Spring:

When tender grass on sunny slopes
    Is thickening day by day,
When baby ferns are half uncurled,
When early sunbeams warm the world,
    And graceful catkins sway;

Then in the meadows cool and wide
    Springeth the flower I love,
And many folk to seek it go,
And cut it carefully below
    And pluck it from above.

A modest plant, and little known
    To those possessed of means:
Yet welcome to the poor man's wife,
The luxury of humble life,
    Is *dandelion greens*.

            C. A. P.—

[*U. At the top of the following letter, in Charlotte's hand, is written: "After Martha Luther's engagement. This to one Sam Simmons a friend of several year's standing. I had so few———."*]

                    8:30 P.M. Mon. Nov. 14.
                          1881.

Quiet.

Dead quiet; with the cat too fast asleep to purr, my watch, and the still lamp, for company.

Mother and Aunt C. are at the Stoddard Lecture. You see I have changed my mind about writing. It is just this way, I ask no more for help from you, but write as my only outlet for thoughts and feelings which crowd painfully. Like one who has safely passed through a serious amputation——cautery has stopped the *danger*, I complain no longer of the *pain*, but feel the *loss of the limb* as sensibly as ever. So I trespass still further on your kindness. And in very truth I had rather write to you than see you; in this I am free as air, candid, unembarrassed, mistress of expression; but when you are with me it is all a blurr of what the old novellists called "conflicting emotions." I keep crossing my desire to speak with your "undesire" to hear, my wish for things with your probable attitude of reception if I asked, my string of ideas that want to come out with your quiet sufficiency that needs for no one—so there's "a little talking of outward things," and no help.

Don't think me ungrateful. It is not your fault that I find in you no whit of what I so longed for for a few days—no one's fault.

To return to my surgical simile, there's no amount of ingenious machinery, no cork, steel, iron, or wood, that can fill the place of the live warm living thing that is gone; but for all that they are grandly useful, and one would be a mere cripple without them. As I look at it now I think that in my first blind misery I must have actually expected you to step into the vacancy, to calmly hand over an arm of your own to fill my empty sleeve!

And that's one thing I always appreciate and enjoy in you and your brother—you are so *true*. Just keep right on in your own line, and other people *have* to fit. And if they can't fit they drop off, and you trot along as evenly as before. You seem almost reliable enough to be used as a unit for measuring the human character.

Stick to it, and I may possibly get acquainted with you in the course of time.

A good days work today. Up at 5.50, with the shiniest kind of a moon, and a strip to sullen red in the east. Got them a real good breakfast, and found time for a lot of little jobs besides the regular ones.

One of my pupils was away today, so I revelled in the other one, and we covered much ground. I am bound to improve the minds of those infants as much as may be, so I read to them while they draw and write. Sent the lone damsel home a bit early, and so had time for a good dinner. Then meandered gaily over to give a weekly drawing lesson on Bridgham st., doing divers errands on the way. Stopped in at Watermans for a few surplus moments gained by speed, and feasted on costume. "Great Scott!" Wouldn't I wear things if I had 'em though! Such sweeping folds of velvet and fur! such glancing lights of silk and jewels!

Well, I shall have to take it out in October sunsets I suppose. Did you chance to see one day last month that quotation on the Poet's Calendar—

> "The maple swamp glowed like a sunset sea,
> Each leaf a ripple with it's separate flush,"—

Isn't it delicious.

Taught the buxom little Cushmans for an hour, trotted down to the Pub. Li. and got two imposing works on Egypt, made a flying visit to Dr. Brooks, and so home. And *such* a fight as I had all the way along George st.! I was cold and tired and hungry in the first place, and secondly it was just the time when I used to go around by M's, stop and be petted a bit, stay to tea, and go home with a sense of happy possession that made an evening's work mere pleasure.

I hardly cared to go half a mile out of my way tonight just to hear about Hingham, so I trotted on.

Yes, and I conquered, too. Again and again it rose to an absolute whimper, and again and again I sat on it, kicked it, trampled it under foot, and deliberately thought about somebody else.

As simple and plain a cure as mud for a wasp sting, is thought of others in personal distress, and though my ministration was confined to an inquiry after Mr. Manchester, still it was genuine, and efficacious. Home I came and devoured a frugal meal of bread & molasses, saw the family off in high spirits, and studied till eyes and head struck work, and I took an evanescent nap.

And wasn't I thankful that nobody called!

I had rather talk than eat, and rather write than talk, so that even the foregone 12 hours work can hardly counteract the sense of indulgence in this hours relaxation.

You say that it would only bring you closer if your friend were engaged. True, but remember that she would be added to him, he would not go to her. "As the husband is the wife is ——"

Then imagine if you can that you had filled to him in a thousand ways the place that she now would—, not that you covered all of her ground, but she all yours and acres more, and see how you would feel to have everything that you had given, *better* given by some one else.

If you can't compass such an abnormal state of affairs as that, suppose differently; imagining yourself still in your present place, and to find in one week that Harold Childs valued another man ten times as much as ever he valued you.

That there was some one who could give your friend *everything* which you had so gladly rendered, and a world beside.

And then imagine you had noone else—that you lived in antagonism to a greater or less degree with nearly every one else, and furthermore that the whole business was an incredible surprise to you, and perhaps you may form some conception of this little tangle.

Excuse repitition, this is not moan, this time, but explanation with a view to conviction; I have no tears tonight, nor pain. That only comes now under touch of sympathy.

I was at the Hazard's the other night, and talking to Carrie. There's a deal of kindness in those people, and much common ground between Carrie and me, so I told her some little, just to explain my dolorousness, and when she stroked my hand in her soft ones, and said "my poor stormy child!" I could have wilted down into my shoes. Just as you can cut yourself in cold weather, and never know it as long as your hands are numb, but warmth will revive the smart and start the blood with amazing speed.

Goodnight.

You are an immeasurable comfort as far as you go, and I only wish you went farther. Goodnight.

And tell me please with that unmistakakable [*sic*] plainness you so well understand, if you object to being written at in *this* style.

Charlotte A. Perkins

Why under the sun don't you understand what I mean without my saying things, and *in spite* of my saying things?

Martha always did!

CAP.

[*P. Charlotte wrote the following poem to Martha Luther shortly after learning of her engagement to Charles Lane.*]

Dec. 13, 1881

Unsent.

A Merry Christmas Sweetheart! Dearest love! My darling! Little girl! Petit canard!
Chere amie! Engel (Mit ein B der for)! Marfia! Chicken! O the little names!

Tender and small they rise in jostling crowds
Each with a throng of memories at its back.
Tender and small are they, but O my heart!
Each little name and all the thoughts behind
Hath arrows poison tipped.

"My little girl!" *My* little girl! No more,
Never again in all this weary world
Can I with clinging arms & kisses soft
Call you "my little girl!"

"My darling!" O my darling! How my heart
Thrills at the words with sudden quivering pain,
Rises and beats against the doors of speech
And sends hot tears and sobs that will be heard.

"Sweetheart!" You *were* my sweetheart. I am none,
To any man, and I had none but you.
O sweet! You filled my life; you gave me all
Of tenderness, consideration, trust,
Confiding love, respect, regard, reproof,
And all the thousand thousand little things
With which love glorifies the hardest life.

Think dearest, while you yet can feel the touch
Of hands that once could soothe your deepest pain;
Think of those days when we could hardly dare
Be seen abroad together lest our eyes
Should speak too loud. * * There is no danger now.

No danger now. Life spreads before your feet.
As fair and pleasant as—the landscape lay
Before *our* feet that day a year ago
When you and I asked nothing of the world
But room, and one another.

Why sweet, I held your heart
In that large empty space where mine was not.
And you? You must have had mine in your hands,
Keeping it warm until another came
To fill the place, and mine was given back.

Held first a moment closer than your soul,
Closer than it had ever been before——
Then given back. A helpless, newborn, child;

Hungry and desolate, alone and cold.
You cannot wonder that the thing should cry.

And yet believe me love, (and even now
I know I need not tell you to believe)
That if your happiness or smallest good
Depended on my silence, not a word
Would every reach you.

    Why I *love* you, Sweet.
I *love* you; and I see no present cause
To hope for change in that most stubborn fact.

Goodnight. Goodbye. I am too tired now
To tell you all I could. So thank your stars
That watch hands pointing to another day
And all tomorrow's—no, *today's* hard work
Compel my sleep. Goodnight dear love.
        Goodbye.————

[*P. Charlotte wrote this poem the day after she was introduced to Charles Walter Stetson.*]

The Suicides Burial.
Jan. 12, 1882

A yellow twilight damp and still.
    A pale young moon o'erhead
The black monks hurrying over the hill
    To bury the nameless dead.

One before with a flaring torch
    Against the sallow sky.
The wind-blown flame doth almost scorch
    The thing they bear so high.

Too vile a thing for the holy night;
    Too vile for the Blessed day;
In shameful haste, twixt dark and light
    They hurry it away.

[*I. On January 31, 1882, Charlotte wrote "An Anchor to Windward," which is inserted on loose paper in the back of the diary for 1882.*]

An Anchor
to
Windward.

Providence.
Jan. 31st. 1882.*

This is for me to hold to if, as I fore-fear, the force of passion should at any time cloud my reason, and pervert or benumb my will.

Now that my head is cool and clear, now before I give myself in any sense to another; let me write down my Reasons for living single.

In the first place I am fonder of freedom than anything else.—I love to see & be with my friends, but only when I want them. I love to have pleasant faces in my home, but only when I want them. I like to have my own unaided will in all my surroundings—in *dress, habits, diet, hours, behavior, speech,* and *thought.*

I *increasingly* like to feel that my home is *mine,* that I am free to leave it when I will, & for as long as I will.

I like to select for myself, to buy for myself, to provide for myself in every way.

I like to start out in joyous uncertainty of where I am going, & with no force to draw me back—like it beyond words. I like to go about alone—*independantly.*

The sense of individual strength and selfreliance is sweeter than trust to me.

I like to be *able* and *free* to help any and every one, as I never could be if my time and thoughts were taken up by that extended self—a family.

If I were bound to a few I should grow so fond of them, and so busied with them that I should have no room for the thousand and one helpful works which the world needs. As it is now, or rather as it *will* be, I can turn to any one in distress and give them my best help; my love, my time, my interest and sympathy.

I am cool, fearless, and strong; and have power which can do good service in proper circumstances, if I can only trust in them and coming opportunity.

It is a matter of futurity in any case, and I am willing to risk my life—yes, and another's too, to prove the question.

It is after all a simple case, for I *mean* to do right, and if I am on the wrong track, I shall do a lot of good work anyway, and merely miss a few year's happiness.

For reasons many and good, reasons of slow growth and careful consideration, more reasons than I now can remember; I decide to *Live*—Alone.

God help me!

[*U. Inscribed in Walter's hand.*]

Charlotte

Wide was the warm blue Space, and O, how deep!
    The stars were gone, and earth, and sea:
    The solitude was only there with thee and me.
Ere whiles I'd prayed my prayer to Sleep,
Who deigned to come and woo the pains I keep
    Awake, till all departed silently.
Oblivion was until that cry and sweep
    Of wings which brought my soul exultant unto thee.
Ah Love! How vast the Space! And we were dead—
Dead, dead, but all alone—at last alone!
    Thy waiting arms, thy glorious face, thy kiss,
Did quite for bitter weary years atone.
    What tho' I bled awake, and fought! 'twas bliss
To conquor, tho' my life-blood all was shed.

I am awake: I fight, and bleed alone.
    Fight—but shall triumph knowing this:
When we are dead—Ah Love, when dead!
    That primal touch of lips shall all out weigh
The myriad blood-drops slowly shed.

Charles Walt Stetson

Feb. 15. 1882

[*U. Inscribed in Walter's hand.*]

To Charlotte

By the body and shed blood of Christ our Lord!
    By the passionate form and pure heart of Love!
    Would I with this poor script now seek to prove
That of all women thou art most adored.
Could my red blood at thy dear feet out poured
    Assurance greater give, then would I move
To spill't, e'en, tho' thereby the one reward
I crave, for sure, I should for this life lose.
But lack is not, for it thou shouldst refuse
    To quite believe, so shall my every deed—
(Through whatso e'er of days my life is long)—
    And Good-work done, slay any doubts that need
    The slaying, or stay any wounds that bleed,
With arguments effectually strong.

Coda

By the passionate form and pure heart of Love!
Of this poor proof I do not all approve.
Could I in mine thy true hand keep alway
And in thine eyes look fondly night and day,
Then were no need, for sure, my most Adored;
Ah no! By the cross and blood of our dear Lord!

Charles Walt Stetson

Studio, May 9. 82

[*U. Inscribed in Walter's hand.*]

The Bride-ring

Now! Where is the ring—
    The bride-ring I gave thee?
Thy finger is bare!
    Where is the ring that would save thee
If ever the lover and King
    Of my Queen should prove false?
Ah! no bride-ring he gave thee!
And now what shall save thee
    To him, thy hot lover,
    If thou shouldst prove false?

Bride-elect of the bride-ring
    That has not been hammered,
    But which circles thy heart
With its fire and its gold,
In the north and the south
    Who shall find it?
In the east and the west
    Who shall mind it
When the kiss of thy mouth
    Is better than bride-ring?
When the babe on thy breast
    Seals me servant, and lover, and King?

And who cares for the bride-ring
    When round thee shall hover
    My kisses of flame,
Which shall burn thee and burn thee
If ever thou turn thee
    From me, thy lord-lover
Thy servant and king!

And then on thy finger
    Which now is babe-bare
A bright flame shall linger,
    And thou'llt find it to burn thee
    Till all men shall spurn thee;
    And so if thou turn thee—
Then a blood-ring of my blood
    Shalt thou ever and ever wear
            There!
                        Charles Walt Stetson

Studio,
May 13, 1882

[*I. The following poem inscribed in Charlotte's hand is inserted in the front of the diary for 1882.*]

                    9:20 P.M.   Prov.   June 15. 1882.

I'm going straight to bed, dear love
From the parlor warm & bright,
But before I go I must let you know
That I love my love tonight.

With body & heart & brain dear love,
"From the center all round to the sea"
I love you dearly tonight, my love,
A *little* as you love me.

When I'm at my highest & best, dear love,
When the world look fair & free,

I feel it rise in my heart, dear love.
A *little* like yours for me.

I could lay my hand in yours, dear love.
And look you straight in the eye
And give you my lips and kiss dear love
As once beneath the sky.

I'm only just as I am, dear love,
And yet you want me so—
If you're going to marry a child, d. l.
You must wait for the child to grow.

You call me glorious names, d. l.
"Heart's dearest," "Helper," "Queen,"
But all you seem to find, dear love,
Is a transformation scene.

love me and help me & wait, d. l.
And live your own true life;
And pray Our Father in high, d. l.
To fit me to be your Wife!

[*l. The following poem inscribed in Charlotte's hand is inserted in the front of the diary for 1882.*]

And Oh! it seems so strange!
That I who lived so long alone
Should find another heart my own;
Should find the life which I had chosen
—Free if friendless, strong if frozen—
Turn with unexpected change
To such radiance of beauty—
Such united Joy and Duty—
That I kneel with hands on eyes
In a humble deep surprise,
And pray upward that my living
May deserve this wealth of giving
Proving as perfect woman
Worth the gladness superhuman.
Sept. 22, '82.
C. A. Perkins

[*l. The following poem from Walter is dated Sept. 23. '82.*]

The Painting of
The Portrait

These many days I've tried to fix the face
Of her I love on canvas, that it might
Remain to tell of her, and glad the sight

Of those to come with intellectual grace.
Most patiently did she sit, and I did trace
    And study the marvellous eye that's dark and bright;
    The curve from the wide clear brow's fair height
Along the cheek to the eloquent lips' red place;
    And then adown the delicate smooth chin
To the supple throat, until it was so lost
In the hid and heaving breasts' cream white high mounds.
    But Oh! today 'tis not more like to her within
My soul, nor like to what her soul surrounds,
Than 'twas when first my brush the canvas crossed.

II

O what in me the fault, or what the sin,
    That dulls my sight or warps her image fair
    Until my hand may not her lovliness declare—
For which I've prayed e'en since I did begin?
Ah, Lord, and hath it always suchwise been,
    That ne'er within my heart I yet did bear
    An image true of all her shape so rare,
Tho' sure I know her spirit dwells therein?
    What then the hope for eminence in Art
When what I love e'en as my very soul
Is not seen clear, is scarcely understood?
    And while I cannot fix the smallest part
Of her great loveliness what can console,
And what of all my life and Art is good?
Charles Walt Stetson.

[I. *Inscribed in Charlotte's hand and inserted into the journal for 1882, this poem is dated October 20, 1882.*]

Home in the soft wet night with happy heart;
Blest heart that never grieves!
Warm air with Autumn odors sadly sweet
Breathing around me, and my dallying feet
On rain-wet fallen leaves.

'Neath the caressing shadow of tall trees,
Cloud softened sky above;
The tender sweetness of the quiet night
Around me, and within me the delight of our united love.

Oh Sweet! I love you! Love you! trying hard
To show new meaning in the timeworn phrase.
Dear wellworn words! Soft said in listening ears
Down the whole series of the world's long years
    In such unnumbered ways!

I love you. And I see the reason now
Why its forever new.
Though uttered for a million years & more
Here are two factors never used before
—See darling, *I* love *you!*

[*I. Following the "oath" below, Stetson drew a picture of a head and legs next to which he inscribed "my seal." The entry is dated Oct. 22, 1882, and is inserted in the front of the journal for 1882.*]

I hereby take my solemn oath that I shall never in future years expect of my wife any culinary or housekeeping proficiency. She shall never be required, whatever the emergency, to D U S T!

Charles Walt. Stetson

[*I. This poem, dated October 27, 1882, was written by Charlotte for her friend Retta Clarke. Walter Stetson is its subject.*]

Reserved.

My lips are my lover's.
This hand you may hold;
It is proud of your pressing, This girdle enfold
With your strong loving arm. To my cheek
lay your own
And kiss as it likes you all else;
this alone
I reserve for my lover

They were kept from first childhood
Not even the mouth
Of my mother touched mine in
My earliest youth.
And when in the forest in flickering light
My lover first kissed me I answered
the rite
With the freshness of childhood.

Supersensitive say you?
The logic is small;
To be chary of one thing and
generous with all.
To reserve one small piece and
Make public the whole.—
And yet I am glad from the
depths of my soul
I kept these for my lover.

C. A. P.

[U. Inscribed in Charlotte's hand. 1883?]

Dear little boy with pretty mouth
Sweeter than flower of tropic south
And fire-blue eyes and curling hair
And smooth white body soft and fair
I love you—some!

And always when my heart is cold
And I feel hungry as of old
And long for kisses warm & sweet
And close embrace from head to feet
To you I come!

[U. January 1, 1883]

My heart's Love—I want you tonight. I'd so like to draw you close even now and tell you how dear that New Year's greeting is. It was a great wave of rest when I came tired home from the studio. I'd like to draw you close—close—with that passionate closeness that makes me know that I shall never want so long as I have you; and with the feeling that I can never, never get you close enough.

I can scarce wait for our ceremonials. I saw in you and in myself last night what makes me sure waiting *should* not be for long.

Now here is a sonnet. I was feeling *assured* of my place in your life, and was thinking how all the blandishments of many fair lovers else could not surpass my silence with the touch of my hand in yours—for *you know my soul.* And so I put it into that form for you.

Yes, right glad I am that I shall see you tomorrow evening, and sit by you for two hours. God keep you, loveliest!

Charles Walt Stetson

Assurance

If thou shouldst gather all thy lovers, Sweet,
    From field and mount, from fount and dell,
    And ask that they how thee they love should tell,
And let me sit most lowly at thy feet
To listen to the o'erstrong words that'd beat
    Upon mine ear—comparing unto philomel
    Thy voice, on telling of thy lips sweet spell;
Or how thine eyes with pity were replete,
    Or how like the jungle tiger's they gave light
Or glowed with passion's fire, or gleamed like the dove's
Content in still dim hours when the fallen night
Brings home her mate,—tho' they were fair, in thine—
And thou wouldst love me best—this hand of mine
I'd lay—thou'dst feel I said, *My life's my Love's!*
Charles Walt Stetson—
for Charlotte's "New Year" '83

[I. This poem is inscribed on the flyleaf of the journal for 1882.]

April 1st. 1883

O God I wish to do
My highest and my best in life!
⸱Stop not for hinderance or strife:
Be Wise, and Strong, and True.
And can I also be a wife?
Bear children too—?

Can I, who hardly know
If I am truly seeing
The half-formed instincts fleeing
Within me to and fro—
Can I, who've scarce begun to grow
Bring others into being?

Can I, who seem to stand
Just on the borders of the world of Truth;
Can I with neither fear nor ruth
Take little children by the hand
And lead them out into the land—
Am *I* a guide for youth?

Can I, who suffer from the wild unrest
Of two strong natures claiming each its due,
And can not tell the greater of the two;
Who have two spirits ruling in my breast
Alternately, and know not which is guest
And which the owner true;

Can I, thus driven, bring a child to light
Who from the hour of birth until he dies,
Will hear still more these strong opposing cries;
Will have any passionate longing to *do right*
To reach the soul's most perfect Paradise

[U. The next several sonnets were written by Charles Walter Stetson during one of those periods before their marriage when Charlotte asked for a separation so that she might pursue her life's work.]

In Her Exile.

O wide-browed goddess Art! hast jealous grown
And sown this discord 'twixt my Love and me
That 'mid our fragrant flowers harsh weeds should be
To stay the heavenly blossoms lately blown?

Hast taught that tale wherewith she doth disown
    Her woman's heart and cries: "I love e'en thee
    But God doth call and brain shout 'be free',
And so I must, tho' thou went slain, and joy unknown"?
    Hast thou done this, and if so, wherefore done?
Speak! when for love of her did I love less
    Thee, goddess, and the work in me begun?
And when failed I thy glories to confess?
    Oh! what's the crime that thou shoulds't cloud my sense
And flood my weary land with bitterness?
Ap. 9*th* 83

In Pain

O Lady, Love! O fair and absolute Queen!
    Thy hopes of holy, fruitful wedded life,
    Thy joys in faintest thought wherein "thy wife"
Stood sweetlier to thy heart than the demesne
Of dreamland and the whole bright world between
    The east and west—how perished they? How rife
    Grew wish for fame and work unwed, and strife
Of alien thought 'gainst loving heart, and e'en
    Those hateful murmurings of distant dead
    Or living ancestors, interpreted
Be thee clear calls to single life and free?
O tell, my Love, how 'twas they grew in thee!
    Thou canst not tell. God knows the tears thou'st shed
    And all thy pain, and how thou'st anguished me.
Ap. 14*th* 83

*   *   *

II

Yea, Love, thou hadst me all, body and soul:
    I gave thee, as thou sayest naught but sweet
    And tender love; adorned thee as was meet,
And prayed that we might reach the self-same goal
In twin-hearts hearing gracious love as dole,
    Leaping as one, glad countenances and fleet.
    And then thou turnedst back thy faltering feet
And left me hastening alone unwhole.
    Oh grieving heart! weary the way for thee
With me afar, for thou dost love me well,
    And so o'er weary is the way for me
    Thou dost no wrong to fear that it may be

Sure Death our utter parting may compel,
Oh, what remorse were then thy freedom's fee!
Ap. 16th 83

*   *   *

Her Second Letter
I
Further Withdrawal

My God, I feel her drifting, drifting far.
How powerless and bound am I! no hand
Can reach to hold her in my needy land
From whence the sun hath gone, while one faint star,
And that my Art, alone remains as light
Thereof! and I am 'neath the firm command
Of vain desire—and I can not withstand!
And she—dost lead her, God, as she goes bright
Beneath the banner writ with fairest truth?
Dost lead her as she drifts so far away
And takes with her my only hope of youth—
Leaves me to sink and watch the waning day—
Rejoices in her calm and lack of ruth?
Make haste, my God—I faint—I am of clay!
23d Ap. 83

[P]

For Isabel Jackson's mother. [April 17] 1883.

Quick tears,
And long slow hopeless pain.
A hollow place that all recurring years
Will never fill again.
In time the agony is past;
We cannot, if we would, forever grieve.
Where the lost arm was taken heals at last—
But oh! the empty sleeve!

[I. *Inscribed in Charlotte's hand and inserted in the back of the journal for 1883. The notation regarding the date is Charlotte's.*]

Alone am I, chillhearted still, and dreary;
Alone art thou, sadhearted, worn, and weary;
Alone indeed are we.

Alone art thou, by wifely love's desertion;
Alone am I mid life-dreams wide dispersion,
Watching youth's visions flee.

Alone art thou, I know not of thy sorrow.
Alone am I; and all life's long tomorrow
   Looks desolate and grey.

Alone art thou. No one to soothe thy sighing
Alone am I, my heart within me dying.
   O Life! Why dost thou stay!

Nov. or Dec. '83. prob. Dec. 1st week.

[U. 1884?]

[To] Mr. C. W. Stetson from Mrs. the same.

There was a young man in moderate health
Who so abounded and rolled in wealth
That night and morning he scornfully poured
The glittering coins of his countless hoard
Out on the chamber floor!

But he had a wife of a frugal mind!
Who cast about her a way to find
To stop this wild unreasoning waste;
And purchased a wallet wherein could be placed
The rolling coins in his pockets that lay
Whereby he might save them from day unto day
And scatter them broadcast no more!

[U. Inscribed in Charlotte's hand. 1884?]

A loving valentine I've sent
With this O love to thee,
But it showeth not a half I meant
Your heart to see.

It showeth not the lonely nights
Where all unkissed I lie
While the warm-glittering starry lights
Drop slowly down the sky.
It showeth not the lonely days
Sweet-scented, warm, and fair,
Yet all unlit by love and praise
For which I care.
Nor the lonely heart that loveth much
And longeth sore for loves delight!
O love to feel your lighest touch!
O love tonight! tonight!

There be too great lights that shine on me,
One before and one behind;

Lights that I could not choose but see
Though I were more than blind

One is the light of a joyous past,
    Shining below, shining above,
The light of my life that will always last——
    My husband's love!

And one is the light of a future long,
A heaven beneath like the heaven above;
Color and perfume and laughter and song———
O beautiful heaven to which I belong———
    My husband's love!

[P. *"In Duty, Bound" was first published in the* Woman's Journal, *January 12, 1884.*]

In Duty, Bound.

In duty, bound. A weary life hemmed in
Whichever way the spirit turns to look.
No chance of breaking out except by sin.
        Not even room to shirk;
        Simply to live, and work.

An obligation preimposed, unsought,
Yet binding with the force of natural law.
The pressure of antagonistic thought.
        Aching within, each hour,
        A sense of wasting power.

A narrow house with roof so darkly low
The heavy rafters shut the sunlight out.
One cannot stand erect without a blow;
        Until the soul inside
        Shrieks for a grave, more wide.

A consciousness that if this thing endure
The common joys of life will dull the pain;
The high ideals of the grand and pure
        Die, as of course, they must,
        Of long disuse, and rust.

That is the worst. It takes supernal strength
To hold the attitude that brings the pain.
And they are few indeed but stoop at length
        To something less than best,
        To find in stooping, rest.

[*Charlotte added a note, on her manuscript copy of this poem, that the last stanza was appended on October 15, 1883.*]

[U. The envelope that accompanies this letter reads: "To the Lovliest, Dearest, Purest and Best-loved Wife."]

My dear sweet lovely Wife!

I know there is nothing, however costly, nothing that money can buy that you would rather have than the knowledge that I love you more—and more—and more; that I love you far better and more wholly; that you please me and comfort me and help me in every little and great way. You are sweeter to me than in our first bed of love even. You are dear past any simile to express. Oh I love you I love you, you pure, lovely wife!

I tell you so—and I know that no gift you have had this year is beyond this.

God keep you ever, and me make more worthy!

This is your Christmas tribute, the offering forced from me by very love as I bent over your pillow as I made our bed.

All your lover and your husband,
Walter.

Christmas eve.

   1884.

[U. Inscribed in Charlotte's hand.]
Jan. 27th 1885

> I sit and wait,
> The hour grows late
> My lover does not come.
> I'd rather hear
> His footsteps dear
> Than bees in summer hum.
> Than velvet bees
> In chestnut trees
> When days are warm and fair
> I'd rather hear
> His footsteps dear
> Than music anywhere.
>
> The night comes fast, his hour is past
>   He surely must be near!
> More joy to me his form to see
>   Than skies of azure clear.
> Than azure skies with stars that rise
>   From twilights soft and fair;
> More joy to me his form to see
>   Than beauty anywhere.

[U. In her entry for January 1, 1887, Charlotte describes the hand-made calendar bestowed upon her by Walter from which the excerpts below are taken. The six-month calendar (January–June 1887) measures approximately 5½ by 5½ inches; the cover is made of soft, pliable light

bisque—colored leather. In the center of the outside cover, in a red box, has been painted "Charlotte from Walter." The inside cover is lined with pink silk, and the calendar is bound together with a thin pink ribbon. Each page is made of parchment and measures approximately 5 by 5 inches. The calendar is adorned with miniature paintings by Walter in pen and ink, accompanied by little bits of verse inscribed in his hand, which Charlotte described as his "sweetest thoughts in color and verse." The calendar for the month of January 1887, for example, is approximately 2 by 2 inches, and it features a tiny but detailed illustration of Adam on one side and Eve on the other; at the bottom is a miniature painting (approx. 1¹⁄₂ by 1¹⁄₄ inches) of a nude couple embracing before a roaring fire; Walter has written "Speak Low! And lean on me thy head—our love is told. Kiss oft. Then let us to our bed where love's not old!"

A few pages later Walter has included an illustration of Spring, with a 3¹⁄₄ by 2³⁄₈-inch drawing of Adam cupping Eve's right breast in his hands, as they sit in the Garden of Eden. Below the painting he has inscribed the following poem, which is an obvious allusion to the wedding night he and Charlotte had shared two and a half years earlier:

> "Ah Heart! She cannot hear thee beat
> With memories of her silver feet
>   so softly sounding when she came unto thy bed
>   with blushing roses garlanded!
>
> Oh Heart! She cannot feel thee beat
> with memories of her kisses sweet
>   so purely, passionately g'v'n within our bed,
>   Her amorous arm beneath my head!
>
> Ah Heart! She cannot see thee leap
> With memories of our wedded sleep.
>   When long in love and peace we lay in our white bed
>   With my fond arm beneath her head!
>
> Oh Heart! When shalt thou spring to meet
> Her softly sounding silver feet,
>   And lead her clad in Love's white flame unto thy bed
>   With rosy blushes garlanded?

[On one page of the calendar are two poems, one dated "In May 1886" lamenting the fading of their previous love and one pre-dated and titled "In May 1887," celebrating its return.]

In May 1886

> The tulip-beds are bright as flame
>   The daffodils nod all arow:
> But ah, where lie the flowers that came
>   And lightly laughed a year ago?
>   Oh where, my Love, are they
>   This morn of matchless May?
> In one fond heart love liveth on
>   Tho' days be dark, go fast or slow;

But ah, dear Love, where hath it gone,
   The love we had a year ago?
     Love liveth still, you say:
     Oh not the love of yester May!
O God who holdeth all in fee
   By whom all things decrease or grow,
Bring back, bring back to her and me
   The love we had a year ago!
     Oh let it be, I pray,
     As blossoms come to May!

In May 1887

And now the springing flow'rs I see;
The lilies and the roses blow;
Dear love's come back to her and me,
The sweet fond love of years ago!
And forasmuch as I did pray
I'll thank thee, God, this May!

[I. Inscribed in Walter's hand and inserted in the diary for 1887.]

For my Love
St. Valentine's, 1887

Thro' all the surging sound of debt and wrong,
   'Mid all unrest and all dull pain,
I hear the music of a tender song
   And rise from fear a man again.

Love sings the song, and sings, dear Love, of you,—
   Sings till my joy grows great and clear,—
Till I can breathe my love, my vows renew,
   And homage pay to wifehood here.

You comfort in your "weakness," dear and Wife,
   Far more than all the world in might:
So for the power you are unto my life
   I call you lovliest Love tonight!

What tho' you grieve and feel your work undone!
   What tho' my life seems all distress!
Hold fast to Love—to Love, and all is won!
   Thenceforth our days are pleasantness!

Tho' all the surging sound of debt and wrong,
   'Mid all unrest and all dull pain
We'll hear the music of a tender song
   And rise from fear to hope again!

                        Charles Walt: Stetson.

[*P. 1891?*]

To me at Last
(To A[deline]. E. K[napp].)

To me at last! When I had bowed my head
In patience to all pain—buried my dead—
    Forgotten hope, accepted the long night
    With only stars for guide—far, cold, and bright—
Content to work and love, uncomforted.
Then, in an hour, a brightness came and spread
And all the dark sky flushed with rose and red
    And gold-lit flowers laughed out—so came the light
        To me at last!
No more the empty loneliness, the fight
To live above all loss, for Truth and Right,
    No more the pale cold heart that ached and bled—
    O happy heart! So warmed and kissed and fed!
I thank thee, God, for sending this delight
        To me at last!

[*U. Written in Walter's hand just weeks after Katharine left Charlotte to live with Walter and Grace.*]

9th July 1894—
Late Afternoon.

My dear Charlotte—

We would like to see you—and we send you our love—Kate and I. She sits at arm's length from me—oh so beautiful! It makes tears fill my eyes—drawing for you. We have been to the Park again, she & I. No two persons could be more companionable than we are. I know what she wants before she says it. I can *feel* her completely. And I think she knows it; and she's becoming fonder & fonder of me; and truly, dear, I do not see how I can ever let her leave me again. I wish I need not—rather I wish we could have her *together*. You see, dear Charlotte, I have been with her now most intimately. Grace has no care of her when she is with me, and I have had a chance to

(she interrupted me there to tell me about an "Infant Camel who went to walk with a baby-carriage—"of course it isn't true" she adds. She is drawing you the Park camel "Rachel"—an aged camel verily, so *droll*!—she has drawn Baby Roger, the elephant).

It is now the 10th, dear. I was interrupted by the return of Grace from Bristol where she had been to try to find board & lodging for the dinner—and unsuccessfully. She boldly went to Wm Trotter & found him with his 7th month's old baby—and "another coming" Grace says. Which shall be the 3d since his marriage!! She feels she escaped some thing. Yes, I think she did. We were in a heavy quandary last night as to what we should do. It is impossible for me to work with them in the studio. They have been here now since Friday morning. Saturday we all went to Sakonnet in the search of rooms fruitlessly—and were held up by a highwayman. It was a pleasant trip which cost about $15.00!—We have spent a half a hundred trying to find [*The remainder of this letter is missing.*]

[U]

361 W. 57th St. New York
April 23rd. 1896—

Dear Walter,

I was very sorry to hear such ill news of the San Francisco show—but to say truth, expected nothing better of that "city of dogs."

They buy good pictures? Never. I'd have written you long since but have been "low" for awhile—had to leave the settlement etc.—all of which I wrote the fair Kate. Now I feel quite like myself again, but it is thin—I have no strength to spare. All summer, I shall trot about and visit, loafing and working by turns; and I have a misty hope that I may get over to London for a little—but that's vague. The Internationalist Socialist Reunion or Convention or whatever is there the last week in July, and I'd like to be in it. Meanwhile, I am here in New York, at my stepmothers. She is a dear little lady and I like her much.

Also she likes me.

With her I inherit stepsisters, not ugly and haughty, but sweet little blond damsels, twins, very like, and looking sixteen though twenty two. Father writes me quite affectionately—is pleased that I like the new mother.

I am making this journey on the strength of an engagement in Boston and return—from Chicago. Then I scratched together some other things to do, and here I am. Monday I attended a grand Woman's Club Lunch—annual affair, at a gorgeous Club House in Brooklyn. Was a guest of honor as it were, and made a little speech with great applause—also poems.

The next day I attended a woman suffrage meeting over there, and spoke further. Tonight I lecture, for half the profits, under W. S. auspices. I could have wished it other, but this opening was here and I took it.

Also from it came another—Mrs. Catt, a very prominent suffragist, had an engagement in Providence for the 22nd and didn't want to go. Would I go in her stead? Yes, truly.

So I went on Tuesday night, and came back last night. Eight years in October next since I was there!

How little and pretty it is! So hard-and-fast, so clean, so dead and buried.

And yet the houses spring up to the eastward, and the cove is filled at last! I saw Mary and Anna & Aunt Caroline—and Aunt Caroline [*sic*], with their husbands and young; the eternal "Brown girls," Pardon Jastram, and Eddie. Also Mrs. Diman & Emily. I visited amongst these, ran about town profusely, addressed the Committee on Special Legislation in the Senate Chamber, had four meals and a nap, attended a reception and banquet in the evening and speechified thereat.

And I went about all day on a broad grin. It did seem so like getting into my child's doll house again! Sidney Burleigh and his mother were at the W. S. Banquet. He seemed very glad to see me. But how insignificant he is getting to look!

I traversed many familiar streets including College, Thomas, N. Main,. S. Main, Gov. st. car route, Waterman & Angell sts. Pitman, Ives, Gano, etc. etc. My—my—my! How familiar and funny and pleasant it all was. I'm going back there to visit the Phelon's and Carpenters pretty soon.

I've got a lot of nice visits in hand—enough to last months. And everybody seemed glad to see me. How pleasant it is. I had no idea they'd be so glad.

I hope to build up solid this summer and write a lot. Already I'm lots better.

As ever
Charlotte.

Isn't the enclosed the key of your studio? Keep it—you may want to call some day.

[U]

Harrisburg Pa—
April 23rd. 1897.

Dear Walter,

Here is the two dollars—much travelled and exchanged!

Thank you very much for the proofs. I looked at them before I read the letter, and did not recognize Katharine at all! Not till I saw the large side view—sitting, did I suspect. What a beautiful damsel she makes in the one with her hand to her chin! And how like Grace one of the standing ones is (on train)! I should like some of them very much. Also the butterfly ones. You needn't even ask me—any picture of her that is good enough to print will always be warmly welcomed by me. Did you ever make any prints of those Norwich graveyard proofs? Mine are nearly faded out. I particularly liked the three of those which showed her encounter with the grave—and triumph over it. Sort of so [*illustration*], they were. These bicycle ones are lovely. How I'd like to see her on it! And Grace looks as well and strong! I shall have one some day too. But as to being strong—I'm getting almost as well as I used to be. Walked six miles Sunday and rowed half an hour beside. Can carry a 150 lb. man. Can put up a twenty pound dumbbell with either hand, even lying flat on my back & doing it with the arm laid straight overhead. I begin to think that I have almost got back to twenty three—fourteen years! And if strength holds it now remains to be seen what I can do.

So the girlie is two inches bigger—latrally or vertically—in diameter or circum-ference—no matter.

Yes, I hope she will be big. And strong.

Grace's school impresses me as a mighty undertaking. My mother used to do the like for us when we were small. Have you no available professional one in Pasadena now? But of course not, or Grace would not add this to her labors.

I am unceasingly grateful to Grace for being what she is—have been ever since I knew her.

Surely I have often said before that there is no person on earth I would rather have my child with.

Your father told me something of Carrie's trouble—or Henry's!—last spring. I am sorry.

And your father is 78! Mine is but 68, and quite broken now. I bade him goodbye last Saturday—for the summer. I've seen a good deal of him this winter—more than I ever did before. He speaks very tenderly of Katharine.

I am truly disappointed not to see your pictures. Indeed I had intended to go to Providence on purpose, but, a postponed engagement came on the 21st—in Harrisburg Pa.—and I had to be in Detroit on the 24th. So that it would have meant straight back on my tracks and more money than I had left over to make the connection.

I simply couldn't.

But I'm most genuinely sorry. I did want to see this California work—and Katharine with Pomegranates—etc. It is a most unusual thing to me to be disappointed—usually I don't care enough about anything personal to mind what happens.

"Canton"!—"Canton"!

Here we are at another little Appalachian town. Barren, hilly sort of country this—I'm on my way from Harrisburg to to [sic] Detroit via Elmira—Canandaigua—Rochester—Buffalo, etc.

Up the Susquehanna part way, and since then it has been through bristly mountains, but when the ledges are near the windows I can see lots of flowers.

So to Chicago Sunday; and then I don't know just what for a month.

As I said before I'm really feeling well; and hope to do much work.

But then—as you sometimes gloomily remark—"probably you won't care for it!" I had a very pleasant little visit with Mrs. Cresson last week. She seemed very glad to see me. Poor lady—she grows old, and suffers much from rheumatism.

Serenely—
Charlotte.

Explanatory Notes

ONE: *"As lonely a heart as ever cried"*

1. While many scholars tend to use the terms *diary* and *journal* interchangeably, for Charlotte the distinction between the two was important. Diaries were commercially prepared books in which daily entries were recorded. Their typically small size, however, restricted the length of the entry that was made. Charlotte's journals, on the other hand, were loose-leaf notebooks that offered her the flexibility to write entries of unlimited length.

2. It was Sidney Putnam who introduced Charlotte to Walter Stetson early in 1882.

3. Aunt Caroline was Caroline Robbins, Mary Perkins's widowed half sister who resided with Charlotte and Mary off and on for many years.

4. Caroline "Carrie" Hazard (1856–1945) was the daughter of Rowland Hazard II, a wealthy philanthropist and manager of the Peacedale Woolen Mills of Rhode Island. Carrie Hazard published books of verse and educational theory and served as president of Wellesley College from 1899 to 1910. Throughout her life Hazard demonstrated enormous generosity toward Charlotte, often sending money during some of Charlotte's worst financial crises.

5. "House and Brain" seems likely to have been a magazine article.

6. Charles A. Fecter (1824–79) was a British actor.

7. Charlotte referred to the youth as simply "W." in her entry for March 28, 1879, as well. It is likely that she was referring to Walter Smith, one of her friends at Harvard University.

8. Kellup: a nickname for Charlotte's friend Caleb Burbank.

9. This allusion to Martha Luther is Charlotte's first. Her diary references to Martha span forty-four years, although most are concentrated between early 1880 and Oct. 5, 1882, the date of Martha's wedding to Charles Lane. Charlotte referred to Martha by a number of nicknames: Marthar, Pussie, Chick, etc.

10. During her youth Charlotte's second cousin Robert Brown made known his attraction to her. Charlotte cited impropriety, on the basis of their kinship, in her refusal to return Robert's affection. (She later overcame this concern when she married first cousin Houghton Gilman in 1900.) Robert was persistent, however, and Charlotte often struggled with the question of propriety and with her own ambivalence. See, for example, her entries dated Aug. 24, 1879, March 4, 1880, and Jan. 30 and Feb. 17, 1881. Over the

years her feelings toward Robert ranged from quiet tolerance (particularly when they formed a brief business partnership) to mild annoyance (see, for example, April 2, 1881,) to unbridled contempt (see, for example, her entry dated Oct. 22, 1886.)

11. Grace Channing, who married Walter Stetson after Charlotte's 1894 divorce, remained a lifelong friend of Charlotte's. See the chapter entitled "Grace" in Ann J. Lane's biography of Gilman, *To Herland and Beyond*, for an account of their friendship.

12. Although Charlotte's friend May Diman survived this mishap, she was killed less than two years later in a similar accident. See Charlotte's entries for April 29 and 30, May 1 and 2, and July 7, 1881.

13. Charlotte went to visit her aunt Katie Gilman (and her cousins Houghton and Francis) on Nov. 17. On Dec. 2, just twelve days after returning to Providence, Charlotte learned that her aunt had died. During the fall of 1879 she began exchanging frequent letters with Houghton Gilman.

14. Charlotte may be alluding to Emily Jolly's novel *My Son's Wife*, published in 1877.

15. See Appendix B for the text of "To D——— G———," which was Charlotte's first published poem.

16. Charlotte's second cousin Robert Brown designed advertising cards for Soapine, a household cleaning product manufactured by the Kendall Manufacturing Company of Providence, R.I. Brown commissioned Charlotte to draw the concepts that he envisioned. Several of her original sketches survive in the Gilman collection at the Schlesinger Library. Original Soapine advertising cards, designed by Charlotte and Robert Brown, can still be found at flea markets and antique shows throughout the northeast United States.

17. *The Confessions of a Frivolous Girl*, by American lawyer and novelist Robert Grant (1852–1940), was first published in 1880.

18. Charlotte occasionally used pins to keep herself awake. See *Living*, pp. 10–11.

19. Ada Blake was a friend of Charlotte's. A newspaper account of Blake's Feb. 24, 1881, wedding to her "swain" spelled her first name "Ehda."

20. Peut-être-pas: [Fr.] perhaps not.

21. *A Fair Barbarian*, by American writer Frances E. Burnett (1849–1924), was first published in 1877.

22. *Sevenoaks: A Story of To-Day*, by American author Josiah G. Holland (1819–81), was first published in 1875.

23. Brown University history professor J. Lewis Diman was the father of Charlotte's close friend May Diman, who died less than three months later.

24. *The Guardian Angel*, by American writer Oliver Wendell Holmes (1809–94), was first published in 1867.

25. *My Wayward Partner*, by American writer Marietta Holley (1836–1926), was published in 1878.

26. Oui mon ami, il est. Quelquefois: [Fr.] Yes my friend, it is. Sometimes.

27. The bride's father was Eli Whitney Blake, a professor of physics at Brown University.

28. Charlotte's second cousin Robert Brown devised a variety of business "enterprises" to help Charlotte and her mother make ends meet in their financially impoverished household. The pie business was short-lived.

29. *Phantasmagoria* (1869) was written by English author Lewis Carroll (1832–98).

30. Charlotte maintained racist views throughout her life. See, for example, her account of a visit to a "Negro Lunatic Asylum" in *Living*, where she writes: "I was told that insanity had increased greatly among the Negroes since they were freed, probably owing to the strain of having to look out for themselves in a civilization far beyond them" (p. 245). Also of interest is Susan A. Lanser's essay, "Feminist Criticism, 'The Yellow Wallpaper,' and the Politics of Color in America," in *Feminist Studies* 15, no. 3 (Fall 1989): 415–41.

31. See Appendix B for a sample of one of Charlotte's numerous valentine poems to May Diman.

32. *The Story of Avis*, by American writer Elizabeth Stuart Phelps (1844–1911), was first published in 1877.

33. Charlotte is alluding here to a $100 loan that she was attempting to secure from Bissell at her brother Thomas's request.

34. James Abram Garfield (1831–81), twentieth president of the United States, was shot in a Washington, D.C., railroad station on July 2, 1881. He died Sept. 19, 1881.

35. Charlotte was instrumental in seeing that the Providence Ladies Gymnasium became a reality (*Living*, pp. 67–68; note, however, that the correct date on p. 67 of *Living* should be 1881, rather than 1891).

36. Martha Luther married Charles Lane on Oct. 5, 1882.

37. Charlotte sketched at the bottom of this entry a mountain peak surrounded by clouds. Considering her emotional state the next day, Charlotte probably conceded that Martha should continue to pursue her relationship with Charles Lane. Just three days later, on Nov. 1, Charlotte learned of Martha's engagement to Lane.

38. Charlotte is probably alluding to her poem dated Dec. 13, 1881, titled "Unsent." See Appendix B for the text of the poem.

39. This is Charlotte's first reference to Charles Walter Stetson.

TWO: *"In Duty, Bound"*

1. Charlotte composed a poem this date (the day after being introduced to Charles Walter Stetson) titled "The Suicides Burial." See Appendix B for the text.

2. Herodotus was one of Charlotte's nicknames for Charles Walter Stetson. Charlotte had been reading a book about Herodotus, the Greek 5th century B.C. historian, when she was introduced to Stetson.

3. Although Stetson includes a lengthy paraphrase of their discussion that evening in his own diary, which included the subject of marriage (*Endure*, pp. 30–36), he does not specifically say that he asked Charlotte to marry him. On Jan. 31, 1882, Charlotte composed "An Anchor to Windward," which lists her reasons for wishing to remain single. See Appendix B for the text.

4. John Stuart Mill (1806–73), English philosopher and economist, was an advocate of women's suffrage. Among his many books was *The Subjection of Women*, published in 1869.

5. Hamilton MacDougall was a close friend of Stetson's.

6. Charlotte, her mother, and Aunt Caroline left for Martha's Vineyard, off the coast of Massachusetts, the following morning.

7. Charlotte variously referred to Charles Walter Stetson as Love, Herodotus, He., Charles Walt, C. W., Mr. Stetson, and later as "my boy."

8. *"Bella"* may have been *Bella Trelawney; or Time Works Wonders*, by J. F. Smith, published in 1882. *Mosses from an Old Manse*, by American writer Nathaniel Hawthorne (1804–64), was first published in 1846. *Sesame and Lilies*, by English sociological writer John Ruskin (1819–1900), was published in 1865. *Littells Living Age* was a reprint series of primarily British works.

9. According to Walter Stetson's diaries (*Endure*, p. 98), Charlotte had asked Walter to purchase a peninsula at Malagawatch, Nova Scotia, where they could build a log cabin and lead a simple life.

10. Charlotte's inclusion of a poem in her diary entry of this date seems to have been inspired by Walter's poem to her, "The Painting of the Portrait," also dated Sept. 23, 1882. See Appendix B for the text of Walter's poem.

11. Charlotte wrote Thomas and his bride, Julia, a poem for their wedding.

12. See *Endure*, pp. 110–13, for Walter's account of Mary Perkins's visit to his studio.

13. *A Blot in the 'Scutcheon* was a play by English writer Robert Browning (1812–89).

14. Charlotte is referring to her first cousin and second husband, Houghton Gilman, and his brother Francis.

15. *Romola* (1881) was written by English writer George Eliot (1819–80).

16. Walter Stetson reported in his journal that Charlotte confessed that evening to having a "relapse"; i.e., her affection for him was waning as she felt an increasing desire to pursue her life's ambition to work (*Endure*, p. 143).

17. Julia Ward Howe (1819–1910) was a leader of the women's suffrage movement and an activist for international peace.

18. Charlotte and Walter, although corresponding frequently, remained apart until May 14, 1883.

19. See Appendix B for the text of the poem to Mrs. Jackson.

20. Belinda was the family cat.

21. Charlotte "murdered" a number of cats over the years, beginning with "Brinnle," when she was 17. On July 18, 1877, she wrote: "I try to chloroform Brinnle. Brinnle wont. He dances over that fence. What shall I do with him?" Two days later, on July 20, she reported, "Brinnle is drowned! No tears are shed. Nevertheless I mourn slightly." The last mention of putting a cat to death is in the diary entry for July 29, 1925, when Charlotte was sixty-five years old. See also the entry for Aug. 11, 1883.

22. Marcus Aurelius Antoninus (188–217 A.D.) was a Roman emperor and author of *Meditations*, a collection of precepts of practical morality.

23. It was Sidney Putnam who introduced Charlotte to Charles Walter Stetson on Jan. 11, 1882. Stetson appeared to be somewhat more grieved over Putnam's death than was Charlotte and surmised that his drowning death might have been a suicide (*Endure*, pp. 221–22).

24. Jane Baillie Carlyle (1801–66) was the long-suffering wife of Scottish essayist and historian Thomas Carlyle (1795–1881).

25. Although it was rejected by *Century*, the poem "In Duty, Bound" was accepted a few weeks later for publication in the *Woman's Journal*.

26. See Appendix A for the complete text of "A Word to Myself."

27. Charlotte's painting of a howling wolf on a frozen lake at night is housed with the Gilman Papers at the Schlesinger Library.

28. Charlotte looked in vain for this picture many years later for inclusion in her autobiography. It is not among the papers in the Schlesinger Library. Walter Stetson described the picture in his diary as depicting "a wan creature who had traversed a desert and came, worn out, to an insurmountable wall which extended around the earth. . . . It *was* powerful. . . . I know it was a literal transcript of her mind" (*Endure*, p. 244).

29. Stetson reported in his diary that he and Charlotte had spent a "painful evening" because of a remark he had made about "harlotry" leading her to believe that he might resort to enlisting the services of a prostitute as a result of the long wait before consummating their relationship. Charlotte apparently convinced Stetson that in his case such a recourse would be unjustifiable (*Endure*, p. 245).

30. "One Girl of Many," a poem in defense of the "fallen woman," was published in the Feb. 1, 1884, edition of *Alpha*. Charlotte cites "One Girl of Many" as her first published poem in *Living* (p. 62). Her memory, however, is faulty. "In Duty, Bound" was published just over two weeks earlier in the Jan. 12, 1884, issue of the *Woman's Journal*, followed by "My View" in the Buffalo *Christian Advocate* a few days later. Moreover, her poem "To D—— G——" was published in the May 20, 1880, issue of the *New-England Journal of Education* when Charlotte was only nineteen. See Appendix B for the text of "To D—— G——" and "In Duty, Bound."

31. Chester was Martha Luther Lane's infant son, born Aug. 6, 1883.

32. Biographers' assertions that Charlotte was 5 feet 6½ inches tall are likely based on her journal entry of Jan. 1, 1879. That entry, however, reports her height with shoes, making her an inch and a half taller than she actually was.

33. See Appendix B for the text of "In Duty, Bound."

34. *On Liberty* (1859) was written by John Stuart Mill.

35. Henry Irving (1838–1905) was a popular English actor whose first tour of America was in 1883–84. He was the first actor to be knighted (in 1895) and is buried in Westminster Abbey.

36. Ich liebe dich: [G.] I love you.

THREE: *"By reason of ill health"*

1. Mary and Ray Phelon were friends and neighbors of Charlotte and Mary Perkins.

2. *Phantastes* (n.d.) was published by writer George Macdonald.

3. Walter had been commissioned to make etchings of paintings by various European master artists, including one by French painter Thomas Couture (1815–79).

4. This is the first allusion to Charlotte's possible suspicion that the sickness she was experiencing might be the result of her being pregnant. A few days later, however, on Aug. 5, she attributed her sickness to "inter-susception of the intestine."

5. In January, Charlotte weighed 118 pounds; her inability to keep food down during the early stages of her pregnancy most likely caused her weight loss.

6. *Dr. Zay* (1882) was written by Elizabeth Stuart Phelps.

7. *A Perilous Secret*, a novel by Charles Reade (1814–84), was published posthumously in 1884.

8. Charlotte's mother, Mary Perkins, left the next day for an extended trip west to visit her son, Thomas, and his family.

9. The letter was probably from Frank Purinton, a friend, who had accused Walter of slighting his work, being uncommunicative, etc. (*Endure*, p. 272).

10. Gus Stetson was Walter's brother.

11. Mary Perkins was en route from Utah, where she had been visiting Charlotte's brother, Thomas, and his wife, for several months.

12. *The Bostonians*, by American author Henry James (1843–1916), was first published separately in 1886.

13. Walter was hoping to sell some of his paintings to Tewksbury and to others.

14. Daphne Lynch, the Stetsons' recently hired maid, had announced her resignation.

15. Mary A. Hill, in *Endure*, lists the title of this painting as *Fool's Sermon* (p. 292).

16. *Ramona*, a novel by American writer Helen Maria Hunt Jackson (1830–85), was published in 1884.

17. "On the Pawtuxet," the work for which Charlotte received her first payment, originally appeared in the *Providence Journal* on Aug. 1, 1886. It was later reprinted in *In This Our World*.

18. William Gillette (1855–1937) was an American actor to whom Charlotte attempted to sell a comedy that she had written with Walter. Although Gillette reported being "favorably impressed" by the script, he was not inclined to buy it.

19. Alice Stone Blackwell (1857–1950) was an American advocate of woman's suffrage and assistant editor of *Woman's Journal*. She and Charlotte met a few weeks later; their friendship lasted for many years.

20. Charlotte kept a lock of Walter's hair tucked away in a little envelope. One of his golden curls is among the collection of Gilman memorabilia at the Schlesinger Library.

21. Ouida was the pseudonym of English novelist Marie Louise de la Ramée (1839–1908).

22. A description of this calendar, as well as some excerpts from it, are included in Appendix B.

23. Charlotte eventually became friends with William Dean Howells after corresponding with him in 1890 and finally meeting him on March 20, 1897, after he attended one of her public lectures.

24. *Woman in the Nineteenth Century*, by American critic and social reformer Margaret Fuller (1810–50), was published in 1845.

25. The next day Charlotte contradicted herself by writing that Katharine "makes herself disagreeable as usual."

26. Although Charlotte reported Feb. 14 as being "a dreary and useless day," she did receive from Walter a loving Valentine's poem, which is inserted the diary for 1887. See Appendix B for the text of the poem.

FOUR: *"You are getting to be a famous woman my dear!"*

1. "The Giant Wistaria," a ghost story, was published in the June 1891 edition of *New England Magazine*. For the complete publication history of virtually all of Charlotte

Gilman's published works, readers should consult Gary Scharnhorst's *Charlotte Perkins Gilman: A Bibliography* (Metuchen, N.J.: Scarecrow, 1985).

2. Charlotte's much-lauded poem "Similar Cases," a bitingly satirical verse against social conservatism, was first published in the April 1890 edition of the *Nationalist*. "Women of To-day," a pro-activist poem condemning the obsequious status of women, first appeared in the June 1890 *Woman's Journal*.

3. In a typed note left among her personal papers at the Schlesinger Library, Charlotte reported that "'The Yellow Wallpaper' was written in two days, with the thermometer at one hundred and three—in Pasadena, Cal." Although she wrote nearly two hundred short stories, "The Yellow Wall-Paper," which first appeared in the January 1892 edition of *New England Magazine*, is her best known.

4. Charlotte reports in her autobiography that she placed the manuscript of "The Yellow Wall-Paper" with Henry Austin, a literary agent.

5. Harriet ("Hattie") Howe was a feminist activist and member of the Los Angeles Nationalist Club's program committee. She boarded with Charlotte, and they became very close friends. See, for example, entries dated June 23, 1891, and Sept. 16, 1892.

6. British author and feminist Olive Schreiner (1855–1920) was one of Charlotte's favorite writers. See Gilman's *Forerunner* 2 (July 1911): 197.

7. American poet Ina Coolbrith (1842–1928) was named poet laureate of California in 1915. She and Charlotte socialized frequently during Charlotte's years in California.

8. French actress Sarah Bernhardt (1844–1923), known as "the Divine Sarah," was on tour in the United States in 1891.

9. Pamela Ann Clemens Moffett (1827–1904) was Mark Twain's oldest sister.

10. It was in Pasadena that Charlotte ended her life in 1935.

11. "Delight" was one of Charlotte's nicknames for Delle.

12. Puss was Delle's horse, and not a pet cat as Ann J. Lane contends in *To Herland and Beyond* (p. 175).

13. As the year drew to a close, Charlotte wrote two poems, one dated Dec. 30, 1891, and the other written just before and just after midnight on Dec. 31. Both poems look forward to the new year with a mixture of anxiety about past pain and hope for future strength. See Appendix B for the text of both poems.

14. Edward Bellamy (1850–98) was an American author whose utopian novel, *Looking Backward* (1888), presented a socialist economic plan that would guarantee material and political equality for all citizens. Charlotte was considerably influenced by his theory in the early 1890s.

15. Mary Perkins was growing increasingly weak from the cancer that had been diagnosed earlier in the year. During the last several months of her dying mother's life, Charlotte nursed her.

16. American poet Joaquin Miller (1839–1913) attracted attention for his verse and for his trademark look, which included western clothing, chaps, and a sombrero. He published several volumes of poetry, an Indian romance, and a play.

17. See pp. 142–43 in *Living* for Charlotte's account of the *Examiner* interview.

18. American fiction writer Hamlin Garland (1860–1940) crossed paths with Charlotte at various times over the next several years. Garland was well known as a literary

realist for his stark portrayals of life in the Midwest. He was awarded the Pulitzer Prize in 1921 for *A Daughter of the Middle Border*.

19. "Through This" is a little known but significant story in Gilman's oeuvre. It can be read, in effect, as a companion to "The Yellow Wall-Paper." See Denise D. Knight, "The Reincarnation of Jane: 'Through This'—Gilman's Companion to 'The Yellow Wall-Paper,'" in *Women's Studies* 20 (1992): 287–302.

20. Most likely the German-born actor Richard Mansfield (1854–1907), who performed on the American stage from 1882, including in *Beau Brummell*.

21. See Charlotte's entry dated May 31, 1893, in Appendix A, "Thoughts and Figgerings."

22. "Will Clemens" was probably a nickname for Samuel E. Moffett (1860–1908), a nephew of Samuel Clemens and an editorial writer for the San Francisco *Examiner*. Moffett wrote a biographical sketch of his famous uncle that was used as part of the "Autograph Edition" of Twain's writings. I am indebted to Twain scholar Michael J. Kiskis for his assistance in making this identification.

23. See Charlotte's account of Mrs. Griffes's murder in *Living*, pp. 175–76.

FIVE: *"A prayer of thankfulness for all good things"*

1. Margaret Perkins was the second wife of Charlotte's older brother, Thomas. Basil Perkins was their son. They were visiting California from Ogden City, Utah.

2. *Barbara Dering*, a novel by American writer Amélie Rives (1863–1945), was published in 1892.

3. Charlotte met and became friends with American poet Edwin Markham (1852–1940) before he gained national recognition with *The Man with the Hoe* in 1899. They remained friends for several years.

4. Mary A. Hill, in *Charlotte Perkins Gilman: The Making of a Radical Feminist, 1860–1896*, incorrectly translates this passage as "My Darling over night" and identifies Charlotte's "darling" as "most likely" being Edwin Markham (p. 218). Charlotte, however, was keeping frequent company with her friend Mrs. Darling, whom she mentioned eight times before this date in her diary for 1893. Her diary entry of June 25, 1893, for example, begins precisely the same way: "Mrs. Darling over night."

5. The book to which Charlotte was referring was her first edition of poetry, *In This Our World*. Subsequent editions were published in 1895 and 1898.

6. Charlotte had made a vow to never cooperate with a Hearst-owned publication as long as she lived. See *Living*, pp. 142–45.

7. Charlotte had been told throughout the years that she bore a resemblance to a number of famous women: French writer George Sand (1803–76), English novelist George Eliot (1819–80), the biblical Rachel, and English poet Christina Rossetti (1830–94).

8. Laurie was the pen name of San Francisco *Examiner* columnist Winifred Black.

9. The pages dated Thursday, April 26, through Sunday, May 13, 1894, are blank. It was sometime between these dates that Charlotte sent Kate back east to live with Walter and Grace. Charlotte wrote a brief note to herself dated May 9, 1894, marking the major

changes taking place in her life, including Katharine's departure. See Appendix B for the text of the note.

10. See *Living*, pp. 167–68, for Charlotte's reaction to the reporter.

11. Francis Gilman was the brother of Houghton Gilman, whom Charlotte married in 1900.

12. American journalist and short-story writer Ambrose Bierce (1842-?1914) had made some disparaging remarks about Charlotte's edition of verse, *In This Our World*, in the "Prattle" column of the June 24, 1894, San Francisco *Examiner*. His comments, in part, read: "In looking through Mrs. Charlotte Perkins Stetson's little book of verses 'In This Our World,' for something to poke fun at I found a piece that is admirable. It is entitled 'Similar Cases,' and is a delightful satire upon those of us who have not the happiness to think that the progress of humanity toward the light is subject to sudden and lasting acceleration."

13. The occasionally violent nationwide railroad strike of 1894 had a widespread impact on the country's industry and economy. See pp. 147–50 of *Living* for Charlotte's reaction to the strike.

14. Probably Paul Tyner, a friend of Charlotte's who worked with her on the *Impress*.

15. The woman Charlotte referred to as "mother" was Helen Campbell (1830–1918), an American writer and activist whose works included fiction and nonfictional works on social and economic issues. Some thirty years older than Charlotte, Campbell became both her mentor and the first of several "adopted mothers," as Charlotte affectionately referred to her in her autobiography. See *Living*, pp. 142, 171–72, for Charlotte's account of their friendship.

16. Pyramus and Thisby are played, respectively, by Shakespeare's characters Nick Bottom and Francis Flute, in *A Midsummer Night's Dream* (c. 1595) in his play-within-a-play.

17. Sabine Baring-Gould (1834–1924) was an English author of theological works, studies in legend and folklore, and numerous novels, including *Mehalah* (1880) and *The Broom Squire* (1896).

18. See Appendix B for the text of a letter dated April 23, 1896, that Charlotte wrote to Walter describing her experiences during this trip to Providence.

19. When she was writing her autobiography nearly thirty years later, Charlotte conceded that she was still unable to grasp the meaning of the remark, "Better get your face plated!" (*Living*, pp. 196–97)

20. Edward Rowland Sill (1841–87) was an American poet and essayist.

21. Charlotte reported in *Living* (p. 199) that her cash was down to $10, rather than the $100 which she recorded in her diary.

22. T. Fisher Unwin was Charlotte's London publisher of *In This Our World*.

23. Charlotte socialized with George Bernard Shaw (1856–1950), British playwright, novelist, and critic, several times while she was in England.

24. Harriot Stanton Blatch (1856–1940) was the daughter of American women's rights activist Elizabeth Cady Stanton (1815–1902). Blatch followed in her mother's footsteps by becoming a suffragist leader, lecturer, and the author of several books including *A Woman's Point of View* (1919).

25. James Ramsay MacDonald (1866–1937) was a British statesman and future prime minister.

26. Grant Allen (1848–99) was a British author of philosophical works and novels.

27. William Morris (1834–96), English poet and artist, died just a few weeks later. See *Living*, pp. 209, 212, for Charlotte's account of her meeting with him.

28. Jane Hume Clapperton was an English Reform Darwinist and author of numerous books including *The Vision of the Future* (1904).

29. Alfred Russel Wallace (1823–1913) was an English naturalist and author devoted to natural history and geography. He was responsible for advancing the theory of natural selection.

30. Charlotte dined with women's suffragist leader Elizabeth Cady Stanton (1815–1902).

31. *The Damnation of Theron Ware*, a novel by American writer Harold Frederic (1856–98), was first published in 1896.

32. The "hopeless pessimist" was actor William Gillette.

33. Ruth McEnery Stuart (1849–1917) was an American writer of stories, primarily about southern life.

34. Charlotte and her first cousin Houghton Gilman were married on June 11, 1900.

35. Oliver Herford (1863–1935) was a noted English writer and illustrator.

36. Charlotte often felt "dismal" or "low" shortly before the onset of her menstrual period, which began this month on May 22.

Six: *"The splendid truths I know"*

1. See *Living*, pp. 290–91, for a description of Dr. Jacobi's treatment of depression.

2. The book that Charlotte envisioned evolved into *Women and Economics*, a major feminist polemic on the sexual-economic basis of gender disparity, which, when published in 1898, won her worldwide acclaim. Charlotte began writing the book on Aug. 31, 1897, and completed the first 356-page draft just thirty-nine days later, on Oct. 8. Even more remarkable, however, is that Charlotte worked on the book for just seventeen of those thirty-nine days.

3. Charlotte had first met American suffragist leader Jane Addams (1860–1935) in 1894. She was particularly grateful, however, to have the opportunity to test her economic theory about women on Addams that summer.

4. *Gates Ajar* (1868) was written by Elizabeth Stuart Phelps.

5. See *Living*, pp. 229–31 for Charlotte's description of her stay at Summer Brook Farm.

6. William Bliss Carman (1861–1929) was a Canadian poet and essayist who served, successively, on the staff of *Independent*, *Current Literature*, and *Atlantic Monthly*.

7. Small, Maynard and Co. did, in fact, eventually publish her manuscript in progress, *Women and Economics*, in 1898.

8. Maude Adams (1872–1953) was an American actress. She starred in *Little Minister* in 1897–98.

9. Charlotte is probably alluding to Robert Green Ingersoll (1833–99), who became a noted agnostic lecturer.

10. Lillian D. Wald (1867–1940) was an American social worker and founder, president, and organizer of the public health nursing establishment, Henry Street Settlement, in New York City. Dubbed by some as the "Jane Addams of New York," Wald was author of *The House on Henry Street* (1915) and *Windows on Henry Street* (1934).

11. Annie Smith Peck (1850–1935) was an American mountain climber, born in Providence, R.I. She became a public speaker in 1890, lecturing mountain climbing, archaeology, and South America. She also wrote several books.

12. Ada Rehan (1860–1916) was an American stage actress who was renowned for her comedic roles.

13. Probably Francis Peabody (1847–1936), prominent American Unitarian theologian, Harvard professor, and author of many books.

14. Annie Russell (1869–1936) was an English-born actress whose stage performances included roles in *Major Barbara*, *Much Ado about Nothing*, and *She Stoops to Conquer*. *A Pretty Idiot* was coauthored by Charlotte and Grace Channing in 1890.

15. The third edition of *In This Our World* was published in 1898.

16. Morris Rosenfeld (1862–1923) was a Russian-born (Bokscha) poet who moved to the United States in 1886 and worked as a tailor. Author of such collections as *Die Glocke* (1888) and *Songs from the Ghetto* (1898), he lamented the miseries of the poor and the oppressed in his verse.

17. Abrahan Cahan (1860–1951) was a Vilna-born author who emigrated to the United States in 1882. He was editor of the *Jewish Daily Forward* and author of *Yekl: A Tale of the New York Ghetto*, *White Terror and the Red*, *The Rise of David Levinsky*, and a five-volume autobiography written in Yiddish.

18. Anna Murray married Frederick Douglass (1818?-95) in 1838 after she helped him to escape from slavery. Both Douglass and his wife became leaders of the abolitionist movement. Douglass's *Narrative of the Life of Frederick Douglass, an American Slave, Written by Himself* was first published in 1845.

19. *The White Company*, by British novelist and detective-story writer Sir Arthur C. Doyle (1859–1930), was published in 1890.

20. Horace L. Traubel (1858–1919) was an American author and close friend, associate, and literary executor of Walt Whitman.

21. See Appendix B for the text of a poem that Charlotte inscribed on the frontispiece of the diary for 1899.

22. Charlotte reports traveling to England aboard the SS *Fürst Bismarck* in *Living*, p. 255.

23. See *Living*, p. 267, for Charlotte's account of this episode.

24. Charlotte describes this episode on p. 265 of *Living*.

25. Charlotte is alluding to her menstrual period, which began this day.

26. Booth Tarkington (1869–1946) was a Pulitzer Prize–winning American novelist.

27. John Peter Altgeld (1847–1902) was governor of Illinois from 1892 to 1896.

28. Mrs. Gates was Susa Young Gates, daughter of American Mormon leader Brigham Young.

29. Charlotte writes, with apparent pride, about paying off her debts in *Living*, pp. 274–75.

30. Charlotte still owed Adeline Knapp $800.

31. See pp. 275–76 of *Living* for Charlotte's reaction to being called an "unnatural mother." Several years earlier, in 1895, Charlotte had published a story titled "An Unnatural Mother" based loosely upon what she perceived to be the public's condemnation of her decision to send Katharine east to live with Walter and Grace.

32. *Vesty of the Basins* (1892) was written by Sarah Pratt Greene.

33. Charlotte's menstrual period began this date.

34. *The Forest Lovers*, by English writer Maurice Hewlett (1861–1923), was published in 1898.

35. *What Diantha Did* was originally serialized in the the *Forerunner* 1 (1909–10).

36. Charlotte's *Herland* was originally serialized in the *Forerunner* 6 (1915).

37. Zona Gale wrote the foreword to the first edition of *The Living of Charlotte Perkins Gilman*.

38. Amy Wellington was a writer and a close friend of Charlotte's. Despite her critical condition Wellington did survive the operation that took place several days later.

39. Charlotte reported in *Living* that she left New York "with measureless relief" to live in Norwich Town, Conn. (p. 324).

40. Emily was married to Houghton's brother, Francis Gilman. Charlotte and Houghton shared a house in Norwich Town for several years.

Textual Notes

The purpose of these Textual Notes is to provide to the reader additional information about the diaries which does not appear in the transcribed entries. Scattered throughout the diaries, for example, are sketches and illustrations that Charlotte included which have been impossible to reproduce in the text. The inclusion of these illustrations in her original entries, however, helps to elucidate her activities, her experiences, and, occasionally, her emotional state. Therefore, a note has been provided to cite the existence of such illustrations. Other information that is documented in this section includes the charting of Charlotte's menstrual cycles (which she began tracking in her diaries in 1890 at the age of twenty-nine), her method of denoting in her diaries the death of friends and loved ones, and various editorial emendations she made, including corrected text, insertions or deletions, transpositions, and the like. A physical description of each journal or diary also has been included.

[1879]

The journal for January 1, 1879–October 10, 1879, is a commercial copybook with a gilt-bordered black leather cover, measuring approximately 6½ by 7⅞ inches. The journal for October 11, 1879–December 31, 1879, continues in a commercial notebook that was used originally by Charlotte for studying German. She made the transition from notebook to journal by writing, "Abandoning German perforce, I hereby utilize the remaining sheets as a second edition of my '79 diary, which has given out at this date."

February 17, 1879 Charlotte included in this entry a drawing of teardrops as an illustration of her distress.

June 3, 1879 Charlotte included in this entry two exaggerated sketches of her cold sore.

November 17, 1879 Charlotte included in this entry a sketch of the clothing she had been given: a long dress, a coat, and a hat.

[1880–81]

The journal for January 1, 1880–December 31, 1881, is missing from the Gilman

Papers at the Schlesinger Library. According to Curator of Manuscripts Eva S. Moseley, the journal has been missing for several years. As a result, transcriptions in this edition have been taken directly from, and verified against, microfiched copy of the original journal.

February 9, 1880   Just over a year later, Charlotte appended the following note to this entry: "Feb. 20th. '81. He [Jim Simmons] amounts to a great deal, but is hardly a caller. CAP."

September 23, 1880   Charlotte later appended this entry: "Sam called! Mother doesn't speak to him!!"

February 13, 1881   Charlotte included in this entry a diminutive sketch of Robert seated next to her on a sofa.

May 14, 1881   Charlotte originally skipped this date in her diary; she wrote the entry on a separate sheet of paper and inserted it in the diary with "Omitted!" written above the date.

July 4, 1881   Charlotte included in the middle of this entry a drawing of a marble-sized hailstone followed by an exclamation point.

September 14, 1881   The correct date was September 15.

September 24, 1881   Charlotte scrawled "HOT" in large bold letters over this entry and the next three, as a record of the late September heat wave that had hit Providence.

[1882–83]

The journal for January 1, 1882–December 31, 1883, is a black and marble leather-bound book with gilt inlay and white, lined pages, measuring approximately 6¾ by 8⅜ inches.

January 22, 1882   Charlotte included in this entry a drawing of large bold stars on each side of the date.

April 10, 1883   Charlotte initially wrote "don't think about it," but she subsequently changed "don't" to "wont."

[1884–86]

The journal for January 1, 1884–December 31, 1886, consists of a set of single white, lined leaves loosely bound with white string along the left edge. The journal has a paper cover measuring approximately 5⅝ by 9 inches.

March 24, 1884   Charlotte included in this entry a sketch of herself carrying a girl on one arm and hip.

April 30, 1884   Charlotte inserted "May 3rd." in parentheses presumably to indicate that she was reconstructing the events of the previous three days on May 3, rather than writing the entries as they occurred. She began an entry listing the date for Thursday, May 1, but subsequently crossed it out. Her original entry for Friday, May 2 (which was subsequently replaced by another entry for that date), was crossed out. Originally, it read: "Down at the house all day, sewing mostly. Groceries come, etc. Finish wedding dress. Walter over P.M. A lot of flowers come; and I fix them. Trim bonnet. Get home at about 5.45." These events apparently took place on Thursday, May 1, instead of Friday, May 2, which was Charlotte's wedding day.

May 2, 1884   Charlotte inserted into this entry a sketch of her velvet wedding-night slippers.

May 8, 1884   Charlotte added "hem tablecloth" in the margin of this entry.

June 25, 1884   Charlotte wrote "suspicion," but she crossed it out and substituted "conviction."

August 8, 1884   Charlotte wrote "50 for '*weeeee*,'" but crossed it out and replaced it with "*we*."

September 1, 1884   This sentence originally read "Accts, and arrange photographs." Charlotte subsequently edited it with a transposition symbol.

May 9, 1885   Charlotte originally wrote "hard" instead of "good."

October 10, 1885   Charlotte inserted into the margin of this entry "Annie Vaughn calls."

October 3, 1886   Charlotte drew dark, heavy borders around the entry for October 3, 1886, to denote the death of her sister-in-law, Julia.

November 1, 1886   Charlotte inserted in the margin of this entry, "Century, Woman's Journal and letter from Grace."

December 26, 1886   Charlotte inserted in the margin of this entry, "Dr. Knight in the morning. Kate better, much."

[1887]

The journal for January 1, 1887–April 19, 1887, consists of a set of single white, lined leaves loosely bound with white string along the left edge. The journal has a paper cover measuring approximately 5⅝ by 9 inches.

January 1, 1887   The date, in fact, was January 2.

March 25, 1887   Charlotte inserted in the margin of this entry, "Walter goes to club and I write some."

[1890]

The diary for January 1, 1890, through December 31, 1890, is a small black leather-bound Sunset commercial diary with dated, white, lined pages, measuring approximately 2⅛ by 5⅜ inches.

February 22, 1890   Charlotte initially added "Grace in the afternoon," but she subsequently crossed it out.

February 23, 1890   "X?" appears just before the date of this entry. It is here, in 1890, that Charlotte begins charting her menstrual periods, a practice that does not appear in her earlier diaries. She also marked with Xs the following dates in 1890: March 26, May 30, July 1, July 30, August 30, September 27, October 31, November 30, and December 29. In the February 23 entry, a question mark suggests that she was attempting to remember precisely which day her menstrual period began for that month.

[1891]

The diary for January 1, 1891–December 31, 1891, is a light tan leather-bound Pacific Coast commercial diary with dated, white, lined pages, measuring approximately 3½ by 6 inches. The 1891 diary is badly mutilated along the spine; it seems to have been chewed by mice or termites.

Charlotte placed an "X" at the top of the entry for January 27, 1891, marking the beginning of her menstrual period for that month. She also marked with Xs the following dates in 1891: March 28, April 26, May 29, June 25, July 24, August 20, September 20, October 15, November 11, and December 11.

July 14, 1891   Charlotte drew a banner on the top of this page, above the date, most likely to celebrate Delle's return.

[1892]

The diary for January 1, 1892–December 31, 1892, is a light tan leather-bound Pacific Coast commercial diary with dated, white, lined pages, measuring approximately 3½ by 6 inches. Like the 1891 diary, the diary for 1892 is badly mutilated along the spine. It, too, appears to have been chewed by mice or termites. Inscribed in Charlotte's hand on the frontispiece of the diary for 1892 is a notation that the diary was given to Charlotte by Delle Knapp for Christmas 1891.

January 8, 1892   Charlotte did not chart her menstrual period regularly during 1892, marking Xs to indicate the start of her cycle only occasionally that year: January 8, February 4, July 20, September 15, November 10, and December 7. She resumed the practice of monthly charting in 1893.

November 6, 1892   Charlotte included in this entry a sketch of the robe that she had created.

December 13, 1892   The word "today" from the previous entry actually appears on the page dated Wednesday, December 14, 1892.

December 31, 1892   Charlotte quoted this passage in her autobiography, before the diary was damaged, as reading: "The divorce is pending, undeclared, mother still lives. There is only to go on."

[1893]

The diary for January 1, 1893–December 31, 1893, is a light tan leather-bound Pacific Coast commercial diary with dated, white, lined pages, measuring approximately 3½ by 6 inches. Like the 1891 and 1892 diaries, the diary for 1893 is badly mutilated along the spine. It, too, appears to have been chewed by either mice or termites. Inscribed in Charlotte's hand on the flyleaf of the diary for 1893 is a notation that the diary was a gift from Delle Knapp.]

Charlotte charted her menstrual periods for 1893 by placing an X on the following dates: January 2, January 26, February 23, March 28, April 27, May 25, June 22, July 19, September 20, October 15, and November 17.

February 10, 1893   Charlotte bracketed "Get notification. . . . Write answer" and appended "This tomorrow" to indicate that the entry should have appeared under February 11.

March 7, 1893   Charlotte drew dark, heavy borders around the entry for March 7, 1893, to denote the death of her mother.

May 24, 1893   Charlotte followed this sentence with "Wrote on 'Punishment & Consequences,'" but she subsequently crossed that out.

July 12, 1893   Charlotte wrote "agrees," but she crossed it out and substituted "undertakes" instead.

October 27, 1893   Charlotte wrote "3.45" above the "four."

[1894]

The diary for January 1, 1894–December 31, 1894, is a black, leather, wallet-style Excelsior commercial diary with dated, white, lined pages, measuring approximately 3¾ by 5⅝ inches.

Charlotte charted some of her menstrual periods for 1894 by placing an X on the following dates: March 12, April 6, August 19, September 20, October 16, November 12, and December 8.

January 26, 1894   Charlotte initially preceded "by the Charity Company" with "a performance given," but she subsequently crossed it out.

[1896]

The diary for January 1, 1896–December 31, 1896, is a leather-bound Standard commercial diary with dated, white, lined pages, measuring approximately 3½ by 6 inches.

Charlotte charted her menstrual periods for 1896 by placing an X on the following dates: January 8, February 5, March 5, April 1, May 23, June 19, July 16, September 11, November 9, and December 6.

March 19, 1896   Charlotte drew an arrow across the page to the entry for Wednesday, March 18, and wrote "It was today—Wed." (that she felt "one faint touch of a feeling of happiness—normality").

[1897]

The diary for January 1, 1897–December 31, 1897, is a cordovan leather-bound Excelsior commercial diary with dated, white, lined pages, measuring approximately 2⅞ by 5¾ inches. For the first time Charlotte included on the inside flyleaf of her 1897 diary the names and addresses of people to contact in case of death or accident. She continued the practice in subsequent years. The 1897 diary listed Charles Walter Stetson, George Houghton Gilman ("for *expenses* & *directions*") and Charlotte's stepmother, Mrs. Frederick B. Perkins.

January 2, 1897   Charlotte charted her menstrual periods for 1897 by placing an X on the following dates: January 2, February 3, March 1 (she added a note in parentheses: "about here I think"), March 31, April 27, May 22, June 19, July 15, August 10, September 7, November 2, November 28, and December 21.

March 8, 1897   Charlotte later circled "Look up Houghton Gilman" and drew four exclamation points in blue pencil around the entry.

December 3, 1897   Charlotte included a notation indicating that she had originally started to enter the events of Saturday, December 4, 1897, on the page dated Friday, December 3.

[1898]

The diary for January 1, 1898–December 31, 1898, is a cordovan leather-bound Excelsior commercial diary with dated, white, lined pages, measuring approximately 2⅞ by 5¾ inches. Inscribed in Charlotte's hand on the inside front cover are instructions to notify Houghton Gilman in case of death or accident.

Charlotte charted her menstrual periods for 1898 by marking an X on the following dates: January 16, February 10, March 9, April 2, May 24, June 20, July 16, August 12, September 10, November 25, and December 24.

[1899]

The diary for January 1, 1899–December 31, 1899, is a cordovan leather-bound Excelsior commercial diary with dated, white, lined pages, measuring approximately 2⅞ by 5¾ inches.

Charlotte charted her menstrual periods for 1899 by marking an X on the following dates: January 19, March 12, April 8, May 3, June 23, July 18, August 7, September 28, October 22, November 17, and December 10.

Selected Bibliography

Works by Charlotte Perkins Gilman

The Charlotte Perkins Gilman Reader. Edited with an introduction by Ann J. Lane. New York: Pantheon, 1980.

Concerning Children. Boston: Small, Maynard & Co., 1900.

The Crux. Serialized in *Forerunner* 2 (1911). Reprint, New York: Charlton Co., 1911.

The Diaries of Charlotte Perkins Gilman. Edited with an introduction by Denise D. Knight. 2 vols. Charlottesville: Univ. Press of Virginia, 1994.

Forerunner 1–7 (1909–16). Reprint, with an introduction by Madeleine B. Stern. New York: Greenwood, 1968.

Herland. Introduction by Ann J. Lane. New York: Pantheon, 1979.

His Religion and Hers: A Study of the Faith of Our Fathers and the Work of Our Mothers. New York: Century Company, 1923.

The Home: Its Work and Influence. New York: McClure, Phillips & Co., 1903.

In This Our World. Oakland: McCombs & Vaughn, 1893. 3d ed., Boston: Small, Maynard & Co., 1898. Reprint, New York: Arno, 1974.

The Later Poetry of Charlotte Perkins Gilman. Edited with an introduction by Denise D. Knight. Newark: Univ. of Delaware Press, 1996.

The Living of Charlotte Perkins Gilman: An Autobiography. Foreword by Zona Gale. New York: Appleton-Century, 1935. Reprint, edited with an introduction by Ann J. Lane, Madison: Univ. of Wisconsin Press, 1990.

The Man-Made World: Our Androcentric Culture. In *Forerunner* 1 (1909–10). Reprint, New York: Charlton Co., 1911.

Moving the Mountain. In *Forerunner* 2 (1911). Reprint, New York: Charlton Co., 1911.

Our Brains and What Ails Them. Serialized in *Forerunner* 3 (1911).

Social Ethics. Serialized in *Forerunner* 4 (1914).

What Diantha Did. In *Forerunner* 1 (1909–10). Reprint, New York: Charlton Co, 1910.

With Her in Our Land. Serialized in *Forerunner* 3 (1911).

Women and Economics: A Study of the Economic Relation between Men and Women as a Factor in Social Evolution. Boston: Small, Maynard & Co, 1898. Reprint, with an introduction by Carl Degler, New York: Harper & Row, 1966.

The Yellow Wallpaper. Boston: Small, Maynard & Co., 1899. Reprint, with an afterword by Elaine Hedges, Old Westbury, N.Y.: Feminist Press, 1973.

"The Yellow Wall-Paper" and Selected Stories of Charlotte Perkins Gilman. Edited with an introduction by Denise D. Knight. Newark: Univ. of Delaware Press, 1994.

SECONDARY SOURCES

Bassuk, Ellen L. "The Rest Cure: Repetition or Resolution of Victorian Women's Conflicts?" In *The Female Body in Western Culture: Contemporary Perspectives*, edited by Susan Rubin Suleiman, pp. 139–51. Cambridge: Harvard Univ. Press, 1986.

Ceplair, Larry, ed. *Charlotte Perkins Gilman: A Nonfiction Reader*. New York: Columbia Univ. Press, 1992.

Degler, Carl N. "Charlotte Perkins Gilman on the Theory and Practice of Feminism." *American Quarterly* 8 (Spring 1956): 21–39.

Hedges, Elaine. Afterword to *The Yellow Wallpaper*. Old Westbury, N.Y.: Feminist Press, 1973.

Hill, Mary A. *Charlotte Perkins Gilman: The Making of a Radical Feminist, 1860- 1896*. Philadelphia: Temple Univ. Press, 1980.

———. *Endure: The Diaries of Charles Walter Stetson*. Philadelphia: Temple Univ. Press, 1980.

———. *A Journey from Within: The Love Letters of Charlotte Perkins Gilman*. Lewisburg, Pa.: Bucknell Univ. Press, 1995.

Howe, Harriet. "Charlotte Perkins Gilman—As I Knew Her." *Equal Rights: Independent Feminist Weekly* 5 (Sept. 1936): 211–16.

Karpinski, Joanne B. *Critical Essays on Charlotte Perkins Gilman*. Boston: G. K. Hall, 1991.

———. "When the Marriage of True Minds Admits Impediments: Charlotte Perkins Gilman and William Dean Howells." In *Patrons and Protégées: Gender, Friendship, and Writing in Nineteenth-Century America*, edited by Shirley Marchalonis, pp. 212–34. New Brunswick, N.J.: Rutgers Univ. Press, 1988.

Kessler, Carol Farley. "Charlotte Perkins Gilman, 1860–1935." In *Modern American Women Writers*, ed. Elaine Showalter. New York: Charles Scribner's Sons, 1991.

Knight, Denise D. *Charlotte Perkins Gilman: A Study of the Short Fiction*. New York: Twayne Publishers, 1997.

———. "The Reincarnation of Jane: 'Through This'—Gilman's Companion to 'The Yellow Wall-Paper.'" *Women's Studies* 20, vols. 3–4 (1992): 289–302.

Lane, Ann J. *To Herland and Beyond: The Life and Work of Charlotte Perkins Gilman*. New York: Pantheon, 1990.

Meyering, Sheryl L., ed. *Charlotte Perkins Gilman: The Woman and Her Work*. Foreword by Cathy N. Davidson. Ann Arbor, Mich.: UMI Research Press, 1989.

Moseley, Eva S. Introductory essay to the inventory of Charlotte Perkins Gilman Papers. Arthur and Elizabeth Schlesinger Library on the History of Women in America, Radcliffe College, Cambridge, Mass., 1972.

Scharnhorst, Gary. *Charlotte Perkins Gilman*. Boston: Twayne, 1985.

———. *Charlotte Perkins Gilman: A Bibliography*. Metuchen, N.J.: Scarecrow, 1985.

Stern, Madeleine B. Introduction to the reprint edition of the *Forerunner*, vol. 1. New York: Greenwood Press, 1968.

Index

A JOURNAL OF R  JGH
THE HIGH SIERF .IA

PHELPS, BOLTON, PERKINS, PROF. LECONTE, SOULÉ, LINDERMAN, COBB.
STONE, HAWKINS, POMROY.

A Journal of Ramblings Through the High Sierras of California

BY THE
"University Excursion Party"

Joseph LeConte

Introduction by
Dean Shenk

Afterword by
John Muir

High Sierra Classics Series

Yosemite National Park, California

Yosemite Association
P.O. Box 545
Yosemite National Park, CA 95389

The Yosemite Association is a non-profit, membership organization dedicated to the support of Yosemite National Park. Our publishing program is designed to provide an educational service and to increase the public's understanding of Yosemite's special qualities and needs. To learn more about our activities and other publications, or for information about membership, please write to the address above, or call (209) 379-2646.

This volume reprints the first edition of the book that was published in 1875. Eight of the nine original photographs have been omitted.

LIBRARY OF CONGRESS CATALOGING-IN-PUBLICATION DATA
LeConte, Joseph, 1823–1901
 A journal of ramblings through the High Sierras of California by the "university excursion party" / Joseph LeConte; introduction by Dean Shenk; afterword by John Muir
 p. cm. – (High Sierra classics series)
 "This volume reprints the first edition of the book that was published in 1875. Eight of the nine original photographs have been omitted."
 – T.P. verso.
 Includes bibliographical references and index.
 ISBN 0-939666-70-7:
 1. Sierra Nevada (Calif. and Nev.) I. Title. II. Series.
 F868.S5C665 1994
 979.4'4 – dc20   93-43686
                                                            CIP

Other books in the "HIGH SIERRA CLASSICS SERIES":

Discovery of the Yosemite
by Lafayette H. Bunnell

One Hundred Years in Yosemite
by Carl P. Russell

CONTENTS

INTRODUCTION

Originally published in 1875, *A Journal of Ramblings Through the High Sierras of California by the 'University Excursion Party.'* recounts an eventful visit to Yosemite in 1870. It is an entertaining narrative full of contagious excitement, adventure and love for the Yosemite region. Joseph LeConte's account of this 37-day trip through nineteenth-century California describes a Yosemite familiar in many ways and, at the same time, remarkably different. Through this modest volume we can join "Professor Joe" and his comrades on their timeless journey, relive with them their personal discovery of Yosemite, share LeConte's meeting and friendship with John Muir, and experience the obvious thrill with which an early scientist responded to Yosemite's natural and scenic wonders.

Joseph LeConte, a leading scientist of his time whose name and persona were to become closely associated with the University of California, the Sierra Club and the Sierra Nevada, was born February 26, 1823, in Liberty County, Georgia. The sixth of eight children and the youngest of four sons, LeConte grew up in the wealthy setting of his family's plantation, Woodmanston, attended by some 200 slaves.

As a boy he was intrigued with all he found during frequent wanderings in the surrounding meadows and woods. "As I grew older," he wrote in his autobiography, "this love of nature took on higher forms; first in the study of ornithology, and later in camping trips, undertaken partly in the spirit of adventure and partly for the geological study of mountains."

At the age of fifteen LeConte entered Franklin College of the University of Georgia in Athens, graduating in August, 1841. Four years later he received a medical degree from the College of Physicians and Surgeons, New York.

He married Caroline Elizabeth (Bessie) Nisbet on January 14,

1847, and began work as a doctor in Macon, Georgia. LeConte discovered that he did not enjoy practicing medicine so much as teaching several medical students. After three and a half years, he dissolved his practice and moved to Cambridge to study geology and zoology at Harvard under the famous Louis Agassiz, in preparation for becoming a professor. Over time LeConte became closely associated with Agassiz, traveling extensively with him along the East Coast, venturing as far south as Florida, assisting with Agassiz's study of coral reefs.

LeConte took advantage of every opportunity to learn about the natural world from experts at Harvard and elsewhere. He visited with the famous naturalist J. J. Audubon and with other men of letters and science. "Think of the galaxy of stars in Harvard at that time!" he wrote in his autobiography. "Agassiz, Guyot, Wyman, Gray, Peirce, Longfellow, Lowell, Holmes, and Felton—with all of whom I was in almost daily contact on the most intimate terms. Emerson I saw sometimes, but not often. Richard Dana I met thrice every day at the table of the house at which I boarded after returning from Florida. The effect of this intellectual atmosphere was in the highest degree stimulating, giving incredible impulse to thought." He received both a degree and a diploma and "after a residence of about fifteen months I left Cambridge and all my dear friends there in the middle of October, 1851."

In 1852, LeConte obtained a professorship at Oglethorpe University, Midway, Georgia. "I was to teach all the sciences except astronomy." Soon thereafter he was selected to fill a chair of geology and natural history at his alma mater, Franklin College, University of Georgia, Athens. A peripatetic professor, he next began teaching chemistry and geology at South Carolina College in Columbia, South Carolina, in January 1857.

During LeConte's time at South Carolina College, the Civil War broke out and South Carolina became the first state to secede from the Union. "At first I was extremely reluctant to join in, and was even opposed to the secession movement; I doubted its necessity and dreaded the impending conflict and its result. A large number of the best and most thoughtful men all over the South felt as I did; but gradually a change came about—how, who can say? It was in the atmosphere; we breathed it in the air; it reverberated from heart to heart; it was like a spiritual contagion—good or bad, who can say? But the final result was enthusiastic unanimity of sentiment through-out the South." The College continued to function until June 1862, when all of the remaining students volunteered. Professor LeConte became a chemist with the rank of major in the Army of the Confederacy.

At war's end LeConte became frustrated with elements of recon-struction and concerned about the academic future of the college. Unable to obtain a position at a university in the north, he and his brother John, also a professor, began looking farther afield. At one point they even considered emigrating to South America. Finally, with the help of many of LeConte's respected academic colleagues (particularly his former professor, Louis Agassiz), Joseph and John both obtained positions at the soon-to-open University of California.

John, as the first appointed member of the faculty, had been named Chair of Natural Science and, prior to assuming a role as professor, was to act as president and oversee the organization of the institution. Soon thereafter, Joseph was selected as the Chair of the Geology Department with the added responsibilities of teaching zoology and botany.

In September 1869, at College Hall in Oakland, the University of California entered the world of higher education with 38 students in attendance. Joseph LeConte told a young scholar as he handed him a pen, "You have the honor to be the first student to register in this institution that is destined to be one of the very greatest in the country."

In the summer of 1870, at the end of the first session of the University, eight of the students invited LeConte and professor Frank Soulé, Jr., to join them in a camping trip to the Sierra Nevada. They eagerly accepted. LeConte wrote, "This trip was almost an era in my life. We were gone six weeks and visited the Yosemite, the high Sierra, Lake Mono and the volcanoes in the vicinity, and Lake Tahoe. The trip was made in the roughest style of camp life, each man carrying his bedding and extra clothing in a roll behind his saddle, and a packhorse bearing the food and camp utensils for the party. We had no tent, but slept under trees with only the sky above us. I never enjoyed anything else so much in my life—perfect health, the merry party of young men, the glorious scenery, and, above all, the magnificent opportunity for studying mountain origin and structure.... I subsequently made many similar trips, but this remained the most delightful, because as it was the first, everything was so new to me and so different from anything that I had previously experienced."

LeConte kept notes of his experiences during this special trip, and arranged to have his account published several years later. Bibliographers estimate that the first edition of the book consisted of 120 copies which were presented by LeConte to the members of the "University Excursion Party" as souvenirs of their summer together. Bound in blue cloth, replete with beautiful typography, and illustrated with nine tipped-in photographs by John J. Reilly, first editions of *Ramblings* are handsome and quite rare. This and later editions are admired and coveted by collectors of fine books, as well as by students and lovers of Yosemite and California history.

Unlike other later editions (all of which are out of print), this volume reprints the original text of the first edition, including several archaic usages. For example, when *Ramblings* was first published, the taxonomy of fir trees was not fully understood; these trees were believed to be spruces. LeConte labeled two fir species as *Picea*

Amabiles and *Picea Grandis;* their current names are *Abies concolor* (white fir) and *Abies magnifica* (red fir). Like many of Yosemite's pioneers, LeConte incorrectly referred to the lodgepole pine as the "tamarack," which, surprisingly, is a deciduous tree. Another change resulted from the recognition that the Spanish word "Sierra" in its singular form signifies a mountain range. "Sierras" (which means multiple mountain ranges) is now considered inappropriate as a name for California's grandest mountain chain.

At the time of LeConte's 1870 trip, Yosemite was not the established, century-old, 1,162 square mile national park we know today, but a six-year-old, 48.6 square mile "grant" (embracing only Yosemite Valley and the Mariposa Grove of Giant Sequoias) under the management of the State of California. The annual visitation for 1870 was 1,735—a total almost triple the figure for 1868, occasioned by the completion of the transcontinental railroad in 1869. (Annual visitation to Yosemite National Park has now reached four million. Approximately 7,800 visitors and 1,300 employees sleep in Yosemite Valley each night of the summer.) In LeConte's time, wagon roads linking Yosemite Valley with civilization would not be completed for several years; visitors rode horses or mules or walked along precipitous trails into the valley. It took the "University Excursion Party" seven days to travel on horseback from Oakland to Wawona.

LeConte's excursion was made the summer following the one immortalized by John Muir in his classic work *My First Summer in the Sierra*. Muir, who later achieved international acclaim through his dozen books and numerous newspaper and magazine articles, then had but a single published letter. Due to the efforts of his mentor, Jeanne Carr, wife of University of California professor Ezra Carr, Muir had become a sort of Yosemite "touchstone" for many members of the literary and scientific community who visited Yosemite Valley. The summer of 1870 was the first that the 32-year-old Muir resided in the valley.

Muir was employed by James Mason Hutchings, Yosemite's first true entrepreneur, performing carpentry work at Hutchings' Hotel and operating Hutchings' sawmill near the base of Yosemite Falls. Hutchings had recently returned from Washington, D.C., where he had argued his homestead claim to 160 acres of Yosemite Valley. Muir boarded with the Hutchings family, but resided in his own version of the "Walden" cabin. Built of mill waste and sugar pine shingles, the cabin was located along the eastern bank of Yosemite Creek between Hutchings' cottage and sawmill. Muir considered it "the handsomest building in the valley," and wrote that it had been constructed "at a cost of only three or four dollars." Twenty five years earlier, Thoreau's cabin at Walden Pond had cost a whopping 28.12\frac{1}{2}$!

As recounted in this work, LeConte first met Muir at the sawmill on August 5, 1870, and noted, "Mr. Muir is a gentleman of rare intelligence, of much knowledge of science, particularly of botany, which he has made a specialty.... A man of so much intelligence tending a saw mill! —not for himself, but for Mr. Hutchings. This is California!"

The two men became friends, and LeConte was among the first to give credence to Muir's revisionary theory on the formation of Yosemite Valley. Upon LeConte's death, Muir wrote a tribute which appeared in the September 1901 issue of *The University of California Magazine*. That article, entitled "Reminiscences of Joseph LeConte," is reprinted for the first time as the afterword in this book.

In the year prior to LeConte's visit, there had been much development in and around Yosemite Valley. Black's Hotel had been built on the site of the Lower Hotel (the first in the valley). West of Black's, a third hotel, Leidig's, had been constructed on the valley floor. At the time of LeConte's ramblings, La Casa Nevada, the hostelry operated by Albert and Emily Snow near the base of Nevada Fall, had been open but a few months.

Outside Yosemite Valley, an inn of sorts could be found at Glacier Point, and there were two rustic accommodations along the trail between Glacier Point and what was then commonly called Clark's Station (now known as Wawona). The Mountain View House, located at Peregoy's Meadow, began receiving guests the previous fall (LeConte mistakenly referred to the spot as "Paragoy's"). Another establishment, known as Ostrander's, was also along this trail. Both enterprises soon fell into oblivion because in 1875 they were bypassed by the wagon road between Clark's and the valley.

In 1870, Clark's Station was properly known as Clark and Moore's because Galen Clark had sold part interest to Edwin Moore the previous year. Clark had first visited Yosemite Valley in 1855 and moved one year later to what is now Wawona for his health, believing that he had but six months to live. In 1866 he was appointed "Guardian" of the Yosemite Grant and served in that capacity for over 20 years.

During LeConte's first stay in Yosemite, another visitor, Therése Yelverton Viscountess Avonmore, fell under the spell of the incomparable valley. Yelverton was well known throughout Europe and America at this time because of her husband's highly publicized divorce attempts. While visiting Yosemite during the summer of 1870, she became fascinated with John Muir, whose genius she recognized and appreciated. Yelverton was supporting herself as a travel writer and found much to write about concerning her Yosemite experience. Although thinly disguised as fiction, her classically Victorian novel, *Zanita, A Tale of the Yosemite*, was a remarkably accurate portrayal of life in Yosemite Valley and featured many of its colorful residents. Historians consider her "Kenmuir" to be an accurate depiction of John Muir.

Although LeConte gives only minor acknowledgement of Yelverton's presence in his book, he apparently made a lasting impression upon her. In *Zanita* she assumes the role of "Mrs. Brown," wife of a character obviously inspired by LeConte: "My husband was a Professor of Geology in a College of California, and much of the pleasantest part of my life was spent in bearing him company in his geological excursions. We usually spent the vacations in delightful rambles, occasionally accompanied by a few of the more studious and inquiring of his pupils, sometimes by a fellow Professor, and sometimes alone."

In 1892 LeConte and his son, Joseph N. LeConte (known as "Little Joe"), along with Galen Clark, J. M. Hutchings, D. J. Foley and, of course, John Muir, were among the 182 charter members of the Sierra Club. LeConte and his son each left a long trail of exploration and mountaineering in the Sierra Nevada.

Throughout the rest of his life Joseph LeConte remained closely associated with the University of California. In his lifetime, he wrote eight books and published more than two hundred articles covering a multitude of philosophical and scientific fields. While he considered *Sight: An Exposition of the Principles of Monocular and Binocular Vision* to be his most significant work, he felt that his peers considered *Religion and Science* and *Evolution and Its Relation to Religious Thought* his more important books.

In the early summer of 1901, as members of the first Sierra Club outing explored Yosemite's high country, the 78-year-old LeConte returned to his beloved Yosemite Valley for what would be his last visit. His group included Frank Soulé, who had accompanied him on his initial visit thirty-one years before. Together they reminisced about that first Yosemite trip while they wandered through the Mariposa Grove and spent two days visiting their old valley haunts. There, the aged professor and his entourage slept at Camp Curry.

Edward T. Parsons, for whom Parsons Memorial Lodge would be built and dedicated, recalled in an article for the January 1902 number of the *Sierra Club Bulletin:* "Those who were with him on his last drive about the floor of the valley will never forget their visit to the foot of the lower Yosemite Fall, where, standing on a rock in the spray of the falling waters, he raised his arms aloft and shouted in the exuberance of his joy and delight at the magnificent spectacle before him."

"On the evening of July 5th," remembered Frank Soulé in the same issue of the *Sierra Club Bulletin*, "the sad words were whispered around the camp that 'dear Doctor Joe is very ill.' He was in great physical pain, caused by angina pectoris, but his daughter and their intimate friends did everything possible throughout the night to alleviate his sufferings. In the morning he seemed to be resting comfortably; so much so that his physician left his bedside to procure additional medicine from the hotel. At 10 a.m. Professor LeConte turned on his left side. At once his watchful daughter noticed a great change come over his face and said, 'Do not lie upon your left side, father; you know it is not good for you.' He smiled, and uttered his last words in this life, 'It does not matter, daughter.' In five minutes' time the revered one was dead."

William Colby reported in the January 1904 issue of the *Sierra Club Bulletin:* "Immediately after the death of Professor Joseph LeConte in Yosemite Valley, the construction of a memorial there in his honor suggested itself to his friends.... They decided that instead of a monument of conventional type it would be much more appropriate and more in keeping with the wishes of Professor LeConte, were he there to express them, and also typical of his active and useful life, to erect a lodge which would serve as a memorial and at the same time be of direct benefit to others.... A portion of the Club library, as well as maps and photographs, will be placed there, and a custodian will be in charge during May, June, and July, to give information to visitors concerning the Club and the surrounding mountain region."

LeConte Memorial Lodge in Yosemite Valley was completed in September 1903 and dedicated July 3, 1904. In recent years, it has become known to many as "LeConte Memorial" perhaps to avoid confusing those who would expect to find rooms for rent at a "lodge." Originally located very near to a then much smaller Camp Curry, a new, duplicate LeConte Memorial Lodge was completed at its current location in 1919. The relocation was financed by the Curry Camping Company which wanted it moved further away from that company's establishment. The site and some remains of the original LeConte Memorial Lodge can still be found in Curry Village where the Yosemite Park & Curry Co. has placed a descriptive sign written by Yosemite author and historian Shirley Sargent.

David A. Curry, of the Curry Camping Company, and the noted geologist François Matthes collected a variety of granitic rocks from a moraine in Yosemite Valley near Bridalveil Fall. They placed the rocks around the trunk of an oak adjacent to the tent in which Joseph LeConte died. After the oak fell and was removed, people unfamiliar with the significance of the site often attempted to clear the rocks away. Shortly before her death in 1948, Jennie "Mother" Curry expressed her desire to preserve the historical significance of this spot with a marker.

On March 2, 1949, Newton B. Drury, the Director of the National Park Service, approved Superintendent Carl Russell's proposal (on behalf of Mother Curry) to mark the location by burying a large boulder with its flat upper surface flush with the ground. Because it was not marked with a plaque or other sign, the memorial boulder was later unearthed and moved to make room for an underground electrical cable. There are now efforts underway to return the boulder to its original location.

Mount LeConte in Great Smoky Mountains National Park, LeConte Glacier (the southernmost tidewater glacier in Alaska) that flows into LeConte Bay in Tongass National Forest, Alaska, a second Mount LeConte (this one within Sequoia National Park), LeConte Divide in Kings Canyon National Park, and LeConte Falls in Yosemite National Park, are some of the impressive natural features that have been named in honor of the man who wrote this book. The Yosemite Association's decision to reprint this significant work by Joseph LeConte chronicling his first ramblings in the Yosemite and the Sierra Nevada in 1870 also pays tribute to this special individual. For as long as this narrative is available to be read, Joseph LeConte and the excitement of this "delightful" excursion will remain alive and in the hearts of fellow mountaineers and lovers of Yosemite and the High Sierra.

Dean Shenk
El Portal, California

PREFACE

About a week before the end of the First Session of the University of California, several young men, students of the University, invited me to join them in a camping party for the Yosemite and the high Sierras. The party was to go in regular pioneer style, cooking their own provisions, and sleeping under the open sky, whenever a convenient place was found; each man was to bestride his own horse, carry his own bedding behind his saddle, and his clothing, with the exception of one change of underwear, on his back.

This was, it is true, a little rougher and harder than anything I had ever undertaken, but still I was fond of adventure, and longed to enjoy the glories of Yosemite and the beauties of the Sierras, and, more than all, to study mountain structure and mountain sculpture, as exhibited there on a magnificent scale. I therefore at once accepted the offer. The party was forthwith organized, ten in number. Mr. Hawkins, who understood something of mountain life, was commissioned to buy the necessary supplies, and the general outfit, such as camp utensils, pack-horse and pack-saddle, and have all in readiness that we might start the very first day after commencement.

To while away my idle moments in camp, and to preserve some *souvenir* of the party, of the incidents, and of the scenery, I jotted down, from time to time, these wayside notes.

J. L'C.

A JOURNAL OF RAMBLINGS.

Amid many kind and cheering words, mingled with tender regrets; many encouragements, mingled with earnest entreaties to take care of myself, and to keep out of *drafts* and *damp* while sleeping on the *bare ground* in the *open air;* many half-suppressed tears, concealed beneath bright smiles, I left my home and dear ones this morning. Surely I must have a heroic and dangerous air about me, for my little baby boy shrinks from my rough flannel shirt and broad-brim hat, as did the baby son of Hector from *his* brazen corslet, and beamy helm, and nodding plume. I snatch a kiss and hurry away to our place of rendezvous.

After much bustle, confusion, and noisy preparation, saddling, sinching, strapping blanket rolls, packing camp utensils and provisions, we are fairly ready at 10 A.M. Saluted by cheers from manly throats, and handkerchief-wavings by the white hands of women, we leave Oakland at a sweeping trot, Hawkins leading the pack; while the long handle of our frying-pan, sticking straight up through a hole in the bag, and the merry jingling of *tin* pans, *tin* cups and coffee pot—"tintinnabulation"—proclaimed the nature of our mission.

We are in high spirits; although I confess to some misgivings when I heard from the Captain that we would ride thirty miles to-day, for I have not been on horseback for ten years. But I am determined not to be an encumbrance to the merry party. We started from Oakland seven in number. One will join us to-night in Livermore Valley. Two others, having gone to Stockton to procure horses, will join us at Graysonville. Without any remarkable incident we rode along the level plain which borders the bay about fifteen miles, and reached our lunch ground, near Hayward, at

1 P.M. Here we fed our horses and rested two hours.

Started again at 3 P.M. Our ride took us over the Contra Costa Ridge, by Hayward Pass, into Amador and Livermore valleys, and then along these valleys, the noble outline of Mt. Diablo looming finely in the distance on our left. I observe everything narrowly, for all is new to me, and so different from anything in the Eastern states. Livermore Valley is an extensive, rich, level plain, separating the Contra Costa from the Mt. Diablo Ridge. It is surrounded by mountains on every side, and the scenery is really fine. Much pleased to find the mountains, on their northern and eastern slopes, so green and well wooded. I have been accustomed to see them from Oakland only on their southern and western slopes, which are almost treeless, and, at this season, brown and sure. Much interested in watching the habits of burrowing squirrels and burrowing owls, especially the amicable manner in which they live together in the same burrows.

After riding about ten miles, we arrived, a little before sunset, at Dublin, a little village of a few houses. Here we found tolerable camping ground, and ought to have stopped for the night; but, against my advice, the party, buoyant and thoughtless, concluded to go on to Laddsville,* where one of the party would join us, and had promised to prepare forage for our horses and camp for ourselves. It was a foolish mistake. From this time our ride was very tedious and fatiguing. The miles seem to stretch out before us longer and longer. The hilarious and somewhat noisy spirits of the young men gradually died away. After some abortive attempts at a song, some miserable failures in the way of jokes, we pursued our weary way in silence. Night closed upon us while we were still many miles from Laddsville. Lights ahead! Are these Laddsville? We hope so. Onward we press; but the lights seem to recede from us. Still onward,

*This place is now called Livermore.

seemingly three or four miles; but no nearer the lights. Are these *ignes fatui* sent to delude us? But courage! here comes some one. "How far to Laddsville?" "Three miles." Onward we pressed, at least three miles. Again a wayfarer. "How far to Laddsville?" "Three and a half miles." Again three or four miles onward; three or four miles of aching ankles, and knees, and hips, and back, but no complaint. "How many miles to Laddsville?" "Five." Again three or four miles of aching knees, and hips, and back. Wayfarers are becoming more numerous. "How far to Laddsville?" "Two miles." "How far to Laddsville?" "A little over a mile." "How far to Laddsville?" "How far to Laddsville?" — "To Laddsville?" — Ah! here it is at last. Yes, at last, about 10 P.M., that now celebrated place was actually reached; but too late for good camping. The companion who was to join us here was nowhere to be found. We hastily made arrangements for our horses in a neighboring stable, and camped on the bare, dusty ground, in an open space on the outskirts of the town. A good campfire and a hearty meal comforted us somewhat. About 11:30 P.M. rolled ourselves in our blankets, and composed ourselves for sleep.

To our wearied spirits, we seem to have traveled at least fifty miles to-day. From the most accurate information we can get, however, the actual distance is only about thirty-five miles. Very foolish to go so far the first day.

———

July 22.

Estimating the whole mammalian population of Laddsville at two hundred, I am sure at least one hundred and fifty must be dogs. These kept up such an incessant barking all night, around us and at us, as we lay upon the ground, that we got little sleep. Near daybreak I sank into a deeper, sweeter sleep, when whoo! — oo — oo —

oo—whoo!!! the scream of a railroad train, passing within fifty feet, startled the night air and us. It is not surprising, then, that we got up reluctantly, and rather late, and very stiff and sore. Our breakfast, which consisted this morning of *fried bacon, cheese, cold bread*, and *good tea*, refreshed and comforted us greatly. While eating our breakfast, whoop! whoop! hurrah! our expected companion, Dell. Linderman, came galloping in, with gun slung on shoulder. He did his best, by whip, and spur, and noise, to make a dashing entry, but his heavy, sluggish mare did not in the least sympathize with his enthusiasm. He had been looking for us the evening before, but had given us up, and went back to a friend's house, a little out of Laddsville.

Soon after sunrise, all the inhabitants of Laddsville, including, of course, the one hundred and fifty dogs, came crowding around us: the men to find out who we were, and where bound; the dogs to find out what it was they had been barking at all night. After we had severally satisfied these, our fellow creatures, both biped and quadruped—our fellow-men and Darwinian cousins—we saddled and packed up, determined to profit by the experience of yesterday, and not to go more than twenty miles to-day. Our horses as well as ourselves have suffered from the travel of yesterday. We started late, about 8 A.M., proceeded only five miles, and stopped, 10 A.M., under the shade of a clump of oaks, near a mill. The air is still this morning, and the sun insufferably hot. We here took cold lunch, and rested until 1 P.M. A cool breeze now springing up, we started, passed over the summit of Corral Hollow Pass and down by a very steep grade, I think about fifteen hundred feet in a mile, into "Corral Hollow" a very narrow cañon with only fifty to sixty yards width at the bottom, with high rocky cliffs on either side, which cuts through Mt. Diablo Range to the base. The road now ran in this cañon along a dry stream bed for many miles, until it finally emerges on the San Joaquin plains.

In Amador and Livermore valleys, I observed the soil was composed of a drift of rounded pebbles, in stiff adobe clay—local drift from the mountains. In Corral Hollow the soil consists of pebbles and coarse sand, evidently river deposit. Fine sections showing cross lamination were observed. Mountains very steep on each side the gorge. Perpendicular cliffs of sandstone and limestone exposed in many places, sometimes worn into fantastic shapes, and often into caves. These caves I hear were once the haunts of robbers. Near the bottom of the gorge the irregularly stratified river sands are seen lying unconformably on the sandstone. We passed, on our way, some coal mines, which are now worked. These strata are probably cretaceous, belonging to the same horizon as the Mt. Diablo coal.

We rode ten or twelve miles down Corral Hollow, or about fifteen miles, this afternoon, and camped, 7 P.M., at a teamsters' camp, the permanent camp of the teamsters of the coal mine. From these men we bought feed for our horses; then cooked supper, and went to bed as early as possible.

———

July 23.

The whole party woke up this morning in good spirits, much refreshed by our supper and sleep last night. We got up at 4 A.M., cooked our breakfast and were off by 5:30. At first we really enjoyed our ride in the cool morning air. In about an hour we emerged from Corral Hollow on the San Joaquin plains. There is still a fine, cool breeze. "Why, this is delightful; the San Joaquin plains have been much slandered," thought we. As we advanced, however, we changed our opinion. Insufficiency of rain last winter has produced utter failure of crops. As far as the eye can reach, in every direction, only a bare, desert plain is seen. The heat now became intense; the wind, though strong, was dry and burning. Over the perfectly level, dry, parched, dusty, and now desert plains, with baked lips and bleeding noses, we pressed on toward Grayson, where we expected to noon. "Grayson is on the San Joaquin River. It can't be far off, for yonder is water." Yes, surely yonder is water; do you not see its glistening surface? its rolling billows running in the direction of the wind? the reflection of the trees, which grow on the *farther* bank? Those white objects scattered over the glistening surface, with their images beneath: are these not sails on the river? Alas! No! It is all mirage. There is no water visible at all. The trees are trees which skirt the *nearer* bank of the river; the white objects are cottages on the desert plains. We could hardly believe it until we were deceived and undeceived half a dozen times. Parched with heat and thirst, and blinded with dust, we could easily appreciate the tantalizing effect of similar phenomena on the thirsty travelers of Sahara.

Onward, still onward, with parched throats, baked lips, and bleeding noses, we press. But even with parched throat, baked lips, and bleeding nose, one may enjoy the ludicrous, and even shake his gaunt sides with laughter; at least I found it so this morning. The circumstances were these: Hawkins early this morning killed a rabbit. Phelps, conceiving the idea that it would relish well, broiled on the glowing coals of our campfire to-night, offered to carry it. He did so for some time, but his frisky, foolish, unsteady filly, not liking the dangling rabbit, became restive, and the rabbit was dropped in disgust and left on the road. Stone, good natured fellow, in simple kindness of heart, and also having the delights of broiled rabbit present in his imagination—the *picture* of broiled rabbit before his *mind's eye,* and the *fragrance* of broiled rabbit in his *mind's nose*—dismounted and picked it up. But essaying to mount his cowlike beast again, just when he had, with painful effort, climbed up to his "saddle's eaves," and was about to heave his long dexter leg over and wriggle himself into his seat, the beast aforesaid, who had been attentively viewing the operation out of the external corner of his left eye, started suddenly forward, and Stone, to his great astonishment, found himself on *his own* instead of his horse's back. Then commenced a wild careering over the dusty plain, with the saddle under his belly; a mad plunging and kicking, a general chasing by the whole party, including Stone himself, on foot; a laughing and shouting by all except Stone, until sinch and straps gave way, and saddle, blanket-roll and clothing lay strewed upon the ground.

We had hardly picked up Stone's traps, and mended his sinch, and started on our way; the agitation of our diaphragms and the aching of our sides had hardly subsided; when Pomroy, sitting high enthroned on his aged, misshapen beast, thinking to show the ease and grace of his perfect horsemanship, and also secretly desiring to ease the exquisite tenderness of his sitting bones, quietly detached his right foot from the stirrup and swung it gracefully over the pommel, to sit a while in woman-fashion. But as soon as the shadow of his great top boots fell across the eyes of "Old 67," that venerable beast, whether in the innocency of colt-like playfulness or a natural malignancy, made frantic by excessive heat and dust, began to kick, and plunge, and buck, until finally, by a sudden and dexterous arching of his back, and a throwing down of his head, Pomroy was shot from the saddle like an arrow from a bow, or a shell from a mortar; and sailing through mid-air with arms and legs widely extended, like the bird of Jove, descended in graceful, parabolic curve and fell into the arms of his fond mother earth. Unwilling to encounter the wrath of his master, Old 67 turned quickly and fled, with his mouth wide open, and his teeth all showing, as if enjoying a huge horse-laugh. Then commenced again the wild careering on the hot plains, the mad plunging and kicking, the shouting, and laughing, and chasing. The horse at last secured, Pomroy took him firmly by the bit, delivered one blow of his clenched fist upon his nose, and then gazed at him steadily, with countenance full of solemn warning. In return, a wicked, unrepentant, vengeful gleam shot from the corner of the deep-sunk eye of Old 67.

Onward, still onward, over the absolutely treeless and plantless desert, we rode for fifteen or more miles, and reached Grayson about 12 M. Here we nooned and rested until 4 P.M. Two of our party, viz.: Cobb and Bolton, joined up here from Stockton, where they had gone to procure horses. While resting here, we took a delightful swim in the San Joaquin River. Delightfully refreshing while in the water; but on coming out, the wind felt as hot, and dry, and fiery, as if it blew out of a furnace. Caught a few fish here, and enjoyed them for lunch. Bought some peaches, and devoured them with a kind of ravenous fierceness. Ah! how delicious in this parched country!

Grayson is a small, insignificant village, with a half-dozen or more buildings, among which there is, of course, the hotel and the post office. I took advantage of the latter to send off a letter to my wife—a very short letter—assuring her of my health, and that I was doing as well as could be expected; indeed, much better.

4 P.M., crossed the ferry, and continued on our journey about eight or ten miles, and camped for the night at Mr. Dooly's ranch. Here we found much kindness in Mr. Dooly, much fodder for our horses, a big straw bank for our beds, and a blue, starry sky for our roof. There was no reason, therefore, why we should not be happy. We were so; indeed, we really enjoyed our supper and our beds.

The San Joaquin plains, though the most fertile part of the State, is at this time, of course, completely dry and parched; nothing green as far as the eye can reach, except along the river banks. The crops, this year, have to a great extent failed, on account of the in-sufficient rain of the last rainy season. The only animate things which enlivened the scene this P.M. were thousands of jack rabbits and burrowing squirrels, and their friends, the burrowing owls.

July 24, Sunday.

The day of rest. Rest on the San Joaquin plains! Impossible! We
pushed on this morning—this delightful, cool Sunday morning—
after a refreshing night's rest. Cool in the morning, but hot, oh! how
hot! as the day advanced. Made fifteen miles, and nooned at a large
ranch—Mr. Ashe's. Besides the invariable jack rabbits, burrowing
squirrels, and burrowing owls, I noticed thousands of horned toads
(Phrynosoma). I observed here a peculiarity of California life. Mr.
Ashe is evidently a wealthy man. His fields are immense; his stables
and barns are very ample; his horses and hired laborers are numerous; great numbers of cows, hogs, turkeys, chickens—every evidence
of abundance, good living, and even of wealth, except dwelling
house. This is a shanty, scarcely fit for a cow-house. He doesn't live
here, however, but in San Francisco.

I saw also, to-day, a badger. One of the party tried to shoot him,
but he disappeared in a burrow.

To-day has been insufferably hot. We find, upon inquiry, that
there is a house at which we may stop, seven miles from this. We
concluded to rest until the cool of the evening. We drowse away several hours under a wagon shed, and resume our journey, 5:30 P.M.
On the way this evening we killed two rattlesnakes, one with eight
and one with twelve rattles. Enjoyed greatly the evening ride, and
the glorious sunset. About dark reached the house where we expected to camp; but, alas, no feed for horses. Directed to another
house, two or three miles further on. They must have feed there, for
it is a *stage station*. On we went in the dark, over an exceedingly
rough, ploughed field, full of great adobe clods, and reached the
house, tired and hungry, about 9 P.M. Again "No feed." We were in
despair. Impossible to go farther. "Any other house?" "None within
seven or eight miles." When we spoke of going on, however, the man
in charge (agent) hinted at the existence of a barley stack. "That's

just what we want." "But can't let you have it." He was evidently trying to extort from us in our necessity. This made Soulé, our Captain, so angry that he plainly told him that we would have the use of the stack, and he might get redress in any way he liked. A good deal of useless cursing passed on both sides, when, by word of command, we marched off to the stack, about one quarter-mile distant, and picketed our horses around, with their heads to the stack. It was already so late that we did not attempt to cook supper, but ate it cold. After our cold supper, we threw ourselves upon the stack, and, although late, gazed up into the clear, black sky, studded with brilliant stars, and talked for more than an hour. The young men asked me many questions about stars, and nebulae, and spectrum analysis, and shooting stars, and meteoric stones, which led to quite a dissertation on these subjects. The time and circumstances gave a keener interest to the discussion.

On San Joaquin plains, and, I believe, everywhere in California, however hot the days may be, the nights are delightfully cool.

———————

July 25.

After a really fine night's rest, we got up about 4 A.M. The day was just breaking, and the air very clear and transparent. The blue jagged outline of the Sierras is distinctly and beautifully marked, above and beyond the nearer foot-hills, against the clear sky. In fact, there seemed to be several ridges, rising one above and beyond the other; and above and beyond all, the sharp-toothed summits of the Sierras. Took, again, a cold breakfast, and made an early start, 5 A.M. Went up to the house and offered to pay the agent for the barley. Charged us $25. We had been charged for the same everywhere else $3. Went into the house. Spoke to the ladies (daughters of the owner) on the subject. They were very kind and pleasant, and well satisfied with $3. We therefore paid them and left.

At first, our ride was delightfully pleasant in the cool morning, but gradually the bare, desert plains, now monotonously rolling, became insufferably hot and dusty. The beautiful view of the Sierras, the goal of our yearnings, gradually faded away, obscured by dust, and our field of vision was again limited by the desert plains. Soon after leaving the plains, we stopped for water at a neat hut, where dwelt a real *"old mammy,"* surrounded by little darkies. On inquiry I found she was from Jackson County, Georgia, and formerly owned by a Mr. Strickland. She had come to California since the war. I was really glad to see the familiar old face, and hear the familiar, low-country, negro brogue; and she equally glad to see me. She evidently did not like California, and seemed to pine after the *"auld country."* From this place to Snelling the heat and dust were absolutely fearful. We are commencing to rise; there is no strong breeze, as on the plains; the heated air and the dust rise from the earth and envelop us, man and horse, until we can scarcely see each other. After about fifteen miles travel, arrived at Snelling at 11:30 A.M. Here we washed ourselves thoroughly, and took a good meal at the hotel, the first meal we have thus taken since leaving Oakland. We heartily enjoyed both the cleansing and the meal.

Snelling is the largest and most thriving village we have yet seen. It is in the midst of a fine agricultural district. It supplies the mining district above, without itself being entirely dependent upon that interest. Pleased to notice a very nice, brick, public schoolhouse. The population is probably six or seven hundred. Observed many Chinese laborers, hostlers, waiters, etc.

Continued our ride, 4 P.M., expecting to go only to Merced Falls to-night. Country beginning to be quite hilly: first, only denudation hills of drift, finely and horizontally stratified; then, round hills, with sharp, tooth-like jags of perpendicularly-cleaved slates, standing out thickly on their sides. Here we first saw the auriferous slates, and here, also, the first gravel diggins. The auriferous gravel and pebble deposit underlies the soil of the valleys and ravines. About five miles from Snelling we forded the Merced River. Here were two roads, one along the river and the other over the hills. Two of the young men, Pomroy and Bolton, took the road over the hills; the rest of us thought that along the river the right one. Called after the other two to return; but they thought they were right, and proceeded. Went down the river about one-half mile below the Falls, and camped. About one hour after dark, Pomroy and Bolton returned, and joined us at supper. No straw bank for bed to-night. On the contrary, we camped on the barest, hardest, and bleakest of hills, the wind sweeping up the river over us in a perfect gale. Nevertheless, our sleep was sound and refreshing.

I heard to-night, for the first time, of a piece of boyish folly — to call it nothing worse — on the part of some of the young men, at Ashe's, yesterday noon. While I was dozing under the shed, some of the young men, thinking it, no doubt, fine fun, managed to secure and appropriate some of the poultry running about in such superfluous abundance in the yard. While sitting and jotting down notes under the wagon shed there, I *had* observed Cobb throwing a line to some chickens. When I looked up from my note book, I did observe, I now recollect, a mischievous twinkle in his coal-black eye, and a slight quiver of his scarcely-perceptible, downy mustache, but I thought nothing of it. Soon after I shut up my note book, and went under a more retired shed to doze. It now appears that a turkey and several chickens had been bagged. The young rascals felicitated themselves hugely upon their good fortune, but, unfortunately, last night and this morning we made no camp-fire, and to-day at noon we ate at the hotel table; so that they have had no opportunity of enjoying their ill-gotten plunder until now.

Capt. Soulé and myself have already expressed ourselves, briefly, but very plainly, in condemnation of such conduct. To-night the chickens were served. I said nothing, but simply, with Soulé and Hawkins, refused the delicious morsel, and confined myself to bacon.

Merced Falls is a small village, deriving its importance only from a large mill situated on a rapid of the same name.

July 26.

Really feel quite vigorous and refreshed this morning. Got up at 4:30 A.M. Again refused fat chicken and turkey, though sorely tempted by the delicious fragrance, and ate bacon and dried beef instead. The young men have keenly felt this quiet rebuke. I feel sure this thing will not occur again. Rode, without any remarkable incident, fifteen miles this morning, to the toll-house, on the top of a high ridge. Here we nooned, fed our horses, and rested until 4 P.M. The country is becoming mountainous; we are rising the foot-hills. The soil begins to be well wooded. The air, though still hot, is more bracing. Small game is more abundant. I have become inured to the exercise of riding, and begin really to enjoy the trip. We are now on the famous Mariposa Estate. We have, all along the road today, seen abundant evidence of mining, prospecting, etc., but all abandoned. While at the toll-house, the young men amused and refreshed themselves by bathing in the horse-trough. It was really a fine bathing tub, being about thirty feet long, two feet wide, and two feet deep, and a fine stream of water running through it. We really had a pleasant time here. Nevertheless, every joy has its corresponding sorrow. We here lost the bag containing our *cheese* and *bacon*. How it disappeared is, and probably always will be, a mystery. There are many hounds about the premises; this may furnish a key to the investigator.* The keeper of the toll-house is a rich character, a regular *Paddy*, full of fun and humor.

About 4:30 P.M. started for Mariposa, twelve miles distant. Enjoyed greatly the evening ride. Passed through the decayed, almost deserted, village of Princeton. Witnessed a magnificent sunset; brilliant golden above among the distant clouds; nearer clouds purple, shading insensibly through crimson and gold into the insufferable blaze of the sun itself. Camped near an inn, where we could buy feed for our horses, one and one-half miles from Mariposa. Unfortunately, no straw bank here, but we must lie on the hard, very hard, ground. Our bacon and cheese being lost, it is fortunate that we killed to-day several rabbits, quails, doves, etc., which we enjoyed at supper.

July 27.

After a refreshing night's rest and a hearty breakfast, we started at 6:30 A.M., and created some excitement in the town of Mariposa, by riding through the streets in double file, military-fashion, and under word of command. The Captain was in his glory, and his horse seemed to snuff the battle. Dismounted at grocery store and bought supplies. Mariposa is now greatly reduced in population and importance. It contains from five to six hundred inhabitants, but at one time two or three times that number. The same decrease is observable in all the mining towns of California. Noticed many pleasant evidences of civilization: church spires, water-carts, fire-proof stores, etc.

----

*Just two years after this event I again with a party passed over this road and camped overnight at this place. The hounds were still there, and we again lost our bacon. This is an additional fact in favor of the *hound theory*.

After about an hour's detention in Mariposa, we rode on. A little
way out of town, we stopped to examine a quartz mill. It is about
forty horse-power. In the narrow, confined valleys of the foot-hills,
the air is comparatively still, and the heat and dust is very great.
Both horses and men very much worried by a march, this morning,
of only fourteen miles. I have felt the ride much more to-day than
yesterday. Stopped for noon meal at De Long's (near White &
Hatch) half-way house from Mariposa to Clark's.

In order to avoid the heavy toll on the finely graded road to
Clark's, we determined to take the very rough and steep trail over
the Chowchilla Mountain, which now rose before us. My advice was
to start at 3 P.M., for I still remembered Laddsville and the stage station, but the rest of the party thought the heat too great. The event
proved I was right. Started 4:30 P.M. We found the trail much more
difficult than we expected (we had not yet much experience in
mountain trails). It seemed to pass directly up the mountain, without
much regard to angle of declivity. In order to relieve our horses, we
walked much of the way. Two of the party, Linderman and Cobb,
stopped to refresh themselves at a deliciously cool spring. We gave
them minute directions concerning the trail, and proceeded. We saw
no more of them. The trail passes directly over the crest of the
mountains, and down on the other side. Night overtook us when
about half down. No moon; only starlight. The magnificent forests of
this region, consisting of sugar pines, yellow pines and Douglass firs
(some of the first eight to ten feet in diameter, and two hundred and
fifty feet high) — grand, glorious by daylight; still grander and more
glorious in the deepening shades of twilight; grandest of all by night
— increased the darkness so greatly that it was impossible to see the
trail. We gave the horses the reins, and let them go. Although in
serious danger of missing footing, I could not but enjoy the night
ride through those magnificent forests. These grand old trunks stand

17

like giant sentinels about us. Were it not for our horses, I would gladly camp here in the glorious forest. But our tired horses must be fed. Down, down, winding back and forth; still down, down, down, until my back ached and my feet burned with the constant pressure on the stirrups. Still down, down, down. Is there no end? Have we not missed the trail? No Clark's yet. Down, down, down. Thus minute after minute, and, it seemed to us, hour after hour, passed away. At last the advanced guard, Hawkins, gave the Indian yell: See lights! lights! The whole company united in one shout of joy. When we arrived it was near 10 P.M. It being so late, we did not cook supper, but took supper at Clark's. Supper over, we turned our horses into Clark's meadow; selected our camp ground, in a magnificent grove of pines one hundred and fifty to two hundred feet high; rolled ourselves in our blankets, and slept, with the mournful sighing of the pines as our lullaby.

We have felt some anxiety on account of the young men we left on the trail. After arriving at Clark's we shot off our guns and pistols, to attract their attention, thinking they might be lost on the mountains. We hope they will come in to-morrow. We killed another large rattlesnake, to-day, on the Chowchilla trail.

———

July 28.

The missing men, Linderman and Cobb, came in this morning about 10 A.M. They had missed the trail; wandered over the mountains; reached a mountaineer's hut; been cordially received; slept over night, and been directed on their road to Clark's, this morning. Our party is complete again. Our trip, thus far, has been one of hardship without reward. It has been mere endurance, in the hope of enjoyment. Some enjoyment, it is true—our camps, our morning and evening rides, our jokes, etc.—but nothing in comparison with the dust, and heat, and fatigue. From this time we expect to commence the real enjoyment. We are delightfully situated here, at Clark's; fine pasture for horses; magnificent grove of tall pines for camp; fine river—South Fork of Merced—to swim in; delightful air. We determined to stop here two days; one for rest and clothes-washing, and one for visiting the Big Trees. I have been sufficiently long with the party to become well acquainted with all. I have nothing to do, to-day, except to wash my clothes. I cannot have a better opportunity to describe our party. I do it very briefly.

We are ten in number. Each man is dressed in strong trowsers, heavy boots or shoes, and loose flannel shirt; a belt, with pistol and butcher knife, about the waist; and a broad-brimmed hat. All other personal effects (and these are made as few as possible), are rolled up in a pair of blankets, and securely strapped behind his saddle. Thus accoutred, we make a formidable appearance, and are taken, sometimes for a troop of soldiers, but more often for a band of cattle or horse-drovers. Our camp utensils consist of two large pans, to mix bread; a camp-kettle, a teapot, a dozen tin plates, and ten tin cups; and most important of all, two or three frying-pans. The necessary provisions are bacon, flour, sugar, tea. Whenever we could, we bought small quantities of butter, cheese, fresh meat, potatoes, etc. Before leaving Oakland we organized thoroughly, by electing Soulé as our Captain, and Hawkins his Lieutenant, and promised implicit obedience. This promise was strictly carried out. All important matters, however, such as our route, how long we should stay at any place, etc., was decided by vote, the Captain preferring to forego the exercise of authority in such matters.

The names and descriptions of the members of the party are as follows:

1. *Capt. Frank Soulé.* Strong, well-formed, and straight, with clear-cut features and handsome face. Mounted on a tall, raw-boned,

high-stepping, dapple-gray, with a high head, a high spirit and fine action, he presents a striking appearance. He evidently feels his rank, and so does his horse. As to the latter:

> "We shall not need to say what lack
> Of leather was on his back,
> For that was hidden under pad,
> And breech of Knight, galled full as bad."

    2. *Lieut. Leander Hawkins*. Strong, thick-set, almost herculean in build. Mounted on a fierce, vicious, Indian pony, as wild as a deer, which he rides with a rope around his nose, instead of a bridle, and a blind across the forehead, which may be slipped over the eyes at a moment's notice, he is evidently a most fearless rider and horse-breaker. He is, besides, thoroughly acquainted with camp life and mountain life. He is, therefore, the most indispensable man in the party. At first he did everything; but he has gradually taught us the mysteries of cooking, dishwashing, and, above all, packing a horse. He is also treasurer and commissary, and always rides ahead, to-ward evening, and selects camp ground. Generous almost to a fault, he is ever ready to help every one, and really does more work than any three in the party.

    3. *Myself*. Long and lean, and lantern-jawed, and in search of romantic adventure, I was sometimes called by Linderman, but very secretly, "Don Quixote." I accept the nick-name with pleasure, per-haps with pride. I have a great respect for the old Don. There was nothing remarkable about my horse. A strong, tough, well-made gray, both gentle and careful, he was admirably suited for my pur-poses. My function in the party was that of surgeon and scientific lecturer.

    4. *Everett B. Pomroy*. Short, strong, compact, muscular, with high roman nose, close-cropped hair, and coarse top-boots; very erect,

somewhat grandiose in appearance and stilted in language. He is called "Our Poet." He is "A chiel amang us, takin' notes, and faith he'll prent it." He is mounted on a large, mud-colored mustang, with a broad, flat head, deep-sunk, vicious eyes, and a sprung knee. He stumbles fearfully, and bucks whenever he can, but is a tough, serviceable beast, nevertheless. We call him "Old 67," from a brand on his thigh. Pomroy sits a-stride of this ill-favored, hobbling beast, majestic and solemn, like Jupiter Tonans, shorn of his ambrosial locks.

5. *Dell Linderman.* Full of wit and infinite humor, quick and unfailing at repartee, with a merry twinkle in his eye, and a humorous, reddish knob on the end of his nose. We call him "Our Jester." He keeps our table in a roar. All the nicknames of men and horses are of his invention. His own horse is a very stout, logy mare, with a very rough gait. He calls her "Dolly Ann, the Scabgrinder." A gun, slung over his shoulder, completes his equipment.

6. *George Cobb.* Full of life and spirit, mercurial in temperament, with small, merry, coal-black eyes, and mouth always laughing and always chattering; he rides a neat, trim, round, frisky little mare, which seems well suited to him. He carries a splendid repeating rifle, with which he often shoots at *marks.* He is not known to have hit any living thing. He wears, also, neat strapped leggings. He is the fancy man and amateur sportsman of the party.

7. *Jack Bolton.* Dark, grave, quiet; he rides a strong-boned, steady-going, grave-looking horse, of excellent gait and qualities.

8. *Charles Phelps.* Slender, long-limbed, loose-jointed, gothic in structure of body and features, Linderman calls him "Kangaroo." His horse is a thin, slender-limbed, weak-looking mare, which, in walking, wobbles its hinder parts in a serpentine manner. On each side of his unsteady beast Phelps' long legs dangle in a helpless manner.

9. *Charles Stone.* Tall, erect; very long, curved nose; very long,

straight legs, and very high hips. Linderman calls him sometimes "Crow," from his nose, and sometimes "Tongs," from his legs. His horse is a pinto iron-gray, with whitish, imbecile-looking eyes, head down, nose stuck forward, and a straddling, cow-like action of his hind legs in trotting. A tough, serviceable beast, withal, except that it is impossible to sinch a saddle on his cow-like form so tightly that it will not slip on his neck in going down hill. Linderman calls him "Samson Nipper;" why, I cannot tell; but the name seems to us all very expressive.

10. *Jim Perkins.* A neat, trim figure, both active and strong; a fine face, with well-chiselled features; quiet, unobtrusive, gentlemanly. He was mounted on a compact, well-built horse, of excellent gait and qualities.

11. Last, but not least, is *"Old Pack,"* as we call our pack-horse. A mild-eyed, patient, much-enduring beast, steady and careful, with every quality befitting a pack-horse. We all conceived a great affection for him.

Our party was divided into three squads of three each, leaving out Hawkins, as he helped everybody, and had more duties of his own than any of the rest. Each squad of three was on duty three days, and divided the duties of *cook, dish-washer,* and *pack* among themselves. On arriving at our camp ground, each man unsaddled and picketed his horse with a long lariat rope, carried on the horn of his saddle for this purpose. In addition to this, whoever attended to the pack-horse that day, unpacked him, laid the bags ready for the cook, and picketed the pack-horse. The cook then built a fire, (frequently several helping, for more expedition), brought water, and commenced mixing dough and baking bread. This was a serious operation, to make bread for ten, and bake in two frying pans. First, the flour in a big pan; then yeast powder; then salt; then mix dry; then mix with water to dough; then bake quickly; then set up before the fire to keep hot. Then use frying pans for meat, etc. In the mean-time, the *dish-wash* must assist the cook by drawing tea. Our first attempts at making bread were lamentable failures. We soon found that the way to make bread was to bake from the top as well as the bottom; in fact, we often baked entirely from the top, turning over by flipping it up in the frying pan, and catching it on the other side. Bake them as follows: spread out the dough to fill the frying pan, one-half inch thick, using a round stick for rolling pin and the bottom of bread pan for biscuit board; set up the pan, at a steep incline, before the fire, by means of a stick. It is better, also, to put a few coals beneath; but this is not absolutely necessary.* It is the duty, now, of the *"dish-wash"* to set the table. For this purpose a piece of Brussels carpet (used during the day to put under the pack-saddle, but not next to the horse) is spread on the ground, and the plates and cups are arranged around. The meal is then served, and each man sits on the ground and uses his own belt knife, and fork, if he has any. After supper we smoke, while Dish-wash washes up the dishes; then we converse or sing, as the spirit moves us, and then roll ourselves in our blankets, only taking off our shoes, and sleep. Sometimes we gather pine straw, leaves, or boughs, to make the ground a little less hard. In the morning, Cook and Dish-wash get up early, make the fire, and commence the cooking. The rest get up a little later, in time to wash, brush hair, teeth, etc., before breakfast. We usually finish breakfast by 6 A.M. After breakfast, again wash up dishes, and put away things, and deliver them to Pack, whose duty it is, then, to pack the pack-horse, and lead it during the day. We could travel much faster but for the pack. The pack-horse must go almost entirely in a walk; otherwise his pack is shaken to pieces, and his back is chafed, and we only lose time in stopping and re-

---

* This account of bread-making anticipates a little. At this time we had not yet learned to make it palatable.

packing. By organizing thoroughly, dividing the duties and alternating, our party gets along in the pleasantest and most harmonious manner. After this description, I think what follows will be understood without difficulty.

Soon after breakfast this morning, Profs. Church and Kendrick, of West Point, called at our camp to see Soulé and myself. Soulé had been under their tuition, and afterwards an assistant teacher at West Point. I found them very hearty and cordial in manner, very gentlemanly in spirit, polished and urbane, and, of course, very intelligent. I was really much delighted with them. They had just returned from Yosemite, and are enthusiastic in their admiration of its wonders. They are going to the Big Trees to-day, and return to San Francisco to-morrow. These gentlemen, of course, are not taking it in the rough way as we are. They are dressed cap-a-pie, and look like civilized gentlemen. They seem to admire our rough garb, and we are not at all ashamed of it.

About ten o'clock we all went down to the river, provided with soap, and washed underflannels, stockings, handkerchiefs, towels, etc. It was really a comical scene. I wish our friends in Oakland could have taken a peep. The whole party squatting on the rocks on the margin of the river, soaping, and scrubbing, and wringing, and hanging out. After clothes-washing we took a swim in the river; then returned to camp, wrote letters home, and ate dinner.

In the afternoon, Profs. Church and Kendrick again called at our camp and bade us good-bye. While preparing and eating our supper, two ladies from Oakland, now staying at Clark's, friends of Phelps and Hawkins, called at our camp-fire and were introduced. They seemed much amused at our rough appearance, our rude mode of eating, and the somewhat rude manners of the young men towards each other. Their little petticoated forms, so clean and white; their gentle manners; and, above all, their sweet, smooth, womanly faces, contrasted, oh! how pleasantly, with our own rough, bearded, forked appearance. They tasted some of our bread, and pronounced it excellent. Ah, the sweet, flattering, deceitful sex! It was really execrable stuff; we had not yet learned to make it palatable.

July 29.

Started for the Big Trees at 7 A.M. Five of the party walked, and five rode. I preferred riding, and I had no cause to regret it. The trail was very rough, and almost the whole way up-mountain; the distance about six miles, and around the grove two miles, making fourteen miles in all. The walkers were very much heated and fatigued, and drank too freely of the ice-cold water of the springs. The abundance and excessive coldness of the water seem closely connected with the occurrence of these trees.

My first impressions of the Big Trees were somewhat disappointing, but, as I passed from one to another; as, with upturned face, I looked along their straight, polished shafts, towering to the height of three hundred feet; as I climbed up the sides of their prostrate trunks, and stepped from end to end; as I rode around the standing trees and into their enormous hollows; as we rode through the hollows of some of these prostrate trunks, and even chased one another on horseback through these enormous, hollow cylinders, a sense of their immensity grew upon me. If they stood by themselves on a plain, they would be more immediately striking. But they are giants among giants. The whole forest is filled with magnificent trees, sugar pines, yellow pines, and spruce, eight to ten feet in diameter, and two hundred to two hundred and fifty feet high. The sugar pine, especially, is a magnificent tree in size, height, and symmetry of form.

Of all the big trees of this grove, and, therefore, of all the trees I have ever seen, the Grizzly Giant impressed me most profoundly;

not, indeed, by its tallness, or its symmetry, but by the hugeness of its cylindrical trunk, and by a certain gnarled grandeur, a fibrous, sinewy strength, which seems to defy time itself. The others, with their smooth, straight, tapering shafts, towering to the height of three hundred feet, seemed to me the type of youthful vigor and beauty in the plentitude of power and success. But *this*, with its large, rough, knobbed, battered trunk, more than thirty feet in diameter—with top broken off and decayed at the height of one hundred and fifty feet—with its great limbs, six to eight feet in diameter, twisted and broken—seemed to me the type of a great life, decaying, but still strong and self-reliant. Perhaps my own bald head and grizzled locks—my own top, with its decaying foliage—made me sympathize with this grizzled giant; but I found the Captain, too, standing with hat in hand, and gazing in silent, bare-headed reverence upon the grand old tree.

We lunched at the Big Trees, rested, examined them three or four hours, and then returned to camp. Then went down to the creek, and enjoyed a delicious swimming bath. On the way back to camp, stopped at Clark's, and became acquainted with President Hopkins and his family. He goes to Yosemite to-morrow. We will see him again. After supper, the young men, sitting under the tall pines, sang in chorus. The two ladies already spoken of, hearing the music, came down to our camp, sat on the ground, and joined in the song. Cobb's noisy tenor, fuller of spirit than music; Pomroy's bellowing baritone, and, especially, Stone's deep, rich, really fine bass, harmonized very pleasantly with the thin clearness of the feminine voices. I really enjoyed the song and the scene very greatly. Women's faces and women's voices, after our rough life, and contrasted with our rough forms—ah! how delightful. About 9:30 P.M. they left, and we all turned in for the night. For an hour I lay upon my back, gazing upwards through the tall pines into the dark, starry sky, which seemed almost to rest on their tops, and listening to the solemn murmurings of their leaves, which, in the silent night, seemed like the whisperings of spirits of the air above me.

July 30.

Got up at 4 A.M. My turn to play cook. But cooking for ten hungry men, in two frying pans, is no play. It requires both time and patience. We did not get off until 7 A.M. Captain not very well to-day—too much violent exercise and ice-cold water yesterday. Another bucking farce this morning. Captain's horse, it seems, has more style and spirit than bottom. He has become badly galled, and has been a constant source of annoyance to the Captain, since we left. He therefore concluded to leave his horse here at Clark's, to "heal him of his grievous wounds," and hire a mule, at least while we remain at Yosemite. He no sooner mounted than the mule started off in the contrary direction, kicking and plunging and jumping stiff-legged, until he threw off—not the Captain, indeed, but the pack behind the saddle.

After some delay, however, we started off fairly. No more roads hereafter; only steep, rough, mountain trails. We are heartily glad, for we have no dust. Pres. Hopkins and party started off with us. His party consisted of himself, wife, son, and several other ladies and gentlemen, and a guide, numbering in all eight. Our party numbered ten and pack. Together, we made a formidable cavalcade. The young men were in high spirits. They sang, and hallooed, and cracked jokes the whole way. Rode twelve miles, up-hill nearly all the way, and camped for noon at Westfall's Meadows, over 7,000 feet above sea level. Hopkins' party went on a mile or two, to Paragoy's, (the half-way-house to Yosemite,) to lunch. In this party is a short, stout, round-faced, laughing-eyed, rather pretty, young woman, in very short bloomer costume, which shows a considerable portion of two very fat legs. Her bloomer makes her look still more squat; and to make things worse, she cannot forego the fashionable bunch of knots, and bows, and ribbons, on or below the waist, behind. Altogether, she was an amusing figure. Our young men called her "Miss Bloomer." The Captain, I think, is struck, but he worships, as yet, only at a distance.

In the afternoon we pushed on, to get our first view of Yosemite this evening, from Sentinel Dome and Glacier Point. Passing Paragoy's, I saw a rough-looking man standing in an open place, with easel on thumb, and canvas before him, alternately gazing on the fine mountain view and painting. "Hello! Mr. Tracy, glad to see you." "Why, Doctor, how do you do? where are you going?" "Yosemite, the High Sierras, Lake Mono, and Lake Tahoe." "Ah! how I wish I could go with you." After a few such pleasant words of greeting and inquiry, I galloped on, and overtook our party on the trail to Glacier Point. About 5 P.M. we passed a high pile of rocks, called Ostrander's Rocks. The whole trail, from Westfall's Meadows to Glacier Point, is near eight thousand feet high. From this rocky prominence, therefore, the view is really magnificent. It was our first view of the Peaks and Domes about Yosemite, and of the more distant High Sierras, and we enjoyed it beyond expression. But there are still finer views ahead, which we must see this afternoon – yes, this very afternoon. With increasing enthusiasm we pushed on until, about 6 P.M., we reached and climbed Sentinel Dome. This point is four thousand five hundred feet above Yosemite Valley, and eight thousand five hundred feet above the sea. The view which here burst upon us, of the Valley and the Sierras, it is simply impossible to describe. Sentinel Dome stands on the south margin of Yosemite, near the point where it branches into three cañons. To the left, stands El Capitan's massive, perpendicular wall; directly in front, and distant about one mile, Yosemite Falls, like a gauzy veil, rippling and waving with a slow, mazy motion; to the right, the mighty granite mass of Half Dome lifts itself in solitary grandeur, defying the efforts of the climber; to the extreme right, and a little behind, Nevada Falls, with the cap of Liberty; in the distance, innumerable peaks of the High Sierras, conspicuous among which are Cloud's Rest, Mt. Starr King, Cathedral Peak, etc. We remained on the top of this Dome more than an hour, to see the sun set. We were well repaid—such a sunset I never saw; such a sunset, combined with such a view, I had never imagined. The gorgeous golden and crimson in the west, and the exquisitely delicate, diffused rose-bloom, tingeing the cloud caps of the Sierras in the east, and the shadows of the grand peaks and domes slowly creeping up the valley! I can never forget the impression. We remained, enjoying this scene, too long to think of going to Glacier Point this evening. We therefore put this off until morning, and returned on our trail about one and a half miles, to a beautiful green meadow, (Hawkins had chosen it on his way to Sentinel Dome), and there made camp in a grove of magnificent spruce trees *(Picea Grandis)*.

July 31, Sunday.

I got up at peep of day this morning, (I am dish-wash today), roused the party, started a fire, and in ten minutes tea was ready. All partook heartily of this delicious beverage, and started on foot to see the sun rise, from Glacier Point. This point is about one and a half miles from our camp, about three thousand two hundred feet above the valley, and forms the salient angle on the south side, just where the valley divides into three. We had to descend about eight hundred feet to reach it. We arrived just before sunrise. Sunrise from Glacier Point! No one can appreciate it who has not seen it. It was our good fortune to have an exceedingly beautiful sunrise. Rosy-fingered Aurora revealed herself to us, her votaries, more bright and charming and rosy than ever before. But the great charm was the view of the valley and surrounding peaks, in the fresh, cool morning hour, and in the rosy light of the rising sun; the bright, warm light on the mountain tops, and the cool shade in the valley. The shadow of the grand Half Dome stretches clear across the valley, while its own "bald, awful head" glitters in the early sunlight. To the right, Vernal and Nevada Falls, with their magnificent, overhanging peaks, in full view; while directly across, see the ever-rippling, ever-swaying, gauzy veil of the Yosemite Fall, reaching from top to bottom of the opposite cliff, two thousand six hundred feet. Below, at a depth of three thousand two hundred feet, the bottom of the valley lies like a garden. There, right under our noses, are the hotels, the orchards, the fields, the meadows (near one of these Hawkins even now selects our future camp), the forests, and through all the Merced River winds its apparently lazy, serpentine way. Yonder, up the Tenaya Cañon, nestling close under the shadow of Half Dome, lies Mirror Lake, fast asleep, her polished, black surface, not yet ruffled by the rising wind. I have heard and read much of this wonderful valley, but I can truly say, I had never imagined the grandeur of the reality.

After about one and a half hours' rapturous gaze, we returned to camp and breakfasted. I had left Glacier Point a few minutes before most of the party, as I was dish-wash, and had, therefore, to help cook prepare breakfast. At breakfast I learned that two of the young men, Cobb and Perkins, had undertaken the foolish enterprise of going down into the valley by a cañon just below Glacier Point, and returning by 4 P.M. Think of it! three thousand three hundred feet perpendicular, and the declivity, it seemed to me, about forty-five degrees in the cañon.

After breakfast we returned to Glacier Point, and spent the

whole of the beautiful Sunday morning in the presence of grand
mountains, yawning chasms and magnificent falls. What could we
do better than allow these to preach to us? Was there ever so venerable, majestic, and eloquent a minister of natural religion as the
grand old Half Dome? I withdrew myself from the rest of the party
and drank in his silent teachings for several hours. About 1 P.M.
climbed Cathedral Dome and enjoyed again the matchless panoramic view from this point, and about 2 P.M. returned to camp.

Our camp is itself about four thousand feet above the valley, and
eight thousand above sea level. By walking about one hundred yards
from our camp fire, we get a most admirable view of the Sierras, and
particularly a most wonderfully striking view of the unique form of
Half Dome, when seen in profile. I enjoyed this view until nearly
time to saddle up.

Our plan is to return to Paragoy's, only seven miles, this afternoon, and go to Yosemite to-morrow morning. 3:30 P.M., and the
young men who went down into the valley have not yet returned.
We feel anxious. Will they return, or remain in the valley? Shall we
remain to-night and wait for them, or go on, leading their horses,
with the expectation of meeting them in the valley? We are to leave
at four; we must decide soon. These discussions were cut short by
the appearance of the delinquents themselves, faint with fatigue.
They had been down, taken dinner, and returned. We started immediately for Paragoy's, where we arrived 6 P.M., and camped in a
grove on the margin of a fine meadow. At Paragoy's we bought a
quarter of mountain mutton. We have been living on bacon and
bread for some time. The voracity with which we devoured that
mutton may be more easily imagined than described.

Ever since we have approached the region of the high Sierras,
I have observed the great massiveness and grandeur of the clouds,
and the extreme blueness of the sky. In the direction of the Sierras

hang always magnificent piles of snow-white cumulus, sharply defined against the deep blue sky. These cloud-masses have ever been my delight. I have missed them sadly since coming to California, until this trip. I now welcome them with joy. Yesterday and to-day I have seen, in many places, snow lying on the northern slopes of the high peaks of the Sierras.

August 1.

Yosemite to-day! Started as usual, 7 A.M. Pres. Hopkins and family go with us. They had stayed at Paragoy's over Sunday. I think we kept Sunday better. Glorious ride this morning, through the grand spruce forests. This is enjoyment, indeed. The trail is tolerably good until it reaches the edge of the Yosemite chasm. On the trail a little way below this edge there is a jutting point called "Inspiration Point," which gives a good general view of the lower end of the valley, including El Capitan, Cathedral Rock, and a glimpse of Bridal Veil Fall. After taking this view we commenced the descent into the valley. The trail winds backward and forward on the almost perpendicular sides of the cliff, making a descent of about three thousand feet in three miles. It was so steep and rough that we preferred walking most of the way and leading the horses. Poor old Mrs. Hopkins, though a heavy old lady, was afraid to ride, and therefore walked the whole way. At last, 10 A.M., we were down, and the gate of the valley is before us, El Capitan guarding it on the left, and Cathedral Rock on the right; while over the precipice on the right, the silvery gauze of Bridal Veil is seen swaying to and fro.

We encamped in a fine forest, on the margin of Bridal Veil Meadow, under the shadow of El Capitan, and about one-quarter of a mile from Bridal Veil Falls. Turned our horses loose to graze, cooked our midday meal, refreshed ourselves by swimming in the Merced, and then, 4:30 P.M., started to visit Bridal Veil. We had understood that this was the best time to see it. Very difficult clambering to the foot of the falls, up a steep incline, formed by a pile of huge boulders fallen from the cliff. The enchanting beauty and exquisite grace of this fall well repaid us for the toil. At the base of the fall there is a beautiful pool. Standing on the rocks, on the margin of this pool, right opposite the falls, a most perfect unbroken circular rainbow is visible. Sometimes it is a double circular rainbow. The cliff more than six hundred feet high; the wavy, billowy, gauzy veil, reaching from top to bottom; the glorious crown, woven by the sun for this beautiful veiled Bride. Those who read must put these together and form a picture for themselves, by the plastic power of the imagination.

Some of the young men took a swim in the pool and a shower bath under the fall. I would have joined them, but I had just come out of the Merced River. After enjoying this exquisite fall until after sunset, we returned to camp. On our way back, amongst the loose rocks on the stream margin, we found and killed another rattlesnake. This is the fourth we have killed.

Hawkins, the enterprising and indefatigable, has been, to-day, up to the hotel for supplies. He has returned, bringing among other things, a quarter of mutton and two pounds of butter. These, with a due amount of bread, etc., scarcely stayed our fierce appetites. After supper we lit cigarettes, gathered around the camp-fire, and conversed. Some question of the relative merits of novelists was started, and my opinion asked. By repeated questions I was led into quite a disquisition on art and literature, which lasted until bedtime. Before retiring, as usual, we piled huge logs on the camp fire; then rolled ourselves in our blankets, within reach of its warmth.

Forming part of the cliff, at the base of Bridal Veil Fall, I observed a remarkable mass of dark rock, like diorite, veined in the most complicated manner with whitish granite. In some places the granite predominates, and encloses isolated masses of diorite.

August 2.

Started this morning up the valley. As we go, the striking features of Yosemite pass in procession before us. On the left, El Capitan, Three Brothers, Yosemite Falls; on the right, Cathedral Rock, Cathedral Spires, Sentinel Rock. Cathedral Spires really strongly remind one of a huge cathedral, with two tall, equal spires, five hundred feet high, and several smaller ones. I was reminded of old Trinity, in Columbia. But *this* was not made with hands, and is over two thousand feet high. Stopped at Hutchings' and took lunch. Here I received letters from home. All well, thank God! Here again met Prof. Hopkins and party; also our friend Miss Bloomer greeted us merrily. Soulé seems deeply smitten, poor fellow! We here had our party photographed in costume. The photographer is none the best; but we hope the picture will be a pleasure to our friends in Oakland.

We first tried it on horseback, but found it impossible. We must be content to leave out these noble animals. Captain is secretly glad —he has left his high-stepping gray at Clark's, and now bestrides a sorry mule. Those ears, he thinks, don't look martial. Now, then, for a striking group!

As the most venerable of the party, my position was in the middle, and my bald head, glistening in the sunshine, was supposed to give dignity to the group. I was supported on either hand by Captain and Perkins, as the handsomest. Dignity supported by beauty — fitting union! Beyond these, on one side stood grave Bolton, in stiff attitude, with his hand resting on Hawkins' gun; while on the other, Linderman, with broad-brimmed hat thrown back, and chest thrown forward, and his gun strapped across his back, tried in vain to make his humorous face look fierce. On the extreme wings Cobb, with his inevitable rifle, and Phelps, with his loose-jointed legs, struck each a tragic attitude. In the foreground, at our feet, were placed the other three. Hawkins' burly bulk, in careless position, occupied the middle, while Pomroy gave solemnity to the left; and on the right, Stone, reclining on his elbow, gathered up his long legs to bring them, if possible, within the view of the great eye of the camera, and placed his broad-brim on his knee, in vain attempts to conceal "their utmost longitude." Far in the back-ground was the granite wall of Yosemite, and the wavy, white waters of the fall. The result is seen in the frontispiece.

In the afternoon went on up the valley, and again the grand procession commences. On the left, Royal Arches, Washington Column, North Dome; on the right, Sentinel Dome, Glacier Point, Half Dome. We pitched our camp in a magnificent forest, near a grassy meadow (the same Hawkins had selected from Glacier Point yesterday,) on the banks of Tenaya Fork, and under the shadow of our venerated preacher and friend, the Half Dome, with also North Dome, Washington Column, and Glacier Point in full view.

After unsaddling and turning loose our horses to graze, and resting a little, we went up the Tenaya Cañon about one-half mile, to Mirror Lake, and took a swimming bath. The scenery about this lake is truly magnificent. The cliffs of Yosemite here reach the acmé of imposing grandeur. On the south side the broad face of South Dome rises almost from the water, a sheer precipice near five thousand feet perpendicular; on the north side, North Dome, with its finely rounded head, to an almost equal height. Down the cañon, to the west, the view is blocked by the immense cliffs of Glacier Point and Washington Column; and up the cañon, to the east, the cliffs of the Tenaya Cañon, and Clouds' Rest, and the peaks of the Sierras in the background. On returning to camp, as we expected to remain here for several days, we carried with us a number of "shakes" (split boards,) and constructed a very good table, around which we placed logs for seats. We cooked our supper, sat around our rude board, and enjoyed our meal immensely. After supper, sat around our camp-fire, smoked our cigarettes, and sang in chorus until 9:30 P.M., then rolled ourselves, chrysalis-like, in our blanket cocoons, and lay still until morning.

Already I observe two very distinct kinds of structure in the granite of this region, which, singly or combined, determine all the forms about this wonderful valley. These two kinds of structure are the concentric structure, on an almost inconceivably grand scale; and a rude columnar structure, or perpendicular cleavage, also on a grand scale. The disintegration and exfoliation of the granite masses of the concentric structures gives rise to the bald, rounded domes; the structure itself is well seen on Sentinel Dome, and especially in the Royal Arches. The columnar structure, by disintegration, gives rise to Washington Column, and the sharp peaks, like Sentinel Rock and Cathedral Spires. Both these structures exist in the same granite, though the one or the other may predominate. In *all* the rocks about Yosemite there is a tendency to cleave perpendicularly. In addition to this, in many, there is also a tendency to cleave in concentric layers, giving rise to dome-like forms. Both are well seen combined in the grand mass of Half Dome. The perpendicular face-wall of this dome is the result of the perpendicular cleavage. Whatever may be our theory of the formation of Yosemite chasm and the perpendicularity of its cliffs, we must not leave out of view this tendency to perpendicular cleavage. I observe, too, that the granite here is very coarse-grained, and disintegrates into dust with great rapidity.

I observed, to-day, the curious straw and grass-covered stacks in which the Indians store and preserve their supplies of acorns.

August 3.

This has been to me a day of intense enjoyment. Started off this morning, with six others of the party, to visit Vernal and Nevada Falls. There are many Indians in the valley. We do not think it safe to leave our camp. We therefore divide our party every day, a portion keeping guard. Soulé, Phelps and Perkins were camp guard today. The Vernal and Nevada Falls are formed by the Merced River itself; the volume of water, therefore, is very considerable in all seasons. The surrounding scenery, too, is far finer, I think, than any other fall in the valley. The trail is steep and very rough, ascending nearly two thousand feet to the foot of Nevada Falls. To the foot of Vernal Falls, the trail passes through dense woods, close along the banks of the Merced, which here rushes down its steep channel, forming a series of rapids and cascades of enchanting beauty. We continued our way on horseback, until it seemed almost impossible for horses to go any farther; we then dismounted, unsaddled and hitched our horses, and proceeded on foot. We afterwards discovered that we had already gone over the worst part of the trail to the foot of Vernal Falls before we hitched; we should have continued on horse-back to the refreshment cabin at the foot of Vernal Falls. We arrived at the refreshment cabin very much heated, and took some refreshment before proceeding. Here we again saw the bright face, the laughing eyes and fat legs of Miss Bloomer, which were also a very great refreshment. Alas for Captain! he is not with us to-day.

The Vernal Falls is an absolutely perpendicular fall of four hundred feet, surrounded by the most glorious scenery imaginable. The exquisite greenness of the trees, the grass, and the moss, renders the name peculiarly appropriate. The top of the Falls is reached by step-ladder, which ascends the absolutely perpendicular face of the precipice. From the top the view is far grander than from below; for we take in the fall and the surrounding scenery at one view. An immense natural parapet of rock rises, breast-high, above the general surface of the cliff, near the fall. Here one can stand securely, leaning on the parapet, and enjoy the magnificent view. The river pitches, at our very feet, over a precipice four hundred feet high, into a narrow gorge, bounded on either side by cliffs such as are seen nowhere except in Yosemite, and completely blocked in front by the massive cliffs of Glacier Point, three thousand two hundred feet high; so that it actually seems to pitch into an amphitheatre, with rocky walls higher than its diameter. Oh! the glory of the view! The emerald green and snowy white of the falling water; the dizzying leap into the yawning chasm; the roar, and foam, and spray of the deadly struggle with rocks below; the deep green of the sombre pines, and the exquisite, fresh and lively green of grass, ferns and moss, wet with eternal spray; the perpendicular, rocky walls, rising far above us toward the blue, arching sky. As I stood there, gazing down into the dark and roaring chasm, and up into the clear sky, my heart swelled with gratitude to the Great Author of all beauty and grandeur.

After enjoying this view until we could spare no more time, we went on about one-half mile to the foot of Nevada Falls. Mr. Pomroy and myself mistook the trail and went up the left side of the river to the foot of the falls. To attain this point we had to cross two roaring cataracts, under circumstances of considerable danger, at least to any but those who possess steady nerves. We finally succeeded in clambering to the top of a huge boulder, twenty feet high, immediately in front of the falls, and only thirty or forty feet from it. Here, stunned by the roar, and blinded by the spray, we felt the full power and grandeur of the falls. From this place we saw, and greeted with Indian yell, our companions on the other side of the river. After remaining here an hour, we went a little down the stream and crossed to the other side, and again approached the fall. The view from this, the right side, is the one usually taken. It is certainly the

finest scenic view, but the power of falling water is felt more grandly
from the nearer view on the other side. The lover of intense ecstatic
emotion will prefer the latter; the lover of quiet scenic beauty will
prefer the former. The poet will seek inspiration in the one, and the
painter in the other.

The Nevada Falls is, I think, the grandest I have ever seen. The
fall is six hundred to seven hundred feet high. It is not an absolutely
perpendicular leap, like Vernal, but is all the grander on that account; as, by striking several ledges in its downward course, it is
beaten into a volume of snowy spray, ever-changing in form, and
impossible to describe. From the same cause, too, it has a slight, S-
like curve, which is exquisitely graceful. But the magnificence of the
Yosemite cascades, especially of Vernal and Nevada Falls, is due,
principally, to the accompanying scenery. See Mt. Broderick (Cap
of Liberty) and its fellow peak, rising perpendicular, tall and sharp,
until actually, (I speak without exaggeration,) the intense blue sky,
and masses of white clouds, seem to rest supported on their summits.
The actual height above the fall is, I believe, about two thousand feet.

About 3 P.M. started on our return. There is a beautiful pool,
about three hundred feet long and one hundred and fifty to two hundred feet wide, immediately above the Vernal Falls. Into this pool the
Merced River rushes as a foaming rapid, and leaves it only to precipitate itself over the precipice, as the Vernal Fall. The fury with which
the river rushes down a steep incline, into the pool, creates waves
like the sea. On returning, all of us who were good swimmers refreshed ourselves by swimming in this pool. I enjoyed the bath
immensely; swam across, played among the waves, contended with
the swift current, shouted and laughed like the veriest boy of them
all. The water was of course very cold, but we have become accustomed to this. On coming out of my bath, I took one final look over
the rocky parapet, over the fall, and into the yawning chasm below.

Returned to camp at 5 P.M., fresh and vigorous, and with a keen appetite for supper. After enjoying that most important meal, as usual, we gathered around our camp fire, sat on the ground, and the young men sang in chorus.

———

August 4.

This has been to me an uneventful day; I stayed in camp to-day as one of the camp-guard, while the camp-guard of yesterday visited the Vernal and Nevada Falls. I have lolled about camp, writing letters home, sewing on buttons, etc.; but most of the time in a sort of day-dream — a glorious day-dream in the presence of this grand nature. Ah! this free life in the presence of Great Nature, is indeed delightful. There is but one thing greater in this world; one thing after which, even under the shadow of this grand wall of rock, upon whose broad face and summit line projected against the clear blue sky with upturned face I now gaze; one thing after which even now I sigh with inexpressible longing, and that is Home and Love. A loving human heart is greater and nobler even than the grand scenery of Yosemite. In the midst of the grandest scenes of yesterday, while gazing alone upon the Falls and the stupendous surrounding cliffs, my heart filled with gratitude to God, and love to the dear ones at home; my eyes involuntarily overflowed, and my hands clasped in silent prayer.

In the afternoon we took our usual swim in the Mirror Lake; after which, of course, supper and bed.

———

August 5.

To-day to Yosemite Falls. This has been the hardest day's experience yet. We thought we had plenty of time, and therefore started late. Stopped a moment at the foot of the Falls, at a saw-mill, to make inquiries. Here found a man in rough miller's garb, whose intelligent face and earnest, clear blue eye, excited my interest. After some conversation, discovered that it was Mr. Muir, a gentleman of whom I had heard much from Mrs. Prof. Carr and others. He had also received a letter from Mrs. Carr, concerning our party, and was looking for us. We were glad to meet each other. I urged him to go with us to Mono, and he seemed disposed to do so.

We first visited the foot of the lower fall, which is about four hundred feet perpendicular, and after enjoying it for a half hour or more, returned to the mill. It was now nearly noon. Impossible to undertake the difficult ascent to the upper fall without lunch; I therefore jumped on the first horse I could find, (mine was unsaddled), and rode to Mr. Hutchings' and took a hearty lunch, to which Mr. Hutchings insisted upon adding a glass of generous California wine. On returning, found the rest of the party at the mill. On learning my good fortune, they also went and took lunch.

We now commenced the ascent. We first clambered up a mere pile of loose debris (talus), four hundred feet high, and inclined at least 45° to 50°. We had to keep near to one another, for the boulders were constantly loosened by the foot, and went bounding down the incline until they reached the bottom. Heated and panting, we reached the top of the lower fall, drank, and plunged our heads in the foaming water until thoroughly refreshed. After remaining here nearly an hour, we commenced the ascent to the foot of the upper fall. Here the clambering was the most difficult and precarious I have ever tried; sometimes climbing up perpendicular rock faces, taking advantage of cracks and clinging bushes; sometimes along joint-cracks, on the dizzy edge of fearful precipices; sometimes over rock faces so smooth and highly inclined, that we were obliged to go on hands and knees. In many places a false step would be fatal. There was no trail at all; only piles of stones here and there, to mark the best route. But when at last we arrived, we were amply repaid for our labor. Imagine a sheer cliff, sixteen hundred feet high, and a stream pouring over it. Actually, the water seems to fall out of the very sky itself. As I gaze upwards now, there are wisps of snowy cloud just on the verge of the precipice above; the white spray of the washing cataract hangs, also, apparently almost motionless on the same verge. It is difficult to distinguish wisps of spray from wisps of cloud. So long a column of water and spray is swayed from side to side by the wind; and, also, as in all falls, the resistance of the rocks at the top, and of the air in the whole descent, produces a billowy motion. The combination of these two motions, both so conspicuous in this fall, is inexpressibly graceful. When the column swayed far to the left, we ran by on the right, and got behind the fall, and stood gazing through the gauzy veil, upon the cliffs on the opposite side of the valley. At this season of the year the Yosemite Creek is much diminished in volume. It strikes slightly upon the face of the cliff, about midway up. In the spring and autumn, when the river is full, the fall must be grand indeed. It is then a clear leap of sixteen hundred feet, and the pool which it has hollowed out for itself, in the solid granite, is plainly visible twenty to thirty feet in advance of the place on which it now falls.

We met here, at the foot of the fall, a real typical specimen of a live Yankee. He has, he says, a panorama of Yosemite, which he expects to exhibit in the Eastern cities. It is evident that he is "doing" Yosemite only for the purpose of getting materials of lectures to accompany his exhibitions.

Coming down, in the afternoon, the fatigue was less, but the danger much greater. We were often compelled to slide down the face of rocks in a sitting posture, to the great detriment of the posterior portion of our pants. Reached bottom at half-past five P.M. Here learned from Mr. Muir that he would certainly go to Mono with us. We were much delighted to hear this. Mr. Muir is a gentleman of rare intelligence, of much knowledge of science, particularly of botany, which he has made a specialty. He has lived several years in the valley, and is thoroughly acquainted with the mountains in the vicinity. A man of so much intelligence tending a saw mill! —not for himself, but for Mr. Hutchings. This is California!

After arranging our time of departure from Yosemite with Mr. Muir, we rode back to camp. I enjoyed greatly the ride to camp, in the cool of the evening. The evening view of the valley was very fine, and changing at every step. Just before reaching our camp, there is a partial distant view of the Illilouette Falls—the only one I know of in the valley. Many of the party seem wearied this evening. For myself, I feel fresh and bright. We were all, however, sound asleep by 8 P.M.

[Our party did not visit the Illilouette Falls, but on a subsequent trip to Yosemite I did so. The following is a brief description, taken from my journal, which I introduce here in order to complete my account of the falls of this wondrous valley:

August 15, 1872

Started with Mr. Muir and my nephew Julian, to visit Illilouette Falls. Hearing that there was no trail, and that the climb is more difficult even than that to the Upper Yosemite, the rest of the party *backed out*. We rode up the Merced, on the Vernal Fall trail, to the junction of the Illilouette Fork. Here we secured our horses and proceeded on foot up the cañon. The rise, from this to the foot of the falls, is twelve hundred to fifteen hundred feet. The whole cañon is literally filled with huge rock fragments—often hundreds of tons in weight—brought down from the cliffs at the Falls. The scramble up the steep ascent over these boulders was extremely difficult and fatiguing. Oftentimes the creek bed was utterly impracticable, and we had to climb high up the sides of the gorge and down again. But we were gloriously repaid for our labor. There are beauties about this fall which are peculiar, and simply incomparable. It was to me a new experience, and a peculiar joy. The volume of water, when I saw it, was several times greater than either Yosemite or Bridal Veil. The stream plunges into a narrow chasm, bounded on three sides by perpendicular walls nearly one thousand feet high. The height of the fall is six hundred feet. Like Nevada, the fall is not absolutely per- pendicular, but strikes about half way down on the face of the cliff. But instead of striking on projecting ledges and being thus *beaten* into a great volume of foam, as in the latter, it *glides* over the some- what even surface of the rock, and is *woven* into the most exquisite lace-work, with edging fringe and pendent tassels, ever-changing and ever-delighting. It is simply impossible even to conceive, much less to describe, the exquisite delicacy and tantalizing beauty of the ever-changing forms. The effect produced is not tumultuous excite- ment, or ecstacy, like Nevada, but simple, pure, almost childish delight. Now as I sit on a great boulder, twenty feet high, right in front of the fall, see! the midday sun shoots its beams through the myriad water-drops which leap from the top of the cascade, as it strikes the edge of the cliff. As I gaze upwards, the glittering drops seem to pause a moment high in the air, and then descend like a glo- rious star-shower.]

August 6.

Slept late this morning. Some of the party stiff and sore; I am all right. The camp-guard of yesterday visited Yosemite Falls to-day, and we stayed in camp. Visited Mirror Lake this morning, to see the fine reflection of the surrounding cliffs in its unruffled waters, in the early morning. Took a swim in the lake; spent the rest of the morning washing clothes, writing letters, and picking and eating raspberries in Lamon's garden.

To a spectator the clothes-washing forms a very interesting scene. To see us all sitting down on the rocks, on the banks of the beautiful Tenaya River, scrubbing, and wringing, and hanging out! It reminds one of the exquisite washing scene of Princess Nausicaa and her damsels, or of Pharoah's daughter and her maids. Change the sex, and where is the inferiority in romantic interest in our case? Ah! *the sex!* yes, this makes all the difference between the ideal and common—between poetry and prose. If it were only seven beautiful women, in simple attire, and I, like Ulysses, a spectator just waked from sleep by their merry peals of laughter! But seven rough, bearded fellows! think of it! We looked about us, but found no little Moses in the bullrushes. So we must e'en take Mr. Muir and Hawkins to lead us through the wilderness of the high Sierras.

In the afternoon we moved camp to our previous camping ground at Bridal Veil meadow. We were really sorry to break up our camp on Tenaya Creek. We have had delightful times here. We called it *University Camp*. Soon after leaving camp, Soulé and myself, riding together, heard a hollow rumbling, then a crashing sound. "Is it thunder or earthquake?" Looking up quickly, the white streak down the cliff of Glacier Point, and the dust there, rising from the valley, revealed the fact that it was the falling of a huge rock mass from Glacier Point.

We rode down in the cool of the evening, and by moonlight.

Took leave of our friends *in* the valley—McKee and his party, Mr. and Mrs. Hutchings, Mrs. Yelverton, Miss Bloomer, (whom we again met, and with whom Captain exchanged photographs); sad leave of our friends, now dear friends, *of* the valley; the venerable and grand old South Dome under whose shadow we had camped so long; North Dome, Washington Column, Royal Arches, Glacier Point; then Yosemite Falls, Sentinel Rock, Three Brothers. By this time night had closed in, but the moon was near full, and the shadows of Cathedral Spires and Cathedral Rock lay across our path, while the grand rock mass of El Capitan shone gloriously white in the moonlight. The ride was really enchanting to all, but affected us differently. The young men rode ahead, singing in chorus. *I* lagged behind, and enjoyed it in silence. The choral music, mellowed by distance, seemed to harmonize with the scene, and to enhance its holy stillness.

About half-past 8 P.M. we encamped on the western side of Bridal Veil meadow. After supper we were in fine spirits, contended with each other in gymnastic exercises, etc. Then gathered hay, made a delightful, fragrant bed, and slept dreamlessly.

At Mr. Hutchings' I again received letters from home—very happy to know that they are well.

———

August 7, Sunday.

Got up late—6 A.M.—as is common everywhere on this day of rest. Now about to leave for Mono, Capt. must have his horse or he cannot accompany us. He only hired the mule while in Yosemite. Mr. Perkins volunteered to ride the mule back to Clark's and bring Captain's horse. He started very early this morning, and hopes to be back by bed-time.

About 11 A.M. took a quiet swim in the river; for we think a *clean
skin* is next in importance to a *pure heart.* During the rest of the morning I sat and enjoyed the fine view of the opening or gate of the valley, from the lower side of the meadow. There stands the grand old
El Capitan in massive majesty on the left, and Cathedral Rock and
the Veiled Bride on the right. I spent the morning with this scene
before me. While sitting here I again took out my little sewing case
and darned my pants, a little broken by my experiments in sliding,
day before yesterday. God bless the dear thoughtful one who provided me with this necessary article. God bless the little fingers
which arranged these needles and wound so neatly the thread. May
God's choicest blessings rest on the dear ones at home. May He, the
Infinite Love, keep them in health and happiness until I return.
Surely, absence from home is sometimes necessary to make us feel
the priceless value of loving hearts.

There is considerable breeze to-day; and now, while I write, the
Bride's veil is wafted from side to side, and sometimes lifted until I
can almost see the blushing face of the Bride herself—the beautiful
spirit of the Falls. But whose bride? Is it old El Capitan? Strength
and grandeur united with grace and beauty! Fitting union. But I,
too, thank God, have a bride—nay, much more and better—a tried
and faithful wife.

At 3 P.M. went again alone to the lower side of the meadow, and
sat down before the gate of the valley. From this point I look directly
through the gate and up the valley. There again, rising to the very
skies, stands the huge mass of El Capitan on one side, and on the
other the towering peak of the Cathedral, with the veiled Bride retiring a little back from the too ardent gaze of admiration; then the
cliffs of Yosemite, growing narrower and lower on each side, beyond.
Conspicuous, far in the distance, see! old South Dome and Cloud's
Rest. The sky is perfectly serene, except heavy masses of snow-
white cumulus, sharply defined against the deep blue of the sky,

filling the space beyond the gate. The wavy motion of the Bride's veil, as I gaze steadfastly upon it, drowses my sense; I sit in a kind of delicious dream, the scenery unconsciously mingling with my dream.

5 P.M. Went, all of us, this afternoon, to visit the Bride. Saw again the glorious crown set by the sun upon her beautiful head. Swam in the pool at her feet. Tried to get a peep beneath the veil but got pelted beyond endurance with water drops, by the little fairies which guard her beauty, for my sacreligious rudeness. Nevertheless, came back much exhilarated, and feeling more like a boy than I had felt for many, many years.

Perkins returned with Captain's horse, to supper.

8 P.M. After supper, went again alone into the meadow, to enjoy the moonlight view. The moon is long risen, and "near her highest noon," but not yet visible in this deep valley, although I am sitting on the extreme northern side. Cathedral Rock and the snowy veil of the Bride, and the whole right side of the cañon, is in deep shade, and its serried margin strongly relieved against the bright moonlit sky. On the other side are the cliffs of El Capitan, snow-white in the moonlight. Above all arched the deep black sky, studded with stars gazing quietly downward. Here, under the black arching sky and before the grand cliffs of Yosemite, I lifted my heart in humble worship to the great God of *Nature*. Yes, but also of *Grace*. In the midst of the overwhelming grandeur of nature, let me not forget this.

August 8.

To-day we leave Yosemite; we therefore get up very early, intending to make an early start. I go out again into the meadow, to take a final farewell view of Yosemite. The sun is just rising; wonderful, warm, transparent golden light, (like Bierstadt's picture), on El Capitan; the whole other side of the valley in deep, cool shade; the bald head of South Dome glistening in the distance. The scene is magnificent.

But see! just across the Merced River from our camp, a bare trickling of water from top to bottom of the perpendicular cliff. I have not thought it worth while to mention it before; but this is the Fall called the *Virgin's Tears*. Poor Virgin! She seems *passeé;* her cheeks are seamed, and channeled, and wrinkled; she wishes she was a Bride, too, and had a veil; so near El Capitan, too, but he will not look that way. I am sorry I have neglected to sing her praises.

We experienced some delay in getting off this morning. Our horses have feasted so long on this meadow that they seem disinclined to be caught. Pomroy's ill-favored beast, *Old 67,* gave us much trouble. He had to be lassooed at last. We forded the river immediately at our camp. Found it so deep and rough that several of the horses stumbled and fell down. We now took Coulterville trail; up, up, up, backward and forward, up, up, up the almost perpendicular side of the cañon below the gate. The trail often runs on a narrow ledge, along the almost perpendicular cliff. A stumble might precipitate both horse and rider one thousand feet, to the bottom of the chasm. But the horses know this as well as we. They are very careful. About the place where Mono trail turns sharp back from Coulterville trail, Mr. Muir overtook us. Without him we would have experienced considerable difficulty, for the trail being now little used, except by shepherds, is very rough, and so blind that it is almost impossible to find it, or having found, to keep it. My horse cast two of his shoes to-day. Yet I had examined them before leaving Yosemite, and found them all right.

Made about fourteen miles, and by 2 P.M. reached a meadow near the top of Three Brothers. Here we camped for the night in a most beautiful grove of spruce—*Picea Amabiles and Grandis;* chose our sleeping places; cut branches of spruce and made the most delightful elastic and aromatic beds, and spread our blankets in preparation for night. After dinner, lay down on our blankets, and gazed up through the magnificent tall spruces into the deep blue sky and the gathering masses of white clouds. Mr. Muir gazes and gazes, and cannot get his fill. He is a most passionate lover of nature. Plants, and flowers, and forests, and sky, and clouds, and mountains, seem actually to haunt his imagination. He seems to revel in the freedom of this life. I think he would pine away in a city or in conventional life of any kind. He is really not only an intelligent man, as I saw at once, but a man of strong, earnest nature, and thoughtful, closely observing and original mind. I have talked much with him to-day about the probable manner in which Yosemite was formed. He fully agrees with me that the peculiar cleavage of the rock is a most important point, which must not be left out of account. He farther believes that the valley has been wholly formed by causes still in operation in the Sierra—that the Merced Glacier and the Merced River and its branches, when we take into consideration the peculiar cleavage, and also the rapidity with which the fallen and falling boulders from the cliffs are disintegrated into dust, has done the whole work. The perpendicularity is the result of cleavage; the want of talus is the result of the rapidity of disintegration, and the recency of the disappearance of the glacier. I differ with him only in attributing far more to pre-glacial action. I may, I think, appropriately introduce here my observations on the evidence of glacial action in Yosemite.

It is well known that a glacier once came down the Tenaya Cañon. I will probably see abundant evidences of this high up this cañon, tomorrow and next day. That this glacier extended into the Yosemite has been disputed, but is almost certain. Mr. Muir also tells me that at the top of Nevada Falls there are unmistakable evidences (polishings and scorings) of a glacier. There is no doubt,

therefore, that anciently a glacier came down each of these cañons.
Did they meet and form a Yosemite glacier? From the projecting
rocky point which separates the Tenaya from Nevada cañon, there
is a pile of boulders and debris running out into the valley, near
Lamon's garden, like a continuation of the point. Mr. Muir thinks
this unmistakeably a central moraine, formed by the union of the
Tenaya and Nevada Glaciers. I did not examine it carefully. Again,
there are two lakes in the lower Tenaya Cañon, viz.: Mirror Lake
and a smaller lake lower down. Below Mirror Lake, and again
below the smaller lake, there is an immense heap of boulders and
rubbish. Are not these piles terminal moraines, and have not the
lakes been formed by the consequent damming of the waters of
the Tenaya? These lakes are filling up. It seems probable that the
meadow, also, on which we camped, has been formed in the same
way, by a moraine just below the meadow, marked by a pile of
debris there, also. Whether the succession of meadows in the Yosemite, of which the Bridal Veil meadow is the lowest, have been similarly formed, requires and really deserves further investigation. I
strongly incline to the belief that they have been, and that a glacier
once filled Yosemite. I observed other evidences, but I must visit
this valley again, and examine more carefully.

After discussing these high questions with Mr. Muir for some
time, we walked to the edge of the Yosemite chasm, and out on the
projecting point of Three Brothers, called Eagle Point. Here we had
our last, and certainly one of the most magnificent views of the valley and the high Sierras. I can only name the points which are in
view and leave the reader to fill out the picture. As we look up the
valley, to the near left is the Yosemite Falls, but not a very good
view; then Washington Column, North Dome; then grand old South
Dome. The view of this grand feature of Yosemite is here magnificent. It is seen in half profile. Its rounded head, its perpendicular
rock face, its towering height, and its massive proportions are well

seen. As the eye travels round to the right, next comes the Nevada Falls (Vernal is not seen); then in succession the peaks on the opposite side of the valley: Glacier Point, Sentinel Dome, Sentinel Rock, Cathedral Spires, and Cathedral Rock; then, crossing the valley, and behind us, is El Capitan. In the distance, the peaks of the Sierras, Mt. Hoffman, Cathedral Peak, Cloud's Rest, Mt. Starr King, Mt. Clark, and Ostranders Rocks are seen. Below, the whole valley, like a green carpet, and Merced River, like a beautiful vine, winding through. We remained and enjoyed the view by sunlight, by twilight, and by moonlight. We then built a huge fire, on the extreme summit. Instantly answering fires were built in almost every part of the valley. We shouted and received answer. We fired guns and pistols, and heard reports in return. I counted the time between flash and report, and found it 9-10 seconds. This would make the distance about two miles in an air line.

About 8 P.M. went back to camp and supper, and immediately after, to bed. During the night some of the horses, not having been staked, wandered away, and some of the party, Soulé, Hawkins, and Cobb, were out two hours, recovering them. They found them several miles on their way back to the fat pasture of Bridal Veil meadow. My own horse had been securely staked. On my fragrant, elastic bed of spruce boughs, and wrapped head and ears in my blankets, I knew nothing of all this until morning.

Coming out of the Yosemite to-day, Mr. Muir pointed out to me, and I examined, the Torreya. Fruit solitary, at extreme end of spray, nearly the color, shape, and size of a green-gage plum, and yet a conifer. The morphology of the fruit would be interesting.

August 9.

Got up at daybreak this morning, much refreshed. I am cook again to-day. My bread this morning was voted excellent. Indeed, it was as light and spongy as any bread I ever ate. About 12 M. we saw a shepherd's camp, and rode up in hopes of buying a sheep. No one at home, but there is much sheep meat hanging about and drying. As we came nearer, a delicious fragrance assailed our nostrils, and set our salivaries in action. "A premonitory moistening overflowed my nether lip." What could it be? Here is a pot nearly buried in the hot ashes, and closely covered. Wonder what is in it? Let us see. On removing the cover, a fragrant steam arose, which fairly over-came the scruples of several of the party. Mutton stew, deliciously seasoned! Mr. Muir, who had been a shepherd himself, and had attended sheep here last year, and became thoroughly acquainted with shepherds' habits, assured us that we might eat without com-punction—that the shepherd would be pleased rather than dis-pleased—that they had more mutton than they knew what to do with. Upon this assurance we fell to, for we were very hungry, and the stew quickly disappeared. We all declared, and will always believe, that there never was such mutton stew made in this world before. While we were yet wiping our moustaches (such as had that ornament) the shepherd appeared, and was highly amused and pleased at our extravagant praises of his stew. Our appetites were, however, not yet half appeased. We went on a little farther and stopped for noon at a small open meadow. While I was cooking din-ner, Hawkins bought and butchered a fat sheep. There are thou-sands of sheep in this region. We expect to live upon mutton until we cross the Sierras.

This afternoon we went on to Lake Tenaya. The trail is very blind, in most places detectible only by the blazing of trees, and very rough. We traveled most of the way on a high ridge. When about two miles of our destination, from the brow of the mountain ridge upon which we had been traveling, Lake Tenaya burst upon our delighted vision, its placid surface set like a gem amongst magnificent mountains, the most conspicuous of which are Mt. Hoffman group, on the left, and Cathedral Peak beyond the lake. From this point we descended to the margin of the lake, and encamped at 5 P.M. on the lower end of the lake, in a fine grove of tamaracks, near an extensive and beautiful meadow. We built an immense fire, and had a fine supper of excellent bread and delicious mutton. Our appetites were excellent; we ate up entirely one hind-quarter of mutton, and wanted more.

After supper, I went with Mr. Muir and sat on a high rock, jutting into the lake. It was full moon. I never saw a more delightful scene. This little lake, one mile long and a half mile wide, is actually embosomed in the mountains, being surrounded by rocky eminences two thousand feet high, of the most picturesque forms, which come down to the very water's edge. The deep stillness of the night; the silvery light and deep shadows of the mountains; the reflection on the water, broken into thousands of glittering points by the ruffled surface; the gentle lapping of the wavelets upon the rocky shore — all these seemed exquisitely harmonized with one another, and the grand harmony made answering music in our hearts. Gradually the lake surface became quiet and mirror-like, and the exquisite surrounding scenery was seen double. For an hour we remained sitting in silent enjoyment of this delicious scene, which we reluctantly left to go to bed. Tenaya Lake is about eight thousand feet above sea level. The night air, therefore, is very cool.

I noticed in many placés, to-day, especially as we approached Lake Tenaya, the polishings and scorings of ancient glaciers. In many places we found broad, flat masses, so polished that our horses could hardly maintain their footing in passing over them. It is wonderful that in granite so decomposable these old glacial surfaces

should remain as fresh as the day they were left by the glacier. But if
ever the polished surface scales off, then the disintegration proceeds
as usual. The destruction of these surfaces by scaling is, in fact, con-
tinually going on. Whitney thinks the polished surface is hardened
by pressure of the glacier. I cannot think so. The smoothing, I think,
prevents the retention of water, and thus prevents the rotting. Like
the rusting of iron, which is hastened by roughness, and still more
by rust, and retarded or even prevented by cleaning and polishing,
so rotting of rock is hastened by roughness, and still more by commencing to rot, and retarded or prevented by grinding down to the
sound rock and then polishing.

To-day, while cooking midday meal, the wind was high, and the
fire furious. I singed my whiskers and moustache, and badly burned
my hand with boiling-hot bacon fat.

August 10.

Early start this morning for Soda Springs and Mt. Dana. Phelps
and his mare entertained us awhile, getting off this morning, with an
amusing bucking scene. The interesting performance ended with the
grand climacteric feat of flying head foremost over the head of the
horse, turning a somersault in the air, and alighting safely on the
back. After this exhilarating diversion, we proceeded on our way,
following the trail on the right hand of the lake. Onward we go, in
single file, I leading the pack, over the roughest and most precipitous trail (if trail it can be called), I ever saw. At one moment we
lean forward, holding to the horse's mane, until our noses are
between the horse's ears; at the next, we stand in the stirrups, with
our backs leaning hard against the roll of blankets behind the saddle. Thus we pass, dividing our attention between the difficulties of

the way and the magnificence of the scenery, until 12 M., when we reached Soda Springs, in the splendid meadows of the Upper Tuolumne River.

Our trail this morning has been up the Tenaya Cañon, over the divide, and into the Tuolumne Valley. There is abundant evidence of an immense former glacier, coming from Mt. Dana and Mt. Lyell group, filling the Tuolumne Valley, overrunning the divide, and sending a branch down the Tenaya Cañon. The rocks in and about Tenaya Cañon are everywhere scored and polished. We had to dismount and lead over some of these polished surfaces. The horses' feet slipped and sprawled in every direction, but none fell. A conspicuous feature of the scenery on Lake Tenaya is a granite knob, eight hundred feet high, at the upper end of the lake and in the middle of the cañon. This knob is bare, destitute of vegetation, round and polished to the very top. It has evidently been enveloped in the icy mass, and its shape has been determined by it. We observed similar scorings and polishings on the sides of the cañon, to an equal and much greater height. Splendid view of the double peaks of the Cathedral, from Tenaya Lake and from the trail. Looking back from the trail soon after leaving the lake, we saw a conspicuous and very picturesque peak, with a vast amphitheatre, with precipitous sides, to the north, filled with a grand mass of snow, evidently the fountain of an ancient tributary of the Tenaya Glacier. We call this *Coliseum Peak*. So let it be called hereafter, to the end of time.

The Tuolumne meadow is a beautiful grassy plain of great extent, thickly enameled with flowers, and surrounded with the most magnificent scenery. Conspicuous amongst the hundreds of peaks visible are Mt. Dana, with its grand symmetrical outline, and purplish red color; Mt. Gibbs, of gray granite; Mt. Lyell and its group of peaks, upon which great masses of snow still lie; and the wonderfully picturesque group of sharp, inaccessible peaks (viz.: Unicorn Peak, Cathedral Peaks, etc.), forming the Cathedral group.

Soda Springs is situated on the northern margin of the Tuolumne meadow. It consists of several springs of ice cold water, bubbling up from the top of a low reddish mound. Each spring itself issues from the top of a small subordinate mound. The mound consists of carbonate of lime, colored with iron deposited from the water. The water, contains principally, carbonates of lime and iron, dissolved in excess of carbonic acid, which escapes in large quantities, in bubbles. It possibly, also, contains carbonate of soda. It is very pungent, and delightful to the taste. Before dinner we took a swim in the ice cold water of the Tuolumne River.

About 3 P.M. commenced saddling up, intending to go on to Mt. Dana. Heavy clouds have been gathering for some time past. Low mutterings of thunder have also been heard. But we had already been so accustomed to the same, without rain, in the Yosemite, that we thought nothing of it. We had already saddled, and some had mounted, when the storm burst upon us. "Our provisions—sugar, tea, salt, flour, etc., must be kept dry!" shouted Hawkins. We hastily dismounted, constructed a sort of shed of blankets and india rubber cloths, and threw our provisions under it. Now commenced peal after peal of thunder in an almost continuous roar, and floods of rain. We all crept under the temporary shed, but not before we had gotten pretty well soaked. So much delayed that we were now debating—after the rain—whether we had not better remain here over night. Some were urgent for pushing on, others equally so for staying. Just at this juncture, when the debate ran high, a shout, "Hurrah!" turned all eyes in the same direction. Hawkins and Mr. Muir had scraped up the dry leaves underneath a huge prostrate tree, set fire and piled on fuel, and already, see! a glorious blaze! This incident decided the question at once. With a shout, we all ran for fuel, and piled on log after log, until the blaze rose twenty feet high. Before, shivering, crouching, and miserable; now, joyous and gloriously happy.

The storm did not last more than an hour. After it, the sun came out and flooded all the landscape with liquid gold. I sat alone at some distance from the camp, and watched the successive changes of the scene—*first*, the blazing sunlight flooding meadow and mountain; then the golden light on mountain peaks, and then the lengthening shadows on the valley; then a roseate bloom diffused over sky and air, over mountain and meadow; Oh! how exquisite! I never saw the like before. Last, the creeping shadow of night, descending and enveloping all.

The Tuolumne meadows are celebrated for their fine pasturage. Some twelve to fifteen thousand sheep are now pastured here. They are divided into flocks of about two thousand five hundred to three thousand. I was greatly interested in watching the management of these flocks, each by means of a dog. The intelligence of the dog is perhaps nowhere more conspicuous. The sheep we bought yesterday is entirely gone—eaten up in one day. We bought another here, a fine, large, fat one. In an hour it was butchered, quartered, and a portion on the fire, cooking. After a very hearty supper, we hung up our blankets about our camp-fire, to dry, while we ourselves gathered around it to enjoy its delicious warmth. By request of the party, I gave a familiar lecture, or rather talk, on the subject of glaciers, and the glacial phenomena we had seen on the way.

LECTURE ON GLACIERS AND THE GLACIAL PHENOMENA OF THE SIERRAS.—(Abstract).

In certain countries, where the mountains rise into the region of perpetual snow, and where other conditions, especially abundant moisture, are present, we find enormous masses of *ice* occupying the valleys, extending far below the snow-cap, and slowly moving downward. Such moving icy extensions of the perpetual snow-cap are called *glaciers*.

It is easy to see that both the existence of glaciers and their downward motion is necessary to satisfy the demands of the great universal *Law of Circulation*. For in countries where glaciers exist, the amount of snow which falls on mountain tops is far greater than the waste of the same by melting and evaporation in the same region. The snow, therefore, would accumulate without limit if it did not move down to lower regions, where the excess is melted and returned again to the general circulation of meteoric waters.

In the Alps, glaciers are now found ten to fifteen miles long, one to three miles wide, and five hundred to six hundred feet thick. They often reach four thousand feet below the snow-level, and their rate of motion varies from a few inches to several feet per day. In grander mountains, such as the Himalayas and Andes, they are found of much greater size; while in Greenland and the Antarctic continent the whole surface of the country is completely covered, two thousand to three thousand feet deep, with an *ice sheet*, moulding itself on the inequalities of surface, and moving slowly seaward, to break off there into masses which form *icebergs*. The *icy* instead of *snowy* condition of glaciers is the result of pressure, together with successive thawings and freezings. Snow is thus slowly compacted into *glacier-ice*.

Although glaciers are in continual motion downward, yet the lower end, or *foot*, never reaches below a certain point; and under unchanging conditions, this point remains fixed. The reason is obvious: The glacier may be regarded as being under the influence of two opposite forces; the downward motion tending ever to lengthen, and the melting tending ever to shorten it. High up the mountain the motion is in excess, but as the melting power of sun and air increases downward, there must be a place where the motion and the melting balance each other. At this point will be found the foot. It is

called the lower limit of the glacier. Its position, of course, varies in
different countries, and many even reach the sea-coast, in which
case icebergs are formed. *Annual* changes of temperature do not
affect the position of the foot of the glacier, but *secular* changes cause
it to *advance* or *retreat*. During periods of increasing cold and moisture, the foot advances, pushing before it the accumulating debris.
During periods of increasing heat and dryness it retreats, leaving its
previously accumulated debris lower down the valley. But whether
the *foot of the glacier* be stationary, or advancing, or retreating, the
matter of the glacier, and therefore all the debris lying on its surface
is in continual motion downward. Since glaciers are limited by melting, it is evident that a river springs from the foot of every glacier.

Moraines. On the surface, and about the foot of glaciers, are
always found immense piles of heterogeneous debris consisting of
rock fragments of all sizes, mixed with earth. These are called
moraines. On the surface, the most usual form and place is a long
heap, often twenty to fifty feet high, along each side, next the
bounding cliffs. These are called *lateral moraines.* They are ruins of
the crumbling cliffs on each side, drawn out into continuous line by
the motion of the glacier. If glaciers are without tributaries, these
lateral moraines are all the debris on their surface; but if glaciers
have tributaries, then the *two* interior lateral moraines of the tributaries are carried down the middle of the glacier, as a *medial moraine.*
There is a medial moraine for every tributary. In complicated glaciers, therefore, the whole surface may be nearly covered with debris.
All these materials, whether lateral or medial, are borne slowly onward by the motion of the glacier, and finally deposited at its foot, in
the form of a huge, irregularly crescentic pile of debris known as the
terminal moraine. If a glacier runs from a rocky gorge out on a level
plain, then the lateral moraines may be dropped on either side, forming parallel debris piles, confining the glacier.

Laws of Glacial Motion. Glaciers do not *slide* down their beds, like solid bodies, but *run* down in the manner of a body half solid, half liquid; *i.e.*, in the manner of a *stream* of *stiffly viscous substance*. Thus, while a glacier slides over its bed, yet the upper layers move faster, and therefore slide over the lower layers. Again, while the whole mass moves down, rubbing on the bounding sides, yet the middle portions move faster, and therefore slide on the marginal portions. Lastly, while a glacier moves over *smaller* inequalities of bed and bank like a solid, yet it conforms to and moulds itself upon the *larger* inequalities, like a liquid. Also, its motion down steep slopes is greater than over level reaches. Thus, glaciers like rivers, have their *narrows* and their *lakes*, their rapids and their stiller portions, their *deeps* and their *shallows*. In a word, a glacier is a *stream*, its motion is *viscoid*, and, for the practical purposes of the geologist, it may be regarded as a very stiffly viscous body.

Glaciers as Geological Agent. Glaciers, like rivers, *wear away* the surfaces over which they pass; *transport* materials and *deposit* them in their course, or at their termination. But in all these respects the effects of glacial action are very characteristic, and cannot be mistaken for those of any other agent.

Erosion. The cutting or wearing power of glaciers is very great; not only on account of their great weight, but also because they carry, fixed firmly in their lower surfaces, and therefore between themselves and their beds, rock fragments of all sizes, which act as their graving tools. These fragments are partly torn off from their rocky beds in their course, but principally consist of top-debris, which find their way to the bottom through fissures, or else are engulfed in the viscous mass on the sides. Armed with these graving tools, glaciers behave towards smaller inequalities like a solid body, planing them down to a *smooth surface*, and marking the smooth surface thus made with *straight, parallel scratches*. But to large inequalities it behaves like a viscous liquid, conforming to their surfaces, while it smoothes and scratches them. It moulds itself upon large

prominences and scoops out large hollows, at the same time smoothing, rounding and scoring them. These smooth, rounded, scored surfaces, and these scooped-out rock basins, are very characteristic of
glacial action. We have passed over many such smooth surfaces this
morning. The scooped-out rock basins, when left by the retreating
glacier, become beautiful lakes. Lake Tenaya is probably such a lake.

Transportation. The carrying power of river currents has a definite
relation to velocity. To carry rock fragments, of many tons weight,
requires an almost incredible velocity. Glaciers, on the contrary,
carry on their surfaces, with equal ease, fragments of all sizes, even
up to hundreds of tons weight. Again, boulders carried by water
currents are always bruised and rounded, while glaciers carry them
safely and lay them down in their original angular condition. Again,
river currents always leave boulders in *secure* position, while glaciers
may set them down gently, by the melting of the ice, in insecure
positions, as *balanced stones*. Therefore, *large, angular* boulders, different from the country rock, and especially if in *insecure* positions, are
very characteristic of glacial action.

Deposit. Terminal Moraine. As already seen, all materials accumulated on the surface of a glacier, or pushed along on the bed beneath,
find their final resting place at the foot, and there form the *terminal
moraine.* If a glacier recedes, it leaves its terminal moraine, and
makes a new one at the new position of its foot. Terminal moraines,
therefore, are very characteristic signs of the former position of a
glacier foot. They are recognized by their irregular crescentic form,
the mixed nature of their materials, and the entire want of strati-
fication or sorting. Behind the terminal moraines of retired glaciers
accumulate the waters of the river which flows from its foot, and
thus, again, form lakes. Glacial lakes, *i.e.,* lakes formed by the action
of former glaciers, are, therefore, of two kinds, *viz.:* 1, The filling of
scooped-out rock basins. 2, The accumulation of water behind old
terminal moraines. The first are found, usually, high up; the second,

lower down the old glacial valleys.

Glacial Epoch in California. It is by means of these signs that geologists have proved that at a period very ancient in human, but very recent in geological chronology, glaciers were greatly extended in regions where they still exist, and existed in great numbers and size in regions where they no longer exist. This period is called the *Glacial Epoch*. Now, during this glacial epoch, the whole of the high Sierra region was covered with an ice-mantle, from which ran great glacial streams far down the slopes on either side. We have already seen evidences of some of these ancient glaciers on *this*, the western slope. After crossing Mono Pass we will doubtless see evidences of those which occupied the eastern slope. In our ride, yesterday and to-day, we crossed the track of some of these ancient glaciers. From where we now sit we can follow, with the eye, their pathways. A great glacier, (the Tuolumne Glacier), once filled this beautiful meadow, and its icy flood covered the spot where we now sit. It was fed by several tributaries. One from Mt. Lyell, another from Mono Pass, and still another from Mt. Dana, which, uniting just above Soda Springs, the swollen stream enveloped yonder granite knobs, five hundred feet high, standing directly in its path, smoothing and rounding them on every side, and leaving them in form like a turtle's back; then coming further down overflowed its banks at the lowest point of yonder ridge—one thousand feet high—which we crossed this morning, and after sending an overflow stream down Tenaya Cañon, the main stream passed on down the Tuolumne Cañon, into and beyond Hetchhetchy Valley. From its head fountain, in Mt. Lyell, this glacier may be traced forty miles.

The overflow branch which passed down the Tenaya Cañon, after gathering tributaries from the region of Cathedral Peaks, and enveloping, smoothing, and rounding the grand granite knobs which we saw this morning just above Lake Tenaya, scooped out that lake basin, and swept on its way to the Yosemite. There it united with other streams from Little Yosemite and Nevada Cañons, and from Illilouette, to form the great Yosemite Glacier, which probably filled that valley to the brim and passed on down the cañon of the Merced. This glacier, in its subsequent retreat, left many imperfect terminal moraines, which are still detectible as rough debris piles, just below the meadows. Behind these moraines accumulated water, forming lakes which have gradually filled up and formed meadows. Some, as Mirror Lake, have not yet filled up. The meadows of Yosemite, and the lakes and meadows of Tenaya Fork, upon which our horses grazed while we were at University Camp, were formed in this way. You must have observed that these lakes and meadows are separated by higher ground, composed of coarse debris. All the lakes and meadows of this high Sierra region, were formed in this way. The region of good grazing is also the region of former glaciers.

Erosion in High Sierra Region. The erosion to which this whole high Sierra region had been subjected, in geological times, is something almost incredible. It is a common popular notion that mountain peaks are *upheaved*. No one can look about him observantly in this high Sierra region, and retain such a notion. Every peak and valley now within our view—all that constitutes the grand scenery upon which we now look, is the result wholly of erosion—of *mountain sculpture*. Mountain chains, are, indeed, formed by igneous agency; but these are afterwards sculptured into forms of beauty. But even this gives as yet no adequate idea of the immensity of this erosion; not only are all the grand peaks now within view, Cathedral Peaks, Unicorn Peak, Mt. Lyell, Mt. Gibbs, Mt. Dana, the result of simple inequality of erosion, but it is almost certain that the slates which form the foothills, and over whose upturned edges we passed, from Snelling to Clark's, and whose edges we again see, forming the highest crests on the very margin of the eastern slope, originally covered the granite of this whole region many thousand feet deep. Erosion has removed it entirely, and bitten deep into the underlying granite.

Now, you are not to imagine that the whole, but certainly a large portion, of this erosion, and the final touches of this sculpturing, has been accomplished by the glacial action which we have endeavored to explain.

About 9 P.M., our clothing still damp, we rolled ourselves in our damp blankets, lay upon the still wet ground, and went to sleep. I slept well and suffered no inconvenience.

To any one wishing really to enjoy camp life among the high Sierras, I know no place more delightful than Soda Springs. Being about nine thousand feet above the sea, the air is deliciously cool and bracing. The water, whether of the spring or of the river, is almost ice-cold, and the former a gentle tonic. The scenery is nowhere more glorious. Add to this, inexhaustible pasturage for horses, and plenty of mutton, and trout abundant in the river, and what more can pleasure seekers want?

August 11.

As we intended going only to the foot of Mt. Dana, a distance of about eleven miles, we did not hurry this morning. The mutton gotten yesterday must be securely packed; we did not get started until 9 A.M. Trail very blind. Lost it a dozen times, and had to scatter to find it each time. Saw again this morning magnificent evidences of the Tuolumne Glacier. Among the most remarkable, several smooth, rounded knobs of granite, eight hundred to one thousand feet high, with long slope up the valley, and steep slope down the valley, evidently their whole form determined by an enveloping glacier.

About 2 P.M., as we were looking out for a camping ground, a thunder-storm again burst upon us. We hurried on, searching among the huge boulders (probably glacial boulders), to find a place of shelter for our provisions and ourselves. At last we found a huge boulder which overhung on one side, leaning against a large tree. The roaring of the coming storm grows louder and louder, the pattering of rain already commences. "Quick! quick!!" In a few seconds the pack was unsaddled, and provisions thrown under shelter. Then rolls of blankets quickly thrown after them, then the horses unsaddled and tied; then, at last, we ourselves, though already wet, crowded under. It was an interesting and somewhat amusing sight. All our provisions and blanket rolls, and eleven men packed away, actually piled upon one another, under a rock which did not project more than two and a half feet. I wish I could draw a picture of the scene; the huge rock with its dark recess; the living, squirming mass, piled confusedly beneath; the magnificent forest of grand trees; the black clouds; the constant gleams of lightning, revealing the scarcely visible faces; the peals of thunder, and the floods of rain, pouring from the rock on the projecting feet and knees of those whose legs were inconveniently long, or even on the heads and backs of some who were less favored in position.

In about an hour the storm passed, then sun again came out, and we selected camp. Beneath a huge prostrate tree we soon started a fire, and piled log upon log, until the flame, leaping upwards, seemed determined to overtop the huge pines around. Ah! what joy is a huge camp fire! not only its delicious warmth to one wet with rain in this high cool region, but its cheerful light, its joyous crackling and cracking, its frantic dancing and leaping! How the heart warms, and brightens, and rejoices, and leaps, in concert with the camp fire!

We are here nearly ten thousand feet above sea-level. Our appetites are ravenous. We eat up a sheep in a day; a sack (one hundred pounds) of flour, lasts us five or six days. Nights are so cool that we are compelled to make huge fires, and sleep near the fire to keep warm.

Our camp here is a most delightful one, in the midst of grand trees and huge boulders—a meadow hard by, of course, for our horses. By stepping into the meadow, we see looming up very near us, on the south, the grand form of Mt. Gibbes, and on the north, the still grander form of Mt. Dana. After supper, and dish-washing, and horse tending, and fire replenishing, the young men gathered around me, and I gave them the following

LECTURE ON DEPOSITS IN CARBONATE SPRINGS.

You saw yesterday and this morning the bubbles of gas which rise in such abundance to the surface of Soda Spring. You observed the pleasant, pungent taste of the water, and you have doubtless associated both of these with the presence of carbonic acid. But there is another fact which probably you have not associated with the presence of this gas, *viz.:* the *deposit of a reddish substance*. This reddish substance, which forms the mound from the top of which the spring bubbles, is carbonate of lime, colored with iron oxide. This deposit is very common in carbonated springs. I wish to explain it to you.

Remember then: 1st, that lime carbonate and metallic carbonates are insoluble in pure water, but slightly soluble in water containing carbonic acid. 2d, that the amount of carbonates taken up by water, is proportionate to the amount of carbonic acid in solution. 3d, that the amount of carbonic acid which may be taken in solution, is proportioned to the pressure. Now, all spring water contains a small quantity of carbonic acid, derived from the air, and will therefore dissolve limestone, (carbonate of lime); but the quantity taken up by such waters is so small that it will not deposit except by drying. Such are not called carbonated springs.

But there are, also, *subterranean* sources of carbonic acid, especially in volcanic districts. Now, if percolating water come in contact with such carbonic acid—being under heavy pressure—it takes up larger quantities of the gas. If such waters come to the surface, the pressure being removed, the gas escapes in bubbles. This is a carbonated spring.

If, farther, the subterranean water thus highly charged with carbonic acid comes in contact with limestone or rocks of any kind containing carbonate of lime, it dissolves a proportionately large amount of this carbonate, and when it comes to the surface, the escape of the carbonic acid causes the limestone to deposit, and hence, this material accumulates immediately about the spring, and in the course of the stream issuing from the spring.

The kind of material depends upon the manner of deposit and upon the presence or absence of iron. If the deposit is tumultuous, the material is *spongy,* or even pulverulent; if quiet, it is *dense.* If no iron be present, the deposit is white as marble; but if iron be present, its oxidation will color the deposit yellow, or brown, or reddish. If the amount of iron be variable, the stone formed will be beautifully striped. Suisun marble is an example of a beautifully striped stone, deposited in this way in a former geological epoch.

I have said that such springs are most common in volcanic districts. They are, therefore, commonly warm. Soda springs, however, is not in a volcanic district. In our travels in the volcanic region on the other side of the Sierras, we will find, probably, several others. At one time these springs were far more abundant in California than they are now.

———

August 12.

We had cooked bread, yesterday, for our breakfast and lunch to-day, in anticipation of our ascent of Mt. Dana. We had this morning only to cook meat. This takes but little time. We made an early start, therefore. Rode our horses up as far as the timber extends, staked them out in little green patches of rich grass, very abundant on the mountain slopes, and then commenced the real ascent on foot. I think we ascended about 3000 feet after leaving our horses. Saw a splendid buck—but alas! Cobb has left his rifle. Mt. Dana, as seen from this side, is of a very regular, conical form, entirely destitute of soil, and therefore of vegetation; in fact, from top to bottom, a mere loose mass of rock fragments—metamorphic sandstone and slates. The slope is, I think, 40°; the rock fragments, where small, give way under the foot, and roll downwards; if large, they are difficult to climb over. The ascent is difficult and fatiguing in the extreme. The danger, too, to those below, from boulders loosened by the feet of those above, is very great. A large fragment, at least one hundred pounds, thus loosened by Mr. Bolton, came thundering down upon me with fearful velocity, before I was aware. I had no time to get out of the way; in fact, my own footing was precarious. I opened my legs, it passed between, and bounded on its way down.

There being no trail, each man took his own way. The young men were evidently striving to see who could be up first. I took my steady, even way, resting a moment from time to time. My progress illustrated the fable of the hare and tortoise. I was the third man on the top. Mr. Muir and Pomroy alone had gotten there before me. I really expected to find the whole party there.

The view from the top is magnificent beyond description. To the southwest, the sharp, strangely picturesque peaks of the Cathedral group. To the south, in the distance, Mt. Lyell group, with broad patches of snow on their slopes; and near at hand, the bare gray mass of Mt. Gibbs. To the north, the fine outline of Castle Peak, rising above, and dominating the surrounding summits; and to the east, almost at our feet, the whole interior valley, including Lake Mono, with its picturesque islands and volcanoes. Stretching away to the west, valleys, with grassy meadows and lakes separated by low wooded ridges. I could count thirty to fifty of these lakes; and meadows without number. These meadows, and lakes, and ridges, suggest glacier beds, with moraines, stretching westward down the Sierra slope.

As already stated, the whole mountain is superficially a mass of loose rock fragments. I saw the rock *in situ* only in one place, but this was a magnificent section. About two-thirds way up, the bedrock appears as a perpendicular crag, nearly one hundred feet high. It is here a very distinctly and beautifully stratified sand-stone, and in a perfectly *horizontal* position. The slope on the western and southwestern side is regular and about 40°, but when we arrived on the top we found that on the east and northeast the slope is very precipitous, forming an immense amphitheatre, in which lay immense stores of snow, and in one place we found nestled a clear, deep blue lake, apparently formed by the melting snow. This great snow-field extends a little over the gentle slope by which we ascended. For the last five hundred to one thousand feet we ascended the mountain over this snow. Mt. Dana is thirteen thousand two hundred and twenty-seven feet high. I did not observe any remarkable effect of diminished density of atmosphere upon respiration or circulation. The beating of the heart was a little troublesome. I had to stop frequently to allow it to become quiet; but this seemed to me as bad or worse near the beginning of the climb than near the top. It seemed only more difficult to get my "second wind," as it is called, than usual.

We took cold lunch on the top of the mountain, and commenced our descent, which was less fatiguing, but much more dangerous and trying than the ascent. The shoes of several of the party were completely destroyed. Mine still hold out. Came back to camp at 2 P.M., tired but not exhausted. Soon after reaching camp, we again had thunder and rain. We all huddled with our provisions and blankets again under our rock shed. There was but a sprinkle this time, however, though much threatening of wind and thunder.

After supper we again built up an immense camp fire. Now, while I write, the strong light of the blazing camp fire is thrown upon the tall tamarack trees, and upon the faces of the young men, engaged in various ways. I wish I could draw a picture of the scene now presented: the blazing fire of huge piled logs; the strongly illuminated figures of the party; the intense blackness of sky and forest. Supper is just over; Mr. Stone is squatting on the ground, engaged in washing up dishes. Mr. Linderman, who is cook to-day, is lying on his back, kicking up his heels, and regarding Mr. Stone with intense satisfaction. His work is over, while Stone's is just begun. Mr. Muir is earnestly engaged hollowing out a place under a huge pine tree, which he intends to make his resting place for the night. Capt. is lying down flat on his back, with his clasped hands under his head and his eyes closed. Pomroy is sitting in the strong light of the fire, writing his journal; he is this moment scratching his cropped poll for an idea. Bolton, Phelps, and Perkins are sitting together near the fire, Bolton enjoying his cigarette, and Phelps and Perkins chatting. Cobb is just returning with another log for the fire. Hawkins has been looking after his horse, and is just returning. I am observing the scene, and jotting down these crude notes.

We will see Mono Lake to-morrow. Before going to bed, therefore, the party gathered about the fire, and by request I gave them the following lecture on the formation of salt and alkaline lakes:

———

LECTURE ON SALT AND ALKALINE LAKES.

Salt Lakes may originate in two general ways: either by the isolation of a portion of sea water, or else by the indefinite concentration of ordinary river water in a lake without an outlet. The great Salt Lake, and all the other salt lakes scattered over the desert on the other side of the Sierras, are possibly formed by the first method. It is probable that at a comparatively recent geological epoch the whole of the salt and alkaline region on the other side of the Sierras, which we will see to-morrow, was covered by an extension of the sea from the Gulf of California. When this was raised into land, portions of sea water were caught up and isolated in the hollows of the uneven surface. The lakes thus formed have since greatly diminished by drying away, as is clearly shown by the terraces or old water levels far beyond and above the present limits; and their waters have become saturated solutions of the saline matters contained in sea water.

The Dead Sea, and many other salt lakes and brine pools in the interior of Asia, have probably been formed in the same way. But the Caspian Sea is probably an example of the second method of formation: *i.e.,* by concentration of river water. The reason for thinking so is, that old beach marks, or terraces, show a great drying away of the lake, and yet the water is still far less salt than sea water.

Alkaline Lakes are formed, and can be formed, only by the second method, *viz.:* by indefinite concentration of river water by evaporation in a lake without an outlet. Such concentration, therefore, may form either a salt or an alkaline lake. Whether the one or the other kind of lake results, depends wholly upon the composition of the river water. If chlorides predominate, the lake will be salt; but if alkaline carbonates predominate, it will be alkaline.

Perhaps some of you will be surprised that the pure fresh water

of mountain streams can produce salt or alkaline lakes. I must therefore try to explain.

We speak of spring water as pure and fresh; it is so comparatively. Nevertheless, all spring water, and therefore all river water,
contains small quantities of saline matters derived from the rocks
and soils through which they percolate. Suppose, then, the drainage
of any hydrographical basin to accumulate in a lake. Suppose, farther, that the *supply* of water by rivers be greater than the *waste* by
evaporation from the lake surface. It is evident that the lake will
rise, and if the same relation continues, it will continue to rise until it
finds an outlet in the lowest part of the rim, and is discharged into
the ocean or some other reservoir. Such a lake will be *fresh; i.e.*, it
will contain only an imperceptible quantity of saline matter.

But if, on the other hand, at any time the *waste* by evaporation
from the lake surface should be equal to the supply by rivers, the
lake would not rise, and therefore would not find an outlet. Now the
salting process will commence. The waters which flow in contain a
little, be it ever so little, of saline matter. All this remains in the lake,
since evaporation carries off only distilled water. Thus, age after age
saline matters are leached from rocks and soils, and accumulated in
the lake, which, therefore, must eventually become either salt or
alkaline.

Thus, whether lakes are saline or fresh depends on the presence
or absence of an outlet, and the presence or absence of an outlet
depends on the relation of supply by rain to waste by evaporation,
and this latter depends on the climate. Saline lakes cannot occur
except in very dry climates, and these lakes are rare, because on
most land surfaces the rainfall far exceeds the evaporation, the excess being carried to the sea by rivers. Only in wide plains, in the
interior of continents, do we find the climatic conditions necessary
to produce salt lakes.

I have shown the conditions necessary to the formation of a salt lake by concentration of river water. Now, the very same conditions control the existence of salt lakes, however they may have originated. Even in the case of a salt lake formed by the isolation of a portion of sea water, whether it remain salt or become fresh will depend wholly on the conditions discussed above.

Suppose, for example, a portion of sea water be isolated by an upheaval of the sea-bed; now, if the supply of water to this lake by rivers be greater than the waste by evaporation from the surface, the lake will rise, overflow, and discharge into the sea or other reservoir; the salt water will be slowly rinsed out, and the lake will become fresh. But if the evaporation should equal the supply, the lake will not find an outlet, and will remain salt, and will even increase in saltness until it begins to deposit.

Thus, if the Bay of San Francisco should be cut off from the sea at the Golden Gate, it would form a fresh lake, for the water running into it by the Sacramento River is far greater than the evaporation from the bay. So the Black Sea, and the Baltic Sea, as above shown by the comparative freshness of the waters, would form fresh lakes. But the Mediterranean, as shown by the great saltness of its waters, would certainly remain salt, and become increasingly salt. We have the best reasons to believe that Lake Champlain, since the glacial epoch, was an arm of the sea. It has become fresh since it became separated.

Saltness of the Ocean. Thus, then, we see that the one condition which determines the existence of salt and alkaline lakes is the absence of an outlet. Now, the ocean, of course, has no outlet; the ocean is the final reservoir of saline matters leached from the earth. Hence, although the saltness of the ocean is a somewhat different problem from that of salt lakes, yet it is almost certain that the saline matters of the ocean are the accumulated results of the leachings of the rocks and soils by circulating waters, throughout all geological times.

During my travels through the Sierras I have made many observations on rocks and mountains. One or two of these I think worthy of mention. First, I have seen everywhere the strongest confirmation of the view that granite, and granitic rocks are but the final term of metamorphism of sedimentary rocks. In Yosemite I could trace every stage of gradation from granite into gneiss, and since leaving Yosemite, from gneiss into impure sandstones. On Mt. Dana sandstones are easily traced into gneiss or even curite, and slate into a crystalline rock, undistinguishable from diorite or other traps.

Second, No one who examines the forms of the peaks of the Sierras can come to any other conclusion than that all the mountain forms seen here are the result of *denudation*. Standing at Soda Springs and gazing upon the strange forms of Cathedral Group, the conviction is forced upon the mind that these were not upheaved, but simply left as more resisting fragments of an almost inconceivable erosion—fragments of a denuded plateau. The strange ruggedness of the forms, the inaccessible peaks and pinnacles, have been the result of the very decomposable nature of the granite. Mt. Dana, with its more regular form, consists of more resistant slates. The evidence that Mt. Dana has been formed entirely by denudation, is, I conceive, complete. As already stated, Mt. Dana is composed of undistributed horizontal strata. The grand bulge of a great mountain chain is probably produced by the shrinkage of the earth; the foldings and tiltings of strata in mountain chains by the same cause; but the actual forms which constitute scenery are purely the result of aqueous erosion. Metamorphism is, I believe, always produced in deeply buried rocks by heat, water, and pressure. The universal metamorphism of the rocks in the Sierras is therefore additional evidence of the immensity of the erosion which brings these to the surface.

Since leaving Yosemite we have seen no houses; in fact, no human beings but a few shepherds. As the flocks require to be driven from one pasture to another, these men live only in hastily constructed sheds, covered with boughs. In this shepherd's life there may be something pleasant, when viewed through the imagination only; but in reality it is enough to produce either imbecility or insanity. The pleasant pictures drawn by the poets, of contemplative wisdom and harmless enjoyment, of affectionate care of the flock, of pensive music of pipes; these possibly, probably, once did exist; but certainly they do not exist now, at least in California.

August 13.

Cold last night. We had to sleep near the fire, and keep it up during the night. Considerable frost this morning, for we are in the midst of the snows. We got up early, feeling bright and joyous, and enjoyed our breakfast as only mountaineers can. Over Mono Pass, and down Bloody Cañon to-day. I really dread it, for my horse's sake. Even well-shod horses get their feet and legs cut and bleeding, in going down this cañon. My horse, since leaving Yosemite, has lost three shoes, and has already become very tender-footed. Got off by 6 A.M. Sorry, very sorry, to leave our delightful camp here. In commemoration of the delightful time we have spent here, we name it "Camp Dana."

The trail to the Summit is a very gentle ascent, the whole way along the margin of a stream. Distance, three or four miles. Saw a deer, but Cobb was not on hand. On the very summit, ten thousand seven hundred feet high, there is a marshy meadow, from which a stream runs each way: one east, into the Tuolumne, along which we had ascended; the other west, down Bloody Cañon into Mono Lake, along which we expect to descend. Right on the Summit, and in Bloody Cañon, we found great masses of snow. The trail passes by their edges and over their surfaces. The trail down Bloody Cañon is rough and precipitous beyond conception. It is the terror of all drovers and packers across the mountains. It descends four thousand feet in two or three miles, and is a mere mass of loose fragments of sharp slate. Our horses' legs were all cut and bleeding before we got down. I really felt pity for my horse, with his tender feet. We all dismounted and led them down with the greatest care. In going down we met a large party of Indians, some on horseback, and some on foot, coming up. We saluted them. In return they invariably whined, "Gie me towaca," "Gie me towaca." They were evidently incredulous when told that none of the party chewed.

The scenery of Bloody Cañon is really magnificent, and, in a scientific point of view, this is the most interesting locality I have yet seen. Conceive a narrow, winding gorge, with black, slaty precipices of every conceivable form, fifteen hundred to two thousand feet high on either side. As the gorge descends precipitously, and winds from side to side, we often look from above down into the most glorious amphitheatre of cliffs, and from time to time beyond, upon the glistening surface of Lake Mono, and the boundless plains, studded with volcanic cones. About one-third way down, in the centre of the grandest of these amphitheatres, See! a deep, splendidly clear, emerald green lake, three or four times the size of Mirror Lake. It looks like an artificial basin, for its shores are everywhere hard, smooth, polished rock; especially the rim at the lower side is highly polished and finely striated. There can be no doubt that this lake basin has been scooped out by a glacier which once descended this cañon. In fact, glacial action is seen on every side around this lake, and all the way down the cañon and far into the plains below. The cliffs on each side are scored and polished to the height of one thousand feet or more; projecting knobs in the bottom of the cañon are rounded, and scored, and polished, in a similar manner.

After we had descended the steep slope, and had fairly escaped from the high rocky walls of Bloody Cañon proper; after we had reached the level plain and had prepared ourselves for an extensive view, we found ourselves still confined between two huge parallel ridges of *debris* five hundred feet high and only one-half a mile apart, and extending five or six miles out on the plain.

These are the *lateral moraines* of a glacier which once descended far into the plain towards Mono Lake. A little below the commencement of these moraines, in descending, we found a large and beautiful lake filling the whole cañon. Below this lake the lateral moraines on either side send each a branch which meet each other, forming a crescentic cross-ridge through which the stream breaks. This is evidently a *terminal* moraine, and the lake has been formed by the damming up of the water of the stream by this moraine barrier.

Below this, or still further on the plain, I observed several other terminal moraines, formed in a similar way, by curving branches from the lateral moraines. Behind these are no lakes, but only marshes and meadows. These meadows are evidently formed in the same way as the lake; in fact, may be lakes subsequently filled up by deposit.

After getting from these lateral moraines fairly out on the plains, the most conspicuous objects which strikes the eye are the extinct volcanoes. There are, I should think, at least twenty of them, with cones and craters as perfect as if they erupted yesterday. Even at this distance, I see that their snow-white, bare sides are composed of loose volcanic ashes and sand, above which projects a distinct rocky crater-rim, some of dark rock, but most of them of light-colored, probably, pumice rock. Magnificent views of these cones and of Mono Lake are gotten from time to time, while descending Bloody Cañon. The cones are of all heights, from two hundred to twenty-seven hundred feet above the plain, and the plain itself about five thousand feet above sea level.

We stopped for lunch at a cabin and meadow—a cattle ranch—

about five miles from the lake. While our horses grazed, we cooked our dinner as usual, and then proceeded three miles and camped in a fine meadow on the banks of a beautiful stream — Rush Creek.

In riding down to our camp, I observed the terraces of Lake Mono, former water-levels, very distinctly marked, four or five in number. The whole region about Lake Mono, on this side, is covered with volcanic ashes and sand. It is the only soil except in the meadows. Even these seem to have the same soil, only more damp, and therefore more fertile. Scattered about, larger masses of pumice and obsidian are visible. Except in the meadows and along streams the only growth is the sage brush. Just before reaching camp, Mr. Muir and myself examined a fine section, made by Rush Creek, of lake and river deposit, beautifully stratified. It consists below of volcanic ashes, carried as sediment and deposited in the lake, and is, therefore, a true lake deposit, and beautifully stratified. Above this is a drift pebble deposit; the pebbles consisting of granite and slate from the Sierras. Above this again, are volcanic ashes and sand, *unstratified,* probably blown ashes and sand, or else ejected since the drift. We have here, therefore, certain evidence of eruptions before the drift, and possibly, also, after.

In the picture of the view from Mono Lake, I have yet said nothing about the Sierras. The general view of these mountains from this, the Mono side, is far finer than from the other side. The Sierras rise gradually on the western side for fifty or sixty miles. On the Mono, or eastern side, they are precipitous, the very summit of the range running close to the valley. From this side, therefore, the mountains present a sheer elevation of six or seven thousand feet above the plain. The sunset view of the Sierras, from an eminence near our camp, this evening, was, it seems to me, by far the finest mountain view I have ever in my life seen. The immense height of the chain above the plain, the abruptness of the declivity, the infinitely diversified forms, and the wonderful sharpness and ruggedness of the peaks, such as I have seen nowhere but in the Sierras, and all this strongly relieved against the brilliant sunset sky, formed a picture of indescribable grandeur. As I turn around in the opposite direction, the regular forms of the volcanoes, the placid surface of Lake Mono, with its picturesque islands, and far away in the distance the scarcely visible outlines of the White Mountains, pass in succession before the eye. I enjoyed this magnificent panoramic view until it faded away in the darkness.

From this feast I went immediately to another, consisting of excellent bread, and such delicious mutton chops! If any restaurant in San Francisco could furnish such, I am sure it would quickly make a fortune. Some sentimentalists seem to think that these two feasts are incompatible; that the enjoyment of the beautiful is inconsistent with voracious appetite for mutton. I do not find it so.

After supper I again went out to enjoy the scene by night. As I gazed upon the abrupt slope of the Sierras, rising like a wall before me, I tried to picture to myself the condition of things during the glacial epoch. The long western slope of the Sierras is now occupied by long, complicated valleys, broad and full of meadows, while the eastern slope is deeply graven with short, narrow, steep ravines. During glacial times, therefore, it is evident that the western slope was occupied by long, complicated glaciers, with comparatively sluggish current; while on the east, short, simple, parallel ice streams ran down the steep slope, and far out on the level plain. On each side of these protruded icy tongues, the debris brought down from the rocky ravines were dropped as parallel moraines. Down the track of one of these glaciers, and between the outstretched *moraine* arms, our path lay this morning.

August 14, Sunday.

I have not before suffered so much from cold as last night; yet yesterday the sun was very hot. No grand forests to protect us from wind and furnish us with logs for camp-fire; only sage brush on the plains, and small willows on the stream banks. The winds blow furiously from the Sierras down the cañons, upon the plains. Got up at 4 A.M.; couldn't sleep any more. After breakfast, went to visit the volcanic cones in the vicinity.* The one we visited was one of the most perfect, and at the same time one of the most accessible. It was not more than one hundred fifty to two hundred feet above the level of the sandy plain on which it stands.

I was very greatly interested in this volcano. It seems to me that its structure clearly reveals some points of its history. It consists of two very perfect cones and craters, one within the other. The outer cone, which rises directly from the level plain to a height of two hundred feet, is composed wholly of volcanic sand, and is about one mile in diameter. From the bottom and center of its crater rises another and much smaller cone of lava to a little greater height. We rode up the outer sand cone, then around on the rim of its crater, then down its inner slope to the bottom; tied our horses to sage brush at the base of the inner lava-cone, and scrambled on foot into its crater. Standing on the rim of this inner crater, the outer rises like a rampart on every side.

I believe we have here a beautiful example of cone-and-rampart structure, so common in volcanoes elsewhere; the rampart, or outer cone, being the result of an older and much greater eruption, within the wide, yawning crater, of which by subsequent lesser eruption the smaller cone was built.†

*While on the way, had a very fine view toward the east, of the terraces of Lake Mono. I think there must be five or six very perfect.
†I have recently (1875) again visited this region. My observations on several of the volcanoes confirm my first impressions.

Mr. Muir is disposed to explain it differently. He thinks that this was once a much higher single cone, lava at top and sand on the slopes, like most of the larger cones in this vicinity; and that after its last eruption it suffered *engulfment*; *i.e.*, its upper rocky portion has dropped down into its lower sandy portion.

The lava of this volcano is mostly pumice and obsidian, sometimes approaching trachyte. It was of all shades of color, from black to white, sometimes beautifully veined, like slags of an iron furnace; and of all physical conditions, sometimes vesicular, sometimes glassy, sometimes stony. Wrinkled fusion-surfaces were also abundant. Again; I believe I can fix the date of the last eruption of this volcano. I found on the outer, or ash cone, several unmistakeable drift *pebbles of granite*. At first I thought they might be the result of accidental deposit; but I found, also, several within the *lava crater*. These were reddened and semi-fused by heat. There can be no doubt, therefore, that the last eruption of this volcano was since the drift; it broke through a layer of drift deposit, and threw out the drift pebbles. Some fell back into the crater.

Mr. Muir took leave of us within the crater of this volcano. He goes to-day to visit some of the loftier cones. I would gladly accompany him, but my burnt hand has to-day become inflamed, and is very painful; the climb of twenty-seven hundred feet, over loose, very loose sand, will be very fatiguing, and the sun is very hot. In spite of all this, I had determined to go, but the party are impatient of delays.

I was really sorry to lose Mr. Muir from our party. I have formed a very high opinion of, and even a strong attachment for him. He promises to write me if he observes any additional facts of importance.

We came back to camp about 12 M., and while dinner was preparing, took a delightful swim in the river which runs here by our camp into the lake. Several Indians visited us while at dinner.

This is a favorite time for such visits. They know they will get something to eat. Two younger Indians were full of life and good nature, but one old wrinkled fellow was very reticent, and stood much upon his dignity. He had a beautiful bow, and several arrows. We put up some bread and the younger ones shot for it, but the old Indian would take no notice of it, and even seemed to treat the idea with contempt. He evidently belongs to the "Old Regime." He remembers the time when the *noble* red man had undisputed possession of this part of the country.

About 2 P.M. we started for Alliton's, a small house on the west side of the lake, and about twelve miles distant. Here I hope to have my horse temporarily shod. In this hope I have picked up and preserved three horse-shoes. If we can find nails at Alliton's, Hawkins will shoe my horse. If not, I know not what I shall do, for my horse is so lame he can hardly get on at all to-day. Had it not been for the lameness of my horse, I would have enjoyed the evening ride greatly. The trail runs close along the margin of the lake, sometimes in the very water, sometimes rising on the slopes of the steep mountains, which come down to the very water's edge. From the sides of these mountains the view of the lake and mountains was very fine. The volcanic character of the islands in the lake was very evident, and their craters were quite distinct. It is said that evidences of feeble volcanic activity still exist in the form of steam jets, hot springs, etc. I am anxious to visit these islands, and will do so if I can. My horse was so lame that I made very slow progress, and lagged behind several miles. When I reached Alliton's I found the house empty. Alliton not at home, and the party gone to a house about a mile or two farther on. Alas! what shall I do for my horse? Soon after leaving Alliton's, however, I met Hawkins, riding Cobb's pony, bareback. He said he had found some shoenails at Alliton's, and he would shoe my horse. We therefore exchanged horses; I went on, and he back to Alliton's, and shod my horse very nicely.

On my way along the shores of the lake I observed thousands of birds: blackbirds, gulls, ducks, magpies, stilts, sandpipers. The sandpipers I never saw alight on the shore, but only on the water. They swam, rose in flocks, settled on the water exactly like true ducks. Will not these in time undergo a Darwinian change into webfooters? These birds seem to collect in such numbers to feed upon the swarms of flies which frequent the shores. The number of these is incredible. I saw them in piles three or four inches thick on the water, and in equal piles thrown up dead on the shore. The air stank with them. These flies come here to spawn. Their innumerable larvae form, I understand, the principal food of the Indians during a portion of the year.* All about the margin of the lake, and standing in the water near the shore, I observed irregular masses of rough, porous limestone, evidently deposited from the water of the lake, or else from limestone springs.

Soon after camping we went in swimming in the lake. The water is very buoyant, but the bathing is not pleasant. The shores are flat and muddy, and swarm with flies. These do not trouble one, but their appearance is repulsive. The water contains large quantities of carbonate of soda, a little carbonate of lime, and probably some borax. It therefore is very cleansing, but makes the skin feel slimy, and lathers the head and beard like soap. The presence of volcanic rocks and volcanic sand, all around, and also of soda granite in the Sierras, sufficiently explains why this lake is alkaline instead of salt.

We bought here a little butter, cheese, and corned beef, and enjoyed them very much for supper. We have gotten out of the region of mutton. With the exception of patches of rich meadow, formed by the streams from the Sierras, everywhere is sage, sage,

---

*I have since (1875), observed the gathering of the larvae, or rather pupae, of these flies. About the 1st of July the pupae are cast ashore in immense quantities. They are then gathered, dried, rubbed to break off the shell, and kept for use under the name of *Koo-chah-bee*.

sage. The water, however, is delicious. The streams are formed by the melting snows of the Sierras, and these are so near by that the water is very abundant, and ice-cold. Close by our camp there issues from a large, rough, limestone rock, a magnificent spring of ice-cold water, which runs off as a large brook.

Most of our party concluded to sleep here in a hay-loft. Hawkins and myself preferred a hay-cock. We put our blankets together, and had a deliciously soft, warm, and fragrant bed, under the starlit sky.

I desired very much to visit the islands from this point, but there was no boat. These islands, I understand, are the resort of millions of gulls, which deposit their eggs there in immense quantities. These eggs are an important article of food, and of traffic for the Indians. Mono Lake is about fifteen miles long, and twelve miles across.

———

August 15.

Got up at 4:30 A.M., greatly refreshed by a fine night's rest. Got off about 7 A.M., in fine spirits. My horse is nearly well of his lameness this morning. Soon after leaving our camp, this morning, we passed a rude Indian village, consisting of a few huts. The Indian huts in this region are nothing but a few poles, set up together in a conical form, and covered with boughs. We bought from these Indians several quarts of pine-nuts.* They are about the size and nearly the shape of ground pea kernels. We found them very sweet and nice. On leaving Mono, we struck out nearly northwest. We were therefore soon amongst the foothills of the Sierras again, and consequently in the mining regions. Saw many evidences of superficial mining. The debris of these washings by the whites are washed over by the

*Nut of the *Pinus monophylla*.

Chinese. Passed quite a village of Chinese engaged in this way. The diminutive mud huts were strung along a little stream—Virginia Creek—in the bottom of a ravine, for a considerable distance. The whites call this Dog Town. I observed, even here, almost every hut had its little irrigated garden patch attached to it. I had an opportunity, also, of examining the process of hydraulic mining by the whites, and was much interested.

About 11 A.M. we met a fruit-wagon, loaded with fruit and other supplies, which had come over Sonora Pass, and was on its way to Mono. With a loud yell, the whole party made a simultaneous dash for the devoted wagon, clambered up its sides, and swarmed over the boxes. Peaches, grapes, apples! Ah! how we enjoyed these delicious luxuries!

After making about twenty miles this morning, we camped for noon, about 12¹/₂ P.M., at Big Meadows. This is a beautiful grassy plain, six or seven miles long and three or four miles wide, on which graze hundreds of cattle and horses. The view from this meadow is superb. Now, as I sit here at our noon camp, I am surrounded on every side by mountains. Behind me, to the east, are the foothills we have just crossed; in front stretches the green meadow, and beyond rises the lofty Sierras.

The nearer mountains are immense, somewhat regular masses, smooth and green to the very summits, except where covered with patches of snow. Behind these, and seen through gaps, are the most magnificent group of singularly sharp and jagged peaks, tinged with blue by their distance, with great masses of snow in the deep hollows on their precipitous faces. The appearance of these great amphitheatres, with precipitous walls, suggested at once that these were the wombs from which once issued great glaciers. I wish my dear friends in Oakland could see us now: some eating, some washing up, some playing ball, some lolling about, and our saddles and packs grouped together where we unsaddled, our horses grazing quietly on the green meadow, and the whole surrounded by this really magnificent mountain scenery.

This afternoon we are wanting some supplies. Some of the party are sadly in want of shoes; some of the horses need shoeing. While three of the party, Captain, Pomroy, and Bolton, go to Bridgeport, a small town on Big Meadows—distinctly visible from our camp, and but little out of our way—the main body of the party went straight on, intending to choose camp and make fire before the rest came. Started about 4 P.M., intending to go only about seven miles and then camp in a cañon which we see emerging into Big Meadows, on the northwest—"Tamarack Cañon." As the sun went down behind the Sierras, the view became more and more splendid, and the coolness of the evening air increased our enjoyment of it. The delight of that evening ride, and the glory of that mountain view, I shall never forget.

About 6:30 found a place in the cañon where the grazing was very fine and water abundant—the grass and clover fresh, tall, and juicy, and a little stream gurgling close by. Here we camped, turned our horses loose to graze, with lariats trailing, intending to stake them securely before going to bed. In the meantime it became very dark, and our companions not yet arrived. We made a rousing fire, and waited, hungry and impatient. They had the pack and the supplies. When at last they did arrive, which was about 9 P.M., they came shouting, and yelling, and hurrahing at the sight of the blazing fire. The noise stampeded our horses, and they ran affrighted and snorting up the steep sides of the cañon, over the mountains, and away into the impenetrable darkness of night. We could trace them only by their shrill snorting, and now and then by the flitting form of my old gray. After some fruitless attempts to recover them, which only increased their fright, the night being very dark, and the mountains very rough, we concluded to give it up until morning, and went to bed feeling much uneasiness.

We have been to-day on the first road we have seen since we left Clark's.

August 16.

At daybreak, two of the party, Hawkins and Linderman, went after
the horses. By the time breakfast was ready they returned with them.
They had tracked them over the mountains back to Big Meadows,
where they found them quietly feasting, about three miles from
camp. We started off about 8 A.M., and for eight or ten miles more
traveled on the Sonora road, along the same narrow cañon in which
we had camped. This cañon is not more than one hundred yards
wide, flanked on each side by very steep hills and precipices, yet the
bottom is quite level, and the road good. Passed immense masses of
trap—ancient lava flows. Some places finely columnar. Mostly por-
phyritic lava and amygdaloid.

About ten miles from our camp, we reached Warm Springs.
These are very fine and very large springs. A considerable brook
runs directly from the principal spring. There are, moreover, several
springs, having different properties. The waters seem to be violently
boiling, but this is the result of escaping carbonic acid, rather than
steam. The temperature of the water seems to be about 150° to 160°.
Everything suitable for a watering place is found here; hot baths,
vapor baths, accommodations for visitors, etc., although in somewhat rude style. We have here still another evidence of the decay of
the mines in this region. This was once a flourishing watering place,
or at least expected to become so; but it is now entirely abandoned.
Several parties are now stopping here to make use of the baths, and
to hunt and fish in the vicinity. They bring, of course, their own provisions. Sage hens are very abundant in the brush, and trout in the
streams, in this region. I observe limestone now depositing from
these carbonated springs. Also, near by, immense rough masses of
the same, which have been similarly deposited at some previous
epoch. The immense lava streams in this immediate vicinity, in fact,
all around, sufficiently account for the heat of these springs.

After examining the springs we rode on, leaving the Sonora road and taking a trail for Antelope Valley. Rain now coming on, we galloped on until we came to a good grazing meadow, about three miles from the Warm Springs. There was here a rude pole house—probably a shepherd's lodge—which sufficiently protected us and our provisions from the rain. Here, therefore, we camped for noon. While here, a party of ladies and gentlemen rode by and camped a little beyond. They had a wagon for protection. The ladies seemed to be true Amazons: managed their horses with the utmost ease, dashed about in the most fearless manner, saddled and unsaddled, mounted and dismounted, without assistance. They were, in short, true cavaliers in petticoats.

This afternoon, the rain detained us here a little longer than we had intended. Started about 3:30 P.M. Delightful ride in the cool of the evening. All in high spirits. We reached a ridge overlooking Antelope Valley about sunset. Before us Antelope Valley lay spread out at our feet, (but ah! how far below us we found to our cost that night), behind us the magnificent Sierras, and the sun setting behind them. We stopped and gazed first at one and then at the other.

"Antelope Valley is but a step; what is the use of hurrying?" "Nevertheless, we had better go on; remember Laddsville and Chowchilla Mountain." On we rode. Presently a cañon, right across the way—and such a cañon! "Surely it is impossible to cross that!" A thousand feet deep, and less than a thousand feet wide at the top, and the sides seemingly perpendicular! But across it we must go. Already we see Hawkins and the advanced guard near the top, on the other side. We speak to them across the yawning chasm. The trail wound backward and forward, down one side, across the foaming stream, and then backward and forward up the other side; we followed the trail, though it led us on the dizzy edge of fearful precipices. We have become accustomed to this sort of thing, and so have our horses.

Onward we pushed, next across an inextricable tangle of sage brush and trap boulders; then down another cañon, and across another ridge, then down, down, down, then over another ridge, and darkness overtook us. Then down, down, down. We lost the trail; scattered about to find it. "Here it is!" found again; lost again; scatter; found again, and so on; but always still down, down, down. At last we reached the plain, after descending at least four thousand feet. In the valley at last! But alas! no meadow; nothing but sage, sage, sage. Very dark; neither moon nor stars. Onward we push, guided only by lights we see in the valley. "Hello! where are you?" we hear from behind. "Here! come on!" we answered. We stop awhile until laggers come up. Onward again we urge our tired horses, winding through the sage brush. Onward, still onward, straining our eyes to peer through the thick darkness. Onward, still onward, five long miles, through the interminable sage desert, without trail, and guided only by the lights. One by one the lights disappear. "What shall we do?" "Can't stop here. Push on." At last reached some Indian huts. "How far to white man's house?" "Leetle ways." "How many miles?" "No savé." "One mile? two mile? half mile?" "No savé." Onward, still onward. In despair we stopped to consult. At the Indian huts we had struck a road, but it was leading us away from the direction in which we had seen the lights. We again struck into the pathless sage. Hawkins is reconnoitering, a little in advance. "Here we are!" we heard him cry. "Whoop! A barley field!" It was without a fence. We determined to ride in, unsaddle, make our camp, allow our horses to eat their fill of standing barley, and make it good by paying in the morning. It was 10 P.M. Some of the party were so tired and sleepy that they preferred to go to bed supperless, and therefore immediately threw themselves on the ground and went to sleep. Five of us, however, determined to build a fire and cook supper. Ah! what a glorious fire sage brush makes! Ah! what a splendid supper we cooked that night! Ah! how we

laughed in our sleeves at the mistake that the sleepers had made!
Comforted and happy, and gazing complacently yet compassionately
on the prostrate forms of our companions, moaning in their sleep
with the pangs of hunger, we went to bed at 11:30 P.M., and slept
sweetly the sleep of innocence. If we are trespassing, it is time
enough to think of that in the morning.

We have ridden twenty-eight to thirty miles to-day, and about
the same yesterday. To-day the trail has been very rough. Our
horses are quite tired.

August 17.

Woke up much refreshed by a sound, dreamless sleep. This valley
can't be more than three to four thousand feet high. Last night was
the warmest we have felt since we left Yosemite. I had just waked
up. I was sitting on my blankets, putting on my shoes, and thinking
repentantly of our trespass. The sun was just rising. Yonder comes
swift retribution in the shape of a tall, rough-looking mountaineer,
with rifle on shoulder and pistol in belt, galloping straight toward
us. As he comes nearer, he looks pale, and his lips are firmly com-
pressed. He stops before me suddenly. "You seem to have had a
good thing here last night?" "Why yes, rather—but we intend, of
course, to pay for it." "I am glad to hear it." He was evidently greatly provoked by our trespass, but after we had explained the circumstances, and had paid him four dollars, he seemed very well satisfied,
bade us good morning, put spurs to his horse, and rode off as rapidly as he had come.

We did not get off so early as usual this morning. The supperless
ones slept heavily this morning, and got up growling. Hawkins was
up and out shooting by daybreak, and returned with a fine rabbit,

which, with other camp delicacies, put all in good humor at breakfast.

Started about 8 o'clock. This valley being so deep, of course we had to climb very high to get out of it. The road is, however, tolerably good. We nooned about ten miles from Antelope Valley, at Silver King, a deserted mining town. This is a good example of many similar towns in the mining districts of California. They are rapidly built up—property rising to fabulous price—then as rapidly decay. This one seems to have flashed up and gone out more suddenly than usual. There are several rather pretentious but unfinished buildings —hotels, stores, etc. The lots are all staked out, and a few years ago were held at high prices. Evidences of mining operations close by. I examined these, but saw no evidence of any special value. We took possession of the hotel; used the bar-room as our dining room, and the bar counter as our table. Made a hearty dinner; the young men all the while playing hotel life, laughing and calling "Waitaw! roast beef; Waitaw! bottle of champagne," etc.

3 P.M. Rode rapidly this evening, a good part of the way at an easy lope, and camped at a meadow in Bagsley's Valley, about two miles from Monitor. Here we found, to our great delight, a flock of sheep. We bought one and enjoyed mutton chops for supper again. After supper we all gathered around the camp fire, and I gave the party a talk on the subjects of Bloody Cañon and its glacier, the volcanoes of Mono, and the lava flows and warm carbonated springs we saw yesterday; but as the substance of what I then said is scattered about among these notes, I omit it here.

It being quite cool to-night, Hawkins and myself concluded to bunk together.

———

August 18.

Last night was the coldest we have yet felt. Did not sleep very well
for the cold. This morning, when I woke up, my blanket, hair and
beard were covered with a heavy frost. The meadow was white with
the same. The water left overnight in our tin canister was frozen. A
blazing fire and plenty of mutton chops, bread and hot tea, soon
thawed us, and by the time the sun was up an hour or so, it was
quite warm again. One of the shoes put on my horse by Mr. Hawkins, at Alliton's, being very thin at the point, has broken, and half
of it come off. I found, on leaving camp this morning, that my horse
was painfully lame again. The sharp fragments of rock which cover
the road here make him shrink, and limp and groan at every step.
Fortunately the town of Monitor is only two miles off. I determined
here to get him well shod all around. I stopped at Monitor for this
purpose, while the rest of the party rode on to Markleeville, about
eight miles farther, where they would stop, in order to get supplies
for the party. While he was shoeing my horse, I sat and talked much
with the blacksmith. I delight in seeing any work well done. He was
master of his trade. I also delight in seeing a fine physique. He was a
well made, strong, and really handsome man. He was also a man of
few words and much good sense. I would like to meet that man
again; I often think of him. I wonder if he has thought a second time
of *me?* Probably not.

After shoeing, I hurried on and overtook the party at Markleeville. Here it was inconvenient to cook our own meal, so we all took
dinner at the hotel. The dinner was really excellent, and we all enjoyed it greatly. Think of it! Besides the meats, which we could have
had as good in camp, rice, in genuine Southern style, (my heart
warmed toward mine host), potatoes, beans, corn, pies, cakes, and
sweetmeats. The variety tempted too much.

I received more letters from home at this place. Every one at

home has been perfectly well since I left. I am light-hearted to-day.
I shall be at home in a week or ten days. I wrote to that effect.

All along the road from Monitor to Markleeville, and in
Markleeville itself, I have seen sad evidences of the effects of the
speculative spirit—sad evidences of time, and money, and energies
wasted. Deserted houses and deserted mines in every direction.
The Indians, of whom there are a large number about Markleeville,
occupy these deserted houses. Some of the mines which I saw
seemed to have been undertaken on an expensive scale. They are
mostly quartz mines.

By invitation of Mr. Hawkins, we went on this afternoon only
three miles, and camped at a ranch belonging to his brother. Beautiful ranch, nice meadows for our horses, rich butter and milk for
ourselves, baths, hot, cold, and warm, issuing from fine springs. The
place has been rudely fitted up for bathing.

This is indeed a most delightful place, and the party seem to feel
its effects upon their spirits. While the horses graze and I sit in the
shade and write this, the young men are playing ball on the smooth-
shaven green. The meadow is surrounded by high, almost perpendicular, and apparently impassable mountains on every side except
that by which we came. In such a secluded, beautiful dell, deep sunk
in the mountain top, might a Rasselas dream away his early life.
Over those apparently impassable cliffs must we climb to-morrow,
if we would go on to Tahoe. Hawkins had intended leaving us here,
as he lives in this vicinity, but he has kindly volunteered to lead us
over the mountains into Hope Valley, from which the road onwards
to Tahoe is very good.

I took here a hot bath, so hot I could hardly bear it, and immediately after an ice-cold shower. The effect was delightful. Most of the
party slept here in a hay loft. I preferred sleeping with Hawkins, in
the open air, on a haystack.

———

August 19.

Heavy frost again this morning. Water and milk left from supper, last night, frozen. Took again, early this morning, the hot bath and cold shower. Mr. Hawkins observed, yesterday for the first time, that his horse is badly foundered. He takes another horse here, and by preference a powerful young horse, upon which man never sat before. Think of going over the most terrible mountain trail on such a horse. But he is accounted, I find, the best rider and horse tamer in the county. He mounted his horse just before we were ready to start, and in half an hour he had tamed him completely.

The trail from this place into Hope Valley is one of the steepest we have yet attempted. It is a zigzag, up an almost perpendicular cliff. In many places there can be no doubt that a false step would have been certainly fatal to man and horse. In the steepest parts we dismounted and led the horses a great portion of the way up. In many places there was no detectible trail at all. When once up, however, the trail was very good. From the top of this ridge I saw many fine peaks of columnar basalt, evidently the remnants of old lava streams. The descent into Hope Valley is much more gentle. This valley is a famous resort for fishing and hunting parties. As we entered the valley, and were about to stop for noon, we met one of these—a large party of ladies and gentlemen. Of course we straightened up and dashed by in fine style, and immediately dismounted and camped on a grassy meadow on the banks of the creek. They seemed much amused and somewhat astonished at our wild appearance.

2 P.M. After resting here two hours, we started on our way to Tahoe. Here Hawkins left us. Every one of the party was sincerely affected. He has been the soul of our party. I don't believe we could have gotten along without him. So generous, so efficient, so thoroughly acquainted with camp and mountain life. He scents out a

trail with the instinct of a bloodhound. As he turned, we all waved our hats and cried, "Three cheers for our noble Lieutenant! Hurrah! hurrah!! hurrah!!!" His face flushed and eyes filled; I know he was gratified with the heartiness of the salute.

We now proceeded by a good wagon road, and therefore quite rapidly. About 5 P.M. rode in double file up to Yank's, and reined up. The fat, bluff old fellow cries out: "Hello! where are you fellows from? Where are you going?" "Excursion party to Tahoe; where best to stop?" "You want to have a free, jolly time, don't you?" "O, yes, certainly." "Well! you camp at this end of the lake, near Rowland's." On we went, at a good round pace, and camped at 7 P.M., in a fine grove of tamaracks, on the very borders of the lake.

We have, I observed this evening, passed through the region of slate, (mining region), and the region of lava flows, and are again in the region of granite. The granite about Tahoe, however, is finer-grained than that about Yosemite and Tuolumne meadows, especially the latter.

August 20.

I am cook to-day. I therefore got up at daybreak and prepared break-fast while the rest enjoyed their morning snooze. After breakfast we hired a sail-boat, partly to fish, but mainly to enjoy a sail on this beautiful lake.

Oh! the exquisite beauty of this lake; its clear waters, emerald green, and the deepest ultra-marine blue; its pure shores, rocky or cleanest gravel, so clean that the chafing of the waves does not stain, in the least, the bright clearness of the water; the high granite moun-tains, with serried peaks, which stand close around its very shore to guard its crystal purity; this lake, not *among*, but *on* the mountains, lifted six thousand feet towards the deep blue over-arching sky, whose image it reflects! We tried to fish for trout, but partly because the speed of the sail-boat could not be controlled, and partly because we enjoyed the scene far more than the fishing, we were unsuccessful, and soon gave it up. We sailed some six or eight miles, and landed in a beautiful cove on the Nevada side. Shall we go in swimming? Newspapers in San Francisco say there is something peculiar in the waters of this high mountain lake; it is so light, they say, that logs of timber sink immediately, and bodies of drowned animals never rise; that it is impossible to swim in it; that, essaying to do so, many good swimmers have been drowned. These facts are well attested by newspaper scientists, and, therefore, not doubted by newspaper readers. Since leaving Oakland, I have been often asked by the young men, the scientific explanation of so singular a fact. I have uniformly answered, "We will try scientific experiments when we arrive there." That time had come. "Now then, boys," I cried, "for the scientific experiment I promised you." I immediately plunged in head foremost, and struck out boldly. I then threw myself on my back, and lay on the surface with my limbs extended and motionless for ten minutes, breathing quietly the while. All the good swimmers quickly followed. It is as easy to swim and float in this as in any other water. Lightness from diminished atmospheric pressure! Non-sense! In an almost incompressible liquid like water, the diminished density produced by diminished pressure would be more than counterbalanced by increased density produced by cold.

After our swim, we again launched the boat, and sailed out into the very middle of the lake. The wind had become very high, and the waves quite formidable. We shipped wave after wave, so that those of us who were sitting in the bows got drenched. It was very exciting. The wind became still higher; several of the party got very sick, and two of them *cascaded*. I was not in the least affected, but on the contrary, enjoyed the sail very much. About 2 P.M. we concluded it was time to return, and therefore tacked about for camp.

The wind was now dead ahead, and blowing very hard; the boat was a very bad sailer, and so perhaps were *we*. We beat up against the wind a long time, and made but little headway. Finally, having concluded we would save time and patience by doing so, we ran ashore on the beach about a mile from camp, and towed the boat home. The owner of the boat told us that *he* would not have risked the boat or his life in the middle of the lake on such a day. "Where ignorance is bliss," etc.

After a hearty supper we gathered around the fire, and the young men sang in chorus until bed time. "Now then, boys," cried I, "for a huge camp-fire, for it will be cold to-night!" We all scattered in the woods, and every man returned with a log, and soon the leaping blaze seemed to overtop the pines. We all lay around, with our feet to the fire, and soon sank into deep sleep.

August 21, Sunday.

Sunday at Tahoe! I wish I could spend it in perfect quiet. But my underclothes must be changed. Cleanliness is a Sunday duty. Some washing is necessary. Some of the party went fishing to-day. The rest of us remained in camp and mended or washed clothes.

At 12 M. I went out alone, and sat on the shore of the lake, with the waves breaking at my feet. How brightly emerald green the waters near the shore, and how deeply and purely blue in the distance! The line of demarcation is very distinct, showing that the bottom drops off suddenly. How distinct the mountains and cliffs all around the lake; only lightly tinged with blue on the farther side, though more than twenty miles distant!

How greatly is one's sense of beauty affected by associations! Lake Mono is surrounded by much grander and more varied mountain scenery than this; its waters are also very clear, and it has the advantage of several picturesque islands: but the dead volcanoes, the wastes of volcanic sand and ashes covered only by interminable sagebrush, the bitter, alkaline, dead, slimy waters, in which nothing but worms live; the insects and flies which swarm on its surface, and which are thrown upon its shore in such quantities as to infect the air—all these produce a sense of desolation and death, which is painful; it destroys entirely the beauty of the lake itself; it unconsciously mingles with and alloys the pure enjoyment of the incomparable mountain scenery in its vicinity. On the contrary, the deep blue, pure waters of Lake Tahoe, rivaling in purity and blueness the sky itself; its clear, bright emerald shore waters, breaking snow-white on its clean rock and gravel shores; the lake basin not on a plain, with mountain scenery in the distance, but counter-sunk in the mountain's top itself; these produce a never-ceasing and ever-increasing sense of joy, which naturally grows into love. There would seem to be no beauty except as associated with human life, and connected with a sense of fitness for human happiness. Natural beauty is but the type of spiritual beauty.

Enjoyed a very refreshing swim in the lake this afternoon. The water is much less cold than that of Lake Tenaya or the Tuolumne River, or even the Nevada River.

The party which went out fishing returned with a very large trout. It was delicious.

I observe, on the lake, ducks, gulls, terns, etc., and about it many sand-hill cranes—the white species. The clanging cry of these sound pleasant to me by early association.

———

August 22.

Nothing to do to-day. Would be glad to sail on the lake, or fish, but too expensive hiring boats. Our funds are nearly exhausted. Would be glad to start for home, but one of our party—Pomroy—has gone to Carson City, and we must wait for him.

I went down alone to the lake, sat down on the shore and enjoyed the scene. Nothing to do, my thoughts to-day naturally went to the dear ones at home. Oh! how I wish they could be here and enjoy with me this lovely lake. And Emma, too! dear Emma! She could dream away her life here with those she loved. How delicious a dream! Of all the places I have yet seen, this is the one which I could longest enjoy and love the most. Reclining thus in the shade, on the clean white sand, the waves rippling at my feet, with thoughts of Lake Tahoe and of my loved ones mingling in my mind, I fell into a delicious doze. After my doze I returned to camp, to dinner.

About 5 P.M., took another and last swim in the lake.

Pomroy, who went to Carson, returned at 7 P.M. After supper, again singing in chorus, and then the glorious camp-fire.

August 23.

We all got up very early, this morning. We wish to make an early start. All in high spirits; for we start for home to-day. I wonder if any one is half so anxious and impatient as I am. We wish to make Sacramento in three days. The distance is 110 miles or more. We must start early and ride late, if necessary. After camping three days in the same place, however, there is always much to collect and to fix. In spite of our early rising, we did not get off until about 7 A.M.

Our route lay over Johnson's Pass and by Placerville. We rode rapidly, however, alternately walking and galloping, and made twenty miles by 12 o'clock. About ten miles from Tahoe we reached the summit. We turned about here, and took our last look at the glorious lake, set like a gem in the mountains. From the summit we rode rapidly down the splendid cañon of the South fork of the American River, here but a small brook, and stopped for noon about two miles below Strawberry, on a little grassy patch on the hill-side, "close by a softly murmuring stream." Here we staked our horses, cooked and ate dinner, and "lolled and dreamed" for three hours, and then again saddled up and away.

Every pleasure has its pain, and every rose its thorn. We are in the region of good roads again, but oh! the dust! It is awful! About 4 P.M., saw a wagon coming; our instincts told us that it was a fruit wagon. With a yell, we rushed furiously upon the bewildered old wagoner. "I surrender! I surrender!" he cried, while, with a broad grin, he handed out fruit and filled our extended hats. "A-a-ah! Peaches! grapes! apples!" How delicious on this hot, dusty road. Rode this evening eleven or twelve miles, the cañon becoming finer as we advanced, until, at Sugarloaf Gorge, it reaches almost Yosemite grandeur. Camped at six P.M., near an inn called "Sugar-loaf," on account of a remarkable rock, several hundred feet high, close by. Our camp-fire was not far from the inn. At a window we saw two young ladies giggling and making merry at our cook — Mr. Linderman — mixing dough and baking bread. We sent them a piece, just to show them what we could do. No good ground to sleep on here. We don't relish sleeping in the dusty road. We therefore took our blankets and slept in the hay loft. Although we left the window open, we found it rather close. Alas! alas! no more grand forests, no more grassy meadows, no more huge leaping camp-fires; only dusty roads, dirty villages, and stable lofts and stalls.

I have been observing the cañon down which we came to-day.

Johnson's Pass, like Mono Pass, was a glacial divide. One glacier went down on the Tahoe side, a tributary to the Tahoe Glacier, but a much larger glacier came down the American Cañon. Sugar-loaf Rock has been enveloped and smoothed by it. This great glacier may be traced for twenty-five miles.

————

August 24.

As we got into the region of civilization again, incidents are less numerous. I observed, both yesterday and to-day, very many deserted houses. This was the overland stage road. Two years ago the amount of travel here was immense. I think I heard that there were twelve to fifteen stages a day. Now the travel is small, the railroad, of course, taking the travellers. The road is, however, splendidly graded, but the toll is heavy. This morning the road ran all the way along the American River, sometimes near the water's edge, but mostly high up the sides of the great, precipitous cañon formed by the erosive power of the river. The scenery all the way yesterday and to-day is fine, but especially along the American River it is really very fine. If we had not already drank so deep of mountain glory, we would call it magnificent. Again, this morning, walking and galloping alternately, we made easily twenty miles by 12 o'clock. Stopped for noon at "Sportsman's Hall," a roadside inn. Here, after dinner, we sold "Old Pack" for twenty dollars, exactly what we gave for him, left our cooking utensils, (our supplies were just exhausted), and determined hereafter to take our meals at the inns on the roadsides, or in the villages. Disencumbered of our pack, we could ride more rapidly.

This afternoon we rode sixteen miles; thirteen to Placerville, then through Placerville and three miles beyond, to Diamond Springs. On approaching Placerville, I observed magnificent orchards, cultivated by irrigation. I never saw finer fruit. Saw everywhere about, and in Placerville, abundant evidences of placer mining. The streams are also extensively used for this purpose, and are, therefore, all of them very muddy. Placerville is by far the largest and most thriving village I have seen since leaving Oakland. It probably contains two or three thousand inhabitants. The houses are stuck about along the streams and on the hillsides, in the most disorderly manner, their position being determined neither by regularity, nor beauty, nor picturesque effect, but chiefly by convenience in mining operations. The streets are very few, very long, very irregular, very narrow. Nevertheless, the general effect is somewhat picturesque. As we rode into town, and passed in double file through the streets, Captain at the head, erect, and evidently feeling his dignity, the young men descried a billiard saloon, became suddenly demoralized, broke ranks, incontinently dismounted, frantically rushed in, and immediately the click of the billiard balls was heard. Greatly disgusted at such insubordination, the Captain rode on with me to the Post Office. Here I mailed a letter to my wife, saying I would be at home probably on the night of the 26th. Onward then, through the town, for nearly a mile (it stretches so far along the stream), then up the hill; turned on the top, and took a look at the town, pleasantly nestled below, among the hills; then over the toll bridge, and onwards until about dark we reached the little village of Diamond Springs, and put up our horses at Siesbuttel's inn. Here we got as good a supper as any one could desire; and such coffee!

That night, to any attentive listener there must have been much good music in the stable—nine horses, crunching, crunching, below, and nine sleepers, snoring, snoring, above.

I was surprised to learn from our host that Placerville and vicinity is very sickly. Everybody suffering from chills and fever. He himself is suffering from this disease. Cause seems to be stirring up the earth by mining, and especially damming up waters for irrigation.

August 25.

Early start this morning. Got fairly off by 6 A.M. Rode rapidly, and made twenty-one miles by 11:30 A.M. Stopped for noon at the Half-way House. Took a swim—our very last—in a pond near by, and our dinner at the inn. Slept an hour, lying on the floor of the piazza; rested our horses until 3 P.M., and then again onward for home.

In the afternoon we rode fourteen miles, to Patterson's Ten-mile House. We found this a delightful place. Mr. Patterson is really a very pleasant and courteous gentleman, and gave us a most excellent supper. This put us all in excellent humor. The young men got lively. One of them, Mr. Perkins, played on the piano, while the rest joined in a stag-dance. The clattering of heavy boots on the bare floor was not very harmonious, it is true, but then, it was very enlivening. The host and all the guests in the house seemed to enjoy it hugely.

Two nights past we have been compelled to sleep in the stable loft, or else in the dusty streets. We are more fortunate to-night. There is a magnificent straw bank in the open field, on the other side of the road. "Once more under the starry canopy! Now for a good sleep! Our Father up there in the starry heavens, watch over us. Amen!"

We are again on the plains of Sacramento, but we no longer find the heat oppressive. We have been all along the road mistaken for horse or cattle drovers, or for emigrants just across the plains. We were often greeted with, "Where's your drove?" or "How long across the plains?" We have been in camp near six weeks, and ridden five or six hundred miles. Burned skin, dusty hair and clothes, flannel shirt, breeches torn, and coarse, heavy boots; the mistake is quite natural.

August 26.

"Home to-day! Hurrah! Wake up, all!" After an early breakfast, got off 6:30 A.M. We rode into Sacramento, ten miles, in 1½ hours, galloping nearly the whole way. We went at a good gallop in the regular order—double file—through the streets of Sacramento, the whole length of the city, down to the wharf, and there tied our horses. Everybody crowded around, especially the little boys about the wharf, curious to know "who and what were these in strange attire?"

Having nothing to do until 12 M., when the boat leaves, Captain and myself strolled through town. The Captain, with flannel shirt, bare neck, shocking bad hat, stout brogans, long knife stuck in belt, and a certain erect, devil-may-care air, certainly looked like a somewhat dangerous character. As we sauntered along the streets, a little sharp-looking Jew suddenly rushed out from his store, crying: "Now, gentlemen, I know you are in want of clothes. Here we are, the cheapest and finest in town. This way, gentlemen, this way!" "No, we don't want any clothes, we have plenty at home." "Ar'nt you the party who went galloping down the street, just now?" "Yes." "Where are you from?" "Only a pleasure party." "Why, I thought you were outlaws, or cattle drovers, or horse dealers, or emigrants over the plains, or something of that kind."

We then visited the State House. As we walked along the corridors toward the well-dressed and courteous usher, the Captain looked very grand. The usher seemed instinctively to know that we were not exactly what we seemed. He treated us very courteously, and showed us the fine halls of Representatives and Senate. We read, "Cum ore rotundo," the latin inscriptions, and translated, to the great astonishment of the usher. We now went back to the wharf, and cut and ate cantalopes; then to a restaurant, and had a most delicious dinner, of which we partook very heartily; then on board of the boat for San Francisco, and tied our horses all in a row and gave them hay, then up into the cabin.

Everybody looked at us with interest and surprise. "Who are they?" Gradually it became known who we were, and we were treated with courtesy, and even became lions. Captain of the boat took some of us up to his room, and asked many questions. Dinner at 4 P.M. I went down, and again ate one of the heartiest dinners I ever ate in my life. I cannot get enough to-day. Our rough appearance gave rise to some amusing incidents. I was coming up stairs, from deck to cabin. Superbly dressed mulatto at the landing. "Got a cabin check, sir?" showing me one. "No, I have not." "Can't come up." "But I paid cabin fare." "Can't come up." Here a white official, who knew me, interfered and apologized.

San Francisco at last! We all went in a body ashore. The cabmen thought here was a prize of greenhorn mountaineers. They came round us in swarms. "Lick House?" "American Exchange?" "Cosmopolitan?" "Who wants a hack?" was screamed into our ears. The young men screamed back, "What Cheer House! Russ House! Occidental! This way, gentlemen!" etc. They soon saw that they had better let us alone. We mounted, and dashed off to the Oakland wharf. Not open yet; what shall we do? we shall ride about town. Pomroy and myself rode to the Lick House, where he wished to get a bundle, which he had left in Cobb's room. He dismounted at the ladies' entrance, and I sat on horseback and held his horse. As he opened the door, the porter said: "What do you want?" "Never mind," and he ran up stairs. Porter came out and said to me, "What does that man want?" "Mr. Cobb," said I. Door shuts. Presently, out he comes again. "Who is that man?" I gave him no answer. Again: "Where did that man come from?" I took no notice of him. Door shuts again, and I could see through the glass that he went up stairs to look after *that man*. After a little, Pomroy came and told me that the porter had finally recognized him, and apologized.

Our glorious party is, alas, dissolving. Three, Cobb, Bolton, and Linderman, left us here; the rest of us now rode down again to the wharf, and found the gate open. Went in and tied our horses. Went across the way and again took a cup of coffee, and ate heartily of doughnuts. Back to the waiting room and dozed. 11:30 got on board the boat for Oakland. Landed at the pier, we galoped alongside the swift-moving cars, the young men hurrahing. The race was kept up pretty evenly for a little while, but soon the old steam horse left us behind, and screamed back at us a note of defiance. We went on, however, at a sweeping gallop, through the streets of Oakland, saluted only by barking dogs; dismounted at the stable, bid each other good night, and then to our several homes; and our party, our joyous, glorious party, is no more. Alas, how transitory is all earthly joy! Our party is but a type of all earthly life; its elements gathered and organized for a brief space, full of enjoyment and adventure, but swiftly hastening to be again dissolved, and returned to the common fund from which it was drawn. But its memory still lives; its spirit is immortal.

AFTERWORD

"Beyond all wealth, honor, or even health, is the attachment we form to noble souls."

I have been one of Joseph LeConte's innumerable friends and admirers for more than thirty years. It was in Yosemite Valley that I first met him, not far from the famous rock beneath the shadow of which he died. With a party of his students he was making his first excursion into the high Sierra, and it was delightful to see with what eager, joyful, youthful enthusiasm he reveled in the sublime beauty of the great Valley, and tried to learn how it was made. His fame had already reached me, though he had then been only a year or two in California, and, like everybody else, I was at once drawn to him by the charm of his manners, as to a fine lake or a mountain; and when he kindly invited me to join his party, of course I gladly left all my other work and followed him. This first LeConte excursion, with its grand landscapes and weather and delightful campfire talks, though now far back in the days of auld lang syne, still remains in mind bright and indestructible, like glacial inscriptions on granite.

We left the Valley by the Coulterville trail, then, turning to the eastward, climbed in long, wavering curves and zigzags through the glorious forests of silver fir north of Yosemite, across the dome-paved basin of Yosemite Creek, along the southern slopes of Mt. Hoffmann, down into the bright, icy basin of Lake Tenaya, over the Merced and Tuolumne divide past a multitude of sublime glacial monuments, along many a mile of smooth, flowery meadows, up Mt. Dana, and down Bloody Cañon to the lake and gray plains and volcanoes of Mono. How the beloved Professor enjoyed all this his own story best tells. Sinewy, slender, erect, he studied the grand show, forgetting all else, riding with loose, dangling rein, allowing his horse to go as it liked. He had a fine poetic appreciation of nature, and never tired of gazing at the noble forests and gardens, lakes and meadows, mountains and streams, displayed along the windings of the trail, calling attention to this and that with buoyant, sparkling delight like that of a child, keeping up running all-day lectures, as if trying to be the tongue of every object in sight. On calm nights by the campfire he talked on the lessons of the day, blending art, science, and philosophy with whatever we had seen. Any one of us, by asking a question on no matter what subject, made his thoughts pour forth and shine like rain, quickening, exciting mental action, appealing to all that is noblest in life.

Our camp at Lake Tenaya was especially memorable. After supper and some talk by the fire, LeConte and I sauntered through the pine groves to the shore and sat down on a big rock that stands out a little way in the water. The full moon and the stars filled the lake with light, and brought out the rich sculpture of the walls of the basin and surrounding mountains with marvelous clearness and beauty amid the shadows. Subsiding waves made gentle heaving swells, and a slight breeze ruffled the surface, giving rise to ever-changing pictures of wondrous brightness. At first we talked freely, admiring the silvery masses and ripples of light, and the mystic, wavering dance of the stars and rocks and shadows reflected in the unstable mirror. But soon came perfect stillness, earth and sky were inseparably blended and spiritualized, and we could only gaze on the celestial vision in devout, silent, wondering admiration. That lake with its mountains and stars, pure, serene, transparent, its boundaries lost in fullness of light, is to me an emblem of the soul of our friend.

Two years later we again camped together, when I was leading him to some small residual glaciers I had found. But his time was short; he had to get back to his class-room. I suggested running away for a season or two in time-obliterating wildness, and pictured the blessings that would flow from truancy so pious and glorious. He smiled in sympathy with an introverted look, as if recalling his own free days when first he reveled in nature's wild wealth. I think it was at this time he told me the grand story of his early exploring trip to Lake Superior and the then wild region about the headwaters of the Mississippi. And notwithstanding he accomplished so much in the short excursions which at every opportunity he made, I have always thought it was to be regretted that he allowed himself to be caught and put in professional harness so early.

As a teacher he stood alone on this side of the continent, and his influence no man can measure. He carried his students in his heart, and was the idol of the University. He had the genius of hard work which not even the lassitude of sickness could stop. Few of his scholars knew with what inexorable determination he toiled to keep close up with the most advanced thought of the times and get it into teachable form; how he listened to the speech which day uttereth unto day, and gathered knowledge from every source—libraries, laboratories, explorers in every field, assimilating the results of other men's discoveries and making them his own, to be given out again free as air. He had the rare gift of making dim, nebulous things clear and attractive to other minds, and he never lacked listeners. Always ready for every sort of audience, he lifted his charmed hearers up and away into intellectual regions they had never hoped to see or dared to encounter, making the ways seem easy, paths of pleasantness and peace, like a mountaineer who, anxious to get others onto commanding peaks, builds a trail for them, winding hither and thither through the midst of toil-beguiling beauty to summits whence the infinitely varied features of the landscape are seen in one harmony, and all boundaries are transparent and become outlets into celestial space.

Joseph LeConte was not a leader, and he was as far as possible from being what is called "a good fighter, or hater." Anything like a quarrel or hot controversy he instinctively avoided, went serenely on his way, steeping everything in philosophy, overcoming evil with good. His friends were all who knew him, and he had besides the respect of the whole community, hopefully showing that however bad the world may be, it is good enough to recognize a good man.

In the winter of 1874 or '5 I made the acquaintance of his beloved brother, John. The two with their families were then living together in a queer old house in Oakland, and I spent many pleasant evenings with them. The brothers and John's son Julian were invariably found reading or writing. Joseph, turning down his book, would draw me out of my studies in the Sierra, and we were occasionally joined by John when some interesting question of physics caught his attention, — the carrying force of water at different velocities, how boulders were shoved or rolled on sea beaches or in river channels, glacial denudation, etc. I noticed that when difficulties on these and kindred subjects came up Joseph turned to his brother, and always, I think, regarded him intellectually as greater than himself. Once he said to me: "The public don't know my brother for half what he is; only in purely scientific circles is he known. There he is well known and appreciated as one of the greatest physicists in America. He seems to have less vitality than I have, seldom lectures outside of his classroom, cares nothing for popularity; but he is one of the most amiable of men as well as one of the most profound and orignal of thinkers." In face and manners he was like his brother, and had the same genial disposition and intellectual power. But he was less influential as a teacher than Joseph, held straighter forward on his own way, doing original and purely scientific work, and loved to dwell on the heights out of sight of common minds. Few of his students could follow him in his lectures, for his aims were high and the trails he made were steep, but all were his devoted admirers. Until John's death, some ten years ago, the brothers were always spoken of as "the two LeContes." In my mind they still stand together, a blessed pair, twin stars of purest light. Their writings brought them world-wide renown, and their names will live, but far more important is the inspiring, uplifting, enlightening influence they exerted on their students and the community, which, spreading from mind to mind, heart to heart, age to age, in ever widening circles, will go on forever.

John Muir

Editor's note: This tribute to Joseph LeConte was written on the occasion of his death. It was originally titled "Reminiscences of Joseph LeConte," and was published in The University of California Magazine *in September, 1901.*

Audubon, ✓✓ vii
Agassiz, Louis vii, viii, INDEX

A JOURNAL OF RAMBLINGS THROUGH
THE HIGH SIERRAS OF CALIFORNIA

A PRINTING HISTORY

A. *A Journal of Ramblings Through the High Sierras of California by the "University Excursion Party."* No author named. San Francisco: Francis & Valentine, 1875. 103 pp. Nine photographs. Hard cover in blue cloth, 5¼" x 8½". Preface by "J. L'C."

It is probable that the tipped-in photographs were the work of J.J. Reilly, who in 1870 hired Daniel Folsom to build the first photographic establishment in Yosemite Valley. (See *J.J. Reilly, A Stereoscopic Odyssey, 1838–1894,* edited by Peter E. Palmquist. Community Memorial Museum, Yuba City, California, 1989.)

Joseph N. LeConte, the author's son, told historian and bibliographer Francis P. Farquhar that he believed twelve copies were privately printed for each of the ten members of the "University Excursion Party." This would make the total run about 120 copies and the book an extremely rare edition.

B. "Rough Notes of a Yosemite Camping Trip" By Joseph LeConte. In *Overland Monthly*, New Series, Vol. VI, Nos. 34, 35, & 36 (Oct.–Dec., 1885).

This serialized account of the trip by the university party is a slightly edited version of item "A."

C. "Ramblings Through the High Sierra." By Joseph LeConte. In *Sierra Club Bulletin*, Vol. III, No. 1 (Jan., 1900). 107 pp. 12 illustrations.

This is another slightly revised version of item "A."

D. *Ramblings Through the High Sierra.* By Joseph LeConte. Publication No. 21 of the Sierra Club. San Francisco: The Sierra Club, 1900. 107 pp. Paper bound with buff colored wrappers, 6" x 9⅝".

This is an unmodified reprint of item "C."

E. *A Journal of Ramblings through the High Sierra of California by the University Excursion Party.* By Joseph LeConte. Foreword and bibliographic notes by Francis P. Farquhar. San Francisco: The Sierra Club, 1930. 170 pp. 5 illustrations. Hard bound in blue paper-covered boards with white cloth spine, simultaneous paper bound version in russet wrapper, both with paper label on spine, 5³/4" x 8³/4".

These reprints of the text of item "C" were issued in an edition of 1,500 copies.

F. "Ramblings Through the High Sierra." By Joseph LeConte. New version of item "C." that appeared in Volume III of the reprint edition of the first five volumes of *The Sierra Club Bulletin*. New York: The Sierra Club, 1950. Hard bound in red buckram.

This set appeared in an edition of 500 copies.

G. *A Journal of Ramblings through the High Sierra of California by the University Excursion Party.* By Joseph LeConte. Foreword and bibliographic notes by Francis P. Farquhar. San Francisco: The Sierra Club, 1960. 166 pp. 9 illustrations. Hard bound in tan paper-covered boards with red cloth spine, 5³/4" x 8³/4".

Another small run, this edition was limited to 2,500 copies.

H. *A Journal of Ramblings through the High Sierra of California by the University Excursion Party.* By Joseph LeConte. Foreword and bibliographical notes by Francis P. Farquhar. New York: A Sierra Club/Ballantine Book, 1971. 156 pp. 9 illustrations. Paper bound, 4¹/4" x 7".

I. The present version is a reprint of the first edition (see item "A.") with changes in pagination, the omission of 8 photographs, and the addition of an introduction by Dean Shenk, an afterword by John Muir and an index.

A JOURNAL OF RAMBLINGS THROUGH
THE HIGH SIERRAS OF CALIFORNIA

This reprint was prepared for publication by the Yosemite
Association using OmniPage Professional OCR software.

Designed by Michael Osborne Design, San Francisco, CA.
Type composition in Cochin.
Printed on Mustang Vellum Offset 60# text and
bound in Speckletone Cream 80# cover by
Delta Lithograph Co., Valencia, CA.